A Jungian Approach
to Literature

BETTINA L. KNAPP

Southern Illinois University Press
Carbondale and Edwardsville

Library of Congress Cataloging in Publication Data

Knapp, Bettina Liebowitz, 1926–
    A Jungian approach to literature.

    Bibliography: p.
    Includes index.
    1. Archetype (Psychology) in literature. 2. Psycho-
analysis and literature. 3. Jung, C. G. (Carl Gustav),
1875–1961. I. Title.
PN98.P75K6   1984   809   83-20459
ISBN 0-8093-1161-5

90 89 88 87 86 85 84 7 6 5 4 3 2 1

*To my mother
Emily Gresser Liebowitz
whose love was my inspiration*

O my friends! Each teacher
reveals his ideas in his own special way,
and then disappears.

Farid ud-din Attar,
The Conference of the Birds

CONTENTS

INTRODUCTION

There are many different approaches to the teaching and study of literature. These include linguistic, psychological, historical, structuralist, semiotic, hermeneutic, heuristic, and so forth. Each method is valid for the one who finds that it answers an intellectual and emotional need; each is meaningful if it deepens the understanding of the works under scrutiny and broadens the horizons of the scholar, critic, and reader. Whatever the approach, it should act as a catalyst; stimulating and exciting those involved in the pursuit of knowledge and encouraging them to develop their own potential. Criticism, in this manner, becomes a creative act. It turns what could be an intellectual exercise or *tour de force* remaining within the confines of the mind, into *praxis*, thereby acting as a broadening force in the life experience.

Carl Gustav Jung sought to "engage the response of the *whole man*" in the psychoanalytic process, not merely the intellectual nor solely the sexual.[1] To this end he studied myths and legends, cultural manifestations of all kinds in both a personal and universal frame of reference. This exploration gave him insights into primordial images, archetypes of the collective unconscious. Drawing parallels between the workings of the individual unconscious, shown in images produced in the dreams of his patients, with the universal recurrent eternal motifs found in religions and works of art, Jung thereby enlarged the scope of psychotherapy. It became not only a curative agent that relates to "the whole history and evolution of the human psyche in all of its manifestations" but also a technique that could help develop the potential of well-adjusted normal and superior human beings.[2]

A Jungian Approach to Literature is a direct outgrowth of

a course I taught at the Graduate Center of the City University of New York and at Hunter College. The explicit system of investigation into the literature under scrutiny and the fullness and plenitude of the psychoanalytical process was helped by the many and varied questions and suggestions offered me by my students. Their ability or inability to follow certain trends and views, the interest they expressed concerning specific themes, myths, and legends, which evidently responded to an inner need, added a whole new dimension to the teaching experience as well as to my own thought.

The ten essays included in *A Jungian Approach to Literature* are purposefully different. Their diversity illustrates the universality of Jungian archetypal analysis and criticism. Archetypal analysis takes the literary work out of its individual and conventional context and relates it to humankind in general. This unique approach lifts readers out of their specific and perhaps isolated worlds and allows them to expand their vision, and thus to relate more easily to issues that may confront them and to understand their reality as part of an ongoing and cyclical reality. To become aware of the fact that people in past eras had suffered from alienation and identity crises—to mention but two problems—and went through harrowing ordeals before they had a chance to know some semblance of fulfillment may help certain readers to face and understand their own gnawing feelings of aloneness.

The impact of the material evaluated in *A Jungian Approach to Literature* is designed to enlarge the readers' views, to develop their potential, and also to encourage a personal confrontation. Such encounters may be painful or joyous, terrifying or serene; hopefully, they will prove enlightening, involve the readers in the writings discussed so that they may understand how and why certain creative works speak and reach them today and why others do not. Energized in this manner, readers might go a step further and explore the literary work in question and through association relate their discoveries to aspects of their own personalities. Self-awareness may then be increased; and the understanding of the individual's function and role in society may be broadened. Reading now becomes not merely an intellectual adventure but an excitingly helpful living experience.

A Jungian Approach to Literature has been divided into seven parts: the first five are chronological; the sixth and seventh are separately presented because they explore unique psychological experiences. Each essay is divided into two sections: an *ectypal* and an *archetypal* analysis of the work discussed. The ectypal section gives a brief historical summary of the period, thus acquainting readers with the appropriate facts concerning the author's environment and background. An exploration of the structure and nature of the work itself is undertaken in certain cases (poem, play, essay, novel), to determine the reasons each specific genre was used, its potential, and so forth.

Archetypal analysis is the most important aspect of *A Jungian Approach to Literature.* Archetypal or primordial images, which emerge from the deepest layers of the unconscious, are found in myths, legends, literary works the world over and from time immemorial. Although definitions of Jungian terms are given throughout the volume, some clarification of the term *archetype* may be in order at this time. The archetype has been compared by Dr. Edward Edinger to the instinct. He writes:

An instinct is a pattern of behavior which is inborn and characteristic for a certain species. Instincts are discovered by observing the behavior patterns of individual organisms and, from this data, reaching the generalization that certain patterns of behavior are the common instinctual equipment of a given species. The instincts are the unknown motivating dynamisms that determine an animal's behavior on the biological level. An archetype is to the psyche what an instinct is to the body. The existence of archetypes is inferred by the same process as that by which we infer the existence of instincts. Just as instincts common to a species are postulated by observing the uniformities in biological behavior, so archetypes are inferred by observing the uniformities in psychic phenomena. Just as instincts are unknown motivating dynamisms of biological behavior, archetypes are unknown motivating dynamisms of the psyche. Archetypes are the psychic instincts of the human species. Although biological instincts and psychic archetypes have a very close connection, exactly what this connection is we do not know anymore than we understand just how the mind and body are connected.[3]

Archetypes are contained in the *collective unconscious*—also referred to as the objective psyche. The collective, as distinguished from the personal unconscious exists at the deepest level within the subliminal realm. It is "suprapersonal and non-individual" by nature and as such, is usually "inaccessible to conscious awareness." Archetypes are made manifest in *archetypal* (primordial) *images*: experienced in such universal motifs as the *great mother*, the *spiritual father*, *transformation*, the *Self*, and others. These archetypal images and more are to be examined in *A Jungian Approach to Literature* for their import within the literary work under discussion and their meaning, both personal and collective, in contemporary society. Further investigation using this dual view may pave the way for a discussion revolving around the anima/animus dynamism. The *anima* has been defined as "an autonomous psychic content in the male personality which can be described as an inner woman"; the "psychic representation of the contrasexual elements in man and is depicted in symbolic imagery by figures of women ranging from harlot to saint." The *animus* may be looked upon as "the corresponding representative of the masculine contrasexual elements in the psychology of women."[4] Positive and negative anima/animus conditions are probed in terms of the protagonists within the context of the literary work and how these relate to twentieth-century life. Psychological types are studied as well: the extrovert and the introvert, and how their energy flow, both inward and outward, acts and counteracts on the dramatis personae and carries over into the contemporary world.

Persona problems are also broached. The *persona*, which comes from the Latin term meaning the actor's mask, may be looked upon as a "public face" which a person may assume when relating to others. Difficulties arise when an individual identifies too greatly with his persona thereby making it difficult for him to adapt to the outside world. The persona may also mask a weakened ego, leading to its eclipse.

Attention is likewise focused on Jung's concept of the four functions: *thinking* (rational), *feeling* (regulates values especially in relationships), *sensation* (promotes adaptation to reality), *intuition* (faculty which perceives via the unconscious). An exploration of the *shadow*, which includes those characteristics that the *ego* considers negative or unacceptable as personified in dreams and myths within the given work of literature is also undertaken. The ego is that part of the psyche which "stands between the inner world and the outer world, and its task is to

adapt to both."[5] Symbols, images, and motifs are examined relative to their specific and long-range effects in the various literary works under discussion: water, cave, earth, sky, clouds,
mountains, mandalas, and more, and the part these play in the
death/rebirth mysteries, in sacrifice, redemption, salvation. A
religious and philosophical dimension now comes into focus and
with it an understanding of the psychological development or
regression of the various protagonists. The concept of *individuation*, or the process of "psychic differentiation" that distinguishes each individual as unique and separate from the collective, is adumbrated. The inner life of the characters may then
be experienced by the reader as a living entity, provoking reflection as well as a desire to assess the literary masterpiece in terms
of his or her own existential condition.

   Part 1 focuses on Euripides' *Bacchants*. Ectypically, the play
revolves around the period of the Second Peloponnesian War,
the end of the Periclean golden age, the beginning of Greece's
decline. Archetypally *The Bacchants* dramatizes the mystery of
sparagmos (dismemberment) and *omophagia* (eating of the flesh);
it also includes such psychological aberrations as transvestism
and voyeurism. Why and for what reasons do such situations
come into being? Are there parallels to be made with society
today?

   Part 2 is devoted to Wolfram von Eschenbach's *Parzival*.
An ectypal account of the historical conditions existing in Parzival's time in Moorish Spain and Christian Europe is offered,
as well as information concerning the many legends revolving
around this hero figure. Archetypally, *Parzival* takes us through
a young hero's psychological evolution: the child living within
the paradisiac realm created by his mother in the forest; his
"fall" into life, and the maturation process with his encounter
and struggle with the Red Knight; the *feminine principle*; his
first and second entry into the Grail castle. In what way do these
steps have their counterpart in twentieth-century society? How
do they relate to the psychological development or lack of it in
youth today? Interesting, too, is the lack of racial antagonism
existing in *Parzival*. The Moors are darker in skin tone than the
Anglo-Saxons. Yet, a harmonious climate existed between the
two groups. How may one account for this in the light of today's environment and cultural attitudes?

Part 3 focuses on three of Montaigne's *Essays*: "On Solitude," "On Presumption," and "On Repentance." An ectypal
view of the Renaissance is given: its history, philosophy, and the
altering religious factors that gave rise to the Reformation. The
archetypal exploration emphasizes Montaigne's ideas about rel-
ativity, divinity, nature, evil, immortality, reason, the physical
body, and the formation of judgment. His views as well as their
application to the present-day world and the individuation process are also adumbrated. Montaigne's attempt to understand
his psychological makeup through his study of the writings and
ideations of classical antiquity allows us to consider the essays
under scrutiny a form of self-analysis, and his probings as a
precursor of the psychoanalytic method.

Part 4 focuses on Corneille's *Horace* and *Rodogune*. After
the ectypal discussion of the period and the playwright's role in
the cultural sphere, attention is paid to the philosophical and
psychological impact of the archetypal hero and antihero.
Questions concerning patriotism, personal loyalty versus society (the individual as opposed to the collective), the *senex* figure, father/son identification, the *vagina dentata* type, the power
drive, the notion of sacrifice are also discussed. In what forms
do these concepts exist today? What is their impact on both the
personal and transpersonal realm?

Part 5 discusses three works of the nineteenth century and
one twentieth-century one: Goethe's *Elective Affinities*, Novalis's *Hymns to the Night*, Rabbi Nachman's "The Master of
Prayer," and William Butler Yeats's *At the Hawk's Well*.

The interaction of different personality types is concentrated upon in *Elective Affinities* in relation to the volatile or
passive attitudes of the protagonists, their separations and re-
unions, and the transformation process in general. Emotional
contents are sparked by Goethe's use of images (house, lake,
park, tree, and so forth) and color symbolism, each indicating a
level of consciousness.

Novalis's attitude toward his dead fiancée, Sophie von Kühn,
yields metaphysical insights into the death/life process. For
Novalis, death meant a reentrance into the *prima materia*, or
mother earth—a rebirth of life. Is such a view to be considered
a *regressus ad uterum*, or an example of the *puer aeternus*, or a
prodromal indication of the poet's own early death? Are what

might be considered Novalis's initiation rituals into another frame of being, his Orphic descent into the shadow world, reminiscent of the introverted and regressive paths taken by so many in our society today?

Rabbi Nachman's "The Master of Prayer," a tale recounted by Martin Buber, approaches the psychological problem of the ego's exile from the Self. Viewed in terms of Hebrew mysticism—the Kabbala—the reader is made privy to sequences of apocalyptic visions of extraordinary beauty. Each revelation ushers in the *numinosum*, each centers around man searching for, finding, and talking with God.

At the Hawk's Well by William Butler Yeats is a fusion of Western extroverted drama and the ancient aristocratic art of Japan. Yeats's play dramatizes the hero/poet's battle to attain and experience the source of eternal inspiration—the collective unconscious. He fails in his attempt and instead of using those forces which manifest themselves as archetypal images to his own advantage, he is swept up and captivated by his anima, the female principle that then shapes and defines his destiny.

Part 6 fleshes out the Finnish national epic—*The Kalevala*. The hero in this work is born, paradoxically, old. The events recounted expose the conscious and unconscious impulses, needs, and desires of a people whose world revolves around Shamanistic practices and beliefs, rituals involving man's mysterious relationships with the forces of nature. Specific archetypes are adumbrated (*creation*, *night-sea journey*, the *treasure hard to attain*, and so forth); because they are universal in vein and transpersonal in power, they still act dramatically upon the reader's psyche even today in the most highly industrialized of modern societies.

Part 7 concentrates on a Sufi mystical experience as delineated in *The Conference of the Birds* by Farid ud-din Attar. In sequences of archetypal images the reader is led into the very heart of religious mystery. The rituals evoked and the invisible forces invoked during the course of Attar's allegorical work disclose an entire Sufi system based on seven levels of religious experience. The psychological process which emerges takes readers from an ego-centered condition in the world of objective reality, to its annihilation within the Self—a dehumanizing experience.

Since the works studied in *A Jungian Approach to Litera-*

ture point up both the negative and positive sides of the creative forces experienced throughout history in a variety of cultures, the reader's unconscious will hopefully be aroused and the knowledge gleaned will disclose a whole new frame of reference. Those "knots" that previously bound and blinded readers, depriving or denying them awareness, may then be untied.

A Jungian Approach to Literature may pave the way for an active participation between text and reader in the learning adventure—as does a work of art and the therapeutic technique. Considered in this dual role, literature is not merely a means of broadening knowledge but a way of discovering one's own ground-bed and of developing one's potential and spiritual élan— of helping a personality to grow and individuate—which are the fruits and goals of the creative process.

I should like to thank Doris Albrecht, the librarian at the C. G. Jung Foundation in New York, for her help in the research work that went into the preparation of *A Jungian Approach to Literature.*—B. L. K.

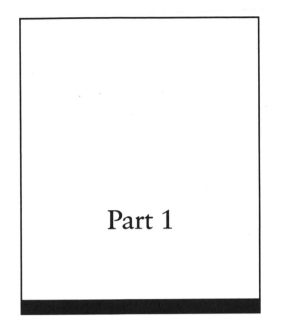

Part 1

Euripides (480–405 B.C.): *The Bacchants—* Fulminating Rage/Outrage

Religious rage/outrage, voyeurism, transvestism, dismemberment, anthropophagy, mark the events dramatized in *The Bacchants*. Such an unhealthy religious and psychological condition resulted, to a great extent, from the prevailing one-sided
patriarchal attitude of the society in power. Lauded was the all-
powerful rational and logical view of life, while the feminine
element, identified with the world of instinct, was undervalued
and repressed. The regressive and punitive measures taken against
womankind by the ruling force were to be returned twofold in
Euripides' work—a most gruesome interplay of opposites. The
action in *The Bacchants* resides in the clash between male/fe-
male principles, religious faith and the lack of it, and the viru-
lence with which these fulminating powers struck at each other.

The Bacchants relates a myth: it enacts a cultural reality, a
sacred story that fuses an *illo tempore*—prehistory—with history, supernatural exploits with natural and human experience.[1]
It is an artist's assessment of the personal and collective feelings
involved in a civilization's decline: the ending of the Periclean
golden age (460–429 B.C.). The fighting of the Peloponnesian
War (431–404 B.C.), that struggle between Athens, a demo-
cratic sea power, and Sparta, a military oligarchical state, that
breaking up of the very fabric and structure of Athenian society,
destroyed the creative spirit of Greece.

ECTYPAL ANALYSIS

Little is known about Euripides' personal life. According to traditional sources he spent much of his time reading and studying,

3

seemingly fascinated by the mysterious hidden elements within the human personality. His great tragedies have been characterized as acidulous satires. They also contain bitter condemnations of those factors in society that were in his view unjust and unwarranted. In *Alcestis* (438 B.C.), Euripides ironizes the subordinate role of women; in *Medea* (431 B.C.), he derides the unfair treatment of foreign women in Athenian society; in *Hippolytus* (428 B.C.), he takes to task the negative fate of illegitimate children; in *The Trojan Women* (415 B.C.), he decries war.

The *Bacchants* was written when Euripides was living in Macedonia in what might well be called exile. It was not performed until 408 B.C., after his death. The subject matter is harrowing. Pentheus, the king of Thebes, the son of Echion and Agave, does not and will not acknowledge the divinity of Dionysus. He rejects the concept of mystical religious faith in general, and adopting a strictly empirical point of view toward life, he orders his people to believe only what they see. The practice of the Dionysian mystery is, therefore, banned. A Stranger soon arrives in Thebes; it is Dionysus, the god now incarnated as man. He is angered that the land where his mother, Semele, was born no longer honors her. Indeed, some Theban citizens consider Semele a wanton woman and deny that her lover was Zeus, maintaining that Dionysus's father was merely a common mortal. In punishment for such a lack of respect, Dionysus strikes the females of Thebes, including his aunt Agave (who is also Pentheus's mother), with holy rage (maenadism). The women have left their homes to practice their mysterious fertility rites on Mount Cithaeron. Pentheus meets the Stranger and listens to him speak in favor of Dionysian rituals which he considers ignominious. Pentheus has him imprisoned. No god, however, may be kept enchained by a mere mortal, and Dionysus quickly frees himself. Punishment for such an affront is in order. Using great cunning, the Stranger entices Pentheus to go to Mount Cithaeron to observe the Bacchant women perform their secret rites. Since only women may participate, Dionysus tells Pentheus that he must go in disguise, don a dress and wig. He does so, then follows the Stranger to the site. To better watch the activities, the Stranger suggests that Pentheus climb a tree. Agave, the leader of the women, spies Pentheus and in her orgiastic delirium takes her son for a lion cub. She grabs him, and in a state of religious ecstasy, dismembers him; with the help of the other members of the group, she begins eating his still warm flesh.

Why should Euripides have been so fascinated with the Bacchants? With their Maenad rage, their Dionysian frenzy, irrational mystical ecstacy? Certainly there must have been unconscious personal reasons, some psychological condition that Euripides attached to the Dionysian myth, but what it was we shall never know. More easily discernible are the ectypal or cultural reasons that may have motivated his choice of theme. The law in Euripides' time was designed to favor men—property, for example was inherited patrilineally. The woman's role was restricted to the home: it was there that she spent her time, directing the servants, bringing up the children, and so forth. She related to her husband only within this highly circumscribed frame of reference. Aristotle and Xenophon, among many, considered women's reasoning and thinking powers far inferior to those of men. Athenian husbands rarely, if ever, had a serious discussion with their wives. The man's sphere, on the other hand, was identified with physical prowess and intellectual acumen. Since the husband had so little emotional or psychological rapport with his wife, his interests and feelings remained focused on male friends. Such attitudes frequently evolved into homosexual relationships as attested to, for example, in Socrates' statements and in the Platonic dialogues in general (see the *Symposium*). Exception was made for concubines, who saw to the sexual pleasures of the male, and courtesans of the hetaera type like the beautiful and brilliant Aspasia by whom Pericles had a son and who became the pride and joy of Athenian society.[2]

That a culture should so devaluate the role and function of women reflects the unconscious discomfort the male feels with his anima, which Jung defines as "the feminine principle in man," his "contrasexual elements," his "inner woman." The anima is an "autonomous psychic content" in the masculine personality. Anima figures have been portrayed in literary and religious works throughout history in characters ranging from harlot to saint. It is that power within the psyche that encourages the male to relate to others and to fall in love—the *eros* principle. When the anima is experienced unconsciously or when an identification exists between the anima and the ego of which the individual is unaware, the man may become effeminite, overly sensitive, resentful, and behave "as an inferior woman." The anima is a beneficial force when the feminine part of the psyche is acknowledged by the ego, thus allowing and even encouraging the male to understand and indulge in feminine relationships outside himself, as well as to explore his own depths: to discover the profoundest layer within his subliminal realm, that is his collective unconscious.[3]

In *The Bacchants*, the anima is unintegrated. It has been rejected by the ruling conscious order, that of Pentheus, king of Thebes. Unable to relate to the feminine principle in general, he unconsciously fears it and seeks to destroy it. To succeed in his endeavor, he represses those forces he fears both outside himself (society) as well as within his own being (unconscious). To enclose, to seal hermetically such contents, creates an explosive situation. Under these circumstances, the imprisoned elemental powers (or energy centers = archetypes) grow in force and expand in mortality. Their virtually autonomous behavior patterns lead to behavioristic extremes. Pentheus, misled into believing that increasingly restrictive laws guarantee the maintenance of the straight and narrow path, that the rational world can circumscribe the meanderings of the irrational domain, suffers the consequences of his unbending views. The emotional oscillation which lies at the heart of *The Bacchants* leads to a destructive dynamics: the harsher the regulations, the greater the enslavement to conventional attitudes, the more unsure the man is of himself and of his own sexual identity. So, too, the woman feels rejected, thwarted, downtrodden and seeks liberation in protracted and frenzied outbursts, in bacchic orgies— always in extreme measures that she wrongly feels flood her with power and a sense of worth.

When man fears woman or those values she represents for him, in the objective world of reality (a projection of an inner condition caused in part by an unintegrated anima), harsher laws against her may minimize her power for a short period of time. Outwardly she may be denied certain liberties, certain areas of accomplishment; inwardly, however, anger, rage, discontent, are fomenting and building up. The overtly subordinated female will be transformed into a disruptive and chaotic force, thus bringing an end to the smooth-running "rationally" oriented society in power.

ARCHETYPAL ANALYSIS

Dionysus in *The Bacchants*, and gods and goddesses in general, may be viewed as archetypes, universal primordial images of timeless human attitudes and patterns of existence that are part of the structure of the collective unconscious. Archetypal myths take readers into subliminal realms where sacred and eternal time predominates, where the dream of immortality abides, where fabulous lives are recounted and supernatural beings exist and are humanized by personal projection. When a culture either lacks or devaluates certain factors within its society, myths of an archetypal nature usually become popular. They offer people compensatory figures, heroes and heroines whose deeds help them stem the tide of despair, events that rectify the inadequate life experience.

In *The Bacchants*, the logical/rational/thinking function is the prevailing attitude; a male-dominated orientation prevails. There is no room for the feminine principle; everything that the anima represents is suppressed. The female is rejected by the male, who considers it, unconsciously to be sure, a threat to his masculinity. It is at this juncture in the culture's evolution that the Dionysian myth is brought into existence (by Euripides in this case) to restore an imbalance in the society.

Dionysus has always been equated with the dark elemental forces of nature, with what is ecstatic, uninhibited, fruitful in its way. Celebrations in honor of the death and rebirth of this god are also at the root of Greek theater. Festivals and dances took place in the spring and autumn. Originally, priests led these activities; in time, however, actors began indulging in a variety of phallic improvisations in honor of this god of nature. Masks were worn; groups of joyous revelers would beat on cymbals and drums, shouting out in shrieks and cries their passion for the deity; torches were carried as were thyrsus (those staffs with a pine cone attached to the end and frequently entwined with ivy or vine leaves) about the countryside, in frenzied joy. Comedy (*komos*) and tragedy (*tragos*) were had by all, as Dionysus, the divine child, was honored and loved but also became the sacrificial victim in what was to be known as the death and rebirth resurrection mystery.

Mysteries, in general, do not seek to teach a doctrine. They set the stage for an experience to be lived. Esoteric in nature, the word "mystery" stems from the Greek *eisôtheô* (I make enter); the intention being to open the door, to make accessible what has been lying hidden or buried in darkness. The goal of a religious mystery is to allow initiates to experience the death of the profane and temporal self and the rebirth of his spiritual and eternal aspects. Mysteries in Greece were practiced in secret. Only those who have passed the most rigorous initiations were admitted to the group. Initiation (from "to go within") amounts to a descent into Self (Jung defines the Self as the total psyche, an equivalent for God in the religious world), the passing from one level of consciousness to another until the deepest levels within the psyche are penetrated. Such a *katabasis* allowed the initiate to reconnect with his own past and concomitantly with humanity's primordial existence.[4] When Socrates said, "Know thyself," he meant discover the inner person. To gain such knowledge requires deep probing, a sounding out of one's being. The object of an initiation is an illumination; as such, the experience cannot be taught, nor can it be recounted to friends or acquaintances, nor handed down from one generation to another. It can only be experienced. The profounder vision that occurs after the completion of the initiation, endows the individual with a fresh world outlook; emotions cannot be verbally expressed (an emotion cannot be articulated); as such, the entire experience is hermetic.

When Euripides dramatized certain sequences in the Dionysian death/rebirth mystery in *The Bacchants*, he was encouraging those of his audience to experience a religious awakening (from the Latin *religio* "a linking back"); thus enabling them to come into contact with their own roots through an archetypal past, experienced on both a personal and a universal level. The present vanishes, as do individuality and mortality, as the characters and the audience as well share in the divine events enacted. Plunged into a primordial sphere, an epiphany is lived out on the stage. The numinosity of the proceedings are of such a nature as to catalyze the inner world of all those sharing in the stage happenings, frequently forcing contents from the un-conscious to move into the conscious sphere. The impact of the experience thus affects the onlookers emotionally; and in so doing, it may make inroads into their conscious lives, influenc-ing their activities and views. Thus theater becomes *praxis*, and an ancient Greek god is reborn into modern times.

Who was Dionysus that he played such an important role in Greek culture? What was his heritage? Why was he called the thrice-born and identified with death and resurrection? Diony-sian worship was one of the oldest mystery religions in Greece. It is believed to have come from Crete around 3000 B.C. or earlier, then traveled on to Thrace, Phrygia, and other areas in Asia Minor, spreading to Attica and to Athens (the city named after Athena, the goddess of wisdom, that is, the intellect).[5] Dio-nysian mysteries were practiced in areas where the great Earth Mother goddesses (Gaia, Rhea, Cybele, Hera, Demeter, Ishtar, Isis, and the like) held sway—that is the *genetrix*, the devourer of the future *genitor*. These deities are viewed as archetypes and, in their more positive manifestations, may be considered life-giving, fertile, loving, and protective forces. When their negative sides are unleased, however, they become death-dealing and sti-fling, bringing darkness and destruction in their wake.

It was the archetypal Earth Mother that saw to nature's yearly renewal. It was she who allowed the seed, the bud, the germ, to emerge from under the ground and then return there once its terrestrial existence was spent, there to decompose and be reborn the following spring. The death/rebirth rituals that grew out of these beliefs gave rise in agrarian societies such as Greece, to episodes of collective intoxication, sexual orgies, and bloody dismemberments. At Eleusis, such mysteries were de-voted to Demeter and her union with Zeus. The *hieros gamos*, or alliance of heaven and earth, which insured the health and procreative power of the land, thus permitting the human race to continue, was celebrated in secret and only by the selected few permitted entry into the group. During the mysteries, an epiphany frequently occurred: God appears to man.[6]

In *The Bacchants* Dionysus, one of the most popular, pow-erful, and complex gods in the Greek pantheon, makes his pres-ence known when nature—the Earth Mother and, by exten-sion, the feminine principle—is being demeaned or violated; he disappears from view when the balance is restored. The feminine principle in Greece was, for the most part, identified with *tellus mater* and the world of instinct. It is this earth force that attempts to redirect the patriarchal sway in *The Bacchants*: Pentheus's conventional and punitive attitude toward women—his rejection of them. Two extremes, therefore, are being lived out in Euripides' play: an *enantiodromia* will occur, that is, one pair of opposites will turn into its opposite.

Although Pentheus prides himself on fostering and furthering conscious rational thought, his own rigidity forbids any true evaluation on the subject, and he is as irrational in his way as the Bacchants are in theirs. His fixation, therefore, leads to a paralysis in his own psychological development. Agave is a powerful *vagina dentata* type who literally devours her son, as this kind of woman covertly and symbolically so often does, tearing the male psyche to pieces, pulling and tugging at it with her demands, dominating it in the subtlest of ways. Consciousness does not come into being in *The Bacchants*, reason is not used to direct instinct; a positive situation is never realized. When the libido (energy, both psychic and physical) works in harmony with *gnosis*, "knowledge," both the individual and the collective usually benefit. In *The Bacchants* we see a dismemberment of the patriarchal way and a deformed psychological condition come into being.

The thrice-born Dionysus was many-natured as attested by his many cognomens: the Delirious, the Noisy, the Frenzied, each appelation describing a facet of his personality. Though his heritage varies according to the specific legend, in Euripides' play, he is the son of Zeus and Semele, the daughter of Cadmus and Harmonia. When Zeus came down to Semele on Mount Sipylos and the beautiful girl was enraptured and succumbed to his wiles, Hera was beside herself with jealousy and decided upon a clever method of revenge. She transformed herself into Semele's nurse and convinced her to ask her lover to appear to her in all of his light—his dazzling glory—as god. Why should Zeus visit Semele only at night? Hera suggested. Was this god ashamed of his relationship with a mortal? Should not Semele know more about her midnight lover particularly now that she was to bear his child? When Semele finally convinced Zeus to appear to her in all of his radiance, His divine fire consumed

Semele. To save their unborn child, however, Zeus removed the fetus from Semele's womb and placed it in his thigh which he had cut open and then sewed up. The child remained there until term and was born at the appropriate moment to the joy of all. Still, Dionysus was in danger. Hera was bent upon revenge. She sent the Titans to destroy him. They tore him to pieces. After the dismemberment, Dionysus was resurrected and the name Zagreus (torn in pieces) was added to his own. The thrice-born Dionysus, like Osiris and Christ, was a survivor.[7]

Since in *The Bacchants* Dionysus enters Thebes as a Stranger, the cultural situation indicates an imbalance that he must rectify. His first task, as he sees it, is to rehabilitate his mother's memory and, by extension, his own. It now seems in order to explore Semele's condition from the point of view of Jungian psychology in order to understand the role she played in Dionysian life. Why, for example, was Semele consumed by the fire of Zeus when she asked to see him in all his glory? To look upon a god, which Jung identifies with seeing the Self—the whole of the psyche—is a mind-blowing experience for the one who is not prepared for it. When light/electricity is extreme, it fulminates. For a mortal to gain access to an infinite realm may be overwhelming and tantamount to the swallowing of the ego by the collective unconscious. One must know how to cope with the presence of a god, to remain grounded, solid in one's own identity. This was not Semele's case. Instead of expanding her vision, helping her to gain enlightenment or strength from Zeus's presence, she was destroyed, her consciousness was eradicated. In psychological terms, she was dead. When an emotion—love, hate, or another—is too intense, the trauma is so great that in many cases consciousness is lost, all perspective vanishes, objective reality is obliterated. To dig too deeply within the Self, to penetrate those arcane regions to the collective unconscious, sometimes leads to disorientation and the loss of identity. That Zeus should have taken the fetus and placed it in his thigh indicates a need for Dionysus's birth: for some a compensatory force to help nature experience some semblance of balance between the masculine and feminine principles. It also points to the role Dionysus was to play. Athena, let us recall, sprang from Zeus's head, thus her domain and that of her twin brother, Apollo, was the clear Attic light of reason. Dionysus's realm was the thigh: that of the instinct, exuberance, and intoxication in the rhythmic dance of life. In his manifestations as bull, lion, goat, serpent, his power and masculinity came to the fore; when associated with the feminine force—nature—he was identified with all types of liquids (water, honey, milk, wine) conducive to growth and procreation; vital if bountiful crops were to be enjoyed.

Dionysus was worshipped in antiquity as the divinity of vegetation, of spring planting and seasonal renewal. Plutarch alluded to him as the god of the tree; Hesiod suggested he brought excitement and revelry wherever he went. The phallus was his symbol; he was sometimes called Phallen, thereby indicating the sexual role he was to play throughout history.[8] Dionysus is, as we have already mentioned, the antithesis of Athena/Apollo, and who represented light, spirituality, cerebrality, inner perception, and intuition. Dionysus stands for liberty, for uninhibited libido in all its free-flowing manifestations. An extroverted god, as opposed to the introverted Appolo, Dionysus's feelings are bound to sensations; they reveal themselves in affects.[9] For harmony to reign in a personality or civilization, both the Apollonian and Dionysian sides of a culture must work together. In this regard, it is fascinating to note that Dionysus's tomb is located at Delphi, in a temple honoring Apollo. Without light, there is no darkness; without intellect, instinct is nonexistent; without soul, body vanishes.

Dionysus is, however, not only associated with Earth Mother, but because of her, he is also identified with the image of ascension. After Semele's death, she had been taken to Hades. It is from there that Dionysus rescues her, then brings her to Mount Olympus, where she was accepted by the heavenly deities as one of their own. In so doing, he was looked upon as a deliverer, a liberator of the female principle from the chthonic realm. (Semele had been called *chthonia*, "the subterranean," by the Phyrgians and Europeans.) Conductor of souls to Uranian climes, Dionysus (and the feminine principle with respect to Semele) was not only henceforth associated with earth forces (germination and fertility), but also with ascension into the celestial sphere. As such, the Dionysian myth had expanded in meaning, had gained cosmic dimension and become identified with Orphism and humanity's need for spiritual life: the freeing of the soul from terrestrial bondage. When an agricultural society is too strongly rooted to the ground, some form of spiritualization becomes a necessity. A reorientation must take place. Prior to Dionysian worship in Greece, two worlds, it was said, existed as separate entities: the human and the divine, that is, earth and heaven, body and soul—alienation between man and god. It was Dionysus who brought these antipodal forces together, who united the dichotomy.[10]

The Dionysian ritual, which lies at the heart of Euripides' dramatic work, is divided into six parts: (1) the *agon* (contest), the period of conflict when the god fights his enemy; (2) the *pathos* or disaster, which frequently concludes with the dismemberment (*sparagmos*) and the eating of the flesh (*omophagia*) of the god; (3) the *messenger* who arrives to report the news; (4) the *lamentation* followed by songs of rejoicing; (5) the *discovery* or *recognition* of the dismembered god; (6) the *epiphany*.[11]

1. The Agon

The Bacchants opens on a square in front of the royal palace at Thebes. Dionysus, disguised as a Stranger, enters. He has just come to Greece from Lydia and Phrygia in the east. That he enacts the role of the Stranger is significant. He represents a foreign or estranged element to Theban culture. What he stands for is separate, unintegrated into the scheme of things. "All Asia is mine," he observes. His mother's sisters Agave (Pentheus's mother), Ino, Autonoe, anger him because they have blasphemed against his mother and himself by implying that Semele's lover was not Zeus, but a mere mortal, and that her passion had been sinful. Punishment will be meted out by Dionysus upon those that do not honor him—the natural and instinctual side of humankind. He has encouraged the women of Thebes, in the most subtle of ways, to leave their homes in a state of "mad frenzy" and go to Mount Cithaeron where they secretly practice their sacred feminine rituals, their orgies, their rages. Dionysus prods these women to wreak havoc with their pent-up emotions; to unleash their instinctual feelings which lie secret and buried within their collective unconscious. In so doing, they will allow their most regressive aspects, repressed until now, to burst forth. Such an unchanneling spells destruction to consciousness; a dissociation of the personality. The unregenerate instincts given free range overwhelm the ego, obliterate any kind of real relationship with the outside world. Dionysus speaks out: "And all the womenfolk of Thebes, every woman in the city, I have driven from home distraught, to join the daughters of Cadmus; together they sit beneath the silver firs, on the open rocks. This city must learn, whether it likes it or not, that it still wants initiation into my Bacchic rites. The cause of my mother Semele I must defend by proving to mortals that I *am* a god, borne by her to Zeus" (p. 282).

The Stranger/Dionysus is handsome and virile, but his hair is long and flowing, and his countenance bears the softness and tenderness of a girl. As an archetypal figure, he represents the universal attitude of joy in life, potency in sexual encounters, antirational attitudes, and visceral relationships. Both the masculine and the feminine aspects of his personality are well integrated. The former will become manifest during the course of the play when identified with the bull, indicating, psychologically, a strong ego that enables him to confront his enemy with force and vigor as well as with cunning. His feminine aspect (anima), symbolized by his long curly hair, reveals his ability to relate to people with ease, to feel into situations. He is a god, and there is no mistaking this: "he is what he is," beyond good or evil; a transpersonal force upon which humankind may project or identify.[12]

The Chorus, a manifestation of the great Earth Mother, is central to the action of Euripides' play. Composed of a group of women who celebrate the joys of natural life, they move about on the stage dressed in fawn skins, draped with ivy, beating timbrels, and holding their sacred thyrsi high as they dance and sing their hymns of passionate praise to Dionysus. They represent the irrational factor in womankind: vital energy. Undervalued, suppressed for so long, the feminine element manifests itself in the Chorus's eruptive ways.

Chaos reigns in the Bacchants' psyche. There is a fundamental confusion between wine and madness. The women have imbibed their god—Dionysus—through the grapes that have turned into wine; soon the wine will turn into blood, and then holy communion will have been experienced. Orgiastic rituals, such as the one described by the Chorus, were considered by

the ancient Greeks to have curative powers: they liberated repressed instincts and emotions which, if contained, might lead
to madness or other assorted ills. The *enthusiasmos* which paved
the way for the psychic discharge of energy which ensues, referred to as the *ekstasis*, took the worshiper out of himself or
herself—thereby altering the personality.[13] Rhythmic song and
dance, noise of all types, pervade the atmosphere and empower
the participants, as does a narcotic, to obliterate reality, thereby
releasing energy and paving the way for the wildest abandon,
thus encouraging obscure primal forces in their natures to take
complete control.

The psychological situation is rendered all the more concrete by the image of the palace which stands in the center of
the stage. The home of the sovereign Pentheus who represents
rational and logical ways, the palace stands for the ruling principle that obliterates mystery, faith, and rejects the feminine element. His world, therefore, must be uprooted, dismembered,
crushed. To accomplish this mission, Dionysus will have to "reveal" himself to Pentheus and to the Thebans in all of his grandeur. He plans his strategy carefully and intuitively. The desire
for revenge drives Dionysus on. The agon—conflict—now begins.

Tiresias and Cadmus enter. The former, the legendary blind
seer who appears in so many Greek myths and dramas, including that of Oedipus, was blinded for having spied on Athena in
her bath. To offset the punishment, he was given the power of
prophecy or inner sight: intuition, to compensate for his lack of
outer vision. Understandably, then, Tiresias's visionary function
is highly developed; as for his anima, that too is well integrated
into his personality, since he understood the need women have
for joy and sexual fulfillment.

Cadmus, the founder of Thebes, was the son of the king of
Tyre. When a youth, he was asked to search for his sister Eu-
ropa (among other trials) who had been carried off by Zeus. He
complied with the order, indicating a sense of responsibility as
well as a feeling for family ties. It was also said, years later, that
Cadmus was the one who introduced the alphabet into Greece
from his native Phoenicia and accomplished many other technical innovations as well. Psychologically, therefore, we may say
that Cadmus represents the rational order, traditional values,
not in conflict with either the earth force or the instinctual realm,

but working with it to better situations. That he was given Harmonia (the daughter of Ares and Aphrodite) as a wife underscores a need within him, and the culture which created this figure, to retain the existing balance in the existential sphere.

The intuitive Tiresias understands the import of balancing the polarities of life (intellect/instinct, earth/spirit, and so forth). He is cognizant that if judgment is to be sound, consciousness productive, the rational sphere must be joined to instinct, earth, body, and matter. Light alone dries up the life-force; aridity ensues. Duality, when kept in balance, energizes, produces, fructifies both earth and cosmos.

Tiresias and Cadmus have both come to help restore Dionysian worship to the land. They will join forces with the Bacchants and celebrate the greatness of the god of the vine. Though old and feeble, the two men will go to the mountain disguised as women, since men are forbidden to participate in these hermetic rites. They will join in the dance, expressing their faith in Dionysus, celebrating their love for life.

That this wild celebration takes place on a mountaintop rather than in a cave (those damp and dark, secret grottos where so many rituals were enacted) indicates the need to bring this complex situation into the open, to spiritualize raw instinct. The Bacchants are as unrelated to their feminine side as Pentheus is to his masculine one. They only know how to express their needs in the most primitive and anthropoid of ways. For nature to become productive, its libido must be channeled, its values heightened, extremes mitigated by balance.[14] If such excesses are allowed to pursue their course, they may take over, leading to primogenial chaos.

"We alone are right," Tiresias explains. "The others are wrong" (p. 285). Neither he nor Cadmus is an overly rational being. Their concepts, therefore, have not become ossified; nor have their ways been shriveled up by too much exposure to the light of reason, too much logic, which so frequently cuts individuals off from the unconscious or creative factors within their psyches: "We do not rationalize about the gods. We have the the traditions of our fathers, old as time itself. No argument can knock *them* down, however, clever the sophistry, however, keen the wit" (p. 285). As *senex* figures, however, their reign is over; the ruling principle that they represented during their youth and

maturity—relative balance—no longer prevails. It has been ploughed back into the ground. Autonomous forces have taken over.

Pentheus, the king, now enters. His world, as we have seen, focuses on the rational principle alone; all other levels of his psyche have been repressed, rendered inefficient, and fragmented. He has one obsession, one view; as such, the rational has become an irrational force in his life attitude. No evaluation can take place, no objectivity, no understanding of other processes. Upholder of limited conventional values, Pentheus practices what *he* considers to be virtues—at least outwardly. Everything he sees, discusses, approaches, he examines in what he believes to be a logical and thoughtful way. Because his world is divested of all magic and mystery, of sensitivity and of largesse—the capacity to experience other views and values—he is a prisoner of his own rigid system. More important is the fact that he has cut himself off from his own feelings and emotions. Instead of relating to the feminine principle within himself in a natural way, expressing tenderness and compassion when the situation calls for such a reaction, he behaves like an automaton. Everything and anything that does not comply with his own logical frame of reference is simply eradicated from consciousness. Outwardly and superficially, he gives the impression of being very male, of possessing great courage and strength, but such a view is illusory.

When Pentheus first talks to the Stranger/Dionysus, the contrast between the two male figures is blatant. The god is at ease with his anima; as such, he lives in harmony with his sexuality. His long beautiful curls, his charm, and alluring ways do not pose a threat to his so-called maleness; and there is therefore no need to fear what they represent—the feminine element. Pentheus, on the other hand, is always ill at ease with his anima, looking upon it, unconsciously, as a threat to his well-being, to the respect people should have for their king. Yet Pentheus and Dionysus do have certain characteristics in common: they are both the same age; their mothers were sisters; they have the same grandfather.[15]

In Jungian terms, Pentheus may therefore be called Dionysus's *shadow* figure. As such, he represents all those traits that the ego considers negative and would like to annihilate. Eradication and not explication, destruction rather than integration, is the only path open in *The Bacchants*. The pleasure principle is unknown to Pentheus; although he may desire it unconsciously, it is unthinkable as a social factor. Women have but one function to fulfill on this earth: they are vessels, they must procreate and tend to their home and family. That they should be allowed to roam through the woods, live naturally, and adore Dionysus—cavorting in the ways of Aphrodite and indulging in sexual fulfillment—must be stopped. Euripides clearly points to the fact that when these same women are not abused and are not constantly threatened with punishment, but are allowed to live undisturbed according to their own credo, their dominion does not lead to crime. When fecundated, nature blooms and gives her bounty; then, for the most part, normal and well-balanced forms emerge. Only when provoked, castigated, repressed, does womankind's passion for growth transform itself into ubridled energy and ruination.

Pentheus, however, is not only unwilling but also unable to see this point of view. To put a stop to the Bacchants and their "sham ecstasies," their "immoral revelry," is his sole goal. With subdued joy, he states, "I have caught a number of them. Jailers have them safely manacled in the public prison" (p. 286). Such a show of force will certainly prove his kingly powers to the populace; it will also reveal the fact that by fleeing to the mountaintop, these women are expressing their dissatisfaction on other grounds: their husbands are sexually insufficient.

That Pentheus represents a rational, puritanical view is obvious; that he is also impotent or at least sexually unsure of himself now becomes evident. Rather than attempt to relate to the feminine, to understand them, and to try to discover those inoperative elements within himself and the society that he heads, he has tried to eliminate them from his world. Pentheus considers all sexual expression dirty, lascivious, and degrading. The same fate is meted out to all those facets within himself with which he cannot cope. Pentheus is so self-centered, that he is unaware that trouble is brewing in his own kingdom; he is oblivious to his own psychological illness. Incapable of analyzing the turmoil within his subliminal realm, those undisciplined and unaccountable forces that compel him to act in a brutal and "unthinking" manner, emerge helter-skelter. The light of true "reason" never penetrates the damp, dismal, cell-like sphere where his insalubrious instincts reside.

Insofar as Dionysus disguised as the Stranger represents foreign elements in Theban society, he stands as a threat to the status quo. Unlike Pentheus, however, he is in touch with those forces that are beyond the king's understanding. By downgrading them, by describing the Stranger's "fragrant golden curls and ruddy face," a personality that "spells love" (p. 286), Pentheus rises in his own self-esteem and considers himself more virile. But the image which he seeks to fix on the Stranger throughout the kingdom, intended to discredit him, has the opposite effect. Finally, Pentheus threatens to dismember the Stranger, "to cut his neck from his body." Such an image is particularly apt: for Pentheus is in effect seeking to sever the mind—which he identifies with the intellect and reason—from the body, which he associates with the feminine instinctual realm. The rational Pentheus is in effect iconographically devaluating what Dionysus stands for, underestimating the *eros* principle, splintering the twin facets of the human being, which he considers as bulwarks of antagonistic views toward life. As such, Pentheus, solitary and deeply introverted to begin with, and so severed from his anima, grows increasingly divided as the play progresses.[16]

When Pentheus sees Tiresias and Cadmus dressed in women's garb, preparing to join the Bacchants, he becomes still more disoriented. "A new phenomenon," he cries, has come into being. He castigates the men, vilifying their attitude of expectancy and delight—in the ritualistic experience they anticipate. Pentheus's way is punitive: retribution, hanging, dismemberment, and killings.

That Pentheus is out of tune with intuitive principles and with Dionysian instinctuality heightens his fear of these forces. He is a man possessed, fixated, panic stricken.[17] When Tiresias predicts that Dionysus will "be great throughout Hellas," Pentheus recoils at the thought. When approached, he shouts, "Do not lay your hand upon me." (Even physical contact repulses him. He considers that the madness of the Bacchants—a psychological condition—is infectious.) "Do not wipe off your folly on me!" (p. 288). He remains aloof, untouched, unsullied, tightly contained in his rigidity. Rather than facing the situation, he attempts to stay away from it, to escape from its "sickening" ways. Pentheus will deal with the Stranger as he does with all else which poses a threat to him: he will lock him up. "Scour the city and track him down this foreign epicene who has brought this strange madness upon women and is defiling our beds" (p. 288), he commands. That Pentheus uses the word "epicene" (a being who has the characteristics of both sexes and is therefore erroneously considered weak) is indicative of his feelings of pseudostrength and power, as contrasted to those of impotence, feebleness, supposedly represented by the Stranger. He orders the Stranger to be captured, put in chains, and stoned.

The Chorus enters, singing and dancing their praise to mother earth. In rhythmic outcries, they call to the "Queen of Heaven," the "Blessed One," they laugh and revel, ejecting their cares and pain, drinking deeply from the wine of life. For those who have no taste for wine and its pleasures, for the body and its beauty, for nature and its bounty, for the happy dawns and sweet sunsets, then straight is the gate.

In ancient times, dancing, particularly during religious ceremonies, was not merely considered a pastime; it was a way of expressing the deepest felt emotions, the most numinous of feelings. Words are frequently inadequate when attempting to translate feelings; abstractions cannot disclose the sensations involved in describing the physical side of life. Bodily rhythms and pantomimic gestures render the visceral world more adequately.

Pentheus has left the stage during this interlude and returns, delighted. He has caught his prey; he has had the Stranger bound and fettered, or so he believes. Unbeknown to him, however, the contrary is true. His enemy has "surrendered," to be sure; "he even smiled as he consented to be arrested and bound" (p. 290). Dionysus's passivity is only a ploy, a device used to delude Pentheus into believing his action to be a definitive show of strength. To try to outwit a god, is to court danger, whether on a religious or a psychological level. The finite being (viewed as the ego), can only suffer the consequences. Clever and subtle in his ways, the Stranger encourages Pentheus to continue harboring illusions. "Trapped as he is, he cannot have the speed to escape me," Pentheus is convinced (p. 290). Time, however, is on Dionysus's side. The god easily slips through the shackles that encircle him and emerges free.

Meanwhile, Pentheus's curiosity grows. He comments on the Stranger's beauty, his complexion, and long curly hair. "It is in the shade you go hunting, hunting Aphrodite with your beauty" (p. 290). He is smitten with the idea of secret realms, of remote regions where hermetic rituals take place; sexual acts are openly practiced. Pentheus questions the Stranger about his heritage, his dreams, and particularly about the bacchic orgies held in honor of Dionysus. In fact, every time Pentheus utters the words "orgies" or "secret rites," excitement seems to flow from him; suppressed desires fester; emotions are quickly muffled since they represent what he rationalizes as shameful and degrading ways. "It is unlawful for profane mortals to know them" (p. 290), the Stranger adds, arousing Pentheus's further interest in these arcane goings-on in the most cunning of ways.

The more Dionysus speaks of the ecstatic rites taking place on Mount Cithaeron, the more Pentheus's curiosity grows. What does Dionysus look like? What is his nature? he questions. The Stranger looks at him with disgust: "Talk wisdom to the stupid, and they will think you foolish" (p. 291). How can one describe a god? an unlimited transpersonal force, an unfathomable entity that lives outside the spatial-temporal continuum? Pentheus guided by his reason alone, limited by his mortal views, cannot make inroads into the world of the absolute—of divinity.

Moments later, Pentheus makes an about-face. Perhaps as a protective device—or so he may think—he condemns the "barbarians" for celebrating their joyful passions. "They have far less sense than Hellenes" (p. 291), people known for their rational and law-abiding attitudes. Do they practice their rites at night or in the daylight? he queries. In darkness for the most part, the Stranger answers. (Understandably, since the rational world is less effective at night; its dominion weaker, therefore, allowing the subliminal world to flow forward powerfully and provocatively.)

Pentheus angers. He threatens to cut off the Stranger's "pretty curls" which he identifies with the feminine component—the anima—which he fears, since it undermines his straitlaced ways. To cut off Dionysus's curls, as Delilah cut off Samson's locks, is

to symbolically castrate the male. Such an interpretation is cor-
roborated by Pentheus when he decides to throw the Stranger's
thyrsus (phallic symbol) away.[18] By depotentiating or castrating
the Stranger, Pentheus again erroneously believes that he has
proved himself more of a man, when in effect, the reverse is true.

The Stranger informs Pentheus that no earthly force can
enchain him: "don't bind me, you fools" (p. 292). Embedded
in his own sense of power, Pentheus allows his hubris to inflate,
thus blotting out all semblance of common sense. He confronts
the Stranger with a show of strength—a test of wills. He has
him imprisoned "in the horses' stables," where "gloom" and
"darkness" reign. He could not have chosen a more appropriate
area. The lack of light is a perfect breeding ground for unregenerate forces to grow, work, and foment. As for the horses, a
paradigm for energetic principles, primogenial chaos, to block
and seal these energetic factors may lead to an explosive situation. "Dionysus, whom you deny," the Stranger tells him proph-
etically, "will exact full payment for this outrage" (p. 292). One
cannot chain an instinct, an urge, imprison a yearning.

The Chorus enters, singing and dancing in wild frenzy. Again
hymns of praise ring out, dithyrambs of joy and ecstasy—premonitory enunciations of events to come. Pentheus is castigated
for his ironclad attitudes. Who is he to dare provoke a God? to
undermine the worship of deity? They call upon Dionysus to
descend from Mount Olympus to "quell" this parvenu. Recollection of Pentheus's former threat to imprison those who practice religious rites and to sell them into slavery causes their antics to grow increasingly frenzied. They call upon their lord, the
fertile one, "father of waters" and "the giver of wealth and
blessing to man," to assist them (p. 293). They long for his aid,
implore him to join them in their games. "Loveliest of waters
are his streams, they tell me, enriching a land of noble horses"
(p. 293).

That Dionysus is identified with the element of water is
understandable, since he, a fertilizing agent, and water, also a
nourishing principle, are both the very substance of life. The
fons et origo of existence—water being that primal element
without which nothing can exist, that fluid which circulates
throughout the universe, feeding everything in its course. Dionysus is inborn in nature; he is that seminal fluid which is pro-

tected within the amniotic waters, which preserve and protect the fetus. As such, it is implicit in the transformation ritual: from fetus to the creation of the human being.

Dionysus together with the Bacchants, will disrupt Pentheus's rigidly structured rule. To effect such an alteration of components, however, requires a cataclysmic event. Lightening now flashes onto Semele's tomb, which is onstage and situated near the palace. The earth trembles. The Chorus rushes about, frantic, fearful, yet bedazzled and enraptured. A god has been scourged, they cry; his worship has been degraded. Retribution is in store. The earth quakes. Part of the royal palace now crumbles; flames invade it; chaos. A God emerges—an epiphany has taken place.

2. *Pathos*

That the royal palace should have begun to crumble is not an unusual occurrence in plays and myths. Cataclysms occur in most religions when a numinous experience is in the offing: when Moses climbed Mount Sinai, at the time of Christ's crucifixion, and Prometheus's fall into Tartarus. Whirlwinds, earthquakes, storms of the most violent kind, indicate the coming of a new or fresh order that breaks through out of darkness, out of the stratified layers of hard matter—from the unconscious to consciousness, from the unmanifested to the manifested. Comparable to the birth of a child, the unborn who cuts its way through the folds of the skin, nerves, and muscles, rupturing membranes, and blood vessels in the journey; so too, a psychological attitude or a creative idea must travel into harrowing climes to reach its sublime goal.

The Chorus begins its dithyrambs anew, its frenetic supplications. "Admire him!" they shout. "O, we adore him!" they iterate. "Burn, burn down, the palace of Pentheus," the god's voice is heard sounding from within the palace, ringing and reverberating through the air in crystal clarity.

The palace crumbles, Pentheus's principled order has been shaken to its very foundations; authority has been eroded; rigid, unbending attitudes have shattered. Lightning again flashes. Semele's tomb smoulders. An epiphany has taken place as Dionysus shouts: "Raise yourselves and take courage." There is nothing to fear in the sexual experience. It is part of the life process.

Immerse yourself deeply in it, in all of life. Let spirit and matter, soul and body, the sacred and the profane, be one.

A Herdsman enters the stage. Pentheus questions him about the orgies taking place on Mount Cithaeron. As they are described to him, Pentheus asks for more and more details. He listens and lusts, his mouth almost watering as he visualizes the women at their libations, their sexual antics, their frenzied dances. The Herdsman continues:

First they let their hair fly loose about their shoulders and tucked up their fawnskins, those whose fastenings had become unloosed, and girt the speckled skins bout them with serpents that licked their cheek. Others held gazelles in their arms, or the untamed whelps of wolves, feeding them with their white milk. These were young mothers who had left their infants behind and still and their breasts swollen with milk. Then they put on ivy wreaths and crowns of oak and flowery smilax. One took her thyrsus and struck it against a rock, and there sprang from it a dewy stream of water. Another struck her fennel wand upon the ground, and the god sent up a fountain of wine for her. (P. 296)

The Herdsman described the manner in which the Bacchants killed the animals on the mountain, how they drank their blood, then experiencing feelings of purification, of cleanliness as "serpents licked clean the clots from their cheeks" (p. 297).

Serpents, also associated with Dionysus, stand for energy, force, nature in its most elemental state, since snakes creep along the earth's floor, hide in the grass, in tree branches, undulate, hiss, attack their victims if provoked. In Crete, the home of Rhea, priestesses wore snakes coiled around their bodies: Artemis, Hecate, Persephone, and Isis were all featured with reptiles about their person. Representative of the most primitive strata of life, snakes also symbolize the death/rebirth ritual: they shed their skin yearly and are thus reborn into a new being, forever and ever.

Pentheus's own sexual duality emerges into actuality. Ambivalent feelings, a tug of opposites, come to the fore. Until now conflict had been inoperative. Rejection and repression of any identification with the feminine world had previously been his way. Now, however, he both hates and loves the Bacchants; he seeks to destroy them yet is enticed by them and what they represent. It would be wiser, the Stranger tells Pentheus, not "to take up arms against a god" but to "sacrifice to him rather than rage and kick against the pricks—a man against a god" (p. 298). Pentheus, though lured by the idea of viewing the Bacchants, is, nevertheless, outraged. In an about-face, he decides to slaughter all the women. Moments later, however, he changes his mind. He yields to the Stranger's suggestion that he view their orgies. To do so, however, he will have to wear women's vestments. Men are forbidden to see these mysteries. Ashamed to wear feminine garb, at first, the more Pentheus thinks about donning such accouterments, the more he enjoys the experience. "What sort of dress? . . . What dress will you put on my body?" he questions heatedly. "What is the next item in my outfit?" (p. 299).

Transvestism, a form of sexual perversion, is a strong force in Pentheus's psychological makeup. His delight at the thought is virtually uncontrollable. Ashamed at first to disguise himself as a woman, the feeling is quickly dissipated by the thought of the pleasures he is to experience. A singular delight overwhelms him as he dons the gaudy robe, the fawn skin, the wig, and moves about "as if under some strange influence." Although some transvestites unconsciously believe that the donning of feminine clothes symbolizes a conquest of the opposite sex, it actually indicates quite the opposite. The transvestite does not want to become a woman, what he is intent upon doing is wresting her power from her, thus erroneously enabling him to feel more masculine, more of a man. Once Pentheus is dressed in feminine clothing, he seems to grow in self-confidence, identifying perhaps with Agave, his powerful mother, who is the leader of the Bacchants in their frenetic rites. Unconsciously, however, he is projecting phallic attributes upon his mother, thus revealing psychologically what is at the heart of his problem, his incestuous feeling for her.[18]

Real heroes, such as Ulysses and Perseus, reject the great mother—both personal and collective—during the maturation process, when identification with the father or masculine principle is acute. Ideally it is at this period that the male discovers his phallic power and learns to use it in a positive manner; in so doing, he achieves some semblance of independence and wholeness. The feminine principle can then be encouraged to reintegrate itself with the psyche; to add its attributes to the complex whole that forms the conscious personality, thus paving the way for a larger frame of reference and a harmony of being. No such process has ever taken place in Pentheus's psyche. Weakly structured, emotionally undeveloped, stunted and one-sided, he is incapable of psychological growth. His infantile ego, exemplified by his propensity for transvestism, discloses a fundamental inability to identify with either the masculine or the feminine sex. Pentheus, therefore, is neither male nor female. He is nothing but an appendage of the phallic mother and her most terrifying of forms. Castrated, impotent, unrelated to earth and body, Pentheus the transvestite is inadequate as either man or ruler. Symbolically speaking, such a being has to be done away with in his present form. A civilization cannot flourish under the dominion of such a force.

Transvestism, which is implicit in bisexuality, was prevalent in Greek culture: the Lycians, for example, wore feminine clothing during their funeral rituals. Mystically considered, bisexuality represents a union of opposites, a self-generative agent.[19] Identified at times with the phoenix, such a fusion of polarities in religious symbolism, indicates a need for inner unity. When the split between the outer and the inner being, or the feminine and the masculine, seems too great, the urgency for balance is revealed at times in an outer garment—a covering of sorts, a mask. Whether the emotional equivalent takes the form of clothing or of an abstract notion, such as Plato's Ideas, the Stoic's *pneuma*, the mathematical harmonies of Pythagoras, or the hermaphroditic god Phanes in Orphism, depends upon the culture, the period, and the person describing the event. An integration of opposites in Pentheus's case is of course impossible under the conditions dramatized by Euripides.

Pentheus tingles with pleasure. He asks the Stranger more and more questions about the secret antics of the Bacchants while also experiencing concomitant sexual glee. "What do I look like?" he questions narcissistically. "Have I not the pose of Ino? or Agave, yes, my own mother Agave?" (p. 302). He oscillates as he speaks, sways in curved contours, titillated at the thought of seeing things he should not view—his mother in particular, in her most secret poses.

The Stranger comments on the fact that Pentheus's wig has loosened. "I must have dislodged it inside," the king retorts, "while I was tossing my locks up and down in bacchic ecstasy"

(p. 302). No longer arrogant or self-righteous, he anticipates the excitement he will know; he sees himself participating in the frantic frenzied rapture. He asks the Stranger for instruction: how should he hold his thyrsus? in his left or right hand? Does his robe hang too low? Is it straight? Meanwhile, his actions have become more nuanced, his feminine side emerging in covert ways. Subtlety, not threats, will help him to eradicate this band of temptresses. "One does not overcome women by force, I shall conceal myself in the firs," he informs the Stranger (p. 302).

The thought of hiding in the fir, that sacred evergreen, arouses Pentheus still further. The fir tree—a visual duplication of the thyrsus—represents the phallus as well as the spiritual domain: the former because of its furry hair and long branches; the latter, because of its branches which point toward the heavens, indicting a need for unification between man and god, heaven and earth, particularly in Pentheus's case—he who has cut god out of his life.

3. *The Messenger*

The Messenger relates the events. Pentheus with the Stranger's help has climbed the fir tree and is hiding in it, deliriously delighting in the ecstasies which voyeurism has brought him. He grew dissatisfied with the view and wanted to see the women at closer range. The Stranger encourged him to climb to higher branches. The sexual imagery relating the events to come, is most blatant: "When he had set Pentheus on the branches of the fir, he slipped his hands along the trunk, letting it straighten again; but gently, for fear the mount should throw the rider. Aloft into the lofty air rose the sturdy fir, with my master sitting on top. And now he saw the maenads—but not so well as they saw him" (p. 305).

Over the melée Dionysus's voice is heard ringing out, asking the women to wreak vengeance on the being who has profaned their religious rites. No sooner are the words articulated than "a mysterious pillar of fire" begins rising from earth to heaven—a veritable ascension. The Bacchants listen to the command. They run, rush toward the fir tree, throw stones at the figure of Pentheus; they hurl "branches of fir at him," form a circle around the "treed beast," to wrench him from his heights so that they can tear him to pieces. Pentheus's mother, Agave, who does not recognize him as her son, "attacked him" and in her wine-driven frenzy pulls off his wig. "I am your child, mother," Pentheus tells her. "Pity me, mother; do not because of *my* sins, kill *your* child" (p. 306). Agave hears nothing. Possessed by Dionysiac frenzy, she begins dismembering what in her delirium she believes to be a mountain-lion cub, first tearing off one of Pentheus's arms, then with Ino's help, removing his other limbs, one by one. The other Maenads join in the sacramental rite of eating the flesh, drinking the blood. Finally Agave takes the head of Pentheus in her hands and impales it on a thyrsus. She again begins her frenzied dance, holding the thyrsus high—not unreminiscent of Salome's dance with the head of John the Baptist centuries later.

The speed and ecstasy of her dance transform her from a mortal person into an archetypal figure—a transpersonal force. The rotating energy of her dance further disorients and dizzies her, paving the way for a complete obliteration of perspective and lucidity. Differentiation disappears. Unconscious and irrational forces have taken over. A full-flooded orgy is unleashed; drums beat, wails and shrieks echo and reecho throughout the near and distant countryside. Quite literally beside themselves, the Bacchants have been divested of their womanhood and individuality; they have been transformed into forces of the collective unconscious, virtual divinities in their own right.

Mount Cithaeron seems the perfect setting for the bacchic sacramental meal. Since mountain peaks rise so much higher than the rest of the land, they have throughout history been identified with the celestial sphere; their majestic upward sweep suggests heavenly power and blessedness. Certainly mountains have been conducive to numinous experiences, as attested to by Mount Meru for the Hindu, Mount Tabor and Mount Sinai for the Jew, the Mount of Olives for the Christian, Mount Kaf for the Muslim. Invested with divine power—or so it is believed— the Bacchants perform the *sparagmos* (dismemberment) and *omophagia* (eating of the flesh). Pentheus, no longer the ruling power nor the voyeur nor transvestite, has become the sacrificial victim. Agave and the other Maenads tear apart what they believe to be a lion cub and consume its flesh and drink its blood.

From time immemorial, blood sacrifices were used as expressions of intense religious faith. Before the Exodus, for example, the enslaved Hebrews sacrificed the paschal lamb; blood was smeared on the doorsteps of their homes to prevent the angel of death from killing the firstborn (Exod. 12:13). Shed blood is also linked to the Christian notion of redemption and resurrection: when Joseph and Arimathea gathered Christ's blood in the Holy Grail after the Crucifixion. In the Catholic Mass, the wine is Christ's blood during the Eucharistic ritual.[20] The sacramental offering thereby reactualizes the mystery of the incarnate God each time it takes place. "And he took the cup, and gave thanks, and gave it to them, saying, Drink ye all of it. For this is my blood of the new testament, which is shed for many for the remission of sins (Matt. 26:28).

Omophagia, the eating of human flesh, is symbolically looked upon as a way of preserving human life: to kill is to continue living. Because meat is vital to humanity's survival, religions are filled with dismemberment images and omophagic rituals: Osiris, Dionysus, Orpheus, Christ, and many more. The bodies of these divinities are either swallowed or chewed or taken through the host to celebrate a sacramental meal. In Matthew we read: "And as they were eating, Jesus took bread, and blessed it, and brake it, and gave it to the disciples, and said, Take, eat; this is my body" (26:26).

To eat the flesh of a god, whether symbolically or actually, is to assimilate and absorb into one's innermost self that deity's essence. A sacramental meal is a way of binding the human and the transcendental together, of expressing brotherhood, spiritual unity, thereby strengthening ties with the divine and the collective. To eat in general is, psychologically speaking, an integrative act as well as an aggressive one, entailing as it does, masticating, swallowing, digesting. It requires the incorporation of exterior substances. Eating raw flesh in archaic societies, prior to the introduction of cooked meat, has often been considered a measure of primitivism: the distinguishing feature between civilization and the lack of it. Cooking, a transformation ritual, alters the consistency of raw meat, just as civilization supposedly changed instinctuality to a higher plane of action. *Omophagia* has, however, also been equated in societies, both young and old, with the renewal of fertility. In Meiningen today, the flesh of pigs is eaten on Candlemas and Ash Wednesday, the bones are kept and then put into a field or blended with seed in a bag, thus assuring the coming harvest.[21]

What Agave and the Bacchants symbolically accomplished by the *sparagmos* and *omophagia* rituals was a dismemberment of those factors in Greek culture that sought to annihilate *tellus mater*. Blood and meat had to be ingested, thus paving the way for an alteration of ways and views. Once maceration and ingestion have taken place, that is, a breaking up or restructuring of rigid attitudes, multiple or fragmented ideations emerge. The mutilation of the status quo, as symbolized in Pentheus's dismemberment, paved the way for the disappearance of a faulty ruling conscious principle.

In *The Bacchants*, however, Agave behaves entirely opposite from the way one would expect. Mothers, as procreating and life-giving forces, are wholly destructive in *The Bacchants*: they are *vagina dentata* types. Agave has devoured her son as Kronos, the father of the gods, ate his children for fear they would overthrow his rule. Agave's aggressive nature prevailed. Her filicide, however, was unconscious; accomplished in a moment of insanity. Kronos's act was thought out, reasoned, and perhaps more insidious. That Agave impales her son's head, indicates her desire to destroy the rational principle, that factor in him that rejected the instinctual world of feeling.

As Agave makes her way down from the mountainside, still aflame with religious frenzy, she displays Pentheus's impaled head—the remains of a lion cub, she says, torn to shreds—the feat that she and her maenads accomplished "With our bare hands" (p. 308). Cadmus enters with the rest of Pentheus's bones on a bier. Agave sees her father and, with unbridled happiness and expectant of all sorts of praise because of her accomplishment, is surprised by his demeanor, by his excoriating attack upon her. His reaction is unwarranted, given the facts she tells him: "I have left my shuttle by the loom; I have gone to greater things, to hunting animals with my hands. I bring in my arms, as you see, this prize of my courage, to hang on your walls. . . . Exult in my hunting and invite your friends to a feast. You are blessed, in the achievement I have wrought" (p. 308). Agave is as unintegrated in her way as Pentheus was in his. She identifies herself with the masculine element, as he unconsciously longed to do with the feminine. She sees herself as a hunter, thereby assuming a male occupation as in patriarchal societies; but female work in gynocracies. A confusion of functions and sexes has taken place. Chaos reigns as a breaking up and reblending of previous orientations and values is in the offing.

4. *The Lamentation*
Cadmus cries out. His agony is beyond describing as he looks in unabashed horror at his daughter raving-mad holding his grandson's head. In her trance dance, Agave is oblivious of her father's dismal view. She is angered by it, blames his lack of appreciation on his age. Cadmus prevails upon her to "gaze" at her prey—to observe closely the object of her rapture.

5. *Awareness*
Slowly consciousness returns and with it, awareness. Hysteria and frenzy subside. Stricken to the marrow by the result of her insidious act, a sense of bereavement follows her every breath; sorrow infiltrates her feeling world. A threnody ensues. "I see a mighty grief. Ah, miserable am I!" (p. 309). Guilt, retribution, a need for atonement prevails. Dread!

6. *Epiphany*
Dionysus makes his appearance—an epiphany, an apotheosis. The sacred moment of the play takes place. Deity is manifest: "My father, Zeus, ordained these things of old" (p. 311). Thus, we learn that the event was preordained and does exist in a mythical time scheme as is true of other numinous experiences. The disorder and disunity that brought ruination to Thebes will now be withdrawn; calm will emerge and with it, the birth of a new era. It has been ordained at the conclusion of the play that Cadmus and his wife, Harmonia, will be transformed into serpents, thus reemerge as eternal forces in humankind's world. As for Agave, she will go into exile. Her brand of feminism being too extreme to be of further aid in building of new ways, yet important in bringing to an end the ineffective and detrimental society in power.

Friedrich Nietzsche had warned of the dangers involved in depotentiating instinct. He was one of the first to speak of the "denaturalization of natural values" and to suggest that "we must liberate ourselves from morality in order to be able to live morally." [21] To codify morality is to ossify it, to transform it into an absolute. [22] If morality is considered as an end in itself, it can become an evil. To seek perfection indicates a repression of whatever unconscious forces are alive within an individual that do not conform to the collective social outlook. Only by reconciling polarities, rather than rejecting them, can a person or a culture come to terms with the multiple and fluid factors that make up human and social behavior patterns. When an individual (or a group) has a *reservatio mentalis* and refuses to face those forces in him or in his land that may not neatly conform to his way of thinking or feeling, he fails to confront his shadow, that factor within his psyche which doubts, irritates, and provokes him. He is in effect rejecting the whole growth process; evaluation nurtures. In Pentheus's case, it was his anima that became his adversary and defeated him. So traumatized was he by this principle, so obsessive was his fear of the feminine side of his nature, that he came under its dominion, tyrannized, and finally destroyed by it.

Dionysus wandered about the world in Greek times rectifying imbalance in institutions and ways of being. His presence did not die with Greece's decline. It still exists today. It is Dionysus who encourages uninhibited sexual pleasures and inspires the natural world to yield its fruits and display its beauteous form. He must work with his opposite, Apollo, who adds an inner dimension to humanity's visionary destiny and capacity. Only with both Dionysus and Apollo at the helm may the individuation process pursue its course in the most creative of ways.

> *Farewell*
> *son of Semele,*
> *who had such a beautiful face.*
> *Without you,*
> *The way to compose a sweet song is forgotten.* [23]

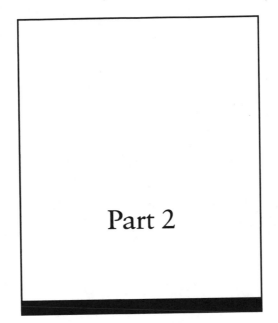

Part 2

Wolfram (1170–1220): *Parzival*— Existence Precedes Essence—The Creation of the Archetypal Hero

Parzival is a treasure trove of philosophical, historical, meta-physical, and psychological material. It is a legend that has been told and retold and forms the basis for Richard Wagner's famous opera. Wolfram von Eschenbach's *Parzival* relates the initiatory steps involved in the creation and evolution of an archetypal hero—the attainment of an integrated physical and spiritual maturity. The present interpretation of Wolfram's work is drawn in large part upon *The Grail Legend* by Marie-Louise von Franz.

Parzival is only one of the group of legends revolving around King Arthur and his Knights of the Round Table and the quest for the Holy Grail. Arthur, a semilegendary and semihistorical figure, was a Christianized Celtic chieftan (sixth century) who led his Welsh kinsmen in defense of their land against the invading Anglo-Saxons. His feats were so heroic that he was raised to the status of king. The Holy Grail was the name of the chalice that Joseph of Arimathea set at the foot of the cross to catch the blood of the crucified Christ. It was also identified with the chalice used by Christ in the institution of the Eucharist at the Last Supper. In *Parzival*, unlike other versions of the Grail story, Wolfram replaces the chalice, which is variously represented as a cup or dish, with an emerald green Grail stone. Whatever the shape, medieval iconography has endowed the Grail with mystical supernatural features. When one is in its presence, life is never-ending; nourishment is plentiful; spiritual illumination and invincibility are complete.

The keeper of the Grail's secret in Wolfram's *Parzival* is the

35

Fisher King, Anfortas, who during the course of his life has become ill from a mysterious and incurable disease. Since the Grail keeps him alive, he cannot die and thus be relieved of his agony. His kingdom, a concrete reflection of his failing physical and spiritual condition, was transformed from a flourishing to an arid and devastated area. Animals no longer procreated; vegetation lay listless. Parzival, the youthful hero, arrives at the Grail castle and, instead of asking Anfortas what troubled him, follows his mother's advice to be polite and stays silent. The Fisher King remains ill, and the land infertile. Aware of his mistake only after the fact, Parzival leaves, distraught. More adventures await him, including the meeting of his great love. Finally, he returns to the Grail castle. This time he is prepared to experience the mystery of the Grail and asks the question: "Uncle, what troubles you?" The Fisher King's health returns. Life is reborn throughout the land. Parzival will become the new keeper of the Grail. His wife, Condwiramurs, his two sons, Kardeiz and Loherangrîn, will join him.

Two important factors are involved in the Grail legend: the Grail stone itself and the quest or search, a process leading to individuation. (The word "quest" from the Latin *quaestus* and "question," *quaestio*, may be associated in this connection.) For Jung, the Grail signifies inner plenitude, the transcendental function, the Self; the ability to synthesize conscious and unconscious contests; to give one's life an inner orientation.[1] Parzival's search for the Grail is tantamount to an individual's quest for the right course to take in life, a journey or pilgrimage that will lead him to his *center*, thereby bringing balance and harmony to an area where chaos might have prevailed. Other quests, notably Osiris's night-sea journey, Orpheus's descent, the Hindu's trajectory to free himself from the world of illusion, the Kabbalist's determination to find the point of creation or Godhead, Dante's *Inferno* and *Paradiso*, can all be related in one way or another to the Grail legend.

The quest for the Grail for some symbolizes the search for the light of Christ. It also possesses a wider psychological significance—a totality—life enriched by the darker, shadowy side of human nature: the syzygy, that is, the double, that other in the pair of opposites which lies buried in the psyche. Spirit without matter, darkness without light, life without death, consciousness without the unconscious, present only half the picture. To find the Grail requires awareness of both aspects of humankind; it demands a very special inner climate marked by *gnosis* as well as by *feeling*. One without the other cannot bring plenitude to an individual, nor can it reveal the treasure hard to attain, that inner wealth that lies dormant within each person and which, when roused from its somnolent condition, brings fullness of being. The tests endured by Parzival during his archetypal journey are here considered as an initiation or as ordeals in a purification process: a filtering that allows the hero to discern those elements in life that help him function as a person and as part of the collective sphere to which he also belongs. In the process, his ego is freed from the bonds that chain it, thus paving the way for a condition of independence and, in so doing, uniting the thinking and feeling function in his psyche.

ECTYPAL ANALYSIS

There are many and varied sources to the Grail legends and the Arthurian romances. Geoffrey of Monmouth in his *History of the Kings of Britain* (1100–1155) intimated that Aeneas's grandson, Brutus, founded Britain, thus reaching far back into classical antiquity, giving stature to the entire group of heroes coming to life. It was Geoffrey also who introduced the characters Merlin the Magician, Lancelot, Perceval, and Gawain. The Welsh priest Nennius (800) in his *Historia Britonum* was also important in relating stories concerning Arthur's parents, King Uther Pendragon (*Pen* in Welsh means "head"; a dragon was featured on the war standard) and Igraine. The Norman poet Wace in his *Roman de Brut* (1155) introduced the image of the Round Table and Arthur's death. Chrétien de Troyes (1160–90) wrote *The Grail Tale* in the ultrarefined court of Marie de Champagne and later at that of Philip of Flanders. His was, however, Wolfram's most important source. The English priest Layamon (1198–1207) translated Wace's work into English, including a host of bloody battles between Arthur and his enemies. Sir Thomas Malory's *Morte d'Arthur* (1485), which excels in artistry, was followed by Edmund Spenser's *Faerie Queene* (1590–96), Tennyson's *Idylls of the King* (1859–85), the works of William Morris, Edward Arlington Robinson, John Masefield, Mark Twain.

Few details are known about Wolfram von Eschenbach's life. He was a Bavarian knight, it is thought, who found patronage with the Landgrave Hermann of Thuringia. He lived in the castle of Wartburg for ten years. It was there that he probably composed *Parzival*. He claimed that he derived the idea for *Parzival* not from Chrétien de Troyes but from a Provençal poet Kiot, whom scholars have never been able to identify. Since Wolfram declared in his work that he did not know how to write, he must have orally transmitted his verse. He was a minnesinger, one of those restless and roving minstrel knights who recited and sang his poetry as he rode from one castle to the next.[2]

The action in Wolfram's *Parzival* spreads over Asia, Europe, Africa, and the Middle East and takes us from the sixth to the eleventh century: a time marked by plague, famine, poverty, and war. The sixth century found the Byzantine world fighting against the Persians, who sought to take over western Asia. With the capture of Jerusalem (614) and with repeated assaults upon Constantinople, the Persians pursued their course until "Greek fire," as these modern instruments of war (flamethrowers) were called, saved the Byzantine capital. Constantinople with its palaces, terraced gardens, gold and silver domes, knew grandeur exceeding that of ancient Rome.[3] The Crusaders helped in the final destruction of Byzantium.[4] Europe, meanwhile, was in a state of ferment. The Moors, who outshone the European peoples in the sciences and the arts, had dominated Spain since the early eighth century when they had driven out the Goths, the Christianized Berbers, and the Iberian Celts.[5] In France, Charlemagne created the most powerful military empire in Europe. He Christianized Bavaria and Saxony, destroyed the Avars, strengthened Francia against the Moors of Spain.

England was primitive by comparison with Spain. In 577 the Angles, Saxons, and Jutes conquered England. It became a divided land. The Danes entered, sacked part of the country, scattering monasteries and libraries. Schools were reduced to a state of virtual destitution. Alfred the Great (849–900), an Anglo-Saxon king, conquered the Danes and unified England. He reorganized the government, built up an army and navy, reformed the administration and judicial systems, and built cities.

It was at this period that the institution of knighthood grew and flourished. The outgrowth, seemingly of an ancient Germanic form of military initiation, it presented the hierophant with a series of rituals, which included both Christian and Muslim concepts: virtue and courage. The knight during the age of chivalry was always from the nobility. Titled and coming from a landholding family, he was a "gentle" man, that is, distinguished by *gens*, his ancestry. The discipline and tasks he had to endure to reach his goal were difficult and lengthy. From the ages of seven to nine, he served in a noble household as a page; from twelve to fourteen, as a squire, he served a lord; he waited on table, bedchamber, manor, learned to joust, strengthening both his body and mind in all kinds of studies, sports, and exercises. Once his apprenticeship was concluded he was received into the knightly order after a complicated ritual: purification in a bath, clothed in white tunic (purity), red robe (blood shed in honor of God), and a black coat (prepared to meet death); fasting, praying, then given his knightly armor (hauber, cuirass, armlets, gauntlets, sword, spurs, and more). The new knight was given his lance, helmet, and horse. Colorful tournaments were organized, as well as festive feasts, songs, dances, trysts, celebrations lasting frequently a week or more. His initiation completed, the knight is called upon to live a heroic and virtually saintly life, in accordance with the classical Roman tradition of physical prowess and martial valor and the Christian emphasis on serving the weak, the poor, the needy, and revering women and church. Although theoretically, the knights were supposed to comport themselves in the highest fashion; in reality, many of them were base, cruel, and corrupt.[6]

ARCHETYPAL ANALYSIS

1. *Parzival's Heritage*
Parzival's father, Gahmuret, was a knight whom Wolfram describes as "gallant and brave" (p. 7). He was beloved by his parents and his brothers. When Gahmuret's father dies, he leaves his kingdom, intent upon forging a life of his own. His older

brother offers him part of his kingdom in the hope he will stay. When he replies in the negative, his family gives him horses, gold, jewels. Gahmuret is filled with the need and desire for adventure: "My heart, however, yearns upward to the heights, I do not know why it is so full of life that the left side of my breast swells to bursting. O where is my desire driving me?" (p. 7)

Gahmuret's ways "were those that moderation dictated, and no other. Boast, he rarely did, great honor he meekly bore, haughtiness had no part in him" (p. 9). He was a noble knight in the best sense of the word. The true knight is master of his mount, which means in Jungian terms that he is master of those aspects of his psyche that his horse symbolized—instinct. It could be said that as master of the horse, an *equestrian*, he acted with *equity*. Aware and conscious of his own actions, he seeks to realize himself, but he is also devoted to the highest ideals.

Gahmuret travels far and wide—to Baghdad, Babylon, Persia, Egypt, Morocco, always fighting and jousting with courage and dignity. It is in Zazamanc, Africa, that he meets his beloved Belacane, a "sweet lady without guile" and "black as night," as are her people (p. 11). She has been attempting to defend her land against Christian invaders from Normandy, Spain, Scotland, and Champagne, but to no avail. Gahmuret drives the enemy out and the people of Zazamanc express their gratitude to him by proclaiming him king. Things go well, but soon, Belacane's love grows so powerful that she becomes overly possessive of Gahmuret. The adventurous type, he yearns to leave and does. Their son, Feirefiz the Angevin, "black and white," is born after his departure.

Gahmuret travels on to Spain and then to Waleis, where he enters a tournament and, being victorious, is offered the hand of Queen Herzeloyde. He has never seen "such radiance," he exclaims. "If all the candles had been extinguished, there would from her alone have been sufficient light" (p. 48). Herzeloyde becomes his second wife. Her love grows all-consuming. Prior to their marriage, however, Gahmuret warns her that he will not give up his life of adventure and that she must not try to hold him back: "you must leave me free of your watchful care. . . . I would like to practice the knightly art. If you do not allow me to go jousting, I still know the old trick that I used when I left my wife. . . . When she applied the chekrein to keep me from battle, I foresook a people and a country" (p. 55).

Gahmuret and Herzeloyde dwell together in complete harmony. She refrains from oversolicitude and together they wisely reign over the three countries of Waleis, Anjou, Norgals. She is very much of a woman—made for love—and when Gahmuret goes away to search for adventure, she does not try to stop him.

Not long after his departure, however, she has a terrible dream. "She thought a falling star was sweeping her into the air where fiery thunderbolts struck upon her with violence" (p. 58). A griffon seizes her right hand and wrenches it off. A dragon claws at her womb, sucking her breast, before fleeing. Herzeloyde writhes in terror. The very next day her husband's squire and another knight come to the castle to announce Gahmuret's death, which occurred while he was fighting for the Saracens in Baghdad. Herzeloyde collapses, unconscious. The right hand which was torn off from her in her dream represents, symbolically, the rational sphere, that force which reaches out into life and relates to the existential domain. In Herzeloyde's case, it was dismembered. Herzeloyde cannot reconcile herself to life without her husband. The falling star and the thunderbolts indicate an attack upon her very being, and destruction and shattering of the spiritual and physical world she has known and enjoyed. As to the meaning of the griffon and the dragon in her dream, their interpretation must wait until later. To discuss it now would be to reveal prematurely the secret involved in the whole process of initiation.

Herzeloyde, bewailing her fate, agonizes over the loss of Gahmuret and the idealized and eternal love that he represented for her. He was destroyed by his masculine drive, his ego, which constantly pushed him on to more and more battles. From their love, however, a son was to be born—Parzival.

2. *Parzival's Childhood*

Herzeloyde's sorrow is not to be assuaged. To preserve her one and only remaining joy—her newborn infant son, Parzival— she decides to relinquish her throne and withdraw into the forest. There she is determined to raise her son far from society and the knightly arts; she even forbids the few servants she brings with her ever to speak of the outside world to him. Her son's realm is to be the primeval forest, a paradisiac world; and the love Herzeloyde bore for her husband is now transferred to her son.[7]

The deep forest, the domain of the great mother, the remote lunar realm, which is left in its natural state in contrast to the cultivated garden with its ordered, planned and restricted vegetation, represents a womblike sphere. Fertility luxuriates and thrives, but chaotically, in the world of the "green" mother. Identified with the most primitive feminine level of the psyche, this protective maternal shelter encircles Parzival, holds him in a kind of psychologically incestuous thrall. In such an atmosphere the possessive, destructive devouring mother principle— nature—of which Herzeloyde like many another mother is quite unconscious, dominates. Her excuse is that she is protecting her son against harm; she will provide him with the nourishing and sustaining forces which will see to his long and "safe" life. Should Herzeloyde's way prevail, it would lead to psychological strangulation.

Parzival's mother, the bearer of the boy's first anima projection, is fostering a dangerous situation.[8] Lacking a father—even a father image—Herzeloyde is determined to fill both roles in her son's life. In so doing, she becomes the so-called protectress, but by the same token, she stunts his psychological development by keeping him in a regressive environment. Parzival's childhood in the forest is tantamount to a state of psychological introversion and complete dependence upon the mother or feminine principle. Not only is he oblivious to the outside world— the conscious realm—but he is also ignorant of his own heritage, even his name. He is always called "good son, beautiful son, dear son"; his mother never addresses him directly by his name. In this overprotective environment, which Herzeloyde is adamant in prolonging. Parzival lives in a "neurotic-regressive" infantile climate.[9] Two factors are here involved. Herzeloyde never again wants to suffer the hurt she knew with her husband's death, and she therefore creates an environment for her son in keeping with that need: thus she dominates him, thinking of herself and not of her son's future development. Herzeloyde is, in effect, acting against nature; re-creating a mother/son union that encourages the son to remain a child. In so doing, she is castrating him psychologically—as Cybele did to her son/lover Attis.

Nature, however, has sometimes a way of coming to the aid of the defenseless, although her method seems often strange and tenuous. Parzival has always enjoyed whittling arrows and shooting birds. Yet each time he shoots one, he weeps. He loves to hear the birds' songs, and when silenced, he tells his mother the world seems empty to him. Parzival's passion for birds is wholly understandable. In contrast to such a symbol as the snake, which crawls on the ground and represents the most elemental or primitive condition, the bird flies in the air to light and freedom, enjoying all those factors that Parzival has so far been denied. Important, too, is the fact that the bird is often symbolically identified with a superior stage of development—spirit as opposed to matter—with thought, feeling, ideas, "mental contents that belong to a higher condition of consciousness." [10] Psychologically, the slaying of the birds, which causes Parzival such pain, is an exteriorization of his own unconscious agony: his imprisonment which wounds him to the very depths of his being, which prevents him from growing and developing into adulthood. That his mother tries to keep him physically in the forest indicates an emotional strangulation of which she is unaware—he has no space nor air of his own to breathe.

As Parzival grows in strength and intelligence, he begins to question his mother about God. What is God like? "He is brighter than the daylight," Herzeloyde answers, "yet He took upon Himself the features of man" (p. 68). She also tells him of the "master of Hell" who is dark. The polarities of light and darkness, of good and evil, which existed inchoate in the medieval mind and created a perpetual tension of opposites, compelling humankind to become aware of the struggle to be waged during one's own life time, enabled differentiation and evaluation to come into being. Parzival has been denied this choice. Though he knows light and goodness, the realm of darkness and evil have been entirely hidden from him.

No life can always be circumscribed. On a hunting expedition one day, Parzival happens to see three knights galloping along a road on horseback. Their armor shines so brilliantly in the sun that Parzival is dazzled; the gleam of their helmets, standards, coats of mail, and swords fills him with what he thinks of as divine light. So naïve is he of the ways of the world that to greet them he crouches down on his hands and knees, addressing them as God. The knights, thinking him a fool, a country bumpkin, an ignorant lad, laugh. A fourth knight arrives and Parzival addresses him as God. The knights tell him that they are merely mortal men, and they begin to describe King Arthur's court and the life they lead there. Parzival is entranced. He rushes home to his mother and tells her of the incident: "I saw four men more shining than God, and they told me about knighthood. The royal power of Arthur shall in knightly honor turn me to chivalric service" (p. 71). Herzeloyde swoons when she hears her son talk in this way. To faint symbolizes the eclipse of the rational sphere; an inability to accept a situation consciously. The time has come when she can no longer keep her hold over her son.

The fact that there are at first three knights and that these are then joined by a fourth is significant in terms of Jungian numerological analysis. Numbers are not invented by the conscious mind but emerge from the unconscious spontaneously, as an archetypal image does, when the need arises. Numbers arouse energy, foment a dynamic process; they are "idea forces"—that is, they are a concretization or development of virtualities of spatial possibilities. They are also experiences or shapes that lie latent in the unconscious until consciousness experiences them in the form of "images, thoughts, and typical emotional modes of behavior."[11] In the conscious domain numbers are "quantitative"; in the unconscious, they are both "quantitative and qualitative," thereby arousing all sorts of sensations and feelings. As ordering devices used by man since the beginning of time, numbers are manifestations of a desire to conquer the world of contingency as well as the one that lies beyond his dominion. In that numbers lend order to what might otherwise be considered chaotic, they give a sense of security to those in need of it, and in this way are considered as "archetypal foundations of the psyche."[12]

In Parzival's case, the fact that the original number of knights was three, an uneven number, represents an active, dynamic, unfulfilled sphere: a tension of opposites, an energizing factor, a *coniunctio* of two and one (spirit, soul, and body, a trinity—Osiris, Isis, Horus; Father, Son, Holy Ghost; Siva, Vishnu, Brahma). The three indicates the chaos inhabiting Parzival's psyche at this time; the dissatisfaction and excitement, feelings of enchantment and terror—the numinosum. The arrival of the fourth knight therefore in a sense completes what was incomplete, adding that fourth element (as in the four seasons, the four cardinal points, the four letters in Adam, the four Evangelists, the Four Horsemen of the Apocalypse), giving Parzival the will, the desire, to enter into the active male sphere, to break out of the circumscribed maternal world in which he has up to now been living, and to carve out a life of his own.

Driven by the excitement caused by the sight of the four knights—reminiscent in so many ways of the religious fervor of saints and prophets—Parzival asks his mother for a horse. She is unable to deny him this request. She knows the lad is determined to set forth on the road of life, as was his father. Yet, she is not devoid of guile. She decides to provide him with the clothes of a "fool." She thinks that "People are much given to mockery," and perhaps Parzival will be so embarrassed by such attitudes that he will swiftly return to her. Out of sackcloth, accordingly, she fashions a fool's garmet and hood and provides him with calfskin boots.

Fools and clowns were closely linked in medieval times: they represented a reversal of the normal order of things and, as such, gave the impression of being stupid, ignorant, irreverent, and humorous. Psychologically, their variegated and colorful costumes are symbolic of fragmentation and lack of cohesion within the psyche. Featured on Tarot cards, the fool is considered to be the epitome of unconventional existence, living outside any hierarchical system or society; Parzival thus is ill equipped to set out into the world alone.

Herzeloyde also provides Parzival with advice designed to underscore his innocent nature. She tells him to be careful of dark fords, to ride swiftly into them if shallow and clear, to be polite when greeting people, to take advice from an old man, and to win a good woman's greeting by taking her ring and then embracing her. When Parzival leaves the following day, his mother is so grief-stricken that as he disappears from view, she drops dead on the ground.

Youth, acting purely on impulse, is unaware of the impact that its acts and desires may have upon its parents, and this is natural. So intent was Parzival upon breaking away from his *uroboric* condition (his endogamous and regressive situation), so intense was his desire for life that the severing of the umbilical cord must take place at all costs. If he were to have pursued his old ways, continued his introverted existence, burrowing ever more deeply into Mother Nature, he would have been doomed to remain at a psychologically infantile level. Herzeloyde's death is the fate meted out to those silver-cord mothers who never allow their sons to grow up, to develop a life of their own; who transfer their own love from their husband to their son, and, as such, experience a kind of arrested development in their own right.

Parzival, gratifying his urgent need for masculine companionship and adventure, has but one concern—to leave the domain of the forest, of the great mother, in which his own personal mother holds him captive. He must create a life of his own, experience the trials and tribulations required of the knight—those disciplines designed to strengthen both body and spirit, to prepare for emotional and spiritual maturity by creating a hierarchy of values—about which he now knows nothing. He has indeed a very long way to go before achieving his goal.

3. The Fool Emerges from the Forest

Parzival rides forth. He comes to a green in which is pitched a luxurious tent. He dismounts, walks inside, and sees a beautiful woman asleep. Remembering his mother's advice, he leaps into her bed, "forces her mouth to his," hugs her, and removes her ring and broach. Terrified, the lady in question, Lady Jeschute, feels horribly ashamed. Parzival gives her another kiss, takes some food for himself and rides off. "God shield you," he says. "That's what my mother told me to say" (p. 74).

This first action after leaving his mother's domain, reveals his simple nature, his naïve ways, and his unworldly manners. Not only was he ignorant of the ways of the world, but he offends the feminine principle by kissing the lady without her knowledge and permission, and by taking her jewels he is completely unaware of the suffering he has caused. That he thinks only of following his mother's advice to the letter, indicates that he is still bound to her emotionally.

When Lady Jeschute's husband, Duke Orilus de Lalander, returns long after Parzival's departure, he accuses her of infidelity and informs her that she has disgraced him. He no longer will live with her as husband and wife. He refuses to listen to what she tries to say in her own defense. He turns against her. His arrogance, egoism, and pride reveal his own unthinking attitude toward women. Caught up in his so-called manly honor, the *logos* principle—devoid of feeling or *eros*, that relating quality—egocentricity prevails. Sorrow is Lady Jeschute's lot now that her husband has rejected her; injustice has been done to a blameless person.

Meanwhile, Parzival rides on, oblivious to the suffering he has caused. He comes upon another lady, Sigune, seated with her dead lover's head and body lying on her lap, reminiscent of the *Pietà* and of the tapestry of the unicorn also resting on the lady's lap, symbolizing in the Middle Ages spiritual suffering and loss when psychic energy (libido) is no longer attracted to the outside world but is entirely indrawn. Sigune tells Parzival of her great sorrow at the death of Schianatulander, the knight whose bride she was to be. Looking up at Parzival's gentle trustful countenance, she tells him that his life will be "rich in blessings." What is his name? she questions. "*Bon fils, cher fils, beau fils,*" he answers. That Parzival is still unaware of his real name is indicative, as we have already mentioned, of his lack of personal identity. He has been so closely linked with his mother that he knows himself only by what she called him, by what she projected on to him. Not ever having experienced any life of his own, he is only his mother's good son, dear son, handsome son. Sigune recognizes the appellations, however, and she now informs him that Herzeloyde is her aunt—she and Parzival are cousins. She tells him that his name is Parzival (meaning *percer à val*, "to pierce right through the middle"). Such is to be his destiny: to pierce, cut, break down the veil—the wall—the circumscribed wall. One day, she predicts, he will reign over his parents' kingdom. She also tells him that Parzival's uncle, his father's brother and her own beloved, has been treacherously slain by Orilus, duke of Lalander, husband of Lady Jeschute. When Parzival hears this, his whole being is set afire by the need to avenge his uncle's death. For the first time he has a cause for which to fight. As Sigune tells him of his father, Gahmuret, of his heroism and Parzival's illustrious heritage, a new sense of awareness invades his being; feelings of identity with his paternal heritage give him a sense of obligation. The greater becomes his desire for a life of knightly action, the more violently he is drawn away from the matriarchal fold. He feels an urgency to take up his calling: the father principle, masculine *logos*, must now be fostered and brought into being.

Although Parzival is ready to pursue his journey, to continue on to King Arthur's castle about which the four knights had told him, Sigune, in her wisdom, realizes that he is as yet unprepared to deal with the dangers which will confront him. She, therefore, does not tell him to take the direct road leading to King Arthur's castle but another, indirect way. He must have experience, he must strengthen both mind and body before dealing with the dichotomies of life. Otherwise he will only come to harm. So Parzival takes his leave and turns to the "smooth-trodden and wide road" (p. 79), following once again the direction of the feminine principle—not of his mother this time but of a member of his own family.

Parzival's next stop is at a fisherman's house, where the fisherman refuses to give the young lad food which he demands without payment. Only after Parzival gives him Lady Jeschute's brooch as payment, is he given food, then directed to King Arthur's court. That the fisherman requires payment for his service is, in psychological terms, a step in the right direction—a further preparation for the cold, objective, outside world. Everything in life must be paid for in one way or another. Parzival, like everyone else, has to learn this difficult lesson: all mothers are not giving; all strangers are not feeling. That he gives the fisherman the brooch (with its pin), rather than the ring, indicates his first act of piercing through the world of infantilism and illusion, thus enabling him to experience the outer world as it is.

The fact that a fisherman is the one to give Parzival this first important lesson is also significant. Christ was associated with the age of Pisces and with fish, as his name indicates: *Jesus Kristus Theou Uios Soter* (Jesus Christ, Son of God, Savior) based on the anagram drawn from the name of fish in Greek, *ichthys*, the initials representing J.K.T.U.S. Fish was also indentified with Christ because of the miracle of the fish (Matt. 14:19). Fish represent fecundity, inner riches, instruments of regeneration, always altering in consistency, renewing in form, ready to nourish those who seek them out. Fish also suggest the Levi-

athan rising from the sea, the antithesis of light, those unre-
deemed, unregenerate, and unchanneled unconscious forces
within man.[13] Parzival might experience the fisherman in either
of these ways.

The fisherman points to the direction that Parzival must
take to reach the court of King Arthur. "You must lead me further than this" (p. 81), the young man tells him. No, the fisherman replies: the mighty high-bred knights who guard the castle
would be offended were he, a peasant, to approach King Arthur's virtually sacred domain. Symbolically, this means that only
those who have passed the tests required, who have been initiated into the chivalric order, are worthy of joining King Arthur
and his knights at the Round Table. Important, psychologically,
is the fact that one can direct a person so far, and that after
that, the initiative must come from the person. To find one's
own way alone obliges one to distinguish between personal feelings and attitudes and universal values.[14] Once questions are
posed, one begins to learn how to relate to the world at large,
without losing one's own still shaky identity in the process. Re-
liance upon oneself is the beginning of maturity.

Although as he rides, Parzival sits erect on his horse like a
knight, his fool's garb is often the target for laughter. Unaware
of the meaning of contempt or derision, he pursues his path
undaunted. When he chances to meet Ither of Gaheviez, the Red
Knight—so-called because his hair, armor, shield, trappings, and
horses are red—Parzival learns that the Red Knight was brought
up by Uther Pendragon and that he now claims the land of Britain as his own. In his hand the Red Knight holds a red-gold
goblet that he has snatched from King Arthur's Round Table
and, in so doing, spilled some of the wine on Queen Ginover's
gown, thus offending her.

Medieval man loved brilliant colors, and red was one of his
favorites, representing war, love, energy, flame, fire, excitement,
as well as passionate feeling. The Red Knight is thus the antithesis of Parzival who is the innocent fool, the pure white knight,
and who stands out by contrast in all his naïveté. Psychologically, the Red Knight may be considered Parzival's shadow, the
composite of his negative characteristics: those affects which have
never been allowed to emerge into consciousness. The goblet
that the Red Knight holds in his hand is a kind of chalice, sym-

bolizing the human heart; that he spilled its contents (the wine), unintentionally on the queen's lap, offending her sense of dignity, represents an affront to the feminine principle. Just as Parzival unintentionally brought harm to Lady Jeschute, so the Red Knight equally unconsciously had hurt the queen. Since both wine and blood are life-preserving forces, the Red Knight has also poured out in effect his own energetic power, a premonitory image of his death. His action was as rude and unbefitting a knight as Parzival's was. They are, indeed, doubles in behavior.

The Red Knight tells Parzival that no one in King Arthur's court has yet attempted to retrieve the goblet, thus avenging the theft and the stain on the queen. Parzival leaves the Red Knight and enters the castle. He finds disorder and chaos reigning: that the feminine principle has been sullied may be considered, symbolically, an attack upon Arthur's power; the fact that no one tried to rectify the situation indicates a state of lethargy and passivity within the court. Indeed, Arthur's power—that of the king, which represents supreme consciousness and the ruling principle in life—is no longer a noble force. His rule has grown weak, his ideals have degenerated indicating a concomitant state in the psychological sphere. The inner court (or the unconscious in man) is no longer working in harmony with the outer world (the conscious sphere).

Parzival approaches King Arthur and asks him for armor and for the rank of knighthood. The king acquiesces. All these things will be his, he tells him—the following morning. Parzival, however, makes it clear to the king that he only wants the Red Knight's armor and no other. Arthur cannot give it to him, since it is not his to give. Annoyed and behaving like a petulant child, which he still is, Parzival yields to his impulses. His request is in itself thoughtless and senseless, indicating a self-centeredness that befits only the adolescent. Arthur warns Parzival that if he fights the Red Knight and demands his armor, he will experience misfortune and sadness. Parzival refuses to listen to reason. He is in a hurry to win his knighthood and fame. He leaves the castle without thinking of the dangers involved, unprepared and ill equipped as is all too often the case with would-be heroes.

Parzival returns to the Red Knight and demands his armor.

That Parzival confronts the Red Knight in such a brash fashion not only reveals his awkwardness, his lack of insight, but his inability to handle situations. He behaves like the child that he is. The two begin jousting. The Red Knight strikes the lad who falls from his horse. Anger swells within Parzival so powerfully that he strikes back and kills the knight, his javelin piercing through the gap between the helmet and the vizor—through the eye. That rage should have been the force that motivated Parzival's action indicates the extent of Parzival's pent-up aggressive nature. Never before has he allowed himself the luxury of anger; nor has he ever felt so vexed. To allow so strong an instinctive reaction to emerge indicates a step forward in the building of a personality; it is also an expression of his emotionality and power. The killing episode, psychologically speaking, allowed his shadow to emerge; that darker half of his personality, that "fearful" world of instincts which erupted into consciousness.[15]

Parzival is intent upon obtaining the Red Knight's armor, indicating his extreme need for another persona, a covering for his fool's clothing, a strong outer layer or shell that will preserve or hide his still weakly structured and faltering ego. Armor represents the male world, the domain with which his father was so identified—the world of the chivalric warrior. The armor shields the secret, weak, chaotic domain with which Parzival must contend and must understand and live with. The slaying of the Red Knight reveals Parzival's attempt to dominate those unregenerate forces that lived within him; that energy until now contained (hermetically sealed) within him. That *yin* power within him is in conflict for the first time with the *yang*: the tension of opposites that were missing during his stay in the forest under his mother's protective care are emerging and will help him to develop.

Once Parzival has won his battle with the Red Knight, he sees a churl about and asks him to take the goblet back to the queen. Parzival does not return with it himself, the psychological implication being that he is either uninterested or unprepared to relate to the feminine element. Strength, power, the fighting spirit, the outward realm—the world of appearances, of knighthood—are now his to conquer.[16] He has won his armor by killing its owner, but when he tries to remove it from the Red Knight's body, he is powerless to do so. He cries out in his helplessness, and a page comes running from the direction of the castle. "Now tell me what to do?" Parzival says. "I don't know how to go about this. How do I get it from him onto me?" (p. 86). The page strips the Red Knight of his armor with great dexterity, explaining as he does so everything he feels that the future knight may need to know. "You have to wear knightly attire now" (p. 87), he tells Parzival. Before helping him to don the armor, he asks him to remove his crude Welsh garments. Parzival refuses, indicating that he is not yet prepared to separate himself from home and his mother. He is still very much attached to the matriarchal fold, as symbolized by the clothes she gave to him. Still living in a semiuroboric condition, he needs the security of the great mother, as exemplified by his own mother. The tenderness, love, and protection she offered, even, though he may also have experienced her negative side, are still important to him. His armor has not been won by courage or wisdom but by rashness. Parzival is not yet prepared to assume his knightly duties; he has not yet developed the virtues necessary: the finesse, the inner strength, the sense of integrity that chivalry requires.

Starting forth once more, he meets Gurnemanz, who is the lord of a castle. A *senex*, or wise old man, Gurnemanz will instruct Parzival further in the virtues needed for knighthood. Parzival's first statement to Gurnemanz reveals his naïveté. "Mother told me to accept advice from any man having grey hair" (p. 90).

Gurnemanz takes Parzival to his castle, has his armor removed, and when he sees the fool's garments beneath, is shocked. Later, he asks his attendants whether the young lad might have been fighting on behalf of a woman's honor? No, they reply, "He would not know how to ask a woman to accept his service, although his looks are of Love's color" (p. 91). They knew at first sight that the lad had not yet learned to relate to woman; he lacks manner, the insight, the *eros* quality so necessary in getting along with the opposite sex.

Gurnemanz noticed that Parzival was wounded; that he had suffered lacerations during his battle with the Red Knight. Gurnemanz himself "washed and bandaged the wound" with such care "that no father who strove for loyalty to his children could treat them any better" (p. 91). He represented the positive father figure—the serene healer. After Parzival was given his supper and was preparing for bed, maidens tended to his needs. But he was so embarrassed by their presence that he asked them to leave. The following morning Parzival is offered magnificent clothing. Conversing with his host, he speaks so much of his mother, that Gurnemanz finally says, "You talk like a little child. Why not stop talking about your mother and think of other things?" (p. 93). It is at this point that Gurnemanz instructs him on knightly comportment. Physical as well as spiritual attributes—loyalty, faith, integrity, are implicit in the archetype of knighthood. He tells him:

1. Never lose your sense of shame.
2. Shield the needy from distress with generosity and with kindness and strive for humility.
3. Be both poor and rich appropriately.
4. Leave bad manners to their own quarrel.
5. Do not ask too many questions.
6. Do not disdain thoughtful answers. . . . These should bring you wisdom.
7. Let mercy go along with daring.
8. You will frequently have to wear armor.
9. Be manly and cheerful of spirit.
10. Let women be dear to you, for that enhances a young man's worth.

Parzival listens quietly thereafter, and he "gave up talking about his mother—in his speech, but not in his heart, as is a true man's way" (p. 95). Psychologically he has developed considerably since he left his forest domain. He has divested himself of the outer garment—the persona—that his mother fashioned for him and donned those of the Red Knight. Outwardly he now stands for manly and heroic virtues; outwardly he will pursue his journey as a hero. Inwardly, he has not yet learned to relate to the feminine principle; to get in touch with his own world of feeling. Experience in the domain of violence and pain will further develop and strengthen both sides of his personality, pave the way for increased understanding and awareness.

Parzival has, however, already learned some of the meaning of duality and suffering, as well as endured physical pain. He has first met and then slain the Red Knight: he has seen the chaos existing at King Arthur's court; the shame the Red Knight's offense caused the queen. He realizes that life consists of more than that childhood paradisiac realm his mother had created for him—that beautiful infantile world: "All greeness looked withered to him" (p. 99); his life has now lost its simplicity. Parzival has learned to experience discomfort and trouble. As he is thinking about these matters while riding along on his horse, he falls into a trancelike state: it is as though he were being led by the horse and not he directing the animal. The reverie he was experiencing indicated a lack of orientation, a split between the persona and the inner man—virtual unconsciousness prevails. In this condition Parzival traverses mountains, streams, valleys, precipices. Finally he and his horse are confronted by a swaying drawbridge, on the other side of which he sees a band of sixty armed knights who shout, "Go back!" (p. 100). Parzival wants to forge ahead but when he sees that his horse is too frightened to step onto the bridge, he dismounts, takes the animal by the bridle, and leads him across. This is the first time that he has thought about a problem, that he has not acted purely on impulse but considered the matter rationally. The bridge he crosses symbolizes a linkage between the two sides of life, a *rite de passage* from adolescence to maturity, from the world of contingencies to that of immortality. Buddha was called "the Great Bridge," through him one crossed over to the other side, from the known to the unknown. That Parzival succeeds in crossing this treacherous drawbridge successfully indicates that he is ready to take the next step in the initiatory process.

He now arrives at the town surrounding a castle. When he knocks at the gate, a young girl opens it and volunteers to take him to the castle of Pelrapeire and its queen. As they move through the streets, Parzival notices the crowds. Everyone looks pale and sickly, shows signs of hunger and fatigue. He learns from his escort that the entire town is starving. The owner of the castle, Condwiramurs, is in desperate straits. King Clamide, who is her suitor, is unacceptable to her; because of it, he has laid siege to her castle and town and is virtually starving Condwiramurs and the inhabitants into submission. Unless she relents and becomes his bride, all her people will perish. When Parzival meets Condwiramurs, she is more beautiful than any woman he has ever beheld; "in *her* God had not omitted any wish" (p. 103). What perplexes the queen and her court is that Parzival, literally following his mentor Gurnemanz's advice, is so courteous that he does not utter a word in her presence. From one extreme (Lady Jeschute) to another. In other words, he still does not know how to relate to women. Parzival first obeyed his mother's rule of orders; now that of a *senex* figure. To be immured in the patriarchal realm is just as dangerous as to be imprisoned in the matriarchal one.

Condwiramurs, however, misinterprets his silence. She thinks he feels scorn for her and her court. She therefore tries to keep open the conversation, retrieve the impasse, and become the link between the masculine and feminine principles. As an anima figure, she takes it upon herself to act aggressively, to become a catalyst that will bring about the fusion of the two polarities.

That starvation and death existed in Condwiramurs's realm is indicative psychologically of an imbalance in her kingdom, as there was at Arthur's court. The dominant reason in both cases—one, patriarchal; the other, matriarchal—is sterility. New blood is needed, an exogamous force. Although "restraint" and "modesty" mark Condwiramurs's ways, so does "distress." Her anxiety is so great that it moves her to visit Parzival in his room at night. So unskilled, chaste, and ignorant of sex is he that he does not take the beautiful damsel to himself: "They did not join their bodies together" (p. 106). Grief-stricken by the lack of passion in his eyes, she begins to cry. Finally, quieting her sobs, she asks him to listen to her laments. It is at this juncture that she tells him that she would rather die than become Clamide's wife. It is Clamide we now learn who had killed Gurnemanz's son, causing the old man such grief. A challenge has occurred. Parzival once again has a cause. He will serve Condwiramurs and save her kingdom. Psychologically speaking, he is learning to relate to the feminine principle, not only subserviently, as he did when his mother gave him her precepts, but objectively in defense of what appears to him to be right.

Just as for Parzival his mother was once an anima figure, so now is Condwiramurs, representing purity, beauty, integrity in the earthly female he one day hopes to possess. Within her appear the highest virtues. She is unwilling to enslave herself to a man whom she does not love. Nor is she passive. Rather, she is forthright, courageous; she will fight for her ideals. To serve

her then is to come into contact with the highest values of
knighthood: to link together what has formerly been disjointed
within his psyche—the feminine and masculine forces in their
most positive aspects, their most noble manifestation. In so doing,
Parzival revitalizes a condition of stasis, feeds what has lacked
nourishment. He transfers his anima figure from mother to future wife.

Parzival has chosen a dangerous course. First, he jousts with
Clamide's seneschal, Kingrun, bringing him to his knees. Then
rather than killing him he resolves to use him to redress a cruel
act he had unthinkingly perpetrated. He instructs Kingrun to
return to Arthur's court to beg forgiveness for a lady he had
shamed inadvertently, Cunneware of Lalant, during the Red
Knight episode. Parzival's attempt to redress a wrongdoing is
his way of evaluating his impulsive deed, of coming to terms
with the suffering he has caused; of gaining a sense of decorum
and establishing a hierarchy of values.

After his victory, he returns to Condwiramurs who embraces him. "I shall never be the wife of any man on earth unless
it be the one I have just embraced" (p. 109). That night Parzival
lies with the queen in bed, but with "such propriety as would
surely not satisfy any woman who was so treated nowadays"
(p. 110). Such delicacy and sensitivity on Parzival's part indicates that woman is not just a sex object for him, according him
merely a pleasurable experience; she embodies spiritual values,
those that imply consideration, understanding and moderation.
He talks to her in gentle loving terms, with a feeling and tenderness that "suits ladies' ways far better" than a rough coarse
manner. On the third night together, they embrace in complete
love. Parzival is conscious of her feelings and not only of his
sexual urges. Their life together is experienced in plenitude, love,
and mutual care for the other's needs.

Danger is still present, however. Clamide's army attacks.
Not until he crosses the moat and enters into single-handed
combat with Parzival does the crisis begin (p. 114). They fight
for hours on and on. Finally Parzival cries out, "Now my wife
shall be free of you. Now learn what death is!" And Clamide
yields and begs for mercy. Again Parzival displays the sense of
pity he learned from Gurnemanz. He bids Clamide go to King
Arthur's court and redress once again the wrong Parzival had

perpetrated against Cunneware of Lalant which had caused the pretty damsel to be beaten (p. 112). That Clamide's defeat was to be put to positive use once again indicates Parzival's emerging consciousness, his sense of responsibility for his own actions; his growing ability to examine them, evaluate them, and if need be, redress a wrong.

Parzival returns to the queen, Condwiramurs, and together they know great happiness. The land is free of enemies; food is plentiful; the people thrive. "Their love stood in such strength that no wavering could affect it" (p. 120). When Parzival tells Condwiramurs that he wants to return to his mother, to see how she is faring, his wife does not try to restrain him. She is secure in her love and therefore feels no need to be possessive. She refuses to deny him the possibility of realizing himself, of developing his potential, which a confrontation with the outside world and the renewal of his ties with his mother may develop within him.

4. *The Grail Castle*

Each setting forth for Parzival is an initiation into the next sphere of being, a vehicle to lead him into another stage of his development.

As he journeys along, he thinks only of Condwiramurs. So deeply embedded is he in his reverie that he loses all sense of direction. Once again it is his horse who leads him on—instinct knowing the right way. He meets another fisherman but this time the man sitting in the boat is dressed in rich garments and wears a hat trimmed with peacock feathers. In medieval religious iconography, the peacock is pictured as drinking from the Eucharistic chalice; it was also believed to represent eternal beatitude. Its hundred eyes, underscore its visionary and intuitive powers. That the fisherman wears the plumage of a peacock in his hat indicates that he—an illuminating spiritual principle—will take over from the horse the function of guidance. No longer will the instinctual sphere be in charge.

When Parzival asks the fisherman where he can find lodging for the night, he points to a road but urges Parzival to be careful because the way is not clearly marked. Like the psychoanalyst who proceeds on the basis of an anamnesis, so the fisherman, identified with the fertile world of the unconscious, will be that force enabling Parzival to explore his own depths. That Parzival has allowed his horse (instinct) to guide him thus far, that his thoughts have been focused on his wife (feeling), and that the fisherman (intuition) now directs him indicate a momentary eclipse of the rational sphere, the reasoning masculine world. Only by this means can contents of the unconscious flow into consciousness.

More adventures ensue. We learn suddenly that a mountain—Munsalvaesche (the Mount of Salvation)—looms before him as if in vision—it seems to come from nowhere. In keeping with mountain symbolism in general, Munsalvaesche stands for spiritual climes, ascent to sublime heights—a point of contact between heaven and earth, a bridge, a link between macrocosm and microcosm. To gain access to Munsalvaesche is difficult. Only those who can see, who possess an inner dimension, are able to view it. For the others, it remains invisible.

Parzival rides up the mountain and into the Grail castle. When he enters this archetypal edifice, he is given an official welcome. His horse is unbridled, his armor removed. He washes, is then brought a magnificent silk cloak that belongs to Repanse de Schoye, whom we later learn is the keeper of the Grail. It is significant that Parzival dons a woman's cloak, since his has not yet been made for him: another persona must be applied if development is to pursue its course: the world of feminine feeling in its most spiritual form must be reactivated. Compensating for the lack of a father image in his youth, Parzival still has a tendency to overevaluate the masculine element of physical strength and to accept advice from *senex* figures (which as we have seen represent surrogate fathers), without questioning what is involved. He has enjoyed discernment and tenderness from Condwiramurs, but these have yet to be integrated into a spiritual kingdom.

Once his armor has been removed, Parzival is divested of his fighting persona. When a courtly official addresses him in what he considers to be an arrogant tone, he reaches for his sword, automatically forgetting that it was removed along with his armor. He can only clench his fist in anger, both recognizing and consciously restraining his instinctive impulses.

Parzival is now conducted to the great hall. It is here that he will experience a spectacular sight, that something about which he knows nothing will be revealed to him: the Grail. The ceremony begins. Candles are lit throughout the hall, creating an ambiance of incredible luminosity, resplendence—paving the way for a veritable epiphany. Huge marble fireplaces flame. Anfortas, the Fisher King, is carried in. Unable either to sit or to stand, his pain is so excruciating, he can only lean; he is placed close to one of the fires because he is always cold; only there can his body be warmed. His bejeweled clothes glitter, the ruby on his sable hat glows, indicating that he belongs to the spiritual elect.

Anfortas, who is alluded to as both the Fisher King and the Grail King, has been ill for a long time. Although the Grail is housed in his castle, he can no longer derive healing from it. Because he had loved an earthly woman more than he did the Grail, because he went in quest of personal fame and neglected chivalric spiritual values, he was punished for his transgressions. He was wounded by a heathen in his testicles and the wound never healed.[17] When one agrees to serve the Grail, it is the whole psyche that must be called into being, not merely the personal, ego-centered aspect. Anfortas's action indicated a narrowness and lack of discernment on his part. That his wound was in his testicles indicates that he had sinned sexually against Christian values: an attitude characteristic of ascetic Christianity, which so overvalues the spirit and undervalues the sexual or instinctual spheres that it thereby creates a dangerous gulf between them.

Illness, like the starvation in Condwiramurs's domain, the listless in King Arthur's court, indicates a sense of malfunction within the system. Something, therefore, seems to have gone wrong with Anfortas as the regulating force, as the superior conscience, as the authority and ideal he should have represented as the Grail King. The king's sickness underscores some cultural and psychological element that has gone askew. A *renovatio* is needed in both the physical and spiritual realm to energize what has grown arid, inject new life into what has fallen into oblivion.

Parzival observes the strange ritual that now takes place. A squire enters the great hall, carrying a lance in his hand from the point of which blood flows, running down into his sleeve. Weeping is heard as the squire bears the lance around the hall. Two noble maidens enter, wearing wreaths of flowers in their hair, each bearing a golden candelabra with its gleaming candles. Other ladies follow, bow, and set the ivory stools they carry, before the king. Two sharp knives are borne in; six more ladies carry in gleaming candles; six more complete the table settings. Silver, linen, goldenware, are placed on the garnet-colored tables along with crystal vases. Repanse de Schoye enters bearing the Grail "which surpasses all earthly perfection." She places it in front of Anfortas.

Each aspect of the Grail ceremony has its symbolic equivalent. The Grail bearer, Repanse de Schoye, we later discover is Parzival's aunt, his mother's sister. She is the counterpart of Parzival's wife: an impersonalized spiritual figure. To live fully, to become aware of life's dichotomies, Parzival must experience the idealized feminine principle as well as the actual flesh-and-blood woman he has chosen to love. If both are not encountered, the individuation process may not be able to pursue its course.[18]

The beautiful young girls participating in the ceremony represent that feminine element which is no longer barred from consciousness: a world of feeling which belongs to the religious experience and which helps in the initiation into another sphere of being. Parzival will now learn how to combine an individual love with one for humanity, tenderness, and compassion with mystical union: a *hieros gamos*, a marriage between the unconscious and conscious personalities.

The candles illuminating the great hall pave the way for an epiphany: light piercing through darkness, the altar awaiting the presence of divinity. The burning, blazing fires are agents of transformation, rendering what is fixed malleable, what is infected pure, what is in a state of stasis energetic. Fire is the element—the demiurge—that helps to warm what is cold and ailing.[19]

The bloodied lance carried by the squire may be considered a phallic symbol in that it penetrates. Awarded to a knight after the completion of his training, it stands for rectitude. The bleeding lance, it has also been suggested, may refer to that of Longinus, the Roman soldier who pierced the side of the crucified Christ and was later converted to Christianity. The two sharp knives brought into the hall will be used to lance Anfortas's wound, to draw out the pus, thus momentarily reliving him of his pain. Insofar as Parzival is concerned, lances, swords, and knives, instruments that cut and separate, indicate the necessity of dividing or breaking up those undeveloped aspects within the psyche of the young knight. Only then will he be able to grasp certain aspects of the spiritual world that remain beyond his understanding. The knives used in the ceremony, therefore, are brought into the light to dazzle and glisten, almost blinding Parzival by their beauty—reminiscent of his first encounter with the three knights whom he thought must be God. In this way, they point up the religious experience, focus on it, cut it into bits and pieces, so that Parzival can evaluate each aspect of the numinosum in terms of his own life experience.

As for the blood on the lance, it is not only an image of sanctification but the very life principle of sacrifice, of redemption. Blood is vital in religious rituals, whether real or symbolic. For some it represents the Eucharistic blood of Christ's sacrifice, which is the Christian's salvation. The Christian church repeats Christ's sacrifice endlessly; in the Middle Ages when faith was at its height, participants in the Mass were so emotionally moved when taking the sacrament, that they understood the meaning of mystical ecstasy. A whole new realm is now being opened up to Parzival—the energetic factor as symbolized by the blood, activating the God principle—the Self or the whole psyche.[20]

The tables filled with food represent those sustaining factors which pave the way for the Christian agape. Like blood, so bread (host), representing the body of Christ, nourishes and prolongs spiritual life. Tables, reminiscent of the Last Supper of Jesus at which the apostles ate, also have their existential counterpart in the Round Table (Charlemagne's table with his twelve peers, and so forth). Tables and food indicate a highly developed sensation function on the part of the participants, the ability to relate and cope with reality.[21]

The Grail stone possesses a soul; it is alive, a hierophany. Stones bearing religious significance have been associated with megalithic cults: the Celt Stonehenge, the Breton menhirs and dolmens. In antiquity and in the Middle Ages, meteorites were believed to have been sent by the gods. The Grail in Catharistic, Gnostic, and other mystic religious sects was considered to have been a gift of divinity. Only the purest of individuals may pick it up or even approach it and view it.[22]

Stone represents cohesion, hardness, durability, oneness; a reconciliation of opposites. Unlike a living plant or animal, minerals are far less subject to growth and change, birth and death. When a stone shatters or fragments, it may be identified with psychic disintegration; when whole, with orientation, equilibrium, memory of both past and present events. In many religions, stone takes on a sacred aspect: the Kaaba for the Muslim, the Omphalos for the ancient Greek, the Beith-El for the Hebrew, the philosophers' stone for the alchemist. Christ was looked upon as the cornerstone of the church (Matt. 21:42); the angular stone of the Mason stands for the passage from brute to refined material.

That the Holy Grail in Parzival is a green stone associates it with the emerald that fell from Lucifer's head when he was cast out of heaven and also with the *Tabula Smaragdina* of Hermes Trismegistus, the alleged founder of alchemy whose writings set down on the green stone are sacred to the mystic: they include the secrets of the earth, spirit, and soul. Green is also the color of the sea; its reflective soothing hues were used by medieval apothecaries in their medications as well as in the symbol that marked their trade. Green stands for fertility, rebirth, growth, futurity, hope. For the Muslim, the Green Man is half a heavenly and half an earthly being. In Celtic lore, Erin green refers to the place where happy people go. The Book of Revelation may perhaps have given Wolfram the idea of an emerald green stone: 'And he that sat was to look upon like a jasper and a sardine stone: and there was a rainbow round about the throne, in sight like unto an emerald" (4:3).

Although Parzival is aware of the extraordinary vision he has been granted in seeing the Grail, his encounter with the *numinosum* is not strong enough to compel him to act upon his own initiative. He still follows Gurnemanz's counsel, "not to ask too many questions," and refrains from questioning Anfortas about his pain, the sickness he must endure. He still identifies with the aggressive and earthly patriarchal sphere, not yet with the spiritually oriented and wise individual—the mature and thoughtful being.

The feast ends. The tables, settings, light, are removed as ceremoniously as they were brought in. Parzival looks at "the most beautiful old man he had ever beheld" (p. 131), King Anfortas. Although as he looks at him he feels as though he were entering another dimension in time, experiencing the world of his ancestors and is invaded by emotions as yet unknown to him—still he refrains from asking the question which would have healed the king and proven the depth of his own growth.

Courteously treated as always, Parzival is taken to his room, given goblets of mulberry juice, wine, claret, all set on a white cloth, fruits which are so beautiful that he thinks they could only have been grown in paradise (p. 133). Then he falls asleep, has a terrible dream, not unlike the one his mother had prior to her husband's death. It is concerned with sword thrusts inflicted on him during a joust which leaves him in great pain. Parzival awakens in agony. He is alone. Of the luxury he witnessed the previous night, there is no trace. On the carpet lie his two swords, the one given him by Anfortas during the ceremony and the other, taken from the Red Knight. He wonders why he has been treated in this way. He is still too young, too inexperienced to comprehend the extent of his failure. Unaware of the meaning of his dream, he has neglected to filter the pure from the impure, to separate and evaluate those ephemeral and eternal aspects of life. His initiation into the spiritual meaning of knighthood is incomplete.

Offended by what he considers to be a lack of consideration, blaming others for his own lack of discernment, Parzival rushes out of the castle, mounts his horse in grief and anger, then rides away. Outside the gates he sees a squire who tells him he should indeed ride off and calls him a "goose" for not having asked "the" question. Parzival understands nothing of what is going on. He demands an explanation from the stranger. None is forthcoming. Riding on, he comes upon a woman lamenting the death of her dead knight, whom she still holds clasped in her arms. It is Sigune, still caught up in her past dead love. He greets her and she warns him not to venture forth into the wild forest ahead of him. Harm can befall him there; many have lost their lives in this mazelike area: "Turn back if life is dear to you" (p. 136). He is adamant in pursuing his course. He wants to return to the Grail castle, to understand the meaning of his misadventure. Sigune tells him that the castle may never again be found; that not everyone may see it and those who search for it may never realize their goal. Only by chance may it be-

come visible, when one least expects it. Sigune now tells him
that Anfortas, the lord of the castle, has a brother, Trevrizent,
who spends his life atoning for the sin the Fisher King inflicted
on them all.

Parzival asks her why she continues to live with a dead
man. She has lost her strength and color and pursues a negative
course. Sigune's tears stream down her face. An anima figure,
Sigune stands for a too distant, too removed reality. She spends
her time in futile lament of a past that can never be recaptured,
a way and time that are over, an attitude that prevents her from
having any relationship with the present. Archetypally one realizes that her unrealized and impossible love are projections of
dead or dormant aspects within her psyche. That Parzival has
encountered her and will see her several times more during the
course of his quest indicates that she is most meaningful to him
as an anima figure, representing unrealized aspects of his own
subliminal world. That he failed to ask "the" question indicates
neglected or deadened contents in his unconscious, which must
be stirred, disturbed, enlivened, roused so that self-knowledge
may be furthered.

Sigune is a catalyst. She chastises Parzival for not having
questioned Anfortas. "Accursed man," she exclaims; she tells
him he lacks understanding and pity; that he is "too faint of
heart" (pp. 138–39). Now she reveals to him the secret of the
magic sword he carries with him. When he engages in combat,
he need not fear. It was made by the famous smith Trebuchet
and will withstand the first blow but will shatter at the second.
If taken back to a certain spring, the sword will become whole
again. "You must have the water at the source, beneath the rock,
before the light of day has shown upon it—the name of this
spring is Lac" (p. 138).

Water, the source of life, that purifying regenerative agent,
that preformal element which washes, soothes, purifies, and re-
blends elements, must be encountered by Parzival; he must bathe
psychologically speaking, in these restorative waters. Like the
waters of the womb, it nourishes; like the *prima materia* it represents potentiality; and when identified with the unconscious,
it contains infinite riches. Water is a hierophany, a sacred element which will purify that which is tainted in Parzival's soul/
psyche.

Until now, Parzival has identified with physical values, with the classical Roman virtues of courage, valor, prowess, bravery. If he should continue on such a course, heaping adventure upon adventure, perversion of his essentially fine nature would set in; his life would be passed in negative and senseless activity. No sense of any real purpose to living would ever be gained.

If Parzival is to develop further into the knightly order, more tests and great pain are in order. He decides to return to the forest, to try to untangle what is chaotic within this darkened sphere, this subliminal realm. During the course of his wanderings he comes upon a lady dressed in rags, dishonored, and grieving. He recognizes her as Lady Jeschute whose husband, Orilus de Lalander, has so wrongly punished her. He challenges Orilus, wins his fight, and again, instead of killing his enemy, requires that he reconcile himself with his lady. Psychologically, Parzival's struggle with Orilus indicates that he has become conscious of his wrongdoing and wishes to rectify it. He succeeds in his endeavor. Husband and wife are reconciled.

Parzival pursues his course. He notices that a falcon has been following him and that this bird has wounded some geese. The entire area is snow-covered. On the gleaming whiteness before him he notices three drops of blood. Suddenly, he feels great distress; pain overwhelms him. His thoughts center around Condwiramurs. The three red spots of blood feel like searing flame, as if his wife's skin were burning. Blood which represents life is being drained, lost, wasted. Symbolically, we may suggest that since the blood brings his wife to mind, something in his relationship with her must be disfunctioning, altering in consistency, diminishing. The falcon, a bird of prey, used both for hunting and in chivalric games, was frequently identified in medieval times with human relationships. That the falcon has wounded the geese indicates that Parzival has injured the feminine principle: the *yang* has mutilated the *yin*. Two contrary principles are evoked in the red blood and white snow images— red as energy, activity and its opposite, passivity and acceptance. So deeply engrossed is Parzival in his thoughts that the outside world seems temporarily blocked out; his mind begins to waver; his "senses deserted him" (p. 156). He lies down to sleep. A squire finds him some time later in a trancelike state. When he awakens, he could think only of Condwiramurs. She appears to him in all of her spiritual beauty; in her strong and steadfast affection. His relationship with her as attested to by his vision indicates a maturation between husband and wife, which frequently comes to pass in the second half of life—when qualities of spirit and soul coalesce, integrity becomes the rule of the day.[23]

When Parzival has sufficiently recovered, he returns to Arthur's court, to redress the wrongs he committed during his youthful adventures. It is there that he meets Cundrie, *la sorcière*. Although she is highly versed in geometry, astronomy, and languages of every kind, she is also beyond all doubt one of the ugliest creatures ever beheld: she has a nose like a dog's with two boar's teeth protruding from her mouth (p. 169). No man cares to be near her. She has told King Arthur that his honor has been blemished, that "falsity" exists within his ranks, and that Parzival is to blame for the wretchedness that permeates the court. "A curse on the beauty of your face and your manly limbs," she says to Parzival. She also chides him for not having questioned Anfortas. "Your silence earned you there the sin supreme" (p. 171). Interestingly enough, it is she who informs him of the existence of his half brother, Feirefiz, born of his father's union with the queen of Zazamanc.

The fact that it is a witchlike creature who tells Parzival of his half brother's existence and of his misdeeds implies the active participation of the supernatural in the events yet to come. A sorceress or witch usually functions by means of magic, which at least implies a mystical bond and *participation mystique* with nature. She may be identified with repressed consciousness; she also exists in a timeless sphere. Considering that Parzival has lived so long "unconsciously," it is not surprising that he should now be aware of this elemental force. A kind of nature spirit, Cundrie impresses Parzival, not through her beauty but by her ugliness; not with her light but by her darkness. She is a shadow figure who casts a spell about her and in this respect is comparable to an *intercessio divina*. She traumatizes Parzival, shocks him, and eventually forces him into action to view the truth of the situation.[24]

Her insults and brash reflections force Parzival to take stock of his universe. He wonders why she treats him in such a cruel manner, why she curses his "beauty." As Anfortas was physically wounded and so became ill, so Parzival is now emotionally hurt. His adventures have taken him into a masculine world filled with extroverted activity; he has developed his knightly martial skills which are now at the peak of their power. The sight of the red drops of blood on the snow, however, forced him to come into contact with his feelings, thoughts of his wife overwhelmed him. Cundrie activates contents in his subliminal realm which bring his failures to consciousness; a whole segment of his past emerges into the present. A period of indwelling follows in which Parzival's energy, formerly directed outward, is to be experienced inwardly. Parzival must come to terms with those witchlike elements within him, understand them, assimilate those contents which he has projected onto Cundrie—another anima figure.

5. Second Encounter with the Grail Castle

Parzival's archetypal quest is far from over. More battles, adventures, and pain are in store for him. The sword made by Trebuchet, which won both honor and fame for him, is shattered. When, as the lady Sigune directed, he brings it to the spring called Lac, it will be made whole again. The shattering of the sword indicates a fragmentation of those components within his psyche which had previously been undifferentiated; when Parzival immerses his sword in the Lac—a paradigm for the collective unconscious—the broken bits are united once more, ushering in new attitudes and a fresh focus on his situation. Parzival's acts now take on meaning and are not merely repetitions of previous ones. His energy is no longer diffused or scattered but pulled together, so to speak. To return a fragmented part of oneself to the depths of the collective unconscious may be to bathe it with nutritive and healing elements, to create a new perspective. Awareness, discernment, understanding of his multiple activities, as well as of the effect of his actions upon others, must now be Parzival's lot.

Once again Parzival returns to the forest where he meets Sigune still bewailing her lost love. Isolated in her loneliness, sustained only by the spiritual nourishment brought to her, we now learn, every Saturday night from the Grail castle, she is suggestive of a vestal virgin, who sublimates her love. Sigune has experienced only the spiritual side of life, and Parzival's repeated encounters with her, as an anima figure, reinforce his obvious need for what she represents. Overly physical, drawn too greatly to an earthbound existence, it is Sigune who always advises him correctly and who now tells him not to waste any more time but return directly to the Grail castle. This proves easier said than done. Parzival loses his way again, underscoring the fact that he is not yet ready for the supreme test.

Parzival journeys on and meets Trevrizent, his maternal uncle, the pious hermit who has renounced bread and wine to live the life of an ascetic: "He chastened himself with fasting and his continence struggle with the Devil" (p. 243). He is Parzival's spiritual father, the one who was to lead him to the Grail castle, thus initiating him still further into the mystery's of existence. But before he does so, Trevrizent takes Parzival into his cave, warmed by glowing coals. In this womblike area, Parzival will gain in understanding and his suffering will be partially assuaged. Reminiscent of Plato's allegory of the cave, this inner recess, lit indirectly by a candle, allows Parzival's soul to contemplate itself, encourages the whole spectrum to become more understandable. It is in this enclosed area, guided by another *senex* figure that Parzival comes to experience the heart: that eternal rhythmic, pulsating entity of being that teaches him the value of the spiritual attributes that must accompany the physical prowess of knighthood.

Trevrizent gives Parzival a black cloak—another persona—this time symbolizing death. Parzival's rapport with his inner and outer worlds, still askew, must be focused upon: his own mortality. The reality of death must be envisaged, not as an illusion, but as an actuality with which he must cope and therefore upon which he must now concentrate his energies. Garments, Jung has suggested, may be alluded to as "attitudes."[25] Parzival must focus upon developing still another view of the life/death cycle.

In Trevrizent's cave Parzival sees some holy relics, books, an altar stone. He recalls that he has come upon these objects during the course of his archetypal travels; each having signified something in terms of his worldly existence; now they will pave the way for his spiritual development. To recall objects from the past not only adds to an understanding of oneself but forces a kind of confrontation, helping one to piece the puzzle of life together. In that Parzival once again comes into contact with holy relics indicates that he is coming into touch with the spiritual values they symbolize, that they will energize something within him, *pierce the veil* of illusion within which he has lived, and are now becoming integrated into his psyche.

Parzival confesses his lack of direction. He seems to have been riding aimlessly for too long a time; bereft of happiness, the burdens of life have become almost too difficult to bear. Trevrizent counsels him to have faith in God, which psychologically implies to have faith in Self, in his total psyche, that transpersonal sphere within each being. He also tells Parzival: "You can wrest nothing from Him with anger. Anyone seeing you defy Him in hate will think you are weak in your wits" (p. 248). Until now Parzival has rejected God because he blamed him for his own failures, projecting upon deity his own inability to come to terms with life, to earn happiness and serenity: "And toward God I bear great hatred, for He stood godfather to my cares" (p. 247). Psychologically, Parzival has been bearing a grudge against his own being: hating, rejecting those aspects within his personality that his ego considered negative—that shadow factor. Now these so-called destructive forces must be understood, accepted, and integrated into the whole, joined together with other still fragmented elements within his psyche.

Trevrizent now completes Parzival's education: he tells him of the death of Herzeloyde, Parzival's mother. "You were the beast she suckled and the dragon which flew away from her" in her dream (p. 255). Guilt and grief are thus instilled in Parzival, important factors which enable him to wrestle with life's values, understand and evaluate his previous acts. Trevrizent informs him that Anfortas is his uncle (Herzeloyde's brother), that Repanse de Schoye is his aunt (his mother's sister). Just as awareness of his past acts constellates contents within his unconscious, thus paving the way for a broader view of the life experience, so his family also becomes known to him, each member representing some psychological factor within his own subliminal realm.

Parzival, returning to the forest, undergoes yet more adventures. He meets a stranger whose vestments are adorned with precious jewels. His name, Parzival learns, is Feirefiz. He has come to the west to try to discover the whereabouts of his father. Before the two brothers are aware of their kinship, they battle. Although Parzival downs Feirefiz, the struggle remains undecided. The white Christian and the black heathen—in Jungian terms, truly doubles—embrace each other. The positive and negative shadow forces now coexist.

Together the brothers go to Arthur's court. Cundrie, the sorceress, reappears in a spectacular headdress and veil. She speaks with great dignity and blesses both of Gahmuret's sons. She tells Parzival that he will eventually become the keeper of the Grail and that his wife, Condwiramurs, and his son Loherangrîn "have been named therein along with you" (p. 406). Cundrie assuages his guilt and, rather than dwelling on his sins, leads him to the Grail castle.

Anfortas greets Parzival in the great hall, which has been freshly aired and in which a special wood has been burning to eliminate "the stench of the wound" (p. 411). Parzival asks Anfortas, "Uncle, what is it that troubles you," and no sooner has he spoken than Anfortas is healed (p. 415). The Grail ceremony again takes place. Repanse de Schoye's exquisite face shines more brilliantly than before. Feirefiz, who eventually is converted to Christianity, marries her. As for Condwiramurs, she and Parzival, along with their two sons, come to the Grail castle where they live in harmony ever after.

Wolfram's *Parzival* is not only a remarkable literary work, capturing the dreams, fantasies, beauty, and ugliness of the late Middle Ages; it is also a spectacular psychological study depicting the birth and growth of an archetypal hero. Raised in the overprotected paradisiac realm his mother created for him, wrenching himself free from this constricting atmosphere, and causing pain to those close to him in so doing, Parzival roams about the world developing himself both on an existential as well as in a spiritual context. He becomes the perfect knight whose inner and outer development allows him to live fully and on multiple levels—in harmony with his ego or conscious domain, in balance with his Self, the transpersonal sphere, deity. Parzival's existence thus preceded his essence—the creation of his personality, his being, his world.

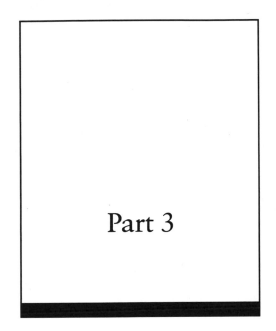

Part 3

Montaigne (1533–1592): *Essays—* The Individuation Process

Montaigne's *Essays* serve as a paradigm of the psychoanalytical technique; they are a way of coming to grips with problems that might otherwise have created havoc within a sensitive psyche. Self-probing and self-insight enabled Montaigne not only to face his torments but to find fulfillment in the process, to grow and evolve in depth and breadth—to individuate. "I study myself more than any other subject," he wrote. "It's my metaphysics and my physics." [1] The deeper his soundings, the greater became his understanding of Self and, as he suggested, of humanity in general: "Each man bears the entire form of man's estate" (p. 611). In contemporary terms we would say, ontogeny recapitulates phylogeny. The development or the course of development of an individual contains and repeats the development and the history of the race: within the individual lives the universal; within the mortal is contained the immortal.

Montaigne's psychological development as expressed in his *Essays* and as experienced in the individuation process calls into being the whole psyche, not merely one aspect or a single facet of it. What remained dormant in the unconscious, he tried to activate; what seemed inferior or what his ego considered to be, he attempted to retrieve and transform into a positive working function. Balance was his goal; harmony of purpose, his intention. Montaigne was no Utopianist, nor did he seek to escape into a world of illusion. He learned through difficult self-education to accept the dualities of life, its torments as well as its pleasures, to lessen its extremes. What he feared most—and understandably so—during his early years were pain and death. To understand the role these forces played in the cosmic process, intellectually, was relatively easy; to experience them emotionally, however, required great thought and courage on his part.

An introverted/thinking type with an inferior feeling function, Montaigne was vulnerable to emotional strain and anxiety. For the modern psychotherapist, the inroads he made into his psyche through self-analysis, as exemplified in his *Essays*, and the insights that emerged are not only fascinating but also creative and innovative. Never resting on his laurels, never experiencing a condition of stasis, Montaigne was always seeking to know himself better, to make conscious the hidden elements in his unconscious; to become increasingly aware of life's patterns via his own psyche.

Each of the three essays discussed in this chapter focuses on specific psychological problems and the way in which Montaigne analyzed and resolved these difficulties. "Of Solitude" deals with the strengthening of a weak ego through introspection; "Of Presumption" is concerned with inflation and deflation; "Of Repentance" broaches such spiritual and religious problems as sin, sacrifice, redemption, as well as ego/persona difficulties.

ECTYPAL ANALYSIS

Montaigne was a child of the Renaissance. He was moved by the spirit of his times—exciting but cruelly divided. An appetite for learning existed along with religious oppression and persecution; beauty with ugliness; progress toward greater individual freedom along with regression. The Renaissance brought into existence a new spiritual, scientific, literary, and philosophical outlook. Such an upheaval, culturally speaking, resulted from two movements: a break with the medieval past based on a relatively unified religious view, that of Roman Catholicism, and a return to classical Hellenic learning and culture previously considered pagan, or simply unknown. Such duality of purpose led to the breakup of traditional attitudes and the embracing of new and vital concepts. It aroused a spirit of adventure and rapture—a longing for beauty in body and soul.

Michel Eyquem de Montaigne first saw the light of day in his family's estate in the Château of Montaigne in Périgord some thirty miles from Bordeaux. His ancestors on his paternal side had been prosperous businessmen. His father, however, went to fight in the Italian wars and upon his return, chose a life of public service. In 1554 he was elected mayor of Bordeaux. A man who enjoyed his home, loved the natural world, and had a great admiration for classical learning, he was also impressively clear of judgment. Years later, Montaigne criticized his father for what he considered his "uncritical worship of learning," quite an understandable propensity given the thirst for acquiring knowledge that prevailed in sixteenth-century France. As for Montaigne's mother, Antoinette de Louppes de Villeneuve, who came from Toulouse, she was a marrano of Spanish-Jewish descent—and her family too were important and prosperous.

Montaigne's father had definite ideas on the education of his son. Believing that it was deleterious to a child's nervous system to be suddenly aroused from sleep, he arranged that the boy should be awakened by the sound of music. Because he wanted him to be fluent in Latin, he hired a German tutor, Dr. Hortastanus, to speak only in this ancient language to the boy. Parents, servants, anyone approaching the young Montaigne, were ordered to speak only Latin. For this reason, Latin may be considered Montaigne's mother tongue. Important, too, was the fact that his father did not believe in beating children; thus a warm and congenial atmosphere reigned in the home. In time, the lad was sent to the Collège de Guyenne in Bordeaux; he then studied law and became a magistrate, attached to the Cour des Aides of Périgueux, counselor at the Parlement of Bordeaux (1554–70). It was in 1559 that Montaigne met the person who was to become his closest and dearest friend, Etienne de La Boétie. A colleague of his in the Bordeaux Parlement, lawyer, humanist, author of *Discourse on Voluntary Servitude*, and happily married as well, died prematurely (1563). His death left an aching void in Montaigne's heart which was never filled save, perhaps, by his *Essays*, which many scholars believe acted as an antidote to his unbearable loneliness.

After La Boétie's death Montaigne tried to assuage his sorrow in various love affairs. These evidently did not bring him the satisfaction he sought. In 1565, he married the bride his parents chose for him, Françoise de La Chassaigne. Belonging to a well-known Bordeaux Catholic family, attractive, vigorous, natural in her ways, it has been said that she remained sexually dissatisfied with the "austere" Montaigne. She remedied this gap, seemingly, by taking his brother, the handsome Captain Saint-Martin, as her lover. Montaigne's ideas on marriage were the conventional ones of the period: love did not enter into the contract, sexual love was offensive to a "sacred alliance," and a profound friendship with a wife cannot be enjoyed because the fair sex (most of them) do not understand the deep feelings involved in such rapport.[2]

When his father died (1568), it caused him great grief, the relationship between father and son had been very close. Montaigne respected him for his humility, kindness and integrity; and courage in the face of disease. His father, who had been vigorous and robust, developed kidney stones which caused him excruciating pain during the last seven years of his life. Montaigne was to inherit this disease. It was because his father before he died had requested it that Montaigne began translating *The Book of Creatures, or a Natural Theology* by the fifteenth-century Spanish theologian Raymond Sebond, a work that proved to be crucial in Montaigne's development.

The question of pain and death would plague Montaigne all his life. Suffering and death were rampant due to the religious wars between Catholics and Protestants throughout France during the sixteenth century; the fact that five of Montaigne's six children died in infancy doubtless also accounts for this preoccupation with death. Montaigne, however, resolved to come to grips with the emotional torment the bereavements caused him. In 1571 he resigned his office of counselor to live on his estate as country squire. It was in these quiet surroundings that he began writing his *Essays*; that he felt a powerful desire to meditate, to understand nature's ways, to find some sort of balance in the chaos of his inner world. He had a fine library built for himself containing books in Greek, Latin, Hebrew, French, Tuscan, Spanish, and more. It was at this juncture that he set about his inquiry into Self—a lifelong endeavor.

Nine years later in 1580, the year that saw the publication of the first two books of his *Essays*, Montaigne visited Italy. He sought to broaden his horizons, refresh his views, acquire greater perspective on certain political, religious, and philosophical questions. He visited both Protestant and Jewish places of worship, as well as Roman Catholic ones. Travel for Montaigne was a *learning* experience in all senses of the word. It was in Italy that he received word that he had been elected mayor of Bordeaux, a post in which he acquitted himself with dignity at a particularly trying period in French history.

During Montaigne's first year as mayor he was able to spend much time on his estate, writing and meditating. The struggle between Henri duc de Guise and his cohorts in the Catholic League and the growing number of Protestants became steadily closer and more alarming. Troops were posted near Montaigne's estate; fighting occurred on his boundaries. The homes and lands of many peasants were pillaged. In addition, the horrors of the plague that broke out in Bordeaux left some fourteen thousand dead. A moral choice arose for Montaigne at the end of his second term in office. Since he had been away from Bordeaux and was to be relieved of his duties on August 1 and the plague had broken out in July, he decided it would be better not to take the chance of going into the city. His reasoning was that he could be of greater service to the citizenry by remaining healthy, outside the city gates, rather than by entering Bordeaux and becoming ill with the plague himself. "I will spare neither my life nor anything else for your service and will leave you to judge whether the service I can render you by my presence at the coming election is worth my risking going into the city in view of the bad condition it is in, especially for people coming from as pure an air as I do."[3] Montaigne was to be much criticized for his decision, yet he remained true to his own powers of reasoning. He did not allow his emotions to dominate his actions and to enslave him. To remain emotionally detached, which was Montaigne's way, was for him to maintain balance.

Montaigne's last years were spent writing, conversing with friends, and transforming his life into an art. To live in harmony with oneself and nature, to discover one's own needs and motivations through psychological investigation, is to enrich life, also to discover one's creative center, to experience serenity of being. For Montaigne, however, *increased consciousness* must work together with *conscience*: questions of morality should never be omitted in the spiritual or empirical realm. Absolute truth is unattainable, he reasoned; an individual, therefore, must rely on human nature once it has been edified through a deeper understanding of Self. The fruits of inner probing may be measured by the life the individual leads.

When death came to Montaigne on September 13, 1592, he seems—from what is known—to have received it serenely, as he had always wished: "I want death to find me planting my cabbages" (p. 62).

ARCHETYPAL ANALYSIS

1. "Of Solitude" (1572–1574): The Identity Crisis

Montaigne's use of both direct and indirect analytical method is particularly evident in his essay "Of Solidute." The technique of personal introspection that he perfected helped him to deal with what today one might call an identity crisis. His procedure seems to have been as follows: first, he chose the path of *indwelling*; he withdrew from the outside world to a great extent in order to devote himself to study, to probe and sound out his ideas, and being in the quiet of his country estate. He then compared his own insights with those held on similar subjects by Seneca, Epictetus, Cato, and other ancients. Antithesis, metaphor, analogy, epigram, and anecdote enabled him to filter his thoughts still further; to question his reasoning, define his problems, refine the conclusions drawn—all of which he believed would be of benefit in both empirical and creative spheres. The mind to Montaigne was not merely an instrument to perfect, however, but one that would help one to lead a fuller, more virtuous life, aid by assuaging fear and sorrow and bringing equilibrium and serenity to the person in need of it.

Because at this juncture Montaigne was experiencing an identity crisis, it was imperative that he assess his own being and discover his own worth and potential. He also needed to learn how to relate to both inner and outer worlds, the subjective as well as the objective, gaining an understanding of many kinds of situations, and a variety of personality types. By so doing, he would be able to discover his own unique qualities, strengthening those aspects within his psyche that were needed: building and structuring. As a thinking personality type, Montaigne proceeded with relative ease in his quest for self-knowledge, by exploring abstract and personal concrete concepts, collating sayings from ancient classical philosophers. An identification with his father, whose ideal had been learning and knowledge, reaffirmed Montaigne's natural mental prowess, his capacity for reasoning and applying logical thought to problematic views and conditions. This same paternal identification, however, was also a negative factor. Montaigne had never really built his own personality—his own code of ethics, views, and emotional conditioning. The time had already passed when the father/son fusion should have ended. Even before his father's death Montaigne needed to build a world of his own, strengthen and structure his ego, thereby developing his own potentialities.

Montaigne was an introverted thinking type; his feeling function was inferior, undeveloped, and vulnerable. He was easily hurt. His lack of *eros* (relating factor) prevented him from engaging in friendships, except the one he had enjoyed with La Boétie. He was aware of the fact that his ego—though, of course, he did not use this term—needed to be protected against incursions made by anxiety and stress—emotional conditions he knew only too well. Plagued by fear of how to endure pain and death, he also suffered, he tells us in "Of Solitude," from a naturally melancholy nature. Sadness and despair frequently overwhelmed him. He realized that if he yielded to these feelings, he might become permanently subject to them; they would dominate his existence, and he would surely succumb to a corrosion of personality structure. Some way of understanding the tensions inhabiting the empirical world and how these affected his psyche had to be found. Montaigne realized that he must develop some sort of discipline that would enable him to handle his self-destructive fears and emotions; to prevent them from gnawing at him. He could not allow himself to be tossed around by every pressure-riddled incident; nor would he allow himself to yield to the temptation of trusting the vagaries of fortune. If he did so, events beyond his control might well destroy him.

Thinking types, according to Jung, are oriented around *logos*, the reasoning power of the mind. Everything in the outer world is related to or associated with the mind. It is the mind that connects and links facts together; it is the mind that structures conceptualizations and abstractions. Such types—and Montaigne was one of them—proceed in an "apperceptive" manner: the mind is conscious of its consciousness.[4] Montaigne's ideas, his mental schema, were able to arouse a re-

sponse within his psyche; as his quest continued, it became progressively more self-stimulating, more self-activating. Never in
stasis, but always in the process of transformation, creating new
operational patterns, an idea for Montaigne was an ordering
experience, a process—a means of growing emotionally.[5]

Two dynamics can be seen at work in Montaigne's thinking
processes: the active and the passive. The first, the product of
his will, was rational, conceptual, ordered thought directed at
formulating judgments. The second, which might be termed intuitive thinking, a kind of "occurrence," when the irrational erupts
into consciousness. Montaigne was guided then by both objective and subjective factors, each in its own way fed by an inner
pulsion, an inner dynamism that bombarded him, disturbing his
supposedly outer orientation. Because he was a subjective introverted type, his thought processes, although directed to the outside world, were in reality often determined by an inner need—
the subjective element.

Like many introverted types, Montaigne often availed himself of an objective idea to which he attached a subjective view,
thereby deforming it; for by projecting his own feelings upon it,
he altered its objective reality. As an introverted type, he selected and determined his conceptualizations in accordance with
special stimuli to which his unconscious predisposed him.[6] To
accuse him of egotism and narcissism is only to reflect an extraverted attitude toward the introverted person. The "normal"
extraverted type relates to objective data and reality; he or she
therefore has little understanding of the problem facing the in-
dweller. Criteria for such judgments are lacking; therefore, views
on these matters, Jung suggests, are usually biased.

"Of Solitude" reveals how much Montaigne was oriented
toward the subjective world, a domain in which his judgment
gradually develops, his conceptualizations structure themselves
and help him to deal with his highly vulnerable nature. To
strengthen his ego—that factor within the psyche that mediates
between the inner and outer worlds—could best be accomplished by Stoic discipline. Its rigid ethic will help him develop
those very characteristics within him that he considers weak or
flawed. Stoicism encourages the authority of the mind and the
will, Montaigne's strong points. To follow Stoic beliefs permits
him metaphorically to flex the muscles of his inner world, to

test and strengthen them by increasing consciousness and, in so doing, toughening the ego.

Founded by Zeno of Citium and advocated by Seneca, Epictetus, Cato the Younger, and Marcus Aurelius, the Stoics believed that reality was material and that a transpersonal force—God—exists throughout the cosmos. Stoicism taught control over passions and desires, renunciation of pleasure and pain, detachment from the external world. Excess emotion was considered harmful and to be overcome by cognitive means. Ethics was achieved by reason and knowledge; morality was a private question; virtue a matter of will and the way to attain true happiness. Montaigne admired the fact that virtue and courage dominated the lives of the Stoics. Cato the Younger, for example, was known for his integrity, incorruptibility, and valiant nature. Seneca was also; when ordered by his former pupil Nero to kill himself, he did so with composure, seated at his table, by letting his blood out. Interesting to note is that Stoicism flourished at a time when the Roman Empire was in a state of political and economic decay, when license bloomed, social and religious armatures were crumbling. It gained impetus to a great extent as a counterforce, as an attempt to rectify an imbalance in the *Zeitgeist.*

One can well understand why Montaigne, a thinking type, would have recourse to such a philosophy—which underscores *logos* and leans so heavily on the will and virtues. There are, nevertheless, important psychological implications in the rigid doctrine of Stoicism. Ego-centered to a great extent, it is based on pride of reason and ethics. An abstract system that sometimes acts contrary to nature in that it disregards human frailties, it gives full reign to a cognitive view of life but gives no credence to man's instinctual world—a part of the whole man. Stoicism attempts to suppress the affective side of humankind which it considers weak (love, affection, relatedness). To divest a person of these characteristics is to dehumanize a being—to starve him.[7]

In Montaigne's case, however, Stoicism was mitigated by humanism, and he saw this philosophy in a more malleable, gentler form. Montaigne did not call for extremes, as practiced by Seneca or Epictetus, but for a more equilibrated attitude, closer to Marcus Aurelius's philosophy as described in his *Med-*

itations. In so far as Montaigne was concerned, the combination of Stoicism and humanism encouraged him to flesh out his feelings as well as his concepts, to bring them to the light of consciousness—thus making them accessible to reason and judgment.

Montaigne's goal at this juncture was to gain control of fears that centered for the most part around pain and death. He sought to become "unreachable" to these passions, to learn to be "above" and "beyond" them; to reject all that could dismember and mutilate his psyche. Exploring and analyzing those factors which bothered him, and making these the object of his analysis, would enable him, he felt, to confront them, thereby accustoming himself to their presence and, in this way, healing the wounds which bled so deeply.

An anamnesis was the opening step: a probing in the manner of a surgeon who seeks to discover significant clues which might lead to a cleansing and healing of an infection. Questions are posed. What distinguishes the individual from the collective? How does one distinguish between friends and acquaintances? family members? Once a person is secure in his own being, Montaigne suggests, he can become involved in outside activity without any ill effects. He should, however, never allow his well-being to be overly disturbed by outside events; never become emotionally victimized by externals. To avoid such a situation, it is wise to think through a problem or situation, thus staying an influx of emotions, evaluating conglomerates of ideas—particularly those which "flourish in the market place" and which offer all types of panaceas—those quick cures for whatever bothers an individual. Only by protracted and concerted exploration of thoughts as they meander about his mind, would Montaigne develop an understanding of Self and pass through the ego crisis plaguing him at this juncture.

How best could Montaigne develop his ego? In the early stages of his self-analysis, he decided to cut the outside world out of his life: to remain in solitude. Thrust upon his own resources, he would not be tempted to rely on external events or diversions that might detract him from his inward trajectory. He must *face himself*, he realized. Travel, therefore, escape mechanisms of any type, would be temporarily cut off. These would lead only to further fragmentation of the psyche and not to an integration of split-offs. Socrates had suggested that voyages do not change a personality, they really do not help find a solution to problems, since people take these heavy burdens along with them wherever they go. To flee a land, therefore, is to prolong a condition of emotional enslavement. Nor does frenetic socializing, amorous attachments, sexual indulgence, or yielding to the opinions of others help clarify thoughts and feelings. Such procedures delete the energy necessary to tend to the healing process.

"Our illness grips us by the soul, and the soul cannot escape from itself," Montaigne wrote. What he meant by "soul" is unclear. It included, certainly, a network of forces: the mind, reason, judgment, and conscience. Using these various factors at his disposal and adding solitude or a period of *introversion* to them were the psychic exercises Montaigne chose to strengthen his ego, thus becoming less vulnerable to emotional heights and depths. "Now since we are undertaking to live alone and do without company, let us make our contentment depend on ourselves; let us cut loose from all the ties that bind us to others; let us win from ourselves the power to live really alone and to live that way at our ease" (p. 177).

Introversion leads to the discovery of what mystics allude to as that *inner point*, that center, that beginning, which when experienced makes for understanding and equilibrium. Montaigne felt that by sequestering himself, cutting himself off from his outside activities, he would better observe the inner convolutions within his psyche; use this knowledge to better his attitude toward the phenomenological world. No room for excuses or evasions; it is within his inner world that he would establish himself and create his constant. During his period of withdrawal, he subsumed his thoughts and feelings. Each problem was broached in a methodical manner: thus he would not be, nor could be, swayed by fanaticism, a force so rampant in his day. "Contagion is very dangerous in the crowd" (p. 175), he wrote, and for this reason, killings may occur at a moments notice: as was the case with the Saint Bartholomew Day Massacre. How could people kill with such ease? he questioned. Without a thorough knowledge of one's inner workings, without airing one's beliefs and feelings, without analyzing one's motivations each step of the way, lucidity and awareness are virtually nonexistent. Any action, therefore, may be performed without the slightest pang of conscience—since it serves an "unreasoned" cause.

Montaigne's seclusion did not preclude his socializing at given periods. He met and invited congenial acquaintances and relatives to his home or attended certain social functions. When, however, he felt that affairs, either personal or collective, disrupted the course he had set for himself, he would again withdraw into his own realm. Such a practice became a valuable instrument in the solidifying of his ego: it forced his well-being to depend upon himself and no one else. It divested him from indulging in overly emotional relationships and took the sting out of involvements which might have torn him apart, thus disorienting him and virtually destroying his inner balance. Each individual, Montaigne wrote, *belongs to himself*. He should not allow any outside force to control his destiny or take control of his emotions when experiencing anxiety and stress. He must learn how to regulate his world, discover his own center of gravity. Life in all of its aspects—including pain and death—must be considered part of a cyclical and unending process. Without death, life is nonexistent; as joy does not come into being without torment.

Volatile temperaments that yield to passing fancies, to fads, who "embrace everything and engage themselves everywhere, who grow passionate about all things, who offer, present, and give themselves on all occasions" are scattered beings (p. 179). Such types have no orientation—no focus. They may become the pawns of movements, of destiny, of friend and foe—overwhelmed and shattered at the slightest provocation.

Since God gives us leisure to make arrangements for moving out, let us make them; let us pack our bags; let us take an early leave of the company; let us break free from the violent clutches that engage us elsewhere and draw us away from ourselves. We must untie these bonds that are so powerful, and henceforth love this and that, but be wedded only to ourselves. That is to say, let the other things be ours, but not joined and glued to us too strongly that they cannot be detached without tearing off our skin and some parts of our flesh as well. The greatest thing in the world is to know how to belong to oneself. (P. 178)

To underscore his view, Montaigne then relates how after Stilpo had survived the burning of his city in which his wife and children lost their lives, Demetrius I of Macedonia, noting the former's untroubled countenance, asked him if he had not suffered a loss in the fire. No, "nothing of his own," was Stilpo's reply. A Stoic to the very core, he had succeeded in so disciplining himself that he was impervious to all outside events. Such behavior might well be characterized as inhuman. Yet, at this stage in Montaigne's development, such complete Stoicism was of great importance as a role model to him.

Throughout the *Essays* and always to prove a point, Montaigne has recourse—as does Plato—to unforgettable archetypal images that remain impressed in the reader's mind long after the abstract argument has faded. In discussing his attempts to make himself mentally and emotionally less vulnerable to his pain and fear of suffering and death, he uses the analogy of a store. A store has two parts to it, he suggests; a front room where outsiders congregate and a back room which is private and to which only the owner has access.

We must reserve a back shop all our own, entirely free, in which to establish our real liberty and our principal retreat and solitude. Here our ordinary conversation must be between us and ourselves, and so private that no outside association or communication can find a place; here we must talk and laugh as if without wife, without children, without possessions, without retinue and servants, so that when the time comes to lose them, it will be nothing new to us to do without them. We have a soul that can be turned upon itself; it can keep itself company; it has the means to attack and the means to defend, the means to receive and the means to give; let us not fear that in this solitude we shall stagnate in tedious idleness. (P. 177)

The front part of the shop can be seen as the center of the conscious personality, the ego, functioning in harmony with the outside world, adapting to public opinion and the needs of the moment: aware, clear, able, and communicative. It allows the individual to display his public face, to reveal those facets of his or her personality with which he or she wishes to be identified; it determines the role and function the person outwardly wants to play. The back room, however, is closed, private, secret, suggestive of those remote cavelike areas in which certain ancient mystery rites took place. Remote, belonging to its owner, and to no one else, it can be equated with the personal and collective unconscious. It is here that solitude is enjoyed, that living, thinking, feeling, on an unconscious level, are experienced in perfect freedom, divested of space/time continuum. Just as the shopkeeper uses the back room as a storage place, to secure his treasures, his unsold articles, so it is also, paradoxically, both limited and unlimited in scope. It represents a world *in potentia*. No one may penetrate this inner sanctum, yet it contains all those elements that sustain the shopkeeper, that allow him to eat and live and to relate to the outside world. So the unconscious is a storehouse, a transpersonal realm, filled with universal contents that have yet to be assimilated by the ego. Accessible to the conscious mind only in archetypal images, the collective unconscious allows its contents to be envisaged in fleeting glimpses that function in the psychological domain as instincts do in the physical one, determining the behavior pattern of the psyche.[8]

Montaigne's image—archetypal, as we have seen, in dimension—expresses the basis of his functioning and his method, his ontology at this phase of his psychic development. It is so apt a comparison that it conveys the exact meaning of his thought. His encounter with the outside world, always difficult because his feeling function was so undeveloped, is to be kept for the present in the back room, compartmentalized, withdrawn, limited. Only those contents that he wants to have known will be visible to the world at large. Montaigne's ego (the front room of the shop) must learn to deal with external forces and take them in stride; the rest of the psyche will be cut off, accessible only when it learns how to disclose its contents in a less destructive manner.

Because archetypal images possess their own psychic energy, Montaigne's analogy aroused different emotional patterns within his unconscious, allowing some of them to flow into consciousness, to be dealt with by the ego, openly and effectively. Montaigne's intuitive perception of the need for withdrawal eventually allowed him to combine the irrational and rational aspects of his psyche, allowing them to function as a cohesive whole. It is interesting to note that Spinoza as well as Henri Bergson considered intuitive knowledge the most perfect form of cognition. In Montaigne's case he was drawing upon his own resources; because of a deep-seated need, an urgency, he became his psyche's self-explorer. As he pursued his method he was convinced that he was on the right path: breaking down, splitting, examining the component parts of each segment or filament of his thought, every emotion, every reaction, and examining them in the light of examples from the classical past. Such a technique allowed him to adapt in a seemingly logical and sequential manner his own private yet universal response to the world at large. Spontaneity and structure, seemingly paradoxical forces, give what sometimes appears to be meandering a ring of authenticity.

The stability Montaigne gained from his period of withdrawal gave him access to a new vantage point; it paved the way for an expansion of consciousness that encouraged him to probe still further. Very early in his self-analysis, Montaigne seems to have realized that answers are not quick to come by: to alter one's ways, particularly when they are so firmly set, takes years of work. As an illustration of this idea—one apt to prove amusing to the modern reader as the same problems remain today—Montaigne alludes to those who are forever carrying pills around with them and taking them at the slightest provocation to fend off a cold or some other simple ailment. They are seeking an immediate cure, an instant removal of a disability that sometimes or other will surely face them. What they do not realize, and what Montaigne knew instinctively, is that it is in the very encounter itself that the cure resides. The strength needed to gain immunity and successfully face ordeals, torments, and anxieties increases and is acquired when dealing with the problem overtly and openly. During difficult periods of stress an individual musters unsuspected powers within the psyche, hidden forces capable of dealing effectively with the trauma at stake. Such emotional upheavals can be beneficial if they prepare the individual for other later adversities; then one learns how to parry, thrust, or fence with the problem. To yield to such a panacea as pills or any other escape mechanism excessively, Montaigne warns, will "strangle us" and sap our very lifeblood (p. 181).

There is no right or wrong road, Montaigne wisely maintains. Everyone must discover his or her own inner being and the treasures it holds. As Sextus Propertius, the Roman elegiac poet wrote: "Let each one know the way that he should go" (p. 181). Each human being alone can come to understand his or her own ground-bed, his or her own center, that area where the person is most at home. Only then can he discover true identity and work at becoming independent. Neither seeking an overly active or ambitious course or its opposite, Montaigne chose for himself the middle way: judgment, understanding, and a sense of integrity and morality. Countering the arguments offered by both Pliny and Cicero, who suggested that personal glory should be the goal in life, Montaigne maintained that "Glory and repose are things that cannot lodge in the same dwelling" (p. 182); by their very nature, the two are at odds with each other.

"Retire unto yourself, but first prepare to receive yourself there; it would be madness to trust in yourself if you do not know how to govern yourself" (p. 182). Isolation without purpose or goal would yield little and might prove deleterious by alienating an individual still further from the collective world, divest him of *eros*. The pragmatic Montaigne, however, found a sort of personal salvation through his self-analytic technique. Rarely acting on impulse, examining his thoughts, feelings, and philosophical views, he never espoused extremes except to help himself over difficult hurdles. Once he had passed his moments of crisis, deep anxiety, and protracted fear, he grew accustomed to the inroads they made upon his psyche, and thus as himself had foreseen, their impact thereby diminished.

The positive result of Montaigne's period of indwelling took root in the life he led. This does not mean that he became less vulnerable, that he developed a hard carapace, that his response to pain and suffering diminished. These factors still coexisted and would always do so; and rather than lessening his life experience, enriched it. He was able to accept the dichotomies that existed in the empirical world: fear of pain and death. His self-analysis not only paved the way for a deeper understanding of the elements involved but also allowed him to accept life's vicissitudes, to look upon the cosmos as a composite of all things forever mobile, according to Heraclitus, forever clashing in accordance with Empedocles' view. So thoughts, feelings, sensations, are likewise fluid and antagonistic. All things alter and are transmuted during the course of existence; all is dialectically in flux, both within and without. The individual must therefore learn to adapt to circumstances and relationships, and he can do so only when he knows how to understand himself; if he feels comfortable within his own being; "to arrest your mind and fix it on definite and limited thoughts in which it may take pleasure" was not Montaigne's way (p. 183). Life in this world means change; it means development. Each phase of existence has its own peculiar excitement and, if examined analytically, broadens consciousness.

The identity crisis that caused Montaigne's initial period of withdrawal and indwelling came to a close. Stoical humanism had helped him over the difficulties that had so deeply troubled him, enabling him to encounter and experience the back room— the unconscious—not as an enemy or stranger but as a friend with whom he could communicate and with whom he felt at ease.

2. *"Of Presumption"* (1570–1580): *Inflation/Deflation*

Montaigne's introversion had a nourishing effect upon his creativity. Each inward probing or thrust made access into his unconscious easier and more fruitful; and he was able to establish a free-flowing relationship between his inner and outer being. As his scapes broadened in feeling tone and *gnosis*, his ego grew in strength. New attitudes were born, fresh ways of viewing life.

Following Socrates' dictum, "Know thyself," a statement that was inscribed on the Temple of Apollo at Delphi, Montaigne wrote: "The world always looks straight ahead; as for me, I turn my gaze inward, I fix it there and keep it busy. Everyone looks in front of him; as for me, I look inside of me; I have no business but with myself; I continually observe myself, I take stock of myself, I taste myself. Others always go elsewhere, if they stop to think about it; they always go forward . . . as for me, I roll about in myself" (p. 499).

As Montaigne grew more comfortable in his own being, the world about him took a less threatening cast. Rather than continuing to adhere to a rigid Stoical point of view, quotations from Plutarch's *Parallel Lives* infiltrated his writings. Plutarch presents a warmer and more appreciative approach to life than do Seneca, Pliny, and Epictetus. For Plutarch life had its pleasures as well as its pains. Worldly existence should not be based on authoritarian stringent discipline but on a flexible, more malleable approach. Important, too, is the fact that Montaigne had discovered that he in his own person could withstand physical suffering; in 1573 he had endured the first signs of kidney disease that was to plague him every now and then and become more severe in time. Pain, therefore, was no longer an unknown quantity. His fear of death was also mitigated. Having been knocked unconscious from a bad fall from his horse, he thereafter equated loss of consciousness with death and compared both with a long sleep—which was not as bad as he had once thought. Philosophically Montaigne realized that death was a necessary part of life—a part of the eternal death/rebirth cycle which all nature knows. Life could not exist without death. Furthermore, fear is never a solution, he reasoned. To live wisely, one must allow for illness and mortality and maintain perspectives; be adaptable to fates' vagaries.

Montaigne's expanded consciousness brought him to a period of greater detachment. He realized that the rigid pat solutions offered by the Stoics no longer answered his needs, either empirically or spiritually. He had grown, evolved, counter arguments begin to infiltrate into the *Essays*. In "A Custom of the Island of Cea" (2. 3), he suggests that Stoicism contains an admixture of spiritual arrogance, allocating as it does to human reason too prominent a place. The human mind has its limitations, and this must always be taken into account. When therefore reason is hailed as the sole and exclusive ruling force in one's life experience, one's outlook tends to become dogmatic and removed from actuality.

"What do I know?" questioned Sextus Empiricus, the third-century poet and Skeptic. Montaigne was so taken by this statement, he tells us, that he had it engraved on a medal that he wore around his neck, it allowed him to broach the entire subject of the reasoning mind and its judgment. In the "Apology for Raymond Sebond," Montaigne is quick to derogate intellectual arrogance, to point out the fact that human beings too often consider themselves superior to every other living creature. Citing Plutarch, he maintains that animals possess intelligence and that they frequently display more courage and kindness than human beings do. Because man no longer lives in harmony with nature, he has disrupted his psychic functioning—his equilibrium. He therefore seeks to dominate the world around him, including all of nature, a highly dangerous course. Humankind's pride and vanity, Montaigne suggests, have been and will be his undoing.

Nor does intelligence make for personal happiness. During the religious wars that plagued France, Montaigne observes, the peasants and the less well educated were better equipped to cope with life than were those who were learned scholars. Reason breeds curiosity, to be sure, but it also paves the way for hubris and wrongdoing. One can be virtuous without being lettered. They are not common denominators. The best lives, Montaigne believes, are the most pliable and adaptable; the least wasteful and extravagant. To follow the cosmic flux and yet maintain one's own identity and independence is Montaigne's ideal. Knowledge must be deepened throughout one's life, but the rational faculty must know its place. It is the *whole individual* that must function in the world—neither the brain nor the brawn exclusively.

Pyrrhon, the founder of skepticism, declared that true knowledge is impossible because our thoughts are always at the mercy of our bodily senses. Our reasoning power, therefore, may alter considerably when either heat or cold is too extreme; when sickness or melancholy takes over. Absolutes, therefore, are impossible to realize in the existential sphere. Life is based on probabilities, and thus, man must try to accept what he cannot control and maintain his calm in the handling of events and emotions under his dominion.

Although a Skeptic in matters of human knowledge—science, philosophy, mathematics, and so forth—when it came to religious belief, Montaigne was a fideist. He had implicit faith in God and rejected any attempt to prove divinity's existence by rational means. To do so, he suggested, was presumptuous: it was to limit the immutable, omniscient, and omnipotent—to render the infinite finite. Only God remains eternally and is unchanged.

Why did Montaigne center his attention on the notion "Of Presumption" when broaching both philosophical and pragmatic questions? Psychologically we may draw an analogy between presumption and inflation—arrogance, hubris. Such inflation indicates an attempt to identify the ego (the center of the conscious personality) with the Self (the total psyche, both conscious and unconscious). Infants and children, some young adults as well, experience a condition of inflation when they believe themselves to be the focal point of their parents' world—or of the world in general. Nothing but their own needs or wants are of import. True ego consciousness, therefore, is virtually non-existent. With maturity, the ego grows, evolves as a separate and independent entity. If it remains in a condition of stasis, the individual continues to live in the paradisiac state of childhood (in unconscious wholeness or an ideal state where everything is taken care of immediately). When such a situation prevails, growth is stunted: it accounts for a *regressus ad uterum* pattern evident today in so many people. With the coming of consciousness, however, a sense of identity arises. Projections on others usually diminish in depth or at least in power as one experiences a sense of one's own unique *oneness*—or *separateness*. As subject and object grow independent of one another, each experiences its own being and essence.

Inflation and its counterpole, deflation, or a sense of worthlessness, involve dependence upon others. Pride thrives only with an audience, and so does a sense of inferiority. Both need strangers or acquaintances to survive; both require comparisons to be made between one individual and another—or one group and many groups. In either case, one cannot live in comfort with oneself. That Montaigne should want to understand the notion of presumption which reveals a condition of dependence on others, as well as an inability to stand firm in one's identity, is understandable. His struggle to affirm his identity during a critical period in his life had also helped him to become emotionally independent and, therefore, able to rely upon his own judgment and reasoning powers to pursue his way in life.

Each time Montaigne takes up a new idea—such as presumption—he proceeds as if he were engaged in a professional analysis: he observes, divides, dissociates, associates his thoughts and feelings, always refining, always aiming for greater objectivity and sounder judgment. Imagery and allusions likewise always come into play to concretize his abstractions. In the case of presumption, he suggests that such escape mechanisms as ambition, hypocrisy, and artificiality detract from the fruit of inquiry: the individual having recourse to these will never focus on the core of his or her problem. To circle around or circumvent the question posed is like separating "the trunk and body of the tree" and forcing someone "to hang on to the branches."

The goal is therefore lost; one's grip becomes unsteady, footing unsure, and the results quite shaky.

Presumption leads Montaigne to consider the entire question of ambition, which he also disparages. "Ambition is neighbor to presumption, or rather daughter" (p. 489), he writes; then he quotes a statement made by Chancellor Olivier: "the French are like monkeys who climb to the top of a tree, from branch to branch, and never stop moving until they have reached the highest branch, and show their rear ends when they get there" (p. 490). To be ambitious implies an unerring confidence in oneself; to the point of believing, perhaps unconsciously, that one is capable of great deeds in life.

Equally presumptuous, writes Montaigne, is humankind's habit of judging others, basing one's conclusions, most frequently, on superficial and exterior criteria: an individual's gesture or his mannerisms. Alexander the Great, Alcibiades, Julius Caesar, and Cicero all had tics and quirks of which they were unaware. Before any judgment of value may be offered, mannerisms of all types must be studied in depth, as part of the whole personality and not merely as an attribute of it. Judgment, therefore, should be reserved, circumspect, and not based exclusively on external attitudes, actions, or comportment.

Nor is hero worship any less presumptuous. It, too, is an example of inflation/deflation, of hasty assessments; indicating a lack of discrimination and insight into people. Hero-worshipers idealize; they look at the object of their admiration from afar; they see their idols only under very special conditions, from a distance and not in an intimate atmosphere. They cannot, therefore, know them whole. Caught up in a vision, they base their value judgments on an illusion, thereby remaining under the dominion of a God figure of sorts.

There are two factors at work, Montaigne remarks, when dealing with presumption: either "we esteem ourselves too highly" or we do not "esteem others highly enough." Laot-ze suggested "high stands on low." Those with inferiority complexes usually conceal an unconscious superiority. "Opposites condition each other," Jung wrote.[9] Montaigne asserted that once the problem had been aired and insight gained, the difficulty could be corrected but not eradicated.

Having studied himself as well as others, Montaigne now proceeds to give one of the most extraordinary self-portraits in French literature: for its clarity, concision, and depth, despite certain conscious and unconscious distortions. The technique of free association, which he uses with felicity, gives a seemingly unstructured feeling to the essay; actually, it is highly ordered, in keeping with Montaigne's reasonable and active mind.

From the very outset, Montaigne wants his readers to know that he does not suffer from presumption, that he is a man like every other. "I consider myself one of the common sort . . . and I value myself only for knowing my value" (p. 481). He knows his worth; he also is aware of his deficiencies. He admits, for example, that he is hard to please. The fact that he cannot appreciate poetry troubles him and so does his writing style. He quotes Ovid:

> *When I reread I blush, for I see quite enough*
> *Fit to erase, though it was I who wrote the stuff.*
> *(P. 482)*

He also deprecates his own thought processes. An idea, he confesses, that seems clear, concise, and perfectly reasonable seems "blurred" once he has put it on paper, as if it had emerged from some sort of dream or vision that he can neither grasp nor exploit. He further reveals his sense of inferiority, when he compares his work to that of classical writers of the past; their imagination and talents "astound" and "transfix" him. He realizes that he must not worship them nor aspire to such heights; yet, he longs to perfect his own technique. In a sweeping, highly derogatory sentence, Montaigne assesses his own work as follows: "Everything I write is crude; it lacks distinction and beauty" (p. 483). Yet were he really to believe this statement, he would never have picked up his pen and written. Montaigne's tendency toward inflation and deflation is clearly present; that he projects these characteristics onto others is his way of facing a situation and clarifying his own emotions about it.

We also learn that although Montaigne is not entertaining, he suffers when he is not the center of attention, when he fails to attract others. If he attempts to tell a story, it is "dull"; he sees himself as devoid of humor. Always serious and intent upon solving philosophical and ethical problems, he cannot enliven or lead conversation. Those at social gatherings do not always want to consider serious problems; nor does he himself introduce such subjects with "ease or polish." His writings are "harsh and disdainful, with a free and unruly disposition" (p. 483); they resemble the style of Seneca rather than that of Plutarch which he more admires (p. 484).

Nor does Montaigne consider himself to be physically attractive. People always congregate around good-looking individuals, he observes. In this respect he takes umbrage with Plato who denigrated the physical body—it was the prison of the soul—and lauded the intellect/spirit, splitting the physical and spiritual asunder, the soma and psyche; his followers, Augustine and Thomas Aquinas, the Patristic Fathers, and others, took this same course. Everything, Montaigne asserts, in a human being is linked and related; nothing is separate—neither the mind nor the body should therefore be ranked. Each serves a purpose; each enhances life. To divide a human being into two parts—his corporeal, earthly, visible body, which is subject to change; and the soul or spiritual part of the being, which is eternal—creates a veritable schism within that may lead to disastrous effects.

Those who want to split up our two principal parts and sequester them from each other are wrong. On the contrary, we must couple and join them together again. We must order the soul not to draw aside and entertain itself apart, not to scorn and abandon the body . . . but to rally to the body, embrace it, cherish it, assist it, control it, advise it, set it right and bring it back when it goes astray; in short, to marry it and be a husband to it, so that their actions may appear not different and contrary, but harmonious and uniform. (P. 485)

The separation of the soul and body, of the spiritual and physical, the immaterial and material, is one of the most significant problems discussed by Montaigne, one that became increasingly crucial in the later development of philosophical thought and is responsible for our own all too often schizophrenic attitude toward ourselves. To cut a being in half, as Plato and Christianity did after him, is to encourage the autocracy of the spiritual half: an *immitatio Christi*, thus creating a one-sided condition. The focus on the soul, the spirit and ethereal realms runs counter to nature and equally counter to the very spirit of the Renaissance, which was so deeply involved in the terrestrial sphere. The Renaissance writers reaffirmed the beauty of body and soul echoing the ancient Greeks and paving the way for harmony of being. The body, they reasoned, should be cared for and not rejected as a vile instrument all too often leading its owner straight to perdition. It is beautiful; as is the soul. The true Christian, Montaigne asserts, cannot really despise the body, for that would preclude all belief in the concept of the resurrection of the body and the life everlasting.

The soul in Montaigne's view is intimately wedded to the body. It participates in our body's physical existence and functioning; it takes on its character and likeness, its capacities for thinking and feeling.[10] In describing himself physically, both body and soul are invoked: "There is no liveliness; there is only a full, firm vigor," Montaigne maintains in his comportment and spiritual climes. Focusing on his temperament, he confesses that it varies "between the jovial and the melancholy." Physically, he is "strong, thick-set, and of medium height," whereas Aristotle, he affirms, admired only tall men. Nor does he possess the "adroitness" or "agility" of his father; furthermore, he is not musically inclined; he cannot dance, play tennis, wrestle, vault, or jump with great ability. In fact, he is clumsy.

Montaigne returns to a subject which did and still does, to a certain extent, preoccupy him: his desire to rid himself of "mental torment and constraint" (p. 487). He cannot "endure worry" (p. 488) and has attempted to overcome this torment. He believes that because as a child he had been brought up in a free and gentle way, with understanding and warmth, he never learned how to harden himself sufficiently to bear anxiety. Worry, for Montaigne sets up sequences of charged energy within him; it triggers stress which disturbs his psychic functioning. His emotions become so powerful that they arouse his unconscious, increasing his sense of misery. Montaigne's self-analysis, however, which allows him to free associate, helps him redress the imbalance brought on by the bouts of anxiety. He encourages his mind to wander, to reflect, to project, to differentiate, and in so doing, the images that frequently arise from his unconscious, the specificity of the words that he later uses to describe his moods, feelings, and thoughts, stimulate fresh sources of psychic knowledge within him, arousing yet other modes of expression. Montaigne's consciousness of his physical body seems to increase whenever he is innervated—that is, experiencing the physical discomfort which arises when there is dissociation in the sense/idea continuum. During these moments, awareness of his body brought *physis* to *nous*: mind helped the body to dissociate from the trauma and objectify it. Unlike Plato, for Montaigne, the body and the spirit worked in a positive way, thereby enabling him for the most part to gain insight into certain situations that might otherwise have remained blocked off to him.

Free and direct association reactivated Montaigne's body and mind, stirred his ego to act, to dissect, sift, examine the momentary turmoil which had seemingly encapsulated him, thereby helping him out of his crisis. Highly sensitive, Montaigne made the most of his technique, adding yet another device to help him assuage his moments of distress: "To expect the worst in everything and to resolve to bear that worst meekly and patiently" (p. 488) is the way he dealt with chance, which he knew must never dominate but to which he intended to adapt. To "expect the worst" would also eliminate the "suspense" that gives rise to dread and all sorts of other unpleasant feelings: "The dread of falling gives me a greater fever than the fall. The game is not worth the candle. . . . The lowest step is the firmest. It is the seat of constancy. There you need nothing but yourself. Constancy is founded there and leans only upon itself" (p. 489). Montaigne thus sets up his guidelines, and it is to this end that he now directs his energies.

Still concerned with self-analysis, as he would always be, and with integrity in the probing process, he turns his attention to humanity's marked propensity for lying. Nature "shuns lying," he writes (p. 491). The Stoics and Skeptics always encouraged the virtues of integrity and forthrightness, qualities in which Montaigne believes in. Had Suleiman, the ruler of the Ottoman Empire, Montaigne writes, regulated his relations with other monarchs in an honest way. He would never have earned distrust and a bad name. To lie is to dissimulate. It is an individual's way of perpetrating a hoax on society, of being presumptuous. Montaigne suggests that one must not be what one is not, nor give a false impression to the world. "I give myself up to being candid and always saying what I think, by inclination and by reason, leaving it to Fortune to guide the outcome" (p. 492).

In so doing, one is dependent upon oneself alone; responsible for one's own decisions and strong enough to bear the reactions of others whatever they may be—whether praise or condemnation. Montaigne's ego has indeed strengthened in the analytical process; his sense of his own identity and worth has grown equally firm.

There are, nevertheless, areas of concern that still remain and always would remain to plague him. To ignore them would be to disregard the life experience. His memory, he writes regretfully, is poor. An instrument that allows an individual to travel through time and space, that permits intellectual displacements in a structured manner, was vital to Montaigne. It did not function as he wished. Yet, he notes—and this insight is fascinating to the psychotherapist—the less confidence he has in his memory, the more confused it becomes. It is far better "to solicit it nonchalantly" than to order it about. He is in effect defining in sixteenth-century fashion what Bergson three centuries later was to discuss: the difference between *voluntary* and *involuntary* memory. If Montaigne "presses" his memory, "it is stunned"; it becomes paralyzed and unreceptive. "It serves me at its own time, not at mine" (p. 493). Not only does memory "flee command, obligation, and constraint" (p. 493), but nature in general also does. Allowed to function according to its own logic and *modus vivendi* it yields its richest fruits.

"Memory is the receptacle and container of knowledge," Montaigne asserts. Because voluntary memory is so capricious, however, he cannot rely upon it exclusively to help him in his probings. His involuntary memory, that which functions autonomously, frequently comes to his aid at its own pace, thereby enlarging his perspective and enabling him to delineate his feelings through images and other sense perceptions.

Free association and involuntary memory work together for Montaigne—both help in his thinking function to discover a way of life and, in so doing, activate his creativity. Each individual, Montaigne suggests, must grope alone, attempt to unearth and then face whatever his characteristics may be, accept these and deal with them in the most positive manner possible. It is Montaigne's "capacity for sifting truth," his ability to doubt, to choose, to compare, that allowed him to develop his ego and to engage in philosophical and psychological speculation as a thinking/feeling being. No belief enslaves him now; neither aesthetic, political, nor religious. He knows what belongs to him, what is harmonious and in keeping with his personality; also, which factors are alien and jar, hurt, and disrupt his balance. He has discovered his center—the psyche's creative point—and feels at home and secure in this position.

For the firmest and most general ideas I have are those which, in a manner of speaking, were born with me. They are natural and all mine. I produced them crude and simple, with a conception bold and strong, but a little confused and imperfect. Since then I have established and fortified them by the authority of others and the sound arguments of the ancients, with whom I found my judgment in agreement. These men have given me a firmer grip on my ideas and a more complete enjoyment and possession of them. (P. 499)

A contemplative being, order, consistency, "tranquility of opinions and conduct," were all important to Montaigne (p. 501). The Pyrrhonist in him, always concerned with ethics, sought detachment from external perturbations, not in the willed manner of the Stoics—through reason exclusively—but mitigated with understanding and feeling; with the idea of accepting life's limitations and rejoicing in the human condition. Montaigne lived in the present, enriching his workaday world by making use of both conscious and unconscious spheres, applying the riches he discovered in both to the art that became his existential experience.

3. "Of Repentance" (1585–1588): Sin/Sacrifice/Redemption and the Persona Problem

When Montaigne wrote "Of Repentance" he was experiencing, what has been labeled, his Epicurean phase. His interests centered around creating a veritable *art of living* for himself that would include metaphysical and spiritual matters. For Epicurean and Skeptic alike, absolute truth is unattainable. What must therefore be focused upon is the human condition—one's lifestyle. What is of import is the practical functioning of one's life, the enjoyment derived from certain events and situations, not to be considered hedonistically, but rather appreciated for itself—to the deepest and fullest extent. Balance and harmony are still important to Montaigne, particularly in the face of dis-

tress; but he had come a long way since his early days, when
Stoicism seemed to be for him the only acceptable answer. Accepting himself as he is, he never attempts to be what he is not.
Moments of happiness come to him through his mind, during
periods of meditation and moments of repose, when undisturbed by an overemphasis on material or emotional factors, he
reaches the "ideal" state—the center of being—that Epicureans
call *ataraxia*.

In the second half of life, according to Jung, most human
beings become increasingly preoccupied with questions of religion and spiritual life. Montaigne was certainly no exception to
this observation. Although he had always been concerned with
the religious questions of sin, guilt, and sacrifice, there seems
now to be a sense of renewed urgency about these problems at
this particular time. Religious wars were taking place throughout France as we have noted. Fighting had broken out in Montaigne's region; his tenants were pillaged, suffering grew acute,
death and cruelties of all types were rampant. Montaigne himself had been accused of favoring the Protestant cause. Such
insinuations were based on fact. He was friendly with Henri of
Navarre, the future Henri IV, a Protestant; one of his brothers
and two sisters had become Protestants.

The problem of repentance particularly preoccupied Montaigne at this juncture: certainly it was closely allied to sin, sacrifice, guilt—means Catholics used in the healing of souls. A
fideist who had experienced periods of grave questioning in existential matters, Montaigne was remarkably secure in his religious faith. He was not, however, bigoted. He accepted the notion of freedom of worship—certainly not a usual outlook in
his age.

The Renaissance, which saw the Reformation and Counter-
Reformation, witnessed the breakdown of the medieval myth:
that there was but a single answer to the life experience, that
there was but one form of universal religious authority—the
Roman Catholic church. No longer was there but a single force,
a unique edifice of belief—or even a single image of God into
which one could pour all one's feelings and find alleviation from
pain. The burden of existence for the Renaissance man, particularly a thinking and intuitive type such as Montaigne, fell
squarely upon his own shoulders. The emphasis during the Ren-

aissance was placed on the *here and now* rather than on the *hereafter and the later*: the empirical domain rather than celestial spheres. The individual, therefore, had to deal with his own pain/pleasure principle, the vagaries of fate. Montaigne's increasing consciousness made him all the more aware of the Empedoclean conflicts which increased psychic tension in his land— particularly in matters of religion.

Blind faith, as it had existed in the Middle Ages, was a thing of the past. The Roman Catholic church was no longer in complete control, no longer the exclusive agent of divine salvation. The meaningfulness of confession and absolution had been questioned by the new sects; the Mass, the divine sacrifice, the *causa efficiens* of the transubstantiation and the gift of God's grace for the Catholic which redeemed him of sin, was still very powerful, yet its dominance over the individual had diminished. The burden of life's fortunes and misfortunes now fell upon the individual—the thinking person was forced to be responsible for his own actions. No one felt the change of focus more powerfully than Montaigne. As his own examiner, his own self-confessor, his own sounding board, Montaigne approaches the problem of repentance in terms of the spirit and its impact upon his life, which he now sought to live as serenely and as fully as possible—in true Epicurean style.

"I rarely repent" Montaigne writes, because "my conscience is content with itself" (p. 612). Repentance or penitence are indulged in to seek pardon for one's misdeeds or moral shortcomings, one's sins. In that guilt-ridden people can no longer thrust their problems into the priest's lap, but must expiate them in their own way, indicates the necessity of viewing the problems of sin and guilt in a fresh manner.

Sin and guilt are two sides of the same coin. In psychological terms, they may be identified with the *shadow* which contains those characteristics that the ego considers to be negative and wishes to hide or rejects by projecting them on others. Blaming someone else or labeling another person a sinner and trying to destroy him verbally or actually, does not, however, solve the problem. The individual so acting believes, erroneously, that he is devoid of any such evil characteristics. Such scapegoat attitudes, however, do not alleviate one's rage or help one cope with the sin/guilt syndrome. Throughout Montaigne's

Essays, he makes a point of examining what he considers to be his own positive and negative characteristics, thereby coming to terms with them and accepting many as part of the life process. His shadow, therefore, does not overly trouble him, rather it works in his favor, allowing antitheses to sharpen insights, conflicts, and comparisons with others and thus to shed further clarity into that darkened interior realm. Good produces evil, and evil good, he reasons, depending upon the circumstances and situations.

The fact that Montaigne castigates "vice" and "malice," labeling them "offensive" for their "ugliness" and the pain they cause others (p. 612), is not an example of his own shadow problem but a very real attempt to understand why they exist, to create certain values, and to establish a kind of norm. In an age "as corrupt and ignorant as this," he writes, "one may never fully understand the meaning of vice." There is no criterion. Each individual must find his own way, live according to the standards he establishes for himself. Montaigne quotes Seneca: "What were vices now are moral acts" (p. 613). Only by constantly confronting one's own inner being, seeking out one's motivations, airing unhealthy and painful areas, can one create a scale of values for oneself and the world at large. If lucidity is not applied to each and every situation, then vice is more likely to be perpetrated. For those who have a conscience, vice arouses repentance, and with it, pain. "Vice leaves repentance in the soul, like an ulcer in the flesh, which is always scratching itself and drawing blood. For reason effaces other griefs and sorrow; but it engenders that of repentance, which is all the more grievous because it springs from within, as the cold and heat of fevers is sharper than that which comes from outside" (p. 612).

Nothing can eradicate the gnawing need for repentance, Montaigne seems to suggest. Only the person who knows he or she is guilty understands the impact of this feeling. In so doing, he or she learns how best to deal with this corrosive, and sometimes illuminating, force. It is a private matter: "Others do not see you, they guess at you by certain conjectures" (p. 613), which is a further reason to examine one's inclinations and motivations constantly and not "cling" to the opinions and judgments of others with regard to virtue or vice. Montaigne substantiates his view by quoting Cicero: "You must use your own judgment. . . . With regard to virtue and vices, your own conscience has great weight: take that away, and and everything falls" (p. 613).

What Montaigne rejects most outspokenly is false repentance: "their penitence, diseased and guilty, almost as much as their sin" (p. 616). Such hypocrisy is more evil than the original misdeed. It not only indicates a lack of vision but points up the fact that such individuals are "glued" to their bad habits, unable to recognize their unhealthy character (shadow), and therefore in no way equipped to alter them. Such beings live in a kind of haze—a life-style quite antipodal to that of Montaigne. "I scarcely make a motion that is hidden and out of sight of my reason, and that is not guided by the consent of nearly all parts of me, without division, without internal sedition. My judgment takes all the blame or all the praise for it; and the blame it once takes, it always keeps, for virtually since its birth it has been one; the same inclination, the same road, the same strength" (p. 616).

Montaigne excoriates "counterfeit" piousness in people. "If conduct and life are not made to conform to it," then piety is worthless and repentance even more so (p. 617). Montaigne does not take repentance lightly. It must "grip" both body and soul if one is to learn from the process. It must "grip me by the vitals and afflict them as deeply and as completely as God sees into me" (p. 617). In psychological terms, it is Montaigne's eye— his mind's eye—that sees clearly and distinctly into Self (the total psyche). There are, therefore, no halfway measures for Montaigne. He does not deny having erred in his life (the running of his estate was not as it should have been, nor were his relationships with his wife and children always harmonious, and so forth). He has not, however, in most instances, acted counter to his reason; whenever at a crossroads or under tension, he tries to examine his actions and feelings as closely as he can, scrutinizing them, weighing them carefully against all possible alternatives. Whatever his mistakes, therefore, he "can do no better" (p. 617); he is conscious of them and acts in good *conscience*, at least as far as he knows. Montaigne's inner voice was his guide. Rarely did he ask others for advice; the burden of responsibility for his behavior was his. "If I do not take advice, I give still less" (p. 618). A responsible person relies upon himself to formulate and form his own criteria, his way of life. Strength comes from clear-sightedness, flexibility in judging others' points of view, thereby increasing still further one's own powers of discernment and of evaluation.

The question of true repentance as opposed to dissimulation or hypocrisy is connected with the *persona problem*. Those who too closely identify themselves with their persona lose sight of their true identity; their egos become swallowed up in the image created for the world at large. Should the dichotomy between the persona and the ego become too great, a sharp imbalance and even a dissociation of the personality may occur. Many weakly structured people suffer from a persona problem. They identify solely with the outside world, attempt to become a successful role model in their cultures and live solely to achieve this ambition—never focusing on their ego and its development. Society projects upon such individuals, and in so doing, the person involved reacts with great pleasure, believing that *he* (his ego) is the object of the collective's admiration when it is his persona. The ego, in such cases, virtually vanishes beneath the mask. Such a fusion between ego and persona encourages deception and may lead to serious psychological problems. Stirrings from the unconscious may disturb the smooth functioning of the persona when least desired, creating deep scars and increasing the pressure on the already alienated ego making the personality still more susceptible, inflexible or inaccessible. A real schism between one's public and private actions may then develop; one may barely recognize an idividual in his disguises. The public persona may perform the most magnanimous of acts for all to see; in private, he may perform the cruelest. "As vicious souls are often incited to do good by some extraneous impulse, so arc virtuous souls to do evil" (p. 615).

To evaluate individuals solely through their outward actions and appearances is to overlook, Montaigne intimates, the persona problem. What is of import is how we function in private during those moments when we are "closest to repose" (p. 615). It is also important in assessing individuals to be able to attribute "common faculties" to so-called outstanding people. All human beings are basically the same. Yet, "we give demons wild shapes." Tamerlaine was looked upon as having "open nostrils, a dreadful face," and being "immense in size" (p. 615) simply because he was a conqueror, a fearful, perhaps demonical force. Imaginations set to work. Nor, on the other hand, should people idealize, Montaigne writes, glorify—divinize individuals.

To know oneself is to know others, Montaigne steadily maintains. "Each man bears the entire form of man's estate" (p. 611). Now that he has grown older, he neither fears condemnation from the outside world nor falls prey to its flattery. He speaks out "as much as I dare speak," he states; "no man ever treated a subject he knew and understood better than I do" (p. 611). Revealing himself to his reader as he has done in his *Essays*, living the life he wanted to, indicate a refusal on his part to conform to the outer world to any great degree. He wore his persona to be sure, but one that suited his psyche; his aim was to seek his own truth. He was psychologically strong enough to be independent and to seek to be consciously. Such an achievement is virtually unique. Society requires "imitation or conscious identification"; it demands that those who wish to gain its approval follow a well-worn path. To choose the solitary way, as Montaigne did, is considered an affront, a rejection of the common attitude, its cultural canon. Montaigne purged himself of any sense of alienation by means of self-examination. He did not bother about society's dictates because he ceased to be affected by public opinion; he was comfortable with himself and his personal world, he had finally cut himself loose from the madding crowd. Troubles, however, did not cease. There still remained the real task—facing of a world of nothingness— his own unconscious. Mimesis allows one's values to be reactivated; when not imitating, one is one's own psychopomp. There are no forces to follow—only the untrodden path. The world is dark for such a being; ominous as well, since one must go it alone; as Kierkegaard stated—in "fear and trembling."[11]

Since life is flux, each day brings new tensions, fresh events, and situations with which to cope. An ability to examine concepts and to express both feelings and ideas helped Montaigne deepen his sense of independence as well as increase his feelings of participating in a universal God-created world. Had Montaigne considered the notion of flux as an intellectual concept alone, and not as a way of life, he would have been faced with staggering problems—with paralyzing uncertainties. He does not therefore "portray being," but rather "I portray passing. Not the passing from one age to another . . . but from day to day, from minute to minute" (p. 611). Montaigne does not rest on past laurels, nor does he make elaborate provision for the future. Every minute represents sequences of multiple eventualities; every second, a variety of courses. Chance, intention, contradiction, mood, feeling—all play their role in the forming of a personality as well as in the life cycle—thus expanding and deepening one's understanding continuously.

Montaigne created a literary masterpiece out of his own well-ordered, honorable, and fulfilled life. "Not to be false to ourselves," was his credo (p. 614). Unlike Alexander the Great, whose watchword seemed to be, "Subdue the world," he chose as his master Socrates, who believed that one should "Lead the life of man in conformity with its natural condition" (p. 614): to be consistent and virtuous in public as well as private life. Let the outer man—the persona—reflect the treasures buried beneath, invisible, but active and present. With such a belief, Montaigne was able to experience serenity even under the most adverse of conditions: "I am nearly always in place, like heavy and inert bodies," he writes. He always returned to the center of gravity. "There is no one who, if he listens to himself, does not discover in himself a pattern all his own, a ruling pattern, which struggles against education and against the tempest of the passions that oppose it" (p. 615). Such a reflective and cogitating frame of reference does not obliterate reactions to events of importance. Emotional upsurges should not be repressed but rather expressed, studied, analyzed, and brought into perspective. "If I am not at home, I am always very near it. My excesses do not carry me very far away. There is nothing extreme or strange about them. And besides I have periods of vigorous and healthy reactions" (p. 615).

Self-analysis and self-recollection allow Montaigne to relate and integrate what otherwise might well have been detached or alienated segments of his personality. To come to terms with his emotional problems as he did, by thinking them through, by using *logos* and intuition to understand his vulnerable feeling world, permitted him to dredge up from his unconscious frequently distasteful elements which must have been frightening to his ego. The process he pursued, as delineated in his *Es-*

says, paved the way for a balance and unity of being rare in any individual in Montaigne's day and equally rare today. That he accepted change, that he was ever open to new ideas and values, that he was constantly creating and renewing himself by increasing his conscious awareness—of both himself and the world at large—is an example of the individuation process at work.

Individuation requires sacrifice, and Montaigne was not spared this ordeal. The approval of the outside world was not always granted him; nor did he experience his withdrawal and his solitude, his inability to relate to others in a joyful manner. Maintaining a nearly constant vigil over himself, he did, however, believe in what he was doing; he was aware of what he was feeling and conscious of his acts. Few surprises, therefore, awaited him in his later years. He felt at ease with himself and others. Continuing to explore and develop aspects of his being, Montaigne might have said with equanimity that he had lived in true Epicurean style—as he understood the concept.

Never a victim of emotional or intellectual stasis, the individuation process experienced by Montaigne allowed him to adapt to both inner and outer reality—to the empirical and mystical realms. Montaigne, it might be said, sought to know the *whole being*: he placed his faith in his own individuality and in God.

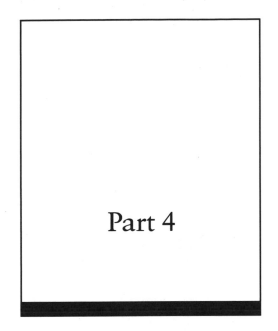

Part 4

Corneille (1606–1684): *Horace* and *Rodogune*—Heroism? Sacrifice? Lust for Power?

Pierre Corneille, the baroque dramatist, was able through his remarkable talent to transform the creatures of his fantasies into flamboyant archetypal beings, unforgettable in their lust for power, their fanatical spiritual zeal. *Horace* (1640), set in the early days of Roman patriarchal society, exalts the will; concentrating on the dialectic of heroism and self-sacrifice implicit in a youthful society. It calls for suppression of personal emotion in the light of public duty. At the time the play opens, Rome is being built, her fame and power are still an ideal. *Rodogune* (1644–45), set in Syria, in the matriarchal sphere, scrutinizes the forces at stake when a political system is on the decline: corruption takes hold, and the power struggle entails the most heinous of crimes.

Corneille's plots and characters are only loosely based on actual historical incidents; this allows him to broaden and deepen the scope of his works, to build tensions, and also to preserve the rules and regulations dominating the theatrical arts of seventeenth-century France. His dramas are ectypal: they are very much products of his time, an expression of the cultural and political forces of his day. The characters, though emanating from ancient times are in reality French aristocrats, with tinges of antiquity occasionally emerging, as they enunciate their thoughts, political aspirations, and spiritual yearnings. Corneille's dramas are also archetypal: they deal with eternal types and values, beings whose essences and characteristics have slumbered in the psyches of uncounted generations in every land, who emerge every now and then into the phenomenological world to force their imprint on an unsuspecting and unprepared public.

ECTYPAL ANALYSIS

Corneille himself lived in a tempestuous time: a period which has been characterized as blood and thunder, one of severe repression and dogmatism. Louis XIII (1601–43) was only nine when his father, Henri IV, was assassinated by a fanatic. Since he was too young to assume the throne, the queen mother, Marie de Medicis, was appointed regent. How could she, superstitious, lethargic, unintelligent, adequately take the place of her husband whom the French regarded as one of their finest kings? Henri IV had instituted religious toleration through the passage of the Edict of Nantes; he created protectionist policies which had helped industry and agriculture; he ordered roads, canals, and bridges built; he restored solvency to a drained treasury. As the center of power and intrigue, Marie de Medicis became the tool of the great French families such as the Condés, the Bouillons, the Longuevilles, who by astute manipulation and with her assent acquired the best offices, posts, finest pensions, and large funds virtually upon demand. Order was only instituted after Cardinal de Richelieu was appointed minister (1624).

Richelieu's dogmatism and his authoritarian rule earned him much hatred, but his aims and politics were nevertheless astute. Although his methods were frequently devious and less than honorable, under his aegis France became the dominant power in Europe. By laying siege and capturing the Protestant strongholds of La Rochelle and Montauban, which had always posed a threat to his iron rule, Richelieu virtually eliminated all Protestant opposition. His manipulations during the Thirty Years' War (1618–48), ended with the Peace of Westphalia, which brought Alsace within the French hegemony and concomitantly weakened both Germany and Austria. Forever involved in quelling conspiracies, such as those melodramatized by Alexander Dumas in *The Three Musketeers*, *Twenty Years After*, and *The Viscount of Bragelone*, Richelieu acted methodically and ruthlessly, the welfare of the nation as a whole being always his chief consideration.

In 1635 Richelieu founded the French Academy, which was

instrumental in forming and sustaining a rigorous literary and grammatical style which laid the foundation stone for French classicism. In order to have their works performed and lauded, French dramatists thereafter had to observe the three unities of time, place, and action—and not trespass against the rules of verisimilitude and decorum. Thanks to the grammarian Vaugelas, French as a language was becoming purified; words were being clearly defined, ideas being set down in rigorous order and logical manner. Guez de Balzac, who wrote lucid and reasoned prose in well-balanced sentences with structure and meter, contributed to the language's intelligibility as did the poet Malherbe who shied from recherché and recondite forms of expression. Although the French language was impoverished, the strictures imposed resulted in concision, density of thought, and clarity of expression.

It was during this highly creative and turbulent period that Corneille arrived in Paris from Rouen, where he was born, to seek his fortune as a playwright. The son of a parliamentarian lawyer, educated by the Jesuits, Corneille had been an outstanding student. Grammar, rhetoric, Latin, had long been his fortes. He had developed a love for literature at an early age; although his father had encouraged him in this field, he was a practical bourgeois and realized that his son had to have some other means of livelihood. The young Corneille had therefore been sent to law school, receiving his degree in 1624. He plead only once. Yet, his training had developed his already logical mind; he reasoned his way through incidents, balanced attitudes in his work as administrator and legal council in a post his father had bought for him. Despite his long working hours, Corneille found time to indulge in what he loved most—playwrighting. His first comedy, *Mélite* (1629–30), was performed in Paris as were nearly all of his succeeding works including both *Horace* and *Rodogune*.

ARCHETYPAL ANALYSIS

Horace

The theme of Corneille's *Horace* is based in part on the account in Titus Livius (*Roman History*, 1) and also perhaps in part from Cicero and Lope de Vega, who were also inspired by the heroic and sacrificial events involved. The plot is as follows. At

the opening of the play, Alba Longa and Rome have declared
war on each other. Camille, the sister of Horace, who is a Roman, is affianced to Curiace, a citizen of Alba Longa, whose
sister, Sabine, is the wife of Horace. Since the personal ties linking these two families are inextricably mixed, the political events
that follow, become the more harrowing. In a dramatic turn of
events, for which Corneille was well known, Curiace informs
both families that the war is not to take place. Instead, three
Roman and three Alban warriors are to be chosen to fight and
thus decide which of the cities is the more powerful. Horace
and his two brothers are selected to fight for Rome; Curiace
and his two brothers, for Alba Longa. Although saddened and
concerned about the situation, Horace, a born hero, is ready to
fight. No thoughts of fear, death, or love intrude. Curiace, equally
courageous, is aware of his emotions. He hesitates, yet, he too
is ready to defend his native land.

The themes of duty, heroism, and sacrifice—as we shall
see—are uppermost in *Horace*. They are based on Roman ideals, which Old Horace and his son consciously seek: strength,
power, fortitude, success. The prevailing archetype in this kind
of society, then, is law and order. To bring this ideal into the
world of reality, the energetic factors activated (body building,
muscular development, physical prowess of all types) are enormous. Emphasis on the physical side does not, however, necessarily mean abandoning the power of reason. On the contrary,
the protagonists in *Horace* are, for the most part, described as
both disciplined and reasoning: they are Stoic types. As such,
their actions and emotional outlook are supposedly controlled
and dictated by *logos*. Once a "rational" decision has been
reached, the application of a strong will ensures control over
any feelings, instincts, or some other form of impulse that is
looked upon as weak.

Corneille's play opens while Horace is still an unproved
and untested hero. He is bound to his city-state; he identifies
with it, upholds its values. For him Rome is the paradigm of
law and order; it represents an organized structure that protects
all within its fold. The city-state in general symbolizes man's
transformation from nomadic to sedentary ways. Introversion
might be said to be the city-state's equivalent in psychological

terms; it replaced the more extroverted view of life, exemplified by nomadic groups moving from place to place. Stability, security, power, are the forces at work, rather than any attempt to discover new and fresh values outside the walled clanlike organization.

The city-state is both patriarchal and matriarchal. In the same way that the mother cares for and nourishes the child in her womb, so the city-state also protects and nurtures those living within its confines. Unlike ancient Babylon, which is referred to in both the Old and New Testaments as "harlot" and "abomination," the Rome of the Horatii was earthy, uncorrupted, and vigorous.

One may well ask, however, whether Horace was fighting to uphold the welfare of the city-state, to protect it from an enemy, or struggling to acquire personal glory. In all fairness, the former seems more likely. Horace, from the very outset, is identified with the patriarchal society which was dominant at this time. He mustered all his strength to defend the values his father and he upheld. Indeed he and his father, a *senex* figure, or the Wise Old Man archetype, are intertwined. Horace is in a sense merely his father's appendage. His ego remains undeveloped, virtually parasitic, as he lives, breathes, and acts under the powerful views of the city-state as these are interpreted by the Old Horace. It is not by chance that Corneille retains the historical name Old Horace for the father figure in his play. The son is his father's offshoot. As such, right or wrong, his allegiance goes to the collective organization and its personal representative, his father. Unicentered, undifferentiated, unthinking, he acts and reacts as one with his father. Never will he become an individual or individuated.

Although Horace looks with horror at the political situation, once war has been declared, he is the first to offer his services to Rome. Never does any cogitation enter into his decisions, never does he weigh the problems involved, his feelings or sentiments for his wife and family come into play. Horace expects this same clear-cut loyalty from his wife, Sabine, though she comes from Alba Longa. One goal, one love, one loyalty—Rome—embodied in its earthly representative, Old Horace. Horace fears neither death nor pain nor loss of any type. Driven by his complete loyalty to his ideal state, it is in the service of this abstract principle that he will win his honors and maintain his integrity.

War, furthermore, will prove Horace's heroism. Without a struggle a hero remains unsung. To fight, to protect his city-state, will bring him glory. His motivations, therefore, are based not only on a collective ideal but on personal aggrandizement. His courage will prove his worth; it will also protect the values he admires: justice, patriotism, virtue—"To die for a country is such a worthy fate" (3. 2). He nearly salivates at the thought of being immolated for a cause. No obstacle is sufficiently great to prevent him from driving straight to his goal: "And breaking all ties"; feelings for his wife and his sister, Sabine, pose no problem. Indeed, they are virtually severed from his psychological makeup. The rush of energy constellated around the power, *senex*, and hero archetypes have seen to that. Glory and honor inflame his being, energizing his blood and stifling all other sentiments.

When Horace learns that Rome has chosen him along with his two brothers to fight its battle, he is proud to the point of blindness. Curiace, should also consider himself honored, Horace suggests, since Alba Longans believe him and his two brothers worthy to fight for their city-state. But Curiace is of a different temperament. Unlike Horace, he finds himself tortured by his feelings, his love for Camille causes conflict within him. Horace considers Curiace's complex and ambivalent reactions timorous. He ridicules Curiace's sensitivity and his subtle and nuanced reasoning. Once war is declared, all relationships between their citizens must be severed; Curiace and Horace are enemies and must henceforth consider themselves as such.

Horace consels his sister, Camille, on how she should treat Curiace and himself. She should honor them both, since each is worthy of the highest dignity and virtue. She also must be strong and face adversity unflinchingly. Never must she yield to her private emotions. Such weakness must be rejected outright; it is unworthy of the high destiny each Roman must fulfill in life. Horace grows increasingly impatient with both Camille and Sabine, annoyed by what he considers to be their hypersensitivity. He is irate at their distress, their pleadings, their tears. They should know better, Horace informs his father, than to weep and bemoan.

Horace is neither Promethean (forethought) nor Epimethean (afterthought) in his comportment. There is nothing unique about him. Because his ego is still so undeveloped, he lives in a state of *participation mystique*. He functions within his father's aura and the city-state's power: he reminds one of a taut rubber band which when stretched to the utmost can only snap. If the state needs his services, he is there heart and soul, certainly not mind. In no way is he an independent person, an integrated individual. (The Latin root for individual is *in* [not] and *dividere* [to divide].)[1] Horace has not freed himself from the paterfamilias. He is still tied to this patriarchal being: the archetypal Wise Old Man, the judge, the elder, who usually rules alone and is rarely if ever associated with women. So Horace being bound to this father figure is unrelated except on a primitive sexual level to his wife. He is dependent upon Old Horace for his way of life, his future, his well-being.

One might say that Horace has never awakened, so to speak, that he is merely an echo of the prevailing father image. He has never challenged his father's values, which is the way of the true hero, nor listened to his own inner voice which emerges from the Self and is sometimes looked upon as divinity speaking through man. Abraham, for example, ushered in the new when he followed his inner voice and heard Jehovah state: "Get thee out of thy country, and from thy kindred, and from thy father's house, unto a land that I will show thee" (Gen. 12:1). Jesus also took an outward route. In both cases, conflict with the status quo ensued; pain and suffering were caused during the birth process. Whenever a cultural canon is broken or a new order comes into being, for better or for worse, disruption and chaos result. The hero in such cases is usually rejected by the society to which he belongs and must find his own way in life, enduring hardships that may symbolically be seen as initiation rites preceding a higher sphere of development.[2]

Since Horace is so unconsciously identified with the prevailing *senex* archetype, his power of judgment, his objectivity, and his perceptions remain undeveloped. Indeed, they are not even his own; they are merely reflections of a vaster sphere. Had

Horace been an individual in his own right, he would have understood the powers at work and sought to unwind or resolve the explosive situation using reason, compassion, and understanding as his armature. Curiace attempted to do so, but fails. As such, Horace remains a puppet, a mirror image of unconscious forces at work in society. Although conscious of his own body, his own physical strength, an indication of the ego's (or the child's) earliest desire to separate from the parent, Horace could not and did not take the vital step in the liberating process which consists in the recognition of one's own identity. He cannot encounter himself nor look within nor understand the values at stake in Rome. An encounter with Self requires an expansion of views, the setting-up of a dialectic: two opposites, each examining the other, extrapolating, explicating their positions, then concluding with the right synthesis. Such a confrontation between Horace and his father or society (ego and Self) requires great strength since it poses a threat to the smooth-running present situation. To face larger forces requires choice; Horace would have to weigh the situation, become accountable for all his acts, evaluate thoughts and motivations; and he does not do so. He never questions, never converses with himself. A truly independent being experiences unity within his personality only after having broken with the status quo, the prevailing archetype, and discovering his own riches, his own individuality. Only then does he reintegrate into a whole. During the period of conflict such a person orients and relates to the workaday world in both a positive and negative tug-of-war.[3]

Old Horace is as bound to the prevailing archetype, as is his son: father and son are in a sense one. Both live through the other's reflection. All Old Horace's hopes reside in his son. When, therefore, the false news of his son's desertion comes, Old Horace is not only abashed but enraged. His son is worthy of death, he states in no uncertain terms. He feels the enormous impact of defeat and shame, all the more powerfully, since he identifies with his namesake, his son. He sees himself placed in this disgraceful role for the rest of his life and prefers death to the agony of disgrace. Old Horace, therefore, welcomes the demise of his other two sons who met their end protecting the city-state and died with honor and glory. Never more shall the name of

Horace, the infamous one, be pronounced in Old Horace's presence, opprobrium is his. When, sometime later, he learns that his son is alive and has slain the Curiace brothers, he is overjoyed. He goes from one extreme to another; polarities are experienced as in a condition of *enantiodromia*. No praise is sufficient for the son whom his father now welcomes as an idol.

To be an individual, to gain one's independence, to become self-sufficient, require stages that include thoughtful self-questioning and loneliness, during which time consciousness develops, nuances come into being, and dichotomies are examined. Frequently, those with emerging egos or who aspire to be youthful heroes cannot stand to be alone; they need others to overcome the solitary state, to protect them from the awareness of their isolation. When the necessity for it is faced and accepted, however, loneliness becomes a positive force that helps one to stand alone and brings growth and maturation.[4] It would be out of character for Horace to want to stand alone; he merely mirrors his father's conventions—the patriarchal formula   the customs that are never questioned as to their propriety, never evaluated for their effect upon others.

Both father and son suffer from a hero fixation; they both harbor certain ideas about how a hero should behave. The hero image which they have depicted for themselves is so powerfully charged that it dictates all their actions. Since any fixation "has an intentionality of its own," anyone subject to one is bound to act in a prescribed way, and if the person fails to carry out this pattern, he or she feels unacceptable to society as well as to himself or herself. No other values, intentions, or qualities are satisfactory.[5] In the case of the Old Horace and his son, aggression and violence are the forces to be used to remove all obstacles to the achievement of their goal.

Father and son cannot objectify the political situation. They are blind to any alternative; their egoes are victimized by the archetype of the Self which becomes the dominating factor, determining that all that is relevant for the individual is for the good of the collective. The individual, therefore, is of little importance. Incapable of thinking things through, of viewing the impact and ramifications of their stand, they cope through coercion—just as many do who possess weakly structured egos.[6]

Their activities, then, are enacted in conformity with the abstract principle that has become their ideal: the preservation of the might of the state, the masculine archetype as they see it.

Hubris is implied in the ego's identification with the Self. Father and son, henceforth, are looked upon as saviors of a way of life, a conditioning functioning society. Viewed by the collective as unique, they become almighty, indispensable. Horace's inflation emerges early in the play. If, by the same token, a hero has no hubris, he can never forge ahead, never consider himself strong enough to commit valorous deeds. A hero, therefore, must necessarily be power-hungry; he must be driven by some energetic principle which is unleashed within him, usually in an aggressive manner. That within the hero's psyche exists a lust for power and violence over which he may be conscious or not is rudimentary. Horace is not a pacifist: as a solar warrior his mettle is as yet undeveloped and unchanneled. It is time—during a period of crisis—for his power to be tested. His purpose at the outset of the drama is to protect his city-state and fatherland—and to win fame in the process. In the same way that Mars possessed dual features, both as the nurturer of life and the destroyer, so Horace will prevail in the war against Alba Longa through force. His inflated ego, however, grows so powerful, his libido becomes overcharged, that when a statement counter to his own view of himself as conquering hero is offered, he flames and flares; his vision of reality vanishes.

The returning Horace—the defender of Rome with freshly flowing blood on his sword—is greeted by his sister, Camille, not with awe and admiration, but with reprimands and condemnations: "Tiger, thirsting for blood . . ." (4. 5). She calls him "barbaric" and demands the return of the body of her beloved Curiace. He is dazed by her attitude, considers it blasphemous. When Camille rushes offstage, Horace follows her and plunges his sword deep into her flesh.

Anyone transgressing or disrupting the hero's fixation—who seeks to alter the patriarchal identification (the ego/Self dynamism)—is unequivocally destroyed. There is no room for questioning; no other alternative possible. Never once does Horace regret having killed his sister. To have allowed her to live would have been to besmirch his and Rome's honor; it would have permitted cowardice, treachery, and blasphemy to prevail.

His honor and glory have been saved; but since murder demands punishment, Horace offers his life for what some in his
entourage consider to be a crime. Indeed, he would be happy to
immolate himself. His glory would then be eternal; he himself
would become immortal. Such an extreme measure is, however,
not required of him. Horace's fratricide is excused by the king
who presides at the trial, because brutality and murder are permitted in a patriarchal society in defense of the city-state. The
king of the land, the judging force, mentions Romulus, Rome's
founding ruler, who slew his brother Remus for the good of the
collective structure. Horace only continues this attitude. Romulus was considered the great "liberator." Horace will also
be looked upon as such—virtuous and glorious—a "magnanimous warrior."

In keeping with Jung's typological theory, both Old Horace
and his son are extroverted sensation types. They are, therefore,
wedded to actuality; they see details rather clearly, noticing all
that is concrete and practical and act accordingly. They know
how to wage war incisively, how to select the best warriors to
rout an enemy. Everything that deviates from the norm—their
vision of things—is considered madness, fantasy and, in their
language, may be viewed as treachery to the state. They are so
cut off from most of their feelings that these virtually do not
exist. Their intuitive faculty is inferior, archaic, and so is their
thinking function. Reasoning is geared to the most elemental
levels. Such extroverted sensation types are frequently overwhelmed by some ideal or spiritual factor or abstract concept;
rarely, if ever, do they bring any reasoning or logic to any situation.[7] These personality traits are eternal, as evident in Corneille's time as they are in today's world. Hero-worshipers and
zealots are outgrowths of this view of life; they seek their goal
no matter what the cost, whether murder is to be carried out or
any other cruel deed. Hitler and Stalin belong to this category.

Curiace's values are different from those of Horace. An introverted thinking and feeling type, he is loyal and warm. Although he is concerned with ideas, with clarity and order, his
emotions are in the forefront. Deeply feeling and cerebral as
well, he is able to evaluate, to understand the various factors
involved. Rather than considering him wise, balanced, and
eclectic in his views, Horace looks down upon Curiace as tim-

orous and inferior because sentiments determine his words and deeds. He loves Alba Longa as much as Horace does Rome; but he dislikes murder of any kind and would do almost anything to avoid it. His loyalty to his city-state is not blind. He seeks to apply reason to his approach. He understands the implications of conflict, suffering, and pain because he has known love and is loved. He searches, therefore, for harmony and balance.

For Horace, Curiace is the antihero par excellence: cowardly, pusillanimous, estranged. He is in Horace's view a man who seeks to escape from historical destiny. What Curiace possesses, because he knows conflict within his psyche (love/war) is that very tension that empowers the ego to grow. The Greek term *agon*, experienced in moments of crises, is nowhere evident in the Horatii father and son. Their rigid and unbending ways strip them of all flexibility.

Curiace, unlike the Horatii, distinguishes between patriarchal and matriarchal consciousness by going through the labors of Hercules, so to speak. He considers Camille's feelings as well as his own; he longs for her warmth and understanding and, in turn, tries to give his to her. Sabine, Horace's wife, is never considered. Inferior to him in all ways, insofar as the existential world is concerned, there is no hesitation about her position in his life. Since Horace never struggled with the trials that make or break a mature being, by means of which individuation may be activated, he never confronted or recognized the unregenerate characteristics slumbering in his or anyone else's psyche. Horace acts impulsively. Anything and everything is valid providing his pragmatic ends are served. Human qualities are driven into the background. Curiace dies during the course of the play because the views he represents are out of keeping with the predominant conscious value of ancient Rome.

Sabine and Camille, also transpersonal forces, are of lesser significance in the patriarchal sphere in which *Horace* is cast. Sabine, the feminine mirror image of Horace, and Camille, the reflection of Curiace, act and react in different ways to Horace's intransigence. Both women try to enlarge his sphere of reference, his understanding of life. Both also are rejected by him, since conflict within his psyche would be engendered should their lives be taken into account.

Although Sabine and Camille are eros figures in that they

attempt to reconcile, and harmonize polarities, their psychic makeup is very different. Sabine, the weaker of the two, is prone to emotional extremes. She either weeps or seeks death as an outlet for her unbearable life. In many ways she represents the *mater dolorosa*. Agonized, suffering, rather than facing facts, she searches for ways to escape it.

Born in Alba Longa and married to a Roman, her emotions are as extreme as her personality: "I fear your victory as much as our loss" (1. 1). She is forever vacillating. Only if she hated Rome or her husband, she states, would she have the strength to choose between the two. Her despair stems in part from her situation, but also from the fact that she does not have the courage to take a stand. She is overwhelmed by events, whichever way she chooses, either her husband or her brothers will die in the struggle. Chaos and despair inhabit her psyche, feelings she tries to hide because they are considered shameful: "I am ashamed to reveal so much melancholy" (1. 1).

Aware of her own weakness, Sabine would be glad to die, but to die heroically, the fate that Horace suggests for himself after he kills Camille, never occurs to her. So unclear, so alienated, are her feelings, that Sabine is forever asking those around her, including her brother, to kill her.

Although Sabine intends to take a firm stand throughout the play, she is incapable of any kind of engagement: "But alas! what side should I take in such a contrary situation" (3. 1). Who is her enemy? Whom should she hate? brother? husband? Imprisoned by her own pathetic weakness, her inability to reason, she is forever a prey to her emotions because of her lack of identity.

Camille, on the other hand, being a mirror image of her beloved Curiace, is endowed with strength as well as with feelings and reason. An introverted feeling type, she adapts to the world through sentiment which is differentiated and affects her inwardly. She is silently loyal; her emotions are not flaunted but reserved. Human beings rather than abstract codes of conduct matter most to her. But because she is also an introverted thinking type, a rare combination, she is concerned with the world of ideas, but only insofar as she can bring order to them. For this reason Camille is always attempting to clarify confusion and to transform chaos, to reconcile polarities. She rebels against the rigid status quo and represents an emerging view of the feminine principle. Unlike the undeveloped Sabine, whose character traits—anger, passion, over emotionality—are undervalued in a patriarchal society, she seeks a middle course, a blend of reason and emotion. Not an advocate of the Christian virtues of suffering, subservience, self-immolation, scourging, and humiliation, she is the most differentiated of all the characters. Within Camille exists the power of evaluation, meditation, and cogitation. She is not easily overwhelmed. Only when grief becomes so acute a force as to lacerate the very fiber of her psyche, does she yield to unreasoning emotionality, and then only for a moment.

Camille's anguish is as strong as Sabine's. Her vocabulary is also constellated with such words as tears, fear, alarm, sigh, death, suffering, disaster. Their energetic power, for the most part, is controlled by her reason and her understanding of the forces at work. She considers the individual, her brother, her fiance, not the collective. Unlike Sabine, she knows where she stands. She is *engagé*. Sabine considers only her own suffering and not the pain experienced by those around her. Camille thinks first of those whom she loves. Functioning in the workaday world, dealing with the realities of life, she has no use for power, glory, sacrifice, or any other force that does not include the *eros* principle of love. She seeks to relate, to experience, to feel, not strongly, but harmoniously. Her hope is for peace, but she knows that this is only an impossible fantasy. She knows that conflict and not stasis is the way of the world.

Camille, like Curiace, knows that where there is glory, there is also loss; heroism requires death; honor, dishonor. It is just this very capacity for thought that Sabine and the Horatii lack. Love, feeling, reasoning, evaluating principles, are all agreeable if they fall within the dominant ruling principle for Horace. As for Old Horace, he subverts feeling, annihilates it, represses it, when it does not live in accordance with Stoic tradition. He disdains love if it fails to adhere to the moral traditions of his patriarchal order. Murder is not an act worthy of punishment as treachery is, since it brings humiliation.

Camille, whose love for Curiace—and his for her—has endowed her with warmth and understanding, as well as with the equilibrium necessary to examine all sides of the situation, opts for death at the end. But death for her is not the hysterical means of escape from life longed for by Sabine but a well thought-out and reasoned eventuality. She emerges the heroine of the drama; the truly moral human being. Moreover, she is the only protagonist who evolves—from an unconscious and unknowing position of dependence to one of self-containment and relative freedom of action. Unafraid to speak the truth to her brother, when in worldly terms it would have been more prudent to remain silent, she exercises her power of choice. Nor is she willing to live enslaved under a regime that is anathema to her, that is unproductive, rigid—where feelings of compassion and understanding not only have no place but are reviled.

Camille has to die because those characteristics that she represents are not yet ready to be born and cannot function openly in the narrow patriarchal society depicted in Corneille's play. No new ethic comes into being in *Horace*: no awareness of fresh value judgments; no relationships requiring an untried center of focus of activity. As in Sparta, or any other society marked by over masculine attachments—where in psychological terms, the father begets the son—the women are virtually powerless and exist only to serve the single function, of being a birthpassage, a procreating agent. The father, in effect, is a modern Kronos who devours his son, imprisoning him in his own outworn obdurate attitude, making it impossible for the youth to develop. Growth, which means change, can only take place when there is a victory over the father. In *Horace* no such situation takes place. Archaic custom and law prevail; masculine power and strength are the focal points.[8] The patriarchal group is the archetypal entity that has taken on social and cosmic dimension. All acts are measured in accordance with this dynamic—that of heroism and sacrifice in a power-driven world.

Rodogune

Rodogune, which was Corneille's favorite among all his plays and one of the most lauded of his tragedies, also focuses on the power archetype, but this time in a matriarchal situation. The historical events that underlie *Rodogune* are mentioned by Marcus Aurelius in his *Roman History*, in Justin's *Universal*

History of Pompeius Trogus, and in Josephus's *History of the Jewish War* and *Antiquities of the Jews.* Corneille never adheres to historical fact in the strict sense of the word.

The action of *Rodogune* takes place in the royal palace at Seleucia on the Tigris, Syria's capital, in the year 125 A.D. The Syrians have been at war with the Parthians before the action of the play begins. Exceptional fighters, the Parthians extended their empire from the Euphrates to the Indus and from the Oxus to the Indian Ocean. The queen of Syria, Cleopatra, is the pivotal being in Corneille's tragedy. She wants to rule her kingdom but is resigned to the fact that she can only do so through a male heir. The historical events revolving around her (prior to the outset of the play) are complicated: Demetrius Nicanor, king of Syria, had been taken prisoner by King Phraates. Condemned to live at the Parthian court, he meets Rodogune, Phraates' sister; they fall in love. A political upheaval occurs and a usurper takes over the government. Nicanor's brother, Antiochus, wars, defeats, and slays the usurper. Cleopatra hears a false announcement, that Nicanor is dead and marries Antiochus. After the fact comes out that Nicanor is alive, Antiochus sets out to free him and, in so doing, is killed. Cleopatra, then, does away with Nicanor and takes Rodogune captive. Both sons she had with Nicanor, Antiochus and Seleucis, are in love with Rodogune whom Cleopatra despises and will seek to kill. Fearful for her welfare, reasonable in her outlook, Rodogune trusts no one even though her confidant, Laonice, who is also Cleopatra's, assures her that the queen has "only the eyes of a mother" when she looks at her. Rodogune loves one of the princes but realizes that to reveal his name would endanger her position. The situation grows acutely dramatic, as we shall see in the course of our analysis.

Cleopatra is one of the most fascinating figures in French classical theater. The equivalent of Medea and Lucrezia Borgia, she has little outward resemblance to the traits of the traditional personal mother, wife, or even queen. Corneille has endowed her with eternal and collective characteristics; he has given her the stature of an archetypal figure. Indeed, the remoteness of the period, the mystery involved in her machinations which are never clear or clarified, the horror of her deeds are so extreme, that they seem not to belong to mortal ways but touch upon superhuman eternal factors. In his "Discours du poème dramatique," Corneille writes: "Cleopatra is very evil; there is not a parricide that would horrify her, providing it could keep her on a throne which she wants above all else, so powerfully is she dominated by the idea; but all of her crimes are accompanied by a greatness of soul which has something so lofty about it, that while hating her actions one cannot but admire the source from which they emerge."[9]

Cleopatra, the terrible mother, is reminiscent of a destructive and deathly womb, one with "gnashing teeth" ready to ingest its prey. Like Scylla, "the devouring whirlpool," or the Graea (those females named Fear, Dread, Terror, whose sisters were the Gorgons), so within Cleopatra—in the deepest areas of her collective unconscious—live monstrous emanations.[10] A *vagina dentata* woman, Cleopatra is driven by a lust for power. Her passionate, ferocious, active, and impulsive nature is supplemented by a will of iron. Nothing can stand in the way of her achieving her ends, not even her sons. Her psychical energy is enormous; it seemingly stems from the divine sphere. It comes into play in all of its vitality each time she strikes, devouring and impetuously crushing everything in sight. This nonrational human being is endowed with demonic qualities that serve her own inner drives and have held fascinated audiences ever since Corneille first created her. Cleopatra's motivations and instinctual ways reach far beyond our ordinary daily world, taking on a mystic dimension: Antiochus as well as others call her "inhuman" (2. 4).

Cleopatra has a numinous quality about her: divine, terrifying. A *mysterium tremendum* is evoked when she is present. She arouses fear in the hearts of all who approach her—as if something extrahuman were imposing itself on the worldly sphere. Nor is Cleopatra immoral. To be immoral would indicate a struggle *against* something, against the status quo. When she cries out, "Nature, leave my heart" (4. 7), she joins the ranks of the "divine" amoral beings; and participates in the superhuman sphere where no limits are placed upon a person since polarities are nonexistent. Acts such as hers, therefore, take on a sacred aura; they belong to the limitless domain of the gods, Otherworldly tonalities resonate from within them. Her presence, therefore gives rise to a theophany or epiphany—EVIL incarnate—triggering acute sensations of awe and horror.[11] When Cleopatra erupts onstage—with tornado and volcanic force, she is resplendent in her brutality, setting her flesh a glaze, her gaze impervious to everything, her subtleties and feigned love bringing a whole scale of ethics and aesthetics of the fore. Her angered and angering deeds are worthy representatives of the *ira deorum* (anger of the gods).

The majesty of Cleopatra's ways stem in part from her remoteness, not only in terms of the human sphere but with regard to time. A superpower, her amoral deeds reign supreme, not in ourpresent phenomenological sphere, but in a world inaccessible to conscious reality—in an atemporal space/time continuum. Extremes are never nuanced; there is no turning back, no recourse to pardon, sin, regret. Like Hera, wounded by Zeus's infidelities, Cleopatra is beyond the limited notions of good and evil as understood in the workaday world.

Cleopatra's drive for power has taken on archetypal dimensions. She seeks to regulate her destiny, to order her kingdom, to dominate the unlimited and indomitable spheres. She is a female Kronos, the god who devoured all his children, except Zeus because his wife had hidden the child. Kronos feared his progenies would usurp the throne; so Cleopatra attempts to grind her own sons into malleable shapes; to dismember them and return them to the great mother. Cleopatra's power drive is unconscious, and therefore, far more dangerous. Her sons for her are merely instruments of power: phallic substitutes.

Cleopatra's passionate drive enslaves her. She is not a free agent. Her *idée fixe* eliminates every other response, desire, or aim. Her lust for power is comparable to a huge vacuum or maw—an area within her being that has never been filled, empty, wounded, pained in part by Nicanor's virtual rejection of her, but also because she has never known or given love, never known or given tenderness, gentleness, as wife or as mother. Deprived of the warmth of love in some early intimate experience, the void left in her psyche must be perpetually replenished. It is, unconsciously filled by the terrible mother's darker side—the shadow—those monstrous emanations emerging from her unconscious—terrifying in their grandeur.

Cleopatra, a negative elementary force, may also be likened

to the uroboric snake woman: the phallus-dominated female who possesses male-identified attributes—a kind of androgyne in this respect, but destructive in her ways. Unlike the gods and goddesses of old or those in modern times, who are usually represented in both beneficent and destructive aspects (Artemis and Hecate), Cleopatra is viewed by Corneille as a wholly negative entity—hunting down her victims. Her sexual drive has been transformed into a devouring womb—an abyss. Reminiscent of the Indian Kali, to whom goats are sacrificed at the Kalighat in Calcutta, thus feeding the newborn and the generations to come. So Cleopatra, as terrible mother, has also become a wet nurse suckling and feeding future peoples, luring and alluring them to follow her in her death-dealing ways.[12]

Cleopatra's speech defines her character: words such as vengeance, hatred, fear, storms, obscurity, violence, thunder, prison, blood, flame, jealousy, crime, furor, abound. A two-sided dynamic is implicit in her energy-charged world: one that enslaves and one that discharges. Because she is obsessed and dominated by her power drive, she cannot act in the open; but must operate and plot in secret, in darkness—in the very mystery of her hidden domain. Shadows give her substance; the dissimulation lurking beneath the clever and endearing phrases reveal her strong persona, engraved with so many niceties. Only when talking with her confidante does she finally begin to reveal herself: "Know me completely . . . "

What does the throne represent that Cleopatra should long so to control it and unleash her fury on those who without her permission seek to attain it? The throne (the kingship), both human and divine, symbolizes supreme power, harmony, balance, the highest values—the supreme ruling principle. Identified with divine science, wisdom, universal knowledge, the king stands for purity, incorruptibility, invincibility—golden qualities. Gold and sun are, therefore, frequently equated with throne symbolism: the Pharaohs in ancient Egypt were believed to have been descended from the sun-god, and so Japanese emperors—even Louis XIV was alluded to as "the sun King." A ruler is a nation's projection of an ideal individual—physically and spiritually—he is the archetype of human perfection.

Cleopatra is the antithesis of this image. She seeks the throne because she is power-hungry and for no abstract reason. She is shadow-dominated and does not live in sunlight; she represents not wisdom and harmony but a corrosive mephitic realm, overrun with unregenerate fungi. Important, too, is the fact that she is never in touch with her feminine side. Animus-possessed, she is unconsciously motivated by what is considered to be male drive. A hypertrophy of the maternal and feminine aspects of her personality have transformed her into a dogmatic, argumentative, domineering, obstinate, and willful woman. So utterly unconscious is she of her actions that the principle of *logos*, which, if objectified, could have brought out her rational and conscious capacities, but reinforces still further her subjective identification of the ego with the animus. She behaves like "an inferior man" and characteristics such as she displayed, are all-powerful in her makeup and actions.[13]

In the prevailing patriarchal society into which Cleopatra was born, consciousness was always considered a masculine characteristic; the unconscious relegated to the female principle. The more powerful consciousness grows, the greater the masculine principle appears. When the woman struggles to develop her consciousness, she also (whether aware of it or not) looks upon her subliminal realm as female, therefore, as a darker, less developed aspect of the psyche and forever struggles against its encroachment. Cleopatra, therefore, is working against a seemingly lost cause from the very outset: not only is she unequipped psychologically to rule, but because she is female she can only rule through a male: Nicanor, Antiochus, or one of her sons. Her dark side dominates all her acts. A vampire figure, a ghoul, frightened and frightening, she can but stand for an unrequited and embittered woman.

Cleopatra knows how to handle people to gain her ends; she is clever, subtle, and devious in her ways, particularly when it comes to her sons. She decides to inform her sons of the price she has paid to assure them the throne—the killing of Nicanor. The crown will be given, she states, to whichever son will do away with Rodogune. When she realizes that Antiochus will never kill Rodogune, she uses another ruse to overcome the hostility she has aroused. All sweetness and light, she confesses to a change of heart: her love for him is all that counts henceforth. She has buried her anger and will no longer seek vengeance. An earthly principle, she senses that Antiochus not only loves Rodogune but is loved by him, and that he is a stronger person because of it. Naïve in all ways, he believes his mother is over-joyed with the prospect of his becoming king and marrying his beloved. Using him as a ploy, Cleopatra then tells Seleucus that he is really the eldest, hoping in this way to incite his jealousy. Seleucus, however, remains serene. He loves his brother and can only wish him well. Cleopatra has now but one course: to de-stroy both her sons, "Let them serve my hatred or let them die" (4. 6).

When the last act opens, Cleopatra has indeed had Seleu-cus secretly put to death. Now she is planning to have both Antiochus and Rodogune poisoned. She has given Antiochus the kingship, and as the crowd awaits the marriage celebration, Cleopatra, with feigned joy, greets the nuptial couple in unc-tuous tones of deceit, "I cease to rule; you begin today" (5. 3), and asks the assembled people to greet her son as ruler and no longer herself. With goblet in hand, she offers it to the royal couple to honor Syrian tradition by drinking from the same goblet. Before they can do so, the prince's tutor rushes forward and announces Seleucus's death and how his last words were, "murdered by a hand dear to us." Deeply troubled and per-plexed, Antiochus does not know whether his brother alluded to Rodogune or to Cleopatra. He picks up the goblet to drink, but Rodogune stops him, asking that a servant drink from the goblet. Angered, Cleopatra drinks it instead. A few minutes later, offstage, she dies in agony. Antiochus tries to help her, and in so doing, she spits out maledictions on him, Rodogune, and Syria, then dies.

Rodogune is also vindictive and power-driven, but she is more balanced in her ways. Having loved and been loved, first by Nicanor and then by Antiochus, she is not ego-centered, but is clearly able to relate to others, to understand and feel for them. Reason is also a working function in Rodogune's psyche. A po-litical prisoner and victim of circumstances, she knows that she must act with restraint and wisdom, as well as with compassion if the need should arise.

Unlike many foreigners who have little or no identity, or those who live as the wife of a ruler or daughter of a sovereign, Rodogune was an entity unto herself. It could be said that she represents Hera's positive side.[14] Strong, steady, committed to her own welfare and only destructive when personal danger to herself or those she loves is involved, Rodogune acts with wisdom. She never allows her own sexuality to be submerged by the male principle; on the contrary, she relates well to her femininity, individuality, and independence and, for this reason, attracts those of the opposite sex. Her ways are winsome; her intellect, exciting; her attitude, healthy.

Rodogune does not hate Cleopatra. She fears her rage and realizes she may be victimized by her. She is motivated by need and the desire to save her life and to parry the fury of a demonic woman. An extraverted thinking type, she is affirmative: she takes a stand and seeks order. Whenever emotions start to overwhelm her, she does not allow herself to be submerged by them but rallies to solve the problems at stake. She knows how to take advice, to experience attachments, and understands relationships. As an introverted intuitive type as well, she sees into situations, understands dangers, and accordingly tries to avoid them. She has prophetic tendencies at times, warning Antiochus, for example, not to drink the poison, sensing that something is amiss.

When Rodogune realizes that Cleopatra is after her blood, her first impulse is to flee and to return to her brother's court; Oronte, the ambassador sent by Phraates, advises her differently. To flee is not only difficult and dangerous, it is also unworthy of Rodogune herself. Stately, majestic, dignified, she must face her situation, must either "reign or perish" (3. 2)—another example of the famous Corneillian antithesis. Her reason now activated, Rodogune attempts to evaluate her situation, to question her feelings on the emotional level as well as on the political one. She calls upon her own regulating principle, her talents to differentiate and examine troubling questions. Oronte had suggested that Rodogune direct the sons' "flame" in a way that would help her. They are adored by the populace, he states, and although Cleopatra dominates them, Rodogune has an advantage; she is loved by them. Cruelty, anger, and hatred are meager weapons against love. Love, then, will be her arm: "If you want to rule, allow love to rule you" (3. 3).

Rodogune finds it difficult to accommodate by deceit. Integrity and not hypocrisy has always been her way. How can she "descend to this cowardly artifice?" (3. 3), she claims. Such an act is unworthy of her station in life; it is "degrading," despicable, a paradigm of a timorous nature. Rodogune despises weakness. Yet, a pragmatist at heart, she quickly realizes that not to act in this way may deprive her and—still more important—the one she loves of the throne. She decides to test the brother's love for her.

When Seleucus and Antiochus separately come to her and avow their love for her, Rodogune tries to calm her own passion, to dominate her instincts and, above all, not reveal the love she herself feels. Her persona functions with relative ease. They must avenge the death of Nicanor, she informs them both. His last words still ring in her ears: "Vengeance! . . . Good-bye: I am dying for you" (3. 3). She loved Nicanor, she tells them, and it is his qualities that she now loves in them. For this reason they must do away with the murderer: "I love the sons of the King, I hate those of the Queen" (3. 4). They must choose; participate in the life experience, become involved, or they will lose her. They must find their own roots, gain strength, earn glory, and no longer pursue their present weak, uncommitted existence. If they decide to follow in their mother's footsteps, "Be cruel, ungrateful, parricide as she" (3. 4), the choice is theirs. Rodogune sees them weakening at the thought of killing their mother; she cannot withdraw her words, however; she cannot change her course; she must test their power.

Rodogune is the one person in the play worthy of kingship. Her ego is not submerged by her instinctual realm; it is sound and strong; when need be, she is guided not by affects but by reason. Her feelings work in consort with logic, her understanding with compassion. If anger arises within her, instincts bubble but are quickly quelled by common sense. Lucidity returns and, with it, equilibrium. Although Rodogune resorts to deceit, it is only out of the necessity to save her life. Love does indeed make her vulnerable, but in the highest sense of the word—it humanizes her. Passion does not blind her; it strengthens her. It arises from natural sources and balances that might otherwise have led to a disastrous clash of wills. Even the imprisoned atmosphere in which she lives serves her: it forces her to confront her own inner world, sound out her being, discover her motivating principles. Introversion thus brings about development, an upsurge of clarity, of focus, of understanding.[15]

Antiochus and Seleucus are *puers*: undeveloped, innocent, passive youths—perpetual mother's boys—takers and not activators, unliberated. They never act contrary to the status quo; they are medium figures and are able only to be acted upon. In *Rodogune* a sexual inversion exists: it is the men who are effeminate and the women who are virile.[16]

Both brothers are introverted feeling types; the other three functions (sensation, thinking, intuition) are so underdeveloped as to be virtually nonexistent. They adapt to all situations and events via feeling; never do they think out a point or event; nor are they intuitive; their sensations never aid them in creating relationships. They have no true scale of values; they only want to be loved. Loyal to both their mother and Rodogune, they are symbolically living in a state of incest; first with their mother, and then later with Rodogune, who is essentially a mother figure. Both men are virtually torn apart by both women, when Cleopatra makes her demands upon them, then, Rodogune, whose equally vindictive needs must also be satisfied. They veer from one to the other—without backbone, with no standards of conduct. They are frail factors in a matriarchal power struggle.[17]

One may look upon Antiochus and Seleucus as one being: each half is kind, gentle, and seeks to bring pleasure to the other, not harm. Their speech is studded with such words as beauty, love, joy, day, light, glory, sacredness. They are essentially pacific, trying to create harmony out of discord, but because they are will-less, they are ineffective; they cannot really act. Each seeks to yield to the other.

Antiochus survives because of Rodogune's love for him and her wise ways. She becomes the instrument of his salvation. It is she who takes a stand against Cleopatra, who prevents him from drinking the poison. Her love paves the way for the transference to take place—from Cleopatra to Rodogune—not overtly but covertly. Seleucus, on the other hand, is castrated, symbolically speaking, when it is reported that his stomach has been gouged out. His murder had to take place since the factors he represented—like those of Attis—were negative.

Antiochus and Seleucus in a sense are antiheroes, types prevalent in mid-twentieth-century literature, appearing in the works of William Burroughs, Allen Ginsberg, Jack Kerouac, and Ferdinand Céline. Seleucus is uninterested in surviving; indeed, he becomes virtually self-destructive. Tired, exhausted, uninterested in the kingship once he has resolved to let Antiochus marry Rodogune, he is overcome by a deep sense of futility. He awakens to the real dangers involved only when he is dying. It is then that valor bursts forth and he warns his brother of the similar fate that may well be awaiting him.

In both *Horace* and *Rodogune* Corneille portrays the many forces at stake in a power-driven world: the patriarchal situation destroyed what was most beautiful and sensitive in humankind to prove an ethos; the matriarchal group, led by a demonic queen, began her destructive course early in life and pursued her destiny until the end. In both *Horace* and *Rodogune*, the psychological impact of energetic drives is delineated with depth and precision—and with a composed classical balance of symmetry and grandeur.

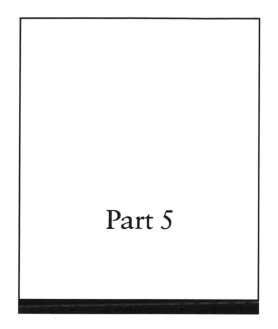

Part 5

1. Goethe (1749–1832): *Elective Affinities*—An Alchemical Process from *Fixatio* to *Dissolutio*

Elective Affinities (1808), a pastoral novel, takes its title from an alchemical process: the blending of certain compounds to cause an alteration in their consistency—from *fixatio* to *dissolutio*. In the human sphere this implies the introduction of new factors or different people into a relationship and, in the process, creation of a climate conducive to a shifting of old affections and allegiances. *Elective Affinities*, written when Goethe was nearly sixty years old, reflects both wisdom and bitterness; his feelings and desire to relive his youthful days and the dangers involved should such feelings be gratified. It is a novel that may well appeal more to the older than to the younger reader, as it deals specifically with the relationship between a middle-aged married couple.

That Goethe should have been interested in alchemy is not surprising. In his *Autobiography*, he tells of an incredible incident which has astounded scholars and might account for Goethe's continuing fascination with the occult sciences. In Leipzig, where he was studying law at the university (1765–68), Goethe began to suffer from a strange illness which included the loss of feeling. Some doctors diagnosed an acute physical depression, and it was believed that a difficult emotional problem accounted for the condition. Meanwhile, Goethe was losing his faith in the church's authority. When he heard that damnation could result if one partook unworthily of the Sacrament, malaise flowed into his being. He suffered from a strange anguish, physically and spiritually.

Goethe's agony was so acute that he was compelled to re-

turn home to Frankfurt. For one and a half years he remained
in an undefinable state of physical and mental collapse. Unable
to relate to his parents or his sister, Cornelia, whom he loved
dearly, he found peace of mind with one of his mother's friends,
the Pietist Fraulein von Klettenberg. She was the only one, he
felt, who succeeded in calming his powerful and unchanneled
passions. They talked of mysticism and alchemy and of the
scientific research being carried out at the time. The teacher—
physician J. F. Metz, who belonged to the Pious Separatist sect
and was adept in treating his patients with what some have called
mysterious medicines—was convinced that a powerful salt solution (considered dangerous if improperly applied) was the
universal element needed to cure Goethe. Salt, for the alchemist/
doctor, represented the principles of nonflammability and fix-
ity: that is, the body and spirit of man. Like Paracelsus, he was
convinced a relationship exists between the body's good health
and that of the soul, and chemicals alone are not potent enough
to cure physical ills; moral lessons must be learned in order to
really comprehend and produce harmony of being.

Dr. Metz's treatment, which fascinated Goethe, consisted
of preparing a small air furnace and a sand bath. Glass alembics
were used to further the operation and placed over a soft fire;
the various blendings were then poured into vessels where they
were left to evaporate. Neutral salts thus came into being in
what could be called the most mysterious of ways. Goethe himself became quite adept in manufacturing the salts needed for
his own cure; he termed them Liquor Solicum (flint juice), which
he made by melting down pure quartz flint with a certain amount
of alkali, producing a transparent and paradoxically fluid glass
which melted away when exposed to air.

Upon his recovery, Goethe was sent in 1770 to Strasbourg
by his father to complete his law studies; however, his interests
lay also in scientific and artistic realms. He therefore attended a
variety of classes, including anatomy, midwifery, chemistry, and
alchemy. He completed his law courses; and still his fascination
with the sciences did not cease, and so he continued to pursue
his studies in medicine, botany, geology, chemistry, and physi-
ognomy. In 1784 he supposedly discovered the intermaxillary
bone in the human skull, which is attached to the upper jawbone by a tiny ligament. Greatly influenced by Lavater, Goethe

collaborated with the Swiss scientist on *Physiognomical Fragments for the Promotion of Knowledge and Love of Man* (1775–78). In botany, Goethe set himself up as leader of the evolutionist theories and devoted his energies to finding the original plant: the archetypal plant that mystics have alluded to as the *Urpflanze*. All other plants, according to Neoplatonists, are variations of the *One* form. Also interested in optics, Goethe believed in the aesthetic and emotional value of colors. He rejected Newton's theory of the light spectrum that breaks light into colors through a prism and labeled it a "spectrum-phantasm." In his *On the Theory of Colors* (1810), he suggests that light is one and indivisible, simple and homogeneous.

The sciences in general always preoccupied Goethe from the time he became ill in Leipzig throughout his older years; alchemy in particular, from a scientific as well as philosophical point of view. He agreed with alchemical theory, which is based on the notion of transmutation: nothing disappears in the cosmos, it merely alters in form and texture. Alchemists, and Goethe, shared these ideas, contended that everything that emerged from the ground, whether animal, mineral, or vegetable, was composed of some *prima materia*. This idea was first formulated by Xenophanes, who believed in a primal unity from which all creation emerged. Such *oneness* implies universality: it also suggests an undifferentiated state, that is, a blend of the pure and the impure. The alchemists who were both scientists and metaphysicians wanted not only to transform the imperfect into the perfect but also to raise man to the paradisiac state he had known prior to his earthly existence or his alienation from God. Metaphysically, the alchemist attempted to redeem his metals, humankind, and himself as well. He longed to become reintegrated into the primordial unity he had known in Eden, but in an altered and sublimed state.

Since for the alchemist, and Goethe as well, everything emerged from original oneness, and becomes differentiated when entering the manifest world and returns to its undifferentiated state after death, everything that is incarnated must necessarily follow the death/rebirth sequence. Metals, for the alchemist, once functioning in the world, are living and breathing substances, as are all other things in the cosmos. Their modalities and stages of evolution are what distinguished mineral, vegetable, and an-

imal. Life, therefore, involves a complex series of transforma-
tions from the minutest particles to the largest of entities, continuous and contiguous within the One. Everything alters through
adaptation. If growth no longer occurs, if a condition of stasis
sets in, which is the situation at the outset of *Elective Affinities*,
then *fixatio* prevails.

ECTYPAL ANALYSIS

Goethe had been living in Weimar for thirty-three years when
he published *Elective Affinities*. He had been invited by Karl
August, duke of Saxe-Weimar (1775–1828), a despot who longed
to transform his principality into a cultural center. Wieland,
Herder, and Schiller also made their home at Karl August's court.
Despite the creativity of the aforementioned writers, however,
the atmosphere at court was traditional and conventional. Initiative and liberty of expression were frowned upon. Anything
that detracted from the smooth-running efficient governmental
world was minimized. Discipline and obedience to the prince
were the rule of the day. Everyone, including such men as Goethe,
was controlled by the absolutism of the duke's rule and by the
stultifying etiquette observed at his court.

The handsome, fascinating, charming, and knowledgeable
Goethe stood out as a Promethean figure in what was otherwise
a dull and tiresome environment. The author of the well-known
Götz von Berlichingen (1773), a drama of love and war, treachery and the zeal for freedom, and of the novel *Werther* (1774),
depicting the sorrows of a young lad in love who finally commits suicide, Goethe was already the idol of the young.

His occupations at Weimar did not, however, allow him
too much time for creative literary activity. He had administrative occupations and was put in charge of the armed forces of
the principality. He wrote plays, verses; organized theatrical
events—including *Iphigenia* (1787) and masquerade balls. He
also read widely.[1]

It was at Weimar that Goethe met Charlotte von Stein, which
was perhaps the single most important event at this period. He
was twenty-six years old when they met; she was thirty-three.
She added another dimension to his vision. Such a Platonic relationship as Goethe enjoyed with Charlotte was encouraged at

Weimar by the atmosphere which was suffused with courtesy, gallantry, and idealized love. Passionate encounters, replete with intrigue and excitement, took place in the imagination rather than in actuality. Goethe was profoundly moved by the experience.

Charlotte was no great beauty: small, thin, her jet black hair accentuated by the pallor of her skin; two dark eyes wore the softest and most arresting of expressions. Graceful in her stance and elegant in her way, she was the essence of dignity. She was married to an equerry who was very much her intellectual inferior (the Baron von Stein, Grand Master of the Horse). She bore him seven children in eleven years of marriage. Only three of her progeny survived. Serious, intelligent, conscientious, virtuous, Charlotte centered her world around her children, piety, idealism, and her profound love for Goethe. It was within this spiritual context that she experienced serenity and consolation: the sphere of abstract notions, or virtualities.

The young and emotionally sensitive Goethe found himself drawn to a woman whose qualities were the very ones he lacked; she responded to a need within him. Their relationship has few parallels in history. In a letter to the poet Wieland, Goethe expressed his feelings toward Charlotte in mystical terms: "I cannot explain the importance and power which this woman has for me except in terms of metempsychosis. Yes, we were once husband and wife. What we know of one another is now veiled in a spiritual cloud. I have no name for what we are: the past . . . the future . . . the Whole."[2]

Charlotte was an anima figure for Goethe. Secure, protective, and understanding and maternal, she gave him the tenderness he needed. She knew how to transform his natural inclination toward passion and emotional involvement, which had brought him such sorrow, into a positive spiritual relationship which broadened his horizons. A mother image, this simple and womanly person helped him assuage his loneliness. Goethe's own mother had always been in close touch with her son; she accepted his ways and fostered his sensitive characteristics. Charlotte also fulfilled another role, the relationship he had enjoyed with his sister Cornelia, who had died at the age of twenty-seven after the birth of her second child. Cornelia had been the carrier of his anima: the love object, the image upon which he

projected. It is no wonder that Goethe, in Weimar, removed
from the two beings on whose affection he had always counted,
unconsciously projected his anima onto Charlotte von Stein. In
some of the seventeen hundred extant letters that Goethe wrote
to Charlotte, he looks upon her as a Madonna ascending to
heaven, a beautiful force in his life. "My love is like the morning
and the evening star. . . . We have never lived such a lovely spring
together before, may it never have an autumn! . . . I cannot tell
you, nor is it given to me to understand what a transformation
your love has wrought in me."[3] In another letter he expresses
his feelings of unity with her: "It's perfectly clear to me that you
have become and must remain my other half. I am no single
independent creature. You support all my weaknesses; you protect my soft qualities; you fill my gaps."[4] There were moments
when he revealed a change of mood; moments of annoyance.
"Dearest lady, be content that I should love you so much. If I
can love anyone else still more I shall tell you."[5]

During Goethe's long devotion to Charlotte,[6] she did,
whether consciously or not, attempt to transform the great writer.
When she first met him, she considered him boorish, unrefined,
a "plebeian," with "vulgar" manners. He became, through her
influence, a tactful and gracious courtier. Indeed, she frequently
insisted he write in French which was then considered to be the
language of the cultured. She also tried to steer him toward the
higher things in life—with regard to love. When she suggested
that he looked down on women and that she sought to remedy
this situation, she seemingly succeeded.[7]

Goethe was so caught up with Charlotte in the first seven
years of their relationship that his own ego diminished in strength.
Jung wrote, which is certainly applicable to Goethe's case at this
period, that the one who projects his anima unconsciously "becomes so lost and submerged in this image that finally its abstract truth is set above the reality of life; and therewith life,
which might disturb the enjoyment of abstract beauty, is wholly
suppressed. . . . In this way he divests himself of his real self and
transfers his life into his abstraction, in which it is so to speak,
crystallized."[8]

It is often easier simply to accept and live out one's projection forever than to try to clarify such a relationship and risk
the ensuing chaos. Goethe, therefore, yielded to Charlotte's im-

placably Platonic views of love, and though he smarted on occasion at her rigid demeanor, he did nothing to alter the situation.[9]

What disturbed the outwardly smooth relationship between Charlotte and Goethe was her husband's return to Weimar (1785). Although Goethe's friendship with Charlotte had been accepted by her husband, upon his return, the poet felt hampered in his presence. Whether or not Goethe wanted the break to be complete, he left on a journey to Italy (1786–88). It seems to have been a kind of quest for wholeness and identity. In any event he felt that his tour of Italy was a tremendous liberation, a release from what had become a life of bondage. In Rome he felt reborn. "One is so to speak, reborn and one's former ideas seem like a child's swaddling clothes."[10]

The period of introspection in Rome gave Goethe the opportunity to reassess his life, to examine each phase of it.[11] His two-year trip permitted him to sort out his tangled emotions, to evaluate the currents and crosscurrents of his relationship with Charlotte as well as his own functions at Weimer. In a letter to her from Rome (June 8, 1787), he mentions the fact that he felt himself to be evolving, developing, no longer in a fragmented way, but as a whole being, toward fulfillment in the Aristotelian sense of *entelechia* (developing of one's potential).

Goethe returned to Weimar a changed man. He asked for, and the duke granted him, release from most of his governmental duties. He wanted to devote his time to writing and scientific experimentation.[12] It was at this period when he was nearly fifty, that he met Christiane Vulpius. Aged twenty-three, she worked in a factory making artificial flowers. A rather stocky young brunette, she answered Goethe's needs at the time. She was an earth principle. She moved into the writer's home. Their son was born on December 25, 1789. All of Weimar was scandalized—not at the birth of an illegitimate child—but that Goethe should have asked her to share his home. Charlotte was angered and jealous; her possessiveness came to the fore. No longer his idyllic love, she had fallen from grace, replacing spirit with earth, the ideal with the real. In 1806, Goethe married Christiane Vulpius. Delighted in Goethe's company, she idolized his every word and could not take her eyes off him. Goethe wrote: "In the whole of *Elective Affinities* there is not a line which I myself did not actually live, and there is far more behind the text than anyone can assimilate at a single reading." [13]

ARCHETYPAL ANALYSIS

As *Elective Affinities* opens, Charlotte and Edward (based at least in part on Charlotte von Stein and Goethe himself) are living on their magnificent country estate. The atmosphere is serene. Edward who is a member of an aristocratic family has been married earlier to a woman he did not love and who has since died. Charlotte, who is likewise of noble birth, also married a man who died and with whom she had little or nothing in common. Now, both middle-aged, Charlotte and Edward have married and are living out what would appear to be an idyllic existence busying themselves with their estate. Charlotte gardens, landscapes, plans walks and roads. Edward also gardens; he is involved with botany and grows rare varieties of flowers. Everything in their horizon spells order and perfection.

The garden, one of the earliest symbols introduced in the novel is symptomatic of their life together. Beautifully ordered and regulated, predetermined in its color, shape, and symmetry, the garden is antithetical to the forest, an expression of nature in its wild, unhampered mood. Identified with conscious planning and measurement, the garden here takes on the dimension of domestication, an imprisoning force. Every now and then, suggestively, Edward and Charlotte imply the need by action or speech to break out of what we realize has become a stultifying style of life.

From the very beginning of the novel something seems askew. Too much attention is centered on the outer world: refurbishing the house, planting, landscaping, and so forth. Too little is focused on the inner being: the ego, psychologically speaking of both protagonists, and their development. Husband and wife are forever *actively* engaged in looking elsewhere, outside themselves, finding things to do to fill up their time. Surface objects are the subject and object of endless conversations, keeping both Edward and Charlotte from becoming aware of the empty vacancy within, from encountering and discovering their own being.

Charlotte and Edward have ceased to evolve; their relationship, therefore, has become perfunctory, routine. Each is virtually unaware of the other's existence—as a unique entity, a force of life. In keeping with alchemical dicta, the introduction of a catalyst is in order, an irritant that will triturate and alter the present condition. When Edward announces to his wife that he has just received a letter from his old friend, the Captain, who has fallen on hard times and needs employment, we know a transformation is about to ensue—the order of things is going to alter.

Edward wants to invite the Captain to his home for an indefinite period. Altruism seems the ostensible reason for the invitation, but suddenly we understand that Edward longs for the warmth of male companionship, his relationship with Charlotte unconsciously weighing heavily upon him. Actually, Charlotte is a mother image for Edward rather than that of a wife. Her attitude toward him is possessive, protective, and nourishing in its own way. Whenever he seeks to strike out on his own— as he does by suggesting he invite the Captain to stay with them— she does not seem to approve. Charlotte asks for time to think the entire situation over. The invitation, she states, is not taken lightly. It is an important step in their lives. If a stranger enters the closed-circuit existence, the perfect balance they now enjoy may be destroyed.

Edward and Charlotte's marriage is not really based on sensuality or passion but rather on an intellectual and spiritual companionship grown arid with time. Little feeling is encountered in their conversations which sound more like debates, discussions concerning social, economic, and aesthetic questions. Theirs, actually, is a pedestrian marriage, the lot frequently of older people who have lived together for years and seem to have little to discover about each other: their *modus vivendi* is their pace of life—a daily plodding along.

Charlotte who rejects change is annoyed at the thought of introducing an alien element (the Captain) into their world; or any factor, organic or inorganic, that may alter the consistency of their relationship. Balance, serenity, immutability, harmony, are functioning at the beginning of *Elective Affinities*, an existence, however, based on isolation, on being cut off from the outside world. To alter this condition is to change the chemistry operating between the protagonists. It is understandable that Charlotte, intuitive in her way, senses tragedy and wants to maintain her uneventful course, the order, the continuity, and pattern of their unchanging existence. Gardening, with its planting and ordering of nature, is sufficient to occupy her days. In the evenings, she and Edward play duets, she at the piano and he on the flute. To invite the Captain will destroy the equilibrium, she maintains. For Edward, however, it will add a new dimension to his life.

If progress is to be made and the human personality to evolve, a *dissolutio* is now in order so as to liquefy and dissolve the arid climate. The alchemical operation intrudes so as to break up hardened attitudes, melt them down, as salt does when placed in a bowl of water. *Dissolutio*, nevertheless, has its dangers: it may lead to regression, to the drowning of the elements involved (that is, the death of the protagonists in Goethe's novel), to a loss of identity, to depression.

Consciously, Edward, dominated by his anima figure, Charlotte, also fears change. He is content to live in the monotony of his circumscribed realm. Unconsciously, however, such stasis begins to prey on his nerves. He needs stimulation to fire his blood and incite his imagination—to make him feel he is still a vital human being and not just stagnating in a narrow world. The Captain who had lived solidly and forcefully in the outer world, who had carved out an existence for himself, represents the new, fresh, and instinctual way of life. When reading the Captain's letter, Edward suddenly feels filled with vigor— volatility, in alchemical terminology—as though he were returning to the fire element of his youth. Indeed, Edward is quickly set afire. Flights of fancy and fantasy seem to swell within him at a moment's notice. Although he is a feeling type, his action and behavior are never the outcome of reasoned thought. Emotionally he still is a *puer*, an undeveloped boy tied to his mother's apron strings, an unthinking youth who lacks independence and foresight, a man who has never matured. Edward constantly adopts different roles in life: for Charlotte, he is her husband; for the Captain, as events will prove, a sort of childlike brother. Edward's identity comes into being via the role he plays; it is not a product of inner growth. He is never himself because he has never discovered his depths. Robust and physically active and strong, he is limp and will-less within. Hiding always behind a mask, he is Charlotte's son/lover, weakly structured, his flaccid ego never comes into his own. Labile, he is readily shattered, crumbling at the slightest provocation, dominated by affects and moods. When he accuses Charlotte of being overly sensitive and of having unjustified forebodings which are simply not there, one can understand why she, as the mother imago, attempts to keep him in place, to dominate him as one does a child. She knows he has a flighty nature and is aware of his need for change and is terrified by it. Charlotte possesses intellectual armor, but she is also intuitive and thus is able to sense the complex interplay of feelings at work.

Charlotte, we learn, also has some news for Edward, which he takes with composure. Her orphaned niece, Ottilie, of whom she is the guardian and whom she has placed in a convent school along with Luciana, Charlotte's daughter by her first marriage, is doing poorly in her work. Since Ottilie has no family of her own to go to, it is decided that both the Captain and Ottilie will be invited to stay with Edward and Charlotte.

The *two* will now become *four*; whatever antitheses exist in the subliminal sphere between Charlotte and Edward, each pulling in his or her direction, will be transformed into what Pythagoras considered the completed or *whole* number—four. Numbers are archetypal as we have already learned. They fix the unpredictable, work with space, have a numinous quality for alchemists and often appear when some form of psychic disorder is occurring. They symbolize the need to compensate for some inner chaotic state. That the dyad is to become a triad, then a quaternity, indicates a potentially inflammatory situation; sparks will ignite; flames will burn; psychic energy will no longer remain stilled and contained.

The *separatio* operation is beginning its mobile and dangerous journey: oneness is to become differentiated, the particular will grow in importance; passivity will become activity; serenity will yield to fear and trepidation. Flame enters the chemical components now, ready to recycle matter, light, energy, and darkness. The alchemists alluded to the burning process as a "baptism in fire," thus an equivalent of the *solutio* or *dissolutio* of that which is imperfect within the holy water.

An example of the fulminating unconscious contents, even before the arrival of the Captain and Ottilie, is implicit in the very evening the letters are received. Charlotte and Edward play their customary duet. Charlotte, as always, performs well at the piano. Neither her thinking nor her feeling functions are disturbed. Edward, however, does not keep time; he hurries here and there, more than usual; he sounds the wrong notes and hesitates frequently. A duet is impossible unless both players keep the same time and play in unison. Rather than make an issue of it, Charlotte tries to follow Edward: she yields to his *puer* tactics, gives in to his caprices as does a mother.

Shortly after the Captain arrives, he expresses his pleasure at the beauty of the estate: the walks, greenery, landscaping. During the course of a conversation he explains the meaning of "affinities," of the alchemical and the magnetic process that draws elements together or tears them apart, that fuses, blends, rejects, or separates them. Edward is unable to understand the profound ramifications of the subject. The Captain interpolates by giving practical examples; water, oil, quicksilver, (mercury) are substances that alter when in the presence of a catalyst in the form of heat, pressure, tension, or the introduction of a particular chemical. The very words *Elective Affinities* provide a case in point: separation occurs paving the way for new combinations to arise from some mysterious realm. Sometimes fusion never takes place, the Captain warns; as when one attempts to combine oil and water. For a moment or two, when shaken together, mechanically or powerfully, they give the impression of *coagulatio*; in reality, *separatio* is clearly in order. Charlotte interprets the Captain's statements concerning alchemical affinities in human terms: she thinks of friendship, hatred, passion and suggests that there are relationships which are considered indissoluble. However, when a third person is introduced into the mixture—inadvertently or by chance—what once was a happily united couple may be forever divided.

The alchemical formulae described by Goethe in *Elective Affinities* are concrete examples of mystical ideations: monism and cosmic unity. A Neoplatonist in the tradition of Paracelsus, Nicholas of Cusa, Giordano Bruno, and Kepler, and alchemists in general, Goethe believed that everything in the universe is linked, that everything in the differentiated world is merely an emanation of the *All*: that universal sympathies act and react on everything, whether these are visible or not, organic or not, conscious or not. The isolated pulsation, thought, sensation, simply do not exist. Each in its own way reverberates, acts, and reacts upon the other: feelings, nerves, particles, like chemical substances such as the alchemist's sulfur, salt, mercury, influence one another.

Man—a microcosm of the macrocosm—possesses his own identity, unity, set of laws and regulations: his own universe. Each being, therefore, is interconnected with others in indefinable ways, through analogy. Although one might not know the general direction of one's life's course, nature is not blind, Goethe felt, every aspect of it is in search of its own perfection or completion. Each entity quests for fulfillment. Plato's ascension toward perfection—in the domain of the idea of the idea or the divine—or Aristotle's concept of *entelechia*, in which reality searches for its own perfection, suggested to Goethe the existence of progress not only in the individual person but in the collective. Nature has its own process of becoming, its own orientating and directing devices, its own unity. The ability to apperceive these paths, to understand one's destiny, may be gained through mystical encounters, each person peering into his or her own depths in search of the divine spark. This does not rule out conflict, abrasion, attraction, ambivalence, which are all part of the life experience.

The condition of stasis existing at the outset of *Elective Affinities* was antithetical to Goethe's own philosophical and scientific beliefs, which posited *entelechia*. The Captain's arrival sets off the alchemical operation. Ottilie's presence would force the events to move on.

Just as Edward and the Captain bore the same first name (*Otto*), so Charl*otte* and *Otti*lie are linked onomastically, thereby underscoring still further the structured nature of the novel and accentuating the affinities involved.

Ottilie's first act, as she steps out of the carriage to greet Charlotte and Edward, is symptomatic of her personality. She throws herself down at Charlotte's feet and embraces her knees. Let us recall that her namesake, Saint Odilia, became blind and was thereafter guided by a powerful inner light so brilliant that it enabled her to experience the deeper realms of being. Similarly Ottilie, although unable to understand studies at the convent school the way that her cousin Luciana (from the Latin, *lux*, meaning "light") does, will find her forte in the subliminal realm and in natural relationships involving the earth. Candid, forthright, Ottilie's character is reminiscent of Marguerite's in Goethe's *Faust*. The home is her domain; she loves to provide food; delights by her charming and domestic ways.

Alchemically, Ottilie is a mediating force. It is she who will liquefy solids, transform the frigid into viable and malleable elements. She may be likened to the following alchemical description drawn from the *Aurora Consurgens*: "I am the mediatrix of the elements, making one to agree with another; that which is warm I make cold, and the reverse; that which is dry I make moist, and the reverse; that which is hard I soften, and the reverse."[14]

When Edward first sees Ottilie, he is overwhelmed by a strange feeling. Unconsciously awed and fascinated by this new anima figure, he feels a kind of dizziness—disorientation; emotions are aroused in him he has not felt for years. She is in the bloom of youth, and she reminds him of his own adolescence when life was just beginning—and the whole world seemed to burgeon. He cannot stop looking at her beautifully shaped face, her soft skin, her gleaming eyes; not to speak of her gentle curves and sensitive stance. Her youth and beauty, her charm and integrity, will rejuvenate him; happiness will be his, the narcissistic Edward feels unconsciously.

As the days turn into weeks and the weeks become months, Edward's pleasure increases. The fact that his ego is undeveloped allows him to plunge into situations rather than consider the consequences of his impulsive self-centered acts or statements. Like a child, he yields to his immediate desires, never directing or channeling his activities. As for Ottilie, she is drawn to him as she would be to the father she no longer has. She anticipates his desires, wants only to please him, to love and be loved. Like a guardian angel, she gives of herself in feeling, building up still further what will become his dependence upon her. Clearly Ottilie is a medium woman: she reflects what is occurring; responds best when she is absorbing Edward's needs, when she can serve and help him, attend to his wants. The antithesis of the narcissist,[15] she may well be associated with echo, responding to but never initiating action. A moon or lunar figure, she only shines by reflected glory.

Needless to say, as an outcome of Ottilie's presence, the

emotional climate alters. On their walks around the estate, Edward and Ottilie stroll ahead followed by Charlotte and the Captain. Edward is the one who now chooses the path; he is the leader, the energizer who longs for unchartered ways, unexplored areas—a sharp departure from his previous staid and conventional attitude, indicating an entirely untried enthusiasm. He now wants and needs fresh vistas; as such we see him stride and step here and there—thoughtlessly, without fear. Every now and then, he looks back to make sure that Charlotte and the Captain are not too far behind. Ottilie follows Edward's footsteps exactly in perfect harmony; when he turns to look at her, it seems to him that he is gazing at some heavenly being. In a sense, Ottilie is just that—another aspect of Edward's anima—the shifting, youthful, untried feminine love that he has never known.

For Edward, Ottilie is pure, untouched, unsullied, virginal femininity. Her life begins and ends with Edward, as his does with hers. Since she is an anima figure, she exists for him only in his imagination, only through his own projection. Such a creature cannot fuction happily in the workaday world. Nor can she develop her own ego; make contacts which will lead to deep-rooted relationships. Reality destroys the harmony implicit in abstract rapports. Remote and virtually diaphanous—a kind of angelic being for Edward—Ottilie is brought into existence when the need arises.

Outwardly Edward believes he feels the same devotion to Ottilie that a father would. He tries to protect her in every way possible, to anticipate her wants. He treats her as he would his own child, admiring her youthful face and delicate ways. Indeed he tells her he wants to share everying with her—his desires, needs, and yearnings—but always in a sublimated and spiritual sense, in a world where virtue reigns and idyllic conditions prevail. The father/daughter theme becomes objectified when Edward suggests she give him the picture of her own father that she always wears in a locket hanging from a chain around her throat. The locket could be dangerous, he suggests, should she trip during one of her strolls through the fields and forests, or climbing mountains. It is too large, he further states, to be comfortable.

Just as the relationship between Edward and Ottilie subtly

alters, so does that between Charlotte and the Captain. Each couple responds to the other's needs. Charlotte is delighted by the Captain's logical mind, by his ability to plan and design improvements on the estate. Both Charlotte and the Captain are rooted in the pragmatic world and understand each other's outlook on life.

A new house will be built, it is decided. The four protagonists are to give their reactions to the projected edifice. Ottilie refuses to comply, since she feels it is not her place to do so. Edward insists, however, that she participate in this momentous endeavor. The new house, she then suggests, should be built on top of the hill: the view of the ponds, the mill, the distant mountains, will become uncluttered; no longer hidden and surrounded by thickly forested spatial areas.

What Ottilie is saying with regard to her plan for the new house is the necessity for a tabula rasa. Destroy the previous contours, let the conventional domain be hidden, and allow youthful enthusiasm, instincts, and untrammeled nature to come to the fore. The heights (spirituality), the ideal reign—since the house is to be built on top of the hill—permits the dream of unattainable beauty, evanescent feelings engendered in this naturally free atmosphere, to remain pure and unsullied. The house, situated on the hill will appear, from a distance, as though emerging from a cloud; it will then take on stature and enter into an existence of its own. As is to be expected, Edward is taken with the idea. The Captain is less so, though he does finally acquiesce, noting that a change is really in order.

Musical evenings are also a paradigm of altering components. Ottilie has learned to accompany Edward on the piano while Charlotte plays duets with the Captain. Ottilie is virtually self-taught, and when she and Edward perform together, they seem to be sharing an emotional experience, each complementing the other—the two fused. Although neither plays according to precise rules, the effect is charming, delightful, and very beautiful. To feel and enjoy the music rather than to play it accurately is their way.

Music represents emotional involvement: feeling replicated in harmonies, polyphonies, and the structured order of tonal phrases. Like Pythagorean music of the spheres, Ottilie and Edward have been attracted into each other's orbit. Music for them symbolizes an intermediary zone between the material and the immaterial, the physical and the spiritual. Music generates love. It is a companion to their sensations; it brings the message of softness to their surroundings.

Charlotte is highly skilled on the piano. At the beginning of the novel, she altered her playing to accommodate Edward's more volatile style, his uneven time, and rhythmic patterns. When he rushed, she hurried her accompaniment, when he slowed down, she retarded. Now she and the Captain, who is a fine violinist, play together in perfect harmony. For Charlotte and the Captain, music stands for the pure light of reason, for harmonious balance, the ordering of the conscious faculties—the Apollonian sphere and not the Dionysian one. Theirs is a true interconnectedness, a music of the spheres in the Pythagorean sense; they bring fullness and practiced skill to their notes; the right tonalities and rhythms are sounded in perfect equilibrium. Spirit, intelligence, are the prime movers; mind rather than body, spiritual rather than earthly ties.

Laying the cornerstone for the new summer house also has its symbolic ramifications. For the mystic and the alchemist, stones denote unity and strength. Unlike living biological entities of the animal or vegetable kingdom, stone seems impervious to change. It is therefore associated with indestructible strength within nature itself, as we have already seen, with regard to the Kaaba in Mecca, the Celtic dolmens and menhirs. Representative of permanence in an ever-changing world, stone evokes a supernatural quality, as if the presence of divinity were ingrained within it—thus making for a magico-religious relationship between object and subject.

The stonecutter, or mason, now mentioned in the book is not simply a worker in stone but belongs to the secret order of Masons to which Goethe himself belonged, which traces its ancestry back to 1000 B.C. and the building of Solomon's Temple. In symbolic terms the mason is constructing not merely a building but a spiritual domain—a soul. He is consciously realizing an as yet unmanifested desire: transmuting a spiritual frame of reference into corporeal being; changing an abstract desire into concrete bedrock. The trials and tribulations associated with the building process are to be looked upon as part of an initiatory ritual—the incarnation of the spiritual experience. Once the mason sets to work and lays the cornerstone of the building, events move swiftly ahead in the existential domain.

During the groundbreaking ceremony—in keeping even today with such rituals—those present are asked to contribute something they consider significant. This item will be looked upon as a talisman and will be buried beneath the building, thereby assuring the success of the work undertaken. Intent upon giving her most precious possession, Ottilie donates the gold chain from which the locket with her father's picture had always hung before she gave it to Edward; she was thus symbolically ridding herself of all earthly objects but, by the same token, of the highest form of morality and the most spiritual of attitudes. Once the gold chain is placed in the earth, it can be relegated to underground areas, to the unconscious. There, with the *prima materia*, it will blend and revert to matter in its unstructured form.

Instincts now will be allowed to prevail: gold blended with earth. For the Mason it is the spiritual world (the underground realm) that allows one to gain knowledge of oneself by testing the forces within. The character of the relationship Ottilie has been enjoying with Edward now comes under scrutiny; the metal and fiber of both are to be tested, their inner core made manifest through their actions. Goethe's focus now alters its course. The scaffolding for the building rises swiftly; the workers perform their jobs with alacrity. Edward asks only that the plane and the poplar trees he planted as a young man not be cut down. He tells Ottilie that they are as old as he is. For Edward the trees are symbolic of his life as well as Ottilie's—their world together. To cut these down would be to divest them of their feeling and sensate worlds.

To pass from one alchemical operation to another, from one psychological or spiritual frame of reference to another, requires pain—even agony. The undifferentiated must become differentiated: the process of evaluation and discrimination must be used to face problems, to look within. It has been said that alchemists, in this stage of their experimentation, cut, torment, and incise their metals, implying in the psychological sphere that duality, ambivalence, and conflict between subjective and objective approaches are part of the process. If Goethe's protagonists are not triturated and lacerated—emotionally speaking—they would remain in their unaltered state and experience a *putrefactio* condition. As such, they would rot, decompose, and disintegrate. This is not the case, however: activity, volatility, fire, are emerging.

Edward's feeling for Ottilie has grown into an uncontrollable sexual urge. On one occasion he knocks at Charlotte's door for the first time in many months. She lets him in and they make love. The only difference between this occasion and previous ones is that Edward envisions it is Ottilie he is holding in his arms; Charlotte, that it is the Captain.

Edward is intent upon celebrating Ottilie's birthday, signalizing the event with festivities of all kinds, culminating in fireworks after a country dance. The evening's celebration has begun when suddenly the embankment upon which the crowd is standing starts to sink—a prelude, symbolically, to the breaking down, the crumbling, of personal relationships. Fortunately all those who fall in the water are rescued, except for one boy who struggles to keep afloat but is so terrified that instead of swimming toward the embankment and safety, he goes in the opposite direction. Seeing him the Captain flings off his coat, jumps into the water, and rescues him. A man of strength, able to brave danger, the Captain thus proves his "mettle."

The alchemical water operation has begun. As land dominates the first part of *Elective Affinities*, with all of its earth elements such as plantings, gardening, construction of all types, so liquid elements—water and lakes—prevail in the latter part of the work. Water for the alchemists means what they call *aqua permanens*, or primordial waters, which are the foundation of the world. Water acts as a dissolving agent; not only does it disperse certain chemicals and obstacles, but it is also empowered to make them disappear. As the fourteenth-century alchemist, Arnold of Villanova wrote in *Rosarium Philosophorum*: "The philosophical work is to dissolve and melt the stone into its mercury, so that it is reduced and brought back to its *prima materia*, i.e., original condition, purest form." Deeply troubled by the near-fatal accident, Charlotte wants to cancel the rest of the festivities, but Edward will hear nothing of it. Determined to make this day memorable for Ottilie, he orders the fireworks to proceed. Standing beneath the plane trees, symbolizing their life together and their love, he speaks to Ottilie with the greatest tenderness. He confesses to her his love for the first time.

The fireworks marking the festivities begin. The hiss and

whizz of Roman candles pour forth, a counterpart to the conflagration within the characters' hearts. Light bursts into the
atmosphere; brilliant flares illuminate the heavens. Rumbling
sounds detonate and deafen in rhythmic reverberation. Alone
with Edward, Ottilie finds her nerves virtually shattered by the
piercing noise and sheets of light floating across the heavens.
Leaning against him, she is overwhelmed with a delightful feeling of belonging.

That night when Ottilie finally retires to her room, she discovers Edward's birthday present: a beautiful chest within which
are various packages containing silk shawls, laces, fabrics, each
one more exquisite than the last; jewels and ornaments of all
kinds, each rivaling the other in beauty. Ottilie can hardly believe her eyes: she replaces everything neatly and carefully. Never,
she decides, will she touch any of these priceless possessions;
they are too incredibly beautiful for her to wear. In time, they
become hierophanies, taking on the sacrality of her love for him
and his for her.

The *separatio* continued. As stated in *The Hermetic Mu-
seum*, "O water of bitter taste, that preservest the elements! O
nature of propinquity, that dissolvest nature! O best of natures,
which overcomest nature herself! . . . Thou art crowned with
light and art born . . . and the quintessence ariseth from thee."
The quaternity breaks up. The Captain leaves and Charlotte
resigns herself to her fate. Ottilie seeks employment in another
household. She realizes Edward has grown so deeply fond of
her as to threaten the stability of the household. Edward is averse
to Ottilie's departure and decides that she must return and that
he will go.

Months pass. When Edward learns that Charlotte is pregnant—the fruit of that one night of tempestuous sexual impulse—emotional chaos overtakes him. He joins the army.
Charlotte gives birth to a son, and it is Ottilie who will take
care of the child. Holding the infant in her arms, she notices
something quite strange; the baby's eyes resemble hers, and its
face is the replica of the Captain's. Symbolically the four have
been joined in one little boy.

Edward returns to the estate after many long months, having convinced the Captain (now Major) that he should marry
Charlotte so that he—Edward—can in turn wed Ottilie. Rather

than greet Charlotte first, he acts impulsively in true *puer* fashion and approaches Ottilie who is reading near the lake. The child is next to her. They converse, and he tells her of his plan to marry her. Never will she agree, she says, if Charlotte will be hurt. Only if both marriages are acceptable to the other two involved will she accept. Uncontrollable passion overtakes Edward. He seizes Ottilie and kisses her. She is so shocked by the incident that she grabs the child and rushes into her little boat. She begins to row away so frantically that the boat, now in the open water, rocks from side to side, and the child is thrown out. Ottilie immediately jumps in to rescue him, but it is already too late. His eyes have closed, his breathing stopped. Half crazed with agony, cut off from any kind of help, Ottilie attempts in vain to revive what is already dead.

Charlotte forgives Ottilie for the accident. Ottilie's sense of guilt is so powerful a force, she vows to sacrifice earthly joy to gain God's forgiveness. Self-denial is her way. She will let herself die from anorexia. Edward lives on mechanically for a short while, but life has lost its luster for him and he dies of despair. He is laid to rest next to Ottilie.

Elective Affinities to a great extent attacks the nineteenth-century view of the sanctity of marriage that does not evolve and deepen but, having once occurred, remains fixed in a closed, sterile, static relationship. There comes a time in life when such a union must be dissolved; personal destruction can only ensue if it is allowed to continue. That Edward and Charlotte devoted so much time to exterior activities—landscaping, for example—at the expense of their inner world was an indication that something was wrong. The catalysts—the Captain and Ottilie—introduced as in the alchemical formulae *solve et coagula*, paved the way for the *dissolutio* that then occurred. Only Charlotte, the thinking and intuitive type, and the Captain, reasonable and objective in his way, survive. Edward and Ottilie, both undeveloped, immature, and unconscious beings die—stunted and unregenerate.

2. Novalis (1772–1801): *Hymns to the Night—A Regressus ad Uterum*

Hymns to the Night (1800), six lyrical poems, expresses Novalis's mystical yearnings for death, reflects his metaphysical beliefs and his search for psychic equilibrium. As a geologist of the soul, each of the hymns cuts through layers of feeling and thought, in spiritual matters: and in so doing, plumbs the poet's inner depths in a desperate search for the mystical *center*, that point within the collective unconscious where the creative élan is experienced.

There were outer cultural reasons as well as inner emotional ones for Novalis's feelings of longing and unrest. Since the Seven Years' War and the French Revolution, Europe had been in a state of political and economic ferment. Spiritually the animosity that had existed between Catholics and Protestants ever since the Reformation remained, and the rise of splinter religious sects added to the poet's uneasiness. Novalis sought answers to these problems, not in terms of an existential scheme, but rather in cosmic dimensions. He attempted to reach out beyond himself, to immerse his being in a triadic universe: heaven, earth, and the spiritual sphere.

Early in life Novalis had come under the influence of Neoplatonism. First as a student, then as a disciple, and finally as a seeker in his own right, he rejected a world of contingencies and enslaved by a growing commercialism and industrial society. He sought to find primal dimensional, atemporal realities in all their mysterious opacities—these he could envision unfolding before him in unending spiraling vortices. Cajoled by his imagination, titillated by his senses, he listened to the inner voice of his unconscious as it whispered its need in hushed tones and silent glimmerings. In Novalis's expanded universe, light gleams in blackness, multiform kaleidoscopic colors emerge from an ever-extending inner universe. The freshness and purity of his inspiration seems never to have lessened nor his yearnings and painful despondencies.

Hymns to the Night is a religious adventure—an excorcism: a record of his Orphic descent first into the world of sleep and then into death. Sleep, both natural and narcotically induced, reveals an oneirosphere replete with dreams, prophetic encounters, and erotic meanderings. Novalis traces his initiatic course, he leads his readers into chthonic regions where rhythms alter, tonalities pulsate, and concatenations multiply in internal groupings. Feelings and nuances, both organic and inorganic in form, possess their own evanescent beauty and meaning in Novalis's hierarchized interior world: enigmatic, oracular, and prodromal. The further the poet departs from the circumscribed land of the living, the more actively and highly charged becomes the nature of the poetry.

Novalis's quest for serenity and for the creative factor is expressed in *Hymns to the Night*, which is in a sense a modern reenactment of an ancient mystery ritual, similar to those experienced in the sanctuaries as Eleusis and those practiced by Orphic and Dionysian cultists. Novalis's seeming goal was also to experience the death of the profane being and rebirth in the divine oriented one. On the aesthetic level, the uncreated *prima materia* would, through the various tests and disciplines required in the sacred ceremonies, become manifest in its most perfected form in the work of art.

Novalis's *regressus ad uterum*, which an Orphic descent requires, was expressed metaphorically through his anima figure: that virginal presence of his beloved fiancée, Sophie von Kühn, who died at the age of fourteen. A hypostasized Marie, she became the poet's psychopomp, leading him to that preexistent sphere of being in which wholeness is linked to love and religion to creativity. It was through the matriarchal fold that Novalis broke through the crust of outside matter and reached a level within his psyche that permitted him to seize his vision, his creation. The numinosity of the spiritual exploration undertaken in *Hymns to the Night* led to a reawakening of his soul, now integrated into his psyche, and its resurrection in the written word.

For Novalis, death was a provisional state. "To die is to be initiated" Plato declared.[1] Death was not an endless nothingness. On the contrary, it was in death that the poet would meet his beloved, share in her embrace, and together was reborn in the created work of art. The initiation process which made such palingenetic feelings possible was arduous, searing, and lacerating. The healing which ensued, like a ripening seed, bursts through the compacted earth, as an idea falls from unconsciousness into consciousness—the *Einfall*. Novalis, the disciple, had experienced the wounds of life as well as those multiple and oppressive forces encountered by the acolyte during his initiation; Novalis, the apprentice, had understood them; Novalis, the poet, expressed them—now that he had become a Master.

ECTYPAL ANALYSIS

Novalis, whose real name was Friedrich von Hardenberg, was the son of an austere, stern, and deeply religious military aristocrat. Having fought in the Hanoverian legions during the Seven Years' War, Baron von Hardenberg suffered deeply when sometime after his return his first wife died of smallpox. Her untimely passing led him to seek comfort in Pietism, a Moravian evangelical sect founded in Bohemia by John Huss (1369–1415), who believed in a return to early Christian simplicity in belief and life-style. Huss was condemned for his religious ideas and burned at the stake. In accordance with Pietism, Novalis's father rejected all formalized religious ritual, as well as a reasoned approach to religious faith, and adopted a Puritanical attitude toward life. When he married again at the age of thirty-two, his second wife was an orphan girl who had lived in the Hardenberg household since childhood. So grateful was she for his attention that she became the most humble, faithful, adoring spouse any husband could possibly have; she also bore him eleven children.

The sensitive and weakly structured Novalis had little in common with his rigid and moralistic father. In keeping with the repressive religious atmosphere of the Hardenberg home, was its architectural gloom—an ancient Gothic convent that the Hardenberg family had acquired during the Seven Years' War.

As a small child, Novalis is said to have learned slowly. He apparently had a relatively poor memory and little taste for study. At the age of ten, however, after a serious illness which forced him to stay in bed for some time, an incredible change was noted, both physically and mentally. Almost overnight, he displayed an enormous desire to learn. His memory grew strong; his attention span increased; his powers of observation became quite remarkable; and his emotional sensitivity deepened. It could no longer be said that his younger brothers were more precocious than he. At sixteen he was sent to the gymnasium at Eiseleben, where he displayed a somewhat rebellious attitude toward Pietism. In any case, the young man seems to have grown weary of the regimentation in general, whether at home or at school. He was then sent to stay with his uncle at Lucklum (Brunswick), where he came in contact with the first of the many creative minds he would encounter during the course of his life.

No longer living in the shadow of the medieval convent and the overly austere and restrictive paternal atmosphere, Novalis began reading the works of the French "philosophes": Diderot and Voltaire among others. It was at his uncle's home that he was also first exposed to Goethe's *Götz von Berlichingen* and *Werther*, to the writings of Wieland, Lessing, and Cervantes. He began to understand the pleasures life could yield to one divested of rigid aceticism and narrow vision. He was ready to step out into the world, into joy, banter, intellectual pursuits, and dialogues, into the world of sunshine, witticism, satire, irony, and fantasy. The rococo style was in full flower and its gaudy, complex, decorative beauty captivated him, as did the women he began meeting.

In 1784 Novalis's father was appointed supervisor of the saltworks at Weissenfels. The Hardenberg children were not averse to leaving the somber convent for the charming little town on the River Saale.[2] Six years passed. In 1790, Novalis was sent to study law in Jena. There he met Schiller who became his idol. Novalis's letters to his family during this period describe Schiller as friend, teacher, creative philosopher. Perhaps because of his overly rigid upbringing, Novalis did not yet know how to use his new-won freedom in a positive way. Outside of the studies he enjoyed, poetry, philosophy, and science, which he pursued—and not law—he indulged in all sorts of amorous adventures and intrigues. These were not to his father's liking. The would-be poet was summoned home, then sent along with his brother Erasmus to the University of Leipzig.

In Leipzig, Novalis met Friedrich von Schlegel (1772–1829), an example of the German romantic poet par excellence, as well as literary critic and scholar. It was he who had traveled with Madame de Staël through Germany, and who had inculcated his ideas to her in giant draughts. He declared romantic poetry to be "progressive" and "universal." It emanated from northern areas, somber, lugubrious, and melancholy climes, where dreams are plentiful and feelings profound. Classicism, born in southern lands, with its rational approach to life and literature, its sunny orientation, was superficial, and frequently arid.

Learning and absorbing the ideas of his literary contemporaries, drawn to the Neoplatonist mystics whose works he both read and heard discussed (Paracelsus, Nicholas deu Cusa, Agrippa von Nettesheim, Giordano Bruno, Jacob Boehme), Novalis was now introduced to new metaphysical dimensions. For the Neoplatonist, the universe is *One*, endowed with a soul; it is a living being. Each individual, animal and mineral, is connected to this one entity—this *All*. Our world of multiplicity is then but a manifestation of this one dynamic force. Connection with the One may be experienced through a network of universal sympathies: via the collective unconscious through which an individual may reach what mystics call the *central point* or the *beginning*, which poets look upon as the *creative principle*, and which Aristotle labeled the "Unmoved Mover."

As monists, the Neoplatonists did not believe that anyone or anything could ever be cut off from this universal All. Each entity, feeling, gesture, stance, breath, was a manifestation, a symbol or sign of that further dimension of existence, that other immortal form of life. The individual was a microcosm within a macrocosm, a unit unto himself but a mirror image of the giant organism which is the All. In the hierarchized world of the Neoplatonist, one could descend or ascend the chain of beings. Only by inner contemplation, through the willed removal of the ego, can an individual perceive and apperceive the uniqueness of life—his or her own as well as that of all humanity—in a descent into Self.

Novalis immersing himself in the works of Boehme, Schelling, Ritter, and Tieck, longed to discover the metaphysical link that existed between himself, a mortal, and the transpersonal All or Self. Such excursions or intuitive forays were attempted in *Hymns to the Night, Disciples of Saïs, Heinrich von Ofterdingen.* During these moments of poetic ecstasy he experienced primordial unity. Past, present, and future were one; the world of contingencies was obliterated and so was his ego; he came face to face with infinite cycles within his psyche—where life and death were but two aspects of a single unified force.

When Novalis was twenty-one years of age his father sent him to the University of Wittenberg, a place made famous because it was here that Martin Luther nailed his Ninety-Five Theses to the church door. Novalis worked assiduously and passed his examinations. He developed an interest for ecclesiastical history, agriculture, gardening, government, and alchemy. Law, however, much to his father's dismay held no fascination for him. Upon graduation, Novalis's father found an administrative post for him. It was on official business that Novalis was sent to Gruningen on November 17, 1794—to levy taxes on Gruningen Castle. It was at this point that he met Sophie von Kühn, the love of his life.

Fair-skinned with black eyes, graceful in her demeanor, charming in her ways, Sophie was not yet thirteen when Novalis first met her. The stepdaughter of Captain von Rockenthien, she and her brothers and sisters had been brought up in the household of military gentry. Hunting and drinking parties were *de rigueur*; the atmosphere was both free and somewhat rowdy; one quite the opposite of that in Novalis's home. Sophie was forthright and naïve, unspoiled and direct in her attitude. Novalis was immediately entranced by her. He was also fascinated by Wilhelmine, who was her stepsister, almost thirty years of age.

Novalis and Sophie became secretly engaged on her thirteenth birthday. In his notebook he jotted down the following impression of her:

Her early maturity. She wishes to please everyone. Her obedience to, and fear of, her father. Her modesty and her blameless fidelity. Her stiffness and her flattery of people whom she appreciates or whom she fears. . . . *She does not desire to be anything*—she is something. She does not allow herself to be bored by my love. My love often oppresses her. She is cold generally. Wonderful power of make-believe: power of

concealment. Great power of women to conceal. Her keen observation. Her real tact. All women have what Schlegel blames in the beautiful soul. They are more perfect than we. Their nature seems to be
our art—our nature, their art. They are born actresses. They individ-
ualise—we universalise. She believes in no future life, but in the wandering of the soul.[3]

Novalis's feelings toward Sophie were complex, and to this day
they have never been fully analyzed. During their engagement,
for example, he not only saw other women but became infat-
uated with some of them, while all the time professing his great
passion for Sophie. When she became ill (1795) with tuberculosis, his attention toward her redoubled, almost as though his
love fluctuated with the state of her health. At fourteen, after
the doctors had pronounced her cured, and Novalis and Sophie
announced their engagement, her condition flared up again, and
rapidly worsened. An operation was ordered. She was taken to
Jena. Her suffering was excruciating. Novalis visited her frequently. Even Goethe came to see her. Novalis's and Sophie's
love flowered. His care and solicitude were unceasing. The doctors, however, could no longer help her. When she was trans-
ported back to her home in Gruningen, Novalis rarely saw her.
Only a few days before her death did he visit her. It was his
brother Erasmus who remained in Gruningen with Sophie until
her death on March 19, 1797, a few days prior to her fifteenth
birthday. Erasmus died a month after her from galloping con-
sumption.

   Novalis not only looked upon Sophie as a beautiful girl, a
pure being, to him she was also the earthly replica of the divine
Sophia—eternal wisdom, for the mystic. Prototype for Dante's
Beatrice, it is by means of Sophie, the meadiatrix, that Novalis
would undertake his descent into the Self—the great mystery.
Five weeks after her death, while visiting her grave, Novalis had
a vision. A week later he began jotting down his feelings when
he contemplated her saintly resting place. Something seemed to
have stirred within his psyche, as if he were haunted by visions
of her. He considered suicide so that he could join her in mystical nuptials beneath the earth.

   On May 19, 1797, he wrote: "What I feel for Sophie is not
love but religion. Absolute love, independent of the heart—love
founded on faith—such love is religion."[4] The feelings which

now welled up within him were religious ones, in the Latin sense of the word *religio*, a linking back into the past, individual as well as universal and cosmic. Sophie was now a divine being—his *femme inspiratrice*. It was she—as an anima figure—who was his catalyst, inciting his thoughts, arousing his feelings, sublimating his sexuality.

It has been suggested that the pain Novalis experienced after Sophie's death, the emotional turbulence of his reaction, the conflicts with which he had to deal, gave rise to a truly numinous experience. The chaos within his psyche had to be sorted out; the intensity of the multiple feelings, each charged with energy, had to be conveyed intellectually, viscerally, and aesthetically. He continued his pilgrimages to Sophie's grave. Seated beside it, he experienced the quietude necessary to untangle the forces confronting him, disengaging the emotions that dominated and blurred his spiritual sight, allowing clarity of perception to emerge in all its power.

Novalis's emotional involvement with Sophie, his concern for his own poetic visions, in no way eliminated his worldly needs and activities, as attested to by the following quotation written on the thirty-ninth day after Sophie's death: "I have not thought of her with emotion; I was almost uneasy, but certainly not in a manner unworthy of her. I thought of her at times in a manly way. . . . This morning I had the fatal oppressive, fearsome feeling of an approaching cold in my head."[5] On the forty-seventh day, Sophie again assumed the role of a poetic vision which became the object of his contemplation. "The whole day I was consecrated to contemplation of Her. . . . I seem to be too much in harmony with everyday life. . . . how short a time I am able to remain in the heights."[6]

Other entries mention the fact that Novalis picked flowers which he placed on her grave, that after spending an entire day seated there he felt himself immersed in a strange sense of joy: "Centuries were as moments—I could feel her near."[7] Time became compressed; space vanished. On the sixty-first day he wrote: "I was not moved at her graveside. . . . I must live ever more and more for her sake. . . . I am for her and for no others. . . . She is the Highest—the only One. . . . If I could only be worthy of her in every moment. My principal exercise should be to bring everything in relation to the idea of her."[8]

The more alienated Novalis felt toward the world around him, the greater his understanding of Sophie became—or that aspect of his psyche which he projected upon her. Novalis did not attempt to divest himself of the grief he felt over her death. On the contrary, he seemed to have tried to cultivate his intense emotions, to nurture them. They fed his inspiration. On the eightieth day, he noted: "The lovers must feel the gap—must ever hold apart the wounds. May God keep me ever in this indescribably sweet pain. Without my Sophie I am nothing; with her everything." [9] Novalis sought consolation in solitude, in isolation. He no longer entertained the idea of suicide. He would wait until his death to celebrate his nuptials with Sophie and gain eternal peace and beatitude.

On December 1, 1779, Novalis arrived in Freiberg to study at the famous mining academy. Chemistry, physics, mathematics, metallurgy, geology, had always fascinated him, and he wanted to deepen his knowledge in these subjects. As administrator of the saltworks, Novalis felt that it was incumbent upon him to strengthen his scientific and technical understanding of the processes with which he was working. In 1799 he was appointed to the staff of the Weissenfels Saltworks. He wrote *Christianity or Europe* (1799) in which his ideas, influenced by Jacob Boehme and other Neoplatonists, as well as the romantics, suggested that the golden age that man had originally known when connected with other forms of nature (animal, vegetable, mineral) would one day be recaptured, that the birth of a new universal church, which would strengthen once again God's spiritual unity that had been known to Christians during the Middle Ages and lost at the time of the Reformation, would again come into being. Novalis was also working on *Heinrich von Ofterdingen*, his *Bildungsroman*, in which he describes a young poet's journey through a fantasized medieval Europe. It was in this novel that the Blue Flower which was to become the symbol of German romanticism appears, standing for feeling, for the imagination's longing for ineffable beauty and the unreachable Ideal. Novalis's philosophical meditation, *The Disciples of Saïs*, where the meaning of life is experienced through the "mother of all things, the veiled Virgin," Isis, who leads the initiate into the land of purity, splendor and mystery, remained unfinished at his death.

In 1800, Novalis became engaged to Julie von Charpentier. He did not marry. He died of tuberculosis the following year. Friedrich von Schlegel wrote in March 1801: "I saw Hardenberg die. . . . One could hardly think it possible to die so gently, so beautifully, for the time I was with him he was unutterably serene. . . . It is beyond all things precious to me to have seen him once more." [10]

ARCHETYPAL ANALYSIS

"Life is the beginning of death," Novalis wrote in his diary on March 25, 1801, a few days before he himself died.[11] He longed for death as he longed for life. Each in its own way acted as a catalyst; each opened him up to the All, the eternal continuum—that single breath of Cosmic Aspiration.

The six hymns to the night are comparable to the six days of creation and the six steps in the ascension of a soul. They take the reader on a pilgrimage, an initiation ritual during the course of which sacrality is experienced. Novalis's undertaking was "galvanic"; it allowed him to embrace qualitative spheres: God/nature/ego, or expressed in another modality: necessity/possibility/reality.[12]

God and nature were not the same for Novalis. God was nature's goal. It was the "condition" into which nature came from and must return. Ego, for Novalis, was that faculty that linked subjective to objective worlds, the bridge which relates an individual's particular identity and conscious contents with the collective world—the unconscious.

> *God is perpetual Activity*
> *Nature is perpetual Object (Matter)*
> *Ego is perpetual condition.*[13]

Novalis's triadic universe may also be divided into other categories: body/breath soul/spirit; in poetic terms: intuition/imagination/intellect (discursive and deductive reasoning). In each case, the poet seeks to experience the most primary levels of being, where unity exists in the inner world; darkness, the uncreated—and the world of multiplicity, light, as well as the created work of art, is still unknown.

Novalis's confrontation with death, first with Sophie's then

with his brother Erasmus's, then with the accidental drowning
of another younger brother, in addition to his own poor health,
dominated his fantasy world. It led him into darker, more somber recesses, to the feeling sphere where objects appeared to him
as signs, symbols, portents of mysterious emanations which he
saw in reflected prismatic colorations, shimmering images—as
if emanating directly from the light of Sophie's radiant soul.
Hymns to the Night is an encounter with Self, as delineated
through the anima. It is the anima—Sophie—who lures the poet
into his own mythic sphere, on his journey to recapture, renew,
revitalize, what has been fragmented and splintered in the empirical sphere—to fuse the triurnal worlds that become One
during the creative impulse.

Novalis not only ushers his reader into the domain of death,
where forms and forces take on their own visibility and consistency, and where hearing, smelling, tasting, and touching coalesce, but also invites him or her to partake in the actual
re-creation of the great mystery beneath ground—in the underworld—into the unknown. During his inner trajectory, spiri-
tuality/sexuality impresses itself upon his being, allowing him
to know moments of true ecstasy.

Psychoanalytically, *Hymns to the Night* is a regression: a
way of returning to the prenatal condition, which allows Novalis the freedom to look upon his as yet unlived life experience.
Within this inner world, the poet knows preconscious existence,
bathed and cradled in the maternal arms. Without worries,
without pain, he slumbers in oblivion. It is within the earth—
the womb—which may also be considered as the unconscious,
that he experiences "a sense and taste for the Unending," a need
for the eternity of death. As a child of nature—like Sophie—
Novalis expresses suicidal tendencies in his *Hymns*, a desire to
end his earthly life. A *puer aeternus*—reminiscent of the ancient
Greek myth of Hyacinth and Narcissus—he could not adapt to
contemporary society, harsh and brutal, and like them was
doomed to die young. Death is the transforming principle through
which Novalis assuages his sorrow—a means of leading to a
world devoid of all temporal anxieties and stress. To be wel-
comed into the warm outstretched arms of the Earth Mother,
and there to be united with his Sophia, is Novalis's goal.

Hymns to the Night is a poetic reenactment of the mythic
birth, death, and dismemberment rituals. It also describes an

Orphic descent to the underworld. Let us recall that it was Orpheus who introduced the "un-Greek doctrine of sin, atonement stain, and purification" into Greece;[14] the followers of Orpheus softened and restrained the wild maenadic elements in the worship of Dionysus; thus ennobling man. It was the divine art of music and poetry that enabled Orpheus to descend to Hades and almost restore to life his beloved Eurydice (anima). When at the last, he failed in his mission, his lamentations were so poignant that they stirred the very rocks to weep. His followers therefore were convinced that everything in the natural world was endowed with a soul that longed to be reunited with the immortal, universal one from which all sprang.

Like Orpheus, Novalis returned to earth after his dark interior journey. Not for long, however. He was dismembered by raging maenads as Novalis was to be physically destroyed by the disease ravaging his lungs—that very organ which allowed him to breathe, to know inspiration—*pneuma, nous*. The pain he endured was great; nevertheless, he accepted death as part of a cosmic process and the tortures accompanying it were implicit in the initiation leading to the mystery of being.[15]

Mystery cults, whether celebrating the memory of Osiris, Dionysus, Demeter, Orpheus, or Christ, have several common factors and frequently follow, as do the *Hymns to the Night*, six separate stages:

1. Entry into the sacred precinct (*temenos*); purification ceremonies.
2. Acolyte becomes associated with other forces of nature through sleep.
3. Trials.
4. Initiate becomes a seer and imparts his visions to others who have not yet experienced the deepest arcanum.
5. Initiate reaches the nonreferential level of experience. He severs relations with the noninitiated, since the ordinary person can no longer communicate with the acolyte or understand him.
6. The initiate dies to the profane world and is reborn to eternal spiritual life.

The transformatory process is experienced in a mystic state of *ekstasis*: each step is lived out in accordance with cosmic flux, as the hierophant ascends/descends (for the mystic space is nondimensional, height and depth do not exist) toward the world of the Absolute. Novalis, the initiate-poet in *Hymns to the Night*, perceives unity/God, through the inner experience, the mystical encounter with the anima—Sophie—which becomes a revelation—an epiphany for him. In the last hymn, the poet "aspires" to reenter the world of the Absolute (or the All), there to blend, to become an element in the perpetually renewed and renewable *prima materia*. Only through death can a superior synthesis come into being, only through analogy, abstraction, or concretion can nature pursue its circulatory trajectory as does the blood through the body, cells in the flesh, and geological layers within the earth.

Hymn 1: Temenos—The Sacred Precinct

The Poet enters the sacred precinct near his beloved's grave. He bursts forth into lyrical song, hymning his joy to the light and the day, to the "marvels of the immense space" unfolding before him. He evokes his feelings in nuanced colorations, rays, waves of light, each falling, shattering, expelling its ideations in emotional equivalents. In the Poet's hierarchized world, ranging from the most distant planetary constellation to the closest earthly pebble, his bipolarized vision is able to encompass the extremes of cold and hot, solid and liquid, thinking and feeling, earth and air in perpetual transmutations. Nature for the Poet is the herald of even more intense splendor. Appearing as the "Queen of terrestrial form," the being responsible for the infinite symphony resounding in the Poet's ears, he declares: "Her presence alone reveals to us the realms of the world in all of their miraculous splendor" (p. 77).

The major, not the minor, key is dominant when the sun is in the ascendant. Its light, its heat, its beauty, and majesty bedazzle the Poet. Graceful forms infiltrate the landscape, sparkle in azured images, shimmer as the sun gazes down, watching, observing, nurturing the new seedlings, paving the way for yet another season of growth and harvest—renewed spiritual plenitude. The solar force, that creative spirit—a father figure—watches over the ceaseless activity and in so doing, strengthens and diminishes, composes and decomposes, intensifies and lessens its light, then weakens and disperses it altogether, paving the way for the oncoming night.

Just as Helios in the Eleusinian mysteries informed Demeter that her daughter Persephone had been ravished by the underworld god Pluto—so the Poet now peers into his own chthonic spheres. Day vanishes. The sun yields its power to night (for the Greeks night was the daughter of chaos, the mother of the heavens [Uranus] and of the earth [Gaia]). Night, in its holiness and mystery, enfolds the Poet. Penumbra, moist and chill, encourages a melancholy flow of tonal feelings. In this shifting atmosphere, the Poet begins reliving his childhood memories, retreating into a dream world. Images inundate his field of vision, capture his attention as they appear before him in cloudy, dark, evanescent glimpses. Once the light of the sun has yielded to the darkness of night, receding, withholding its flaming radiance, the Poet inhales the darkness, seeking within it solace. His fragmented psyche, so dispersed during the sunlit/conscious hours, finds comfort and refuge in the darkness and plenitude of the night/unconscious.

Night, the great mother, healer, protector, emerges in all of her beatific grandeur. She shields the Poet, encourages him to blend with the earth realm; by a sleight of hand, he becomes invisible, fuses with the surroundings, penetrates the very fiber and breath of being. Only through night, the feminine principle, can magic be restored; the hidden made visible; the worn, renewed; the damaged, restored; the arid made fertile. The Poet awakens to the great mystery unfolding before him. He opens himself to occult forces, to those living essences now activated within his subliminal realm.

The great mother night is alluded to as the "Sun of Night" whom the Poet experiences as an inner force, integrating this aspect of his anima into his very essence. In so doing, the Poet celebrates his newfound experience in sequences of premonitory images, hypnagogic dreams, embracing nature in so doing, seeing and feeling beyond the realm of gross matter into a sphere bathed in the softness of contentment. The Poet now begins his "night-sea journey" as had Osiris, Orpheus, Christ, when attempting to penetrate the profoundest levels of the psyche—the collective unconscious. The Poet sees night as the queen mother now, wearing her cloak of darkness; she takes on the contours of a human form, a new reality and from her "ineffable emotion" exudes numinosity. The *temenos*, the sacred precinct, makes

itself known. The "grave" face of this queen of night, now filled
with infinite tenderness and clusters of memories, is framed within
a "forest of curls." The Poet welcomes her and longs for her
embrace, reaching out with infinite joy into the blackness before
him, and in so doing, the last vestiges of the "poor and puerile"
light of day disappear, allowing the shadowy realm of oncoming night to take precedence.

Night opens the Poet's eyes, encouraging him to peer into
infinite spatial realms, far beyond the stars that seem to scintil-
late and infiltrate into his newly expanded vision. What the poet
knew in the daylight hours of his life—in the exterior world of
multiplicity where exterior frames of reference are the sine qua
non of the empirical world—gives way to feelings "of indescribable voluptuousness," to binary rhythmic sequences, each
alive, functioning, activating *the prima materia* of his triadic
universe. The Poet looks into the unearthly eyes shining before
him and he knows he is entering a sacred area—soul-forces.
The eyes of what he alludes to now as the "Queen of the Universe" lead the Poet into sublime regions, there to be lulled,
guided through uneven and unknown paths. "Priestess of a
celestial love" (p. 81), it is night that sends the Poet his beloved,
allowing him to be "consumed" by her "spiritual flame." Forms
are divested of their materiality, substance dispelled, as the Poet
unites in intimate union in this his "nuptial night" with his beloved for "all eternity" (p. 81).

Night/death/marriage are intertwined in Novalis's image of
nature's veiled goddess. Together they fructify the Poet's world
of dreams, celebrate his sexual union with his bride that will
give birth to the poem that ensues. The Poet's initiation continues. Purification now takes place in the deep waters of the earth's
maternal womb; then diffusion into nothingness. The Poet's ego,
now disperses, dissolves into dew, scatters into ash, fades, dismembers, and gestates. His unconscious, now unbound, is free
to roam, to spread out throughout an aspatial continuum.

The Poet now identifies his beloved Sophie/anima with night
and with the earth and its inner recesses. Youth is not obscured,
but lives on in ethereal essences. In the shadowy domain of desire, where fugitive feelings are transformed into hard and crystalline entities, the Poet, too, feels an alteration of mood occurring within his being. He feels the warmth engendered as flames

vibrate within him, luminous globes infiltrate the opaque atmosphere. Friction, involved in the transmutation process, burns away the impurities which still cling to him—the residue from the differentiated world. Only the ash, which in alchemical terminology is the most perfect of elements, the quintessence of being, remains. The fire, that energetic principle which, according to the Gnostic philosopher Simon Magus, was an aspect of universal friction, has charged the Poet's libido—that invisible, unseen, unrealized force that enables him to pursue his journey, to record his trajectory, from the *created* world of multiplicity to the *uncreated* amorphous domain—a world in potentia—where he now exists.

Night, the habitation of Sophie/anima is a fertile realm. It is within the earth that life is stilled; that death becomes a curative force. Here the Poet rids himself of constricting worldly demands and feels he is taking on wholeness. In an analogical vision of himself as Osiris, he too will know rebirth: "I [Osiris] have nourished the herbs and what is withered, I let become green again." [16] It is death that allows body and spirit to unite and in so doing, to fructify into creation the poetic image. Heightened visions, paralleling the Poet's intensity of feeling, now emerges.

It is Sophie/anima that leads him on to full participation in poetic life—psychic nuptials. As in the ancient incubation mysteries enacted in the Aesculepian sanctuaries, [17] so the Poet, too, experiences the healing rituals on and near his *temenos*—Sophie's grave. She encourages the Poet to explore further that divine supernal sphere in death. Sophie now appears to him in all of her beauty—as soul—resplendent as she takes on even greater stature within his psyche. It is at this time that he prepares for physical and spiritual union within the sacred marriage that concludes the first hymn. The necrophilic embrace cuts him off completely from the conscious or daylight realm, enabling him to infiltrate the earth sphere even more deeply, to penetrate night/great mother/beloved—where life begins and ends. Sophie/anima receives the Poet's seed—the word—warms and nurtures it, allows it to germinate in the poem. "Consume my body in your spiritual flame and reduced into an aerial substance, I blend in most intimate union with you, so that our wedding night will last for all eternity" (p. 81).

Hymn 2: Sleep

Once the Poet has rejected day and light, and embraces the ineffable essence of night, the Earth Mother, he experiences in her arms the second level of his inner journey—sleep. Sleep is the earth's way of divesting the Poet of dichotomies, of separations encountered in the differentiated world. An intimate communion with natural forces cloaks the Poet, conditions him to experience a link with his ancestral and primordial past. During his slumber, holding his beloved Sophie/anima close, in tight embrace, he feels part of the cosmic totality—the All. Removed from the cerebral domain, from consciousness, a new orientation takes hold of him—an understanding of the Self (the absolute or objective psyche).

The Poet, divested of his ego, lies dormant in the eerie shadows of the subliminal realm. The rhythm is now slower, dominated by diminished intensities; the agitation is less severe. Feelings of quietude, however, magnify pathos, increase distress. Sleep, which Hesiod alluded to as *hypnos* and the Latins as *somnus*, is the son of night and death's twin brother. It is sleep that lulls the Poet into an undifferentiated state, where bleakness of contours conceals dichotomies and allows for his further dispersion as an individual, into spatial climes.

The Poet mentions the poppy plant that he sees before him. Opium, made from the poppy lessens consciousness, reminiscent of the wine used in Dionysian mysteries; the Poet feels inebriated. Vertigo takes hold of him as if he were in a drunken stupor. Opium not only nullifies lucidity but was considered by the Greeks to have medicinal virtues: its juicy and milky substance was used for curative purposes. So, for the Poet, torpor descends on his high-strung nature, invading his sick soul with sublime ingredients. He succumbs to the narcotic. His fears are smothered; his rational world dulled. He sings of the beatific elements he encounters, mysterious concoctions existing in the shadow of slumber allow him to participate in the *rite d'entrée* that follows. He mentions grapes as well as poppies. Nourishing, delicate in their sweetness, ripe in their fruit, they are used in transubstantiation rituals as divinity's blood—God becoming man—as energy and life itself. The Poet is both sacrificer and sacrificed: the Lamb of God who encounters martyrdom in the hymn—into which he is now transforming the creative life-force.

The Poet now mentions almond oil, a substance referred to as "miraculous" in its perfume, in the delicacy of its fragile flower, glistening in the multiple layers of his darkened realm. It was said that Attis was born of a virgin who conceived from an almond: the same legend has been applied to the Virgin Mary and the Immaculate Conception. Interestingly, too, is the idea that the mysterious city of Luz (almond tree in Hebrew) was the place where Jacob had his vision of the ladder and saw the angels descending and ascending—experiencing the connection between himself and divinity—ego and Self.

The Poet's description of the almond oil, the poppy, the grapes—all narcotics in one form or another—arouse his hallucinatory faculties and enable him to fantasize unheard-of visions and images. The uninitiated cannot comprehend such phantasmagorias; they do not experience these visual particles as nutritive forces—the "golden juice" that inseminates the Poet with soul food, strengthening, intensifying, the fluidity of the modalites which are replicated in the hymn.

Sleep for the Poet is a descent into the great mystery of life itself. From his sleep, however, he finally awakens, refreshed, reborn in the work of art. It has permitted him to rest in spiritual and sexual union with Sophie/anima, his seed inseminating her and fructifying her so that she may help him engender the poem. Sleep, "floating around the tender breast of virgins, transforming this breast into paradise," allows the Poet to embrace her as earth goddess, wife, mother, healer, guardian, sister, and mourner. She becomes a *Mater Gloriosa*, the "bearer of the key which gives access to happy domains, mute messenger of endless mysteries" (p. 83). Neither death nor sleep is to be feared anymore. They do not conclude; they are bridges—into cosmic existence.

Hymn 3: Trials

The Poet, now on the threshold of two worlds—life and death—experiences two energetic intensities, two modalities. His psychic energy functions at a slower as well as at heightened pace: day and night, awake and asleep. Fluidity of feelings alternate in biorhythmic patterns, in spasmodic movements, not yet in harmony with being.

Tears come. Wet, fluid, they are metaphors for pain. As they emerge into the Poet's world as crystals, iridescent transparencies, composites of opposites, both malleable and fixed, transparent and opaque, they help the future hymn to gestate. Water, the source of life, used in baptism and purification rituals, a protective force in the womb, aids the Poet in the transmutation process: from feeling to word to poem.

As a fluid, water denotes infinite possibilities and virtualities, preformal potential; it becomes a medium which immerses and dissolves, prepares the alchemist's *coagulatio* process when the mobile becomes fixed. Water is Prakriti, the Hindus say. All is water prior to manifestation. Water is the *fons et origo* of the universe: it quenches, feeds, bathes particles in its substance and liquidity. As if with a magic wand, it triggers dreams, dissolves opacities, stirs phantoms which flow into the immaterial world to form new universes, warmed by the very excitement of the transmutation process, healing the Poet as if wafting him in some kind of vaporized air. "The landscape seemed to rise, tenderly in the air—above the landscape hovered my spirit, liberated, regenerated" (p. 85).

Solitary, alone, far from the world the Poet once knew, he now slumbers in his beloved's embrace, ascending and descending even more deeply into the inner regions beneath the earth—his collective unconscious—that mythical realm, that beginning point. In these inner chambers which may be likened to the lobes of the brain, to geological strata, the various spheres within his psyche are apprehended. The Poet is suddenly overcome by an "obscure chill," and stepping with trepidation from the known to the unknown world, he reaches the very heart of the mystery. Light vanishes.

Earth in all of its black splendor comes into being, awakens, prepares itself for the cleansed and purified poem that is to be born. Incomprehensible, immutable, the Poet seizes its palpability, understands and responds with "fervor" to the meanings associated with this body. "Sacred slumber" that now inhabits his being, captivates and captures him every so gently, generating and regenerating his élan and finally liberating the seed/semen within his psyche—the creative spark which sexual union with his Sophie/anima has brought about—injecting new life into the poem. Only in the earth do his tears create life, inundate concrete forces which then dissolve the experience—known only in its gross state—allowing the quintessence of the life-force to be disclosed.

"Within the depths of her eyes shone eternity—I took her by the hands, and tears formed a sparkling, infrangible chain between us" (p. 85). The Poet embraces his vision. Her eyes glisten, focusing directly into his being. The eye, the source of vision for the Poet, is not to be compared with the brash intellectual/rational illumination of earthly humans. Rather, it may be likened to Siva's divine eye or the eye depicted on sarcophagi in ancient Egypt: that eye within which a blackened pupil stares into the distance—sees the human in all of his conditions and states—follows him around the universe. Shaped like a mouth, the pupil contains the food: the Word. The poetic eye, then becomes a force that pierces through the imperceptible world, activates the immobile, sensitizes the dull. The "eye of the mind," the "eye of the heart," the eye of the psyche—all are endowed with intense power. The eye is the gateway leading to the source—the All: the omniscient and omnipotent essence of divine existence.

No area is deep enough, no walls sufficiently thick to prevent this cosmic eye which the Poet mentions—God's eye—from peering deeply through matter. So the Poet likewise pierces through opacities and from this new vantage point unearths the marvels which he will embed within his hymn: they will radiate in their prismatic beauty. Dimensionless and horizonless entities come into view; new feelings take on multiple consistencies, as if "the dawn of a new life" were impressing itself upon him. The dream born from night, "the eternal and immutable" experience he now knows bathes him in the renewed light of love (p. 87).

As the Poet experiences two worlds as one (life and death, day and night), the currents of lower and higher frequences are united in his being, forming the very substance that engenders his hallucinations. According to Jung, the psyche—this is true of matter in general—is a form of energy, but "an energy form of an infinitely high frequence of intensity." So powerful is the psyche's intensity, that its speed exceeds that of light. Since "observables" are transcribed around the phenomenon of light and what exceeds this speed remains unknown, Jung has suggested that the psyche "irrealizes" the body. Only if the frequency of intensity of the psyche is slackened or lessened to that of light, can phenomenon be observed. The brain is that instrument, then, which "tunes down the intensity of the psyche," writes Marie-Louise von Franz, "until it becomes bound to lower frequencies which create our experience of space-time." [18] In a letter written on February 29, 1952, Jung states:

It might be that psyche should be understood as *unextended intensity* and not as body moving with time. One might assume the psyche gradually rising from minute extensity to infinite intensity transcending for instance the velocity of light and thus *irrealizing* the body. . . . In the light of this view the brain might be a transformer station, in which the relative infinite tension or intensity of the psyche proper is transformed into perceptible frequencies or "extensions." Conversely, the fading introspective perception of the body explains itself due to a gradual "psychification," i.e., intensification at the expense of extension. Psyche=highest intensity in the smallest space. [19]

The Poet during this period with his beloved has experienced a level of energy intensity far higher than when living in the empirical world. This bears out statements made by literary critics that the poetry of Novalis became more profound after Sophie's death, for it was then that he became capable of projecting his anima (that part of his psyche represented by Sophie) on to outer phenomena. Her departure from the existential realm loosed his anima, allowing it to live on in intensified frequencies which, according to Jung, exist after death.

Heraclitus and Simon Magus inferred that fire was the transforming agent of matter; psychic energy, which is fire, heightens or diminishes the Poet's levels of intensity during his life-in-death experience. It may be suggested that his anima, when *irrealizing* his body, alluded to as a parapsychological revelation by scholars, paved the way for the Poet's leap into the "unobservable."

The Poet's psychological journey may be viewed as follows:

1. Bodily existence in the empirical world; energy intensity is low.
2. The incarnated psyche used in the activities of the brain in

higher and lower frequencies is still observable and understandable, since they are measured in terms of the speed of light.

3. That part of the psyche which is not bound to the brain transcends the speed of light and is *irrealized*, thereby experiencing a domain unknown to those who have not undergone such an initiatory ritual.

Hymn 4: The Seer—The Einfall

The Poet now awakens into another realm. Mediator between life and death, he has become a seer, the *epoptes* of the Eleusinian mysteries—"he who sees."[20] He experiences his awakening as his own "last morning" (p. 89), when neither light nor day will be known as opposites but will have coalesced through the interplay of his beloved Sophie/anima, in his creative spirit. The Poet passes through a painful and languishing condition, as though some strange celestial emotion had taken hold of him, intoxicated and inspired him to the point of *ekstasis*. He undertakes a pilgrimage to the Holy Sepulcher and becomes the cross; the Poet identifies with Christ in the death/resurrection myth.

In an *imitatio Christi*, the Poet now feels himself to be one of the elect, set apart from the vulgar, the rabble, those unable to peer deeply into spatial spheres, those who have not imbibed "from that crystalline spring," who have not immersed themselves in "the obscure heart of this burial mound" (p. 89) where human existence vanishes and the eye is encapsulated within a different sphere. It is here that the Poet who in the third hymn has dismissed the sensate world, peers through walls, screens, obstacles of all kinds, compelling energy to transform itself from one pattern to another, one frequency to another, as all antitheses fuse and the religious experience impresses itself ever more powerfully on the Poet.

The Poet's world now seems to fill with crystals in all forms and shapes; transparencies and opaque fluids that incorporate the visible and invisible into one. He marvels at the supernal appearances before him: "Mary is crystal, her Son, celestial light," writes Angelus Silesius. For the Poet, too, crystal takes on spiritual essences; it may be looked upon as a kind of embryo or diamond within the earth. Rock crystal, the Immaculate Conception, for early Christians, was identified with that highest of earthly forces: a kind of funnel within which or because of which earth and heaven could communicate in an interplay of energetic light patterns.

The internal landscape of Novalis's images dilate, diffuse in prismatic color tones. Verticality takes precedence as the reader mounts with the Poet to the heavens. Crystals appear before the mind's eye as spectacular tonalities in all their evolutive form of decomposed light, and radiant energy is transmuted into a spectrum of hues: violet, indigo, blue, green, yellow, orange, red. Nothing is fixed as this flowing atmosphere mingles with sensations of love and longing, past and present, and the Poet feels himself plunging ever more deeply and directly into the very source of life. Below and above the earth in aerial climes which he traverses, intangibles become infrangible, feelings float, irreality takes on ductile consistencies. As in a collage, so the Poet reveals an assemblage of multiple visions, reminiscent of variegated arteries and capillaries, each activated by the energy particles of a cosmic circulatory system.

Light is personified and sanctified. It "instills life and joy" into the Poet (p. 91). It alights here and there, enticing the body, energizing the nervous system, touching and patting the mossy surface of a stone: that green-gray durable entity upon which a soft wet, succulent bryophytic plant has chosen to root itself. Anterior worlds are evoked and invoked as the Poet, like Jacob during his dream, reaches cosmic heights and depths communicating his sensate feelings in fluctuating fluidities.

Suddenly the Poet is once more seized with a feeling of *ekstasis*, a longing for death, for the enchantment brought upon one with the oncoming night: blackness feeds the hues of his kaleidoscopic passion. He feels uplifted, wafted through infinite space, evanescent, omnipresent in giant cosmic arms, lost in the rhythmic spirals and fantasies of flaming patterns—all within the great mother's heaving breast. "I feel her frenetic activity slacken within me—celestial liberty, blessed return!" (p. 39).

Time for the Poet remains unmarked in an eternal present; sacred and mythological nonlinear sequences of existence. One day the vast sun or moon dial will impress their numbers, hours, studding each fleeting moment with immobility. Watches, barometers, compasses, each orienting and directing mankind into one path or another—these, too, will vanish. The eternal circle, the mandala, the ancient meditative device, will replace them and will further enable the Poet to travel on endlessly in spiraling patterns, reaching out in his creative act still further into space, burning it with the flame of creation. The energy forming the word will appear in his mind's eye as does the image incised throughout the universe in gigantic and impulsive waves.

The Poet leaves the domain of prose for verse. The new abode upon which he has focused is divested of extraneous material: it is clear. The Poet feels some kind of stinging sensation, whether it be that of a bee or wasp, it becomes the catalyst, infusing "celestial voluptuousness" into the heart of his being. Gone are the chains holding him prisoner of conscious reality. "To sleep in the heart of Love" (p. 93) is what he seeks throughout all eternity. A world of infinite spiraling shapes wind and unwind before him; the Poet turns, whirls, twirls through space as if in waves, jarring, searing, luminary groupings, like a ship cutting through the wave and riding the crest. His spherical journey is now experienced in vertical climes. He feels his Sophie/anima vibrate within this darkened realm, the shadowy world of his being. She has placed a "garland" of freshness and purity upon his head.

The Poet asks that his beloved "aspire" and breathe him into her being—into that other realm, death. There he will be inundated, the "restorative flow" will permeate his being. Like sweet-smelling and cooling resin, which he now mentions, a narcotic for him, will help him pursue his poetical trajectory; will cosmify his ego. He will take a world of imponderables into himself, elastify them, liquify and volatilize these subtle elements into aspatial areas. In this condition he will die, enflamed, ablaze in the very heart of mystical illumination.

> *And I die throughout the nights,*
> *Ablaze in sacred flames*
> *(P. 95)*

Hymn 5: Nonreferential Level of Experience

The Poet experiences the nonreferential level of being, perhaps known by the mystes undergoing the Orphic-Dionysiac mysteries. The Poet sings out his cosmogonic creation hymn and tells of the giants who once peopled the earth, the boundless worlds that existed at the dawn of life, when heaven and earth communicated fully, totally in synthetic experience. The human and the divine nature and the universe were one. Each spoke to the other, endlessly. The Poet tells of the giant who carried the divine word up and down, in vertical and horizontal denominations. Giants, primordial beings, represent that which surpasses the normal: Goliath, the Cyclops, Satan, each superhuman in size and strength. Other mystical giants also existed: Adam Kadmon, the universal man, God's first creation according to the Kabbalistic *Zohar*. In those days man lived in "crystalline grottos," visible from afar in every and all ways. Laughing, happy, life seemed to flower—animals, trees, clustered about each other in creative particles—in a womb which grew in beauty and nutritive force. A kind of "holy drunkenness" enables the Poet to prepare himself for the communal meal which is to take place— the agape.

Death "interrupting the orgy" of growth and futurity; it fills the world with "terror" and "pain" as well as with "tears." Dichotomies, dualities, conflicts, tension, separate and torture humankind. Life and death struggle in hopelessly antagonistic polarities—each the implacable foe of the other. The Poet attempts to discover an answer, to beatify and beautify this "hideous/phantom which the world has become.

Change alters the face of the visible world. Ancient cultures decline; new ones arise. God dies. Man remains alone "bound to the iron chain of the arid Number and strict Measure" (p. 101). Hostility, coldness, disturbances, shed darkness and disenchantment. Christ was born of the Virgin Mary, and in this context the Poet rhapsodizes on early death, on the certainty of resurrection. Mother and Son give solace to the lonely in his vision, comfort the wretched, and immortalize the life-span in the realm of love for those who before had only known turmoil and terror. Blazing light infiltrates the atmosphere; flame in chromatic lunar rays aids the Poet in his course. The spectacular metaphor used by that third-century Christian Neoplatonist, Clement of Alexandria, is applicable here: "O truly sacred mysteries! O pure light! In the blaze of the torches I have a vision of heaven and of God. I become holy by initiation."

Religion is the Poet's guide as he and his Sophie/anima merge in all their sexual spirituality into death—the arms of eternity.

The Poet speaks of the flower that he embraces, the petal of his soul, each breathing in that metaphysical melancholia, that child which prefigures the death/rebirth ritual. "Priestess of a celestial love," she becomes the harbinger of the Blue Flower that Novalis will delineate in detail in *Heinrich von Ofterdingen*. Here, the flower is not specified; it does not refer to a definite object but rather to an alchemical process—an individuating soul. The flower opens up, unfolds its layers of understanding, compassion, feelings of infinity as does a mandala. It is within the flower that the fragmentary reaches into the infinite, and life, in its essence, is gleaned; the inner core identifying with the heart, breathing, leaping, and sounding its experiences prior to their creation in the word. As the flower grows and intensifies its hues, exudes its perfume, so the Poet reveals his feelings and ideations in images which seem to alternate in consistency: they become fluid iconographic forms—letters, words, lines—each heralds fresh rhythms, cradles the Poet's rapture. Now sinew, muscle, flesh, filament, flex as the Poet and his Sophie/anima contemplate each other, in intermingling tonal blocks, in vortices of cycloramic fusing forms.

Hymn 6: "Aspiration toward Death"

This, the sixth and last hymn, is the only one Novalis gave a title to and the only one written in its entirety in structured metrical verse; it carries the Poet to his destination. Reminiscent of young Hyacinth, the protagonist in Novalis's *The Disciples of Saïs*, who uproots himself from the land of the living to experience the unexplored universe within his dream world, the Poet consummates his union, reaches into the sacred sleep of eternal duration. He inhales the quietude, the serenity of this new state where Death will overtake him and allow him to participate in the cosmic All.

Celebrants of ancient mysteries who longed for "eternal Night" and "eternal Sleep" (p. 113), seeking to end the turmoil of their quest and travail by their reentry into the maternal earth world, now search as well for the "paternal home" (p. 113). There, when male and female unite, thirst is quenched, dark and light become universals, no longer polarized but each enriching the other in a complex of opposites. The Poet listens to the faint whisperings of nature in her wholeness, the mineral and vegetable world; he shudders, vibrates, empathizes with each. He hears their callings, sobs his answers, like echoing refrains of a beating heart.

> *Let us descend toward the Fiancé,*
> *Toward Jesus-Christ, the Beloved!*
> *Courage! Evening will be heard*
>
> *By loving and pious hearts.*
>
> *A dream, cutting our bonds,*
> *Will plunge us into our Father's breast.*
> *(P. 117)*

The Poet's journey is now culminating. From the realm of the mother to that of the father, from generative meditation to collective immortalization. The Poet has experienced equilibrium in a *unio mystica*—an alchemical marriage where disparate elements coalesce—an apotheosis and a demortalization come into being.

To read *Hymns to the Night* is to undergo a religious experience, personal as well as universal. It is a poet's way of dealing with *Thanatos* and the anima. At first wrenched and divided, the poet allows the experience to take hold of him and in so doing, it becomes a healing device for him, bringing him wholeness in his poetic vision. As a psychological portrayal of a young man of genius unable to face the ache and turmoil of the workaday world, Novalis resorts to the age-old, as we have seen, practices of the mystery religions—Dionysian, Eleusinian, Orphic, Christian. Each in its way transforms the turmoil of individual existence into the serenity and plenitude of the universal, giving "superhuman ontological status" to the myste in his descent/ ascent into Self. As the ritual pursues its course, the initiate is able to reevaluate and spiritualize his past. The secret disciplines he gleans from the inner trajectory and the trials he endured, however, must remain secret, hidden from the multitude. So in Novalis's *Hymns to the Night*, his euphemization of the death experience—an excorcism of sorts—with its complex conduits, its sublimated cryptic images, opens up to him the cosmic experience. His entire being both bodily and spiritually functions as a unity; in the necrophilic act, the sexual urge to drink, eat, and possess his beloved throughout the lyrical verse, his implacable urge to experience the pleroma within the darkened domain, is transmuted into the eternal sphere of art. Novalis the poet who became his own intercessor, his own master of ceremonies, functioning in a sphere devoid of light, arises like the alchemist's quintessential ash from his shadowy world with his philosophers' stone which is the *Hymns*.

3. Nachman (1772–1811): "The Master of Prayer"—A Kabbalistic View of the Ego's Exile from the Self

Rabbi ben Simhah Nachman of Bratislava was regarded as a holy man, a teacher, guide, and master—a zaddik as this sort of rabbi came to be known in the small Jewish communities of eastern Europe. He expressed his theological beliefs in homiletic works and sayings but most poignantly in his tales. In fictional accounts he felt he could best convey the deepseated joy that his religious faith inspired in him: his love for God and the certainty of humanity's eventual redemption and salvation. For Rabbi Nachman, a tale was endowed with a very special power; it was a living organism, a vital force, a mask or garb, enclosing a supernatural mystery. As such, the psychic energy implicit in the words and the events of the narrative could by means of their own catalytic power, flow into hearers imbuing them with feelings of exaltation and sacred awe. Psychologically, in cases of alienation, narration can indeed kindle feelings of belonging—inspiring activity rather than passivity, integration, not fragmentation, life, not death.

"The Master of Prayer" (1809) that Rabbi Nachman told to his disciple Nathan of Nemirov, who transcribed it, can be characterized as a moralizing agent. Inspired and nurtured by Kabbala (Hebrew mystical writings), it is an allegorical and symbolic description of an ecstatic religious experience. Traditional in form, it discloses a revelation—an apocalyptic vision—of a man speaking to and conversing with divinity. The plethora of archetypal images contained in the tale center around the birth and growth of ego-consciousness and its struggles to reintegrate into the Self.

Martin Buber's (1878–1965) recountal of Rabbi Nachman's tale is not a translation in the usual sense of the word. It is literally a retelling of the tale "with full freedom, yet out of his spirit as it is present in me."[1] For Buber, Rabbi Nachman had endowed "The Master of Prayer" with a life of its own: it is filled with messianic spiritual zeal, each word, clause, and sentence shining with fervor and elation.

The events described in "The Master of Prayer" take the reader through what Kabbalists allude to as the "Great Cosmic Catastrophe"—man's exile from God that not only occurred at the time of Adam's fall but also took place prior to that, with God's first creation, Adam Kadmon. Parallels may be drawn in the historical sphere to the many periods of exile and persecution that the Jews have known since Abraham first left the land of Ur. The long years of bondage in Egypt—the Babylonian captivity after Nebuchadnezzar's destruction of the Temple (587 B.C.), the destruction of the Second Temple (70 A.D.) by the Romans and the Diaspora, culminating in modern times with the Holocaust—seem to have created in many Jews a very special psychological condition: an *exile archetype*. Deeply embedded in the psyche, it is expressed in an unconscious fear of the ego's banishment from the Self; of being cut off, rejected, and left to die. The wanderings, encounters, and confrontations, both painful and beneficial in Rabbi Nachman's tale that end with the final reintegration on a higher level of the lost ones or the fragmented psyche into the Godhead/Self may also be considered as a paradigm to a great extent of archetypal exile.

ECTYPAL ANALYSIS

Rabbi Nachman was born in the small town of Medzhibozh where his great-grandfather, the Baal-Shem-Tov (Master of the Good Name), who was the founder of Hasidism, was also born. A kind of mystical religious revival movement, Hasidism spread in the eighteenth-century from southern Poland to Romania, Lithuania, and Russia, perhaps as a result of the terrible pogroms that were taking place in eastern Eurpe, when thousands of Jews were tortured and killed. To survive in such an atmosphere of persecution and terror, a religious outlook had to be developed that would be able to heal the emotional scars left by these harrowing conditions, instilling hope and faith in those who had lost it, and a sense of well-being in those who had been robbed of what should be the birthright of every human being. Hasidism answered this need. Rather than focusing on earthly conditions, it emphasizes a glad spiritual orientation, a delight in the service of God, and the benevolent and blissful heavenly condition awaiting the pure in soul and heart. Hasidism was and is a sect that reaches out to embrace all—the sick and the well, the rich and the poor.

Reared in this Hasidic environment, everything in Rabbi Nachman's childhood indicated a religious destiny for him. It was his mother, Feige, who was the granddaughter of the Baal-Shem-Tov; his paternal grandfather, Nahman of Horodenka, had been his close friend; his paternal uncle, Baruch, was one of the leading zaddiks in the community. The sensitive boy had every reason to take pride in his ancestry and his family; unquestionably, love and affection for them played an important role in his spiritual formation and destiny.

Rabbi Nachman followed Hasidic practices. His great-grandfather had preached prayer as a healing device, its mystical power being able to increase spiritual awareness of the divine, allowing the person praying to feel warmed, understood, accepted: to experience the inward flow of the Godhead throughout his or her being. Prayer for Rabbi Nachman frequently led to rapture and exaltation; it dispelled the sense of utter despair and worthlessness that at that time permeated the psyches of so many inhabitants of the Jewish communities in eastern Europe. Although little is known about Rabbi Nachman's early life, it is said that as a child he used to spend long hours in solitary prayer, intent upon personally experiencing the *numinosum*. Sometimes he wandered to secluded areas on the coldest of nights or prayed beside the grave of the Baal-Shem-Tov, hoping to receive God's impress. More frequently than not, he felt cut off, frozen, isolated. His prayers remained unanswered. Terror seized him because the flow of feeling between himself and God had halted. Not ecstasy but despair ensued. Ascetic practices, such as fasting and praying continually through the night, were indulged in until the gift of the Divine Presence was reawakened once more; it was a fresh flowing, a new light born out of darkness.

At the age of thirteen, when in keeping with Hasidic custom, Rabbi Nachman was married to Sashia, a rabbi's daughter, he went to live with his bride in his parents-in-law's home in Usyatin. In so doing, he left the city ghetto with its imprisoning and stifling cluster of dark damp houses, where sunlight was virtually unknown and a new vision of life was given to him: the sight of green grass in springtime and summer, of flowers opening their petals, of trees welcoming him under their shade. It was there that finally he understood the miracle of God's greatness. In later years, Rabbi Nachman is said to have told his disciples:

When man becomes worthy to hear the songs of the plants, how each plant speaks its song to God, how beautiful and sweet it is to hear their singing! And, therefore, it is good indeed to serve God in their midst in solitary wanderings over the fields between the growing things and to pour out one's speech before God in truthfulness. All the speech of the fields enters then into your own and intensifies its strength. With every breath you drink in the air of paradise, and when you return home, the world is renewed in your eyes.[2]

After the death of Rabbi Nachman's mother-in-law (1790) and the remarriage of his father-in-law, the couple moved to Medvedevka in the province of Kiev, which was to be their home for the next ten years. There Rabbi Nachman began attracting many Hasidim to his fold. His extreme asceticism, the purity of his religious belief, and his simplicity and kindness won for him much admiration. Unlike some of the other zaddiks of the time, who enjoyed being hailed as miracle workers and receiving much adulation from the entourage, Rabbi Nachman preferred a far humbler course. He received his students and disciples only on certain holy days: Rosh Hashanah (the Jewish New Year), the Sabbath of Hannukah, and Shavuot (Pilgrim Festival).[3] These occasions were devoted to prayer and instruction, song and dances in praise of God's glory. When his followers broached such sacred topics as God's mysteries revealed in Scripture and in Kabbalistic writings, Rabbi Nachman's exposition seemed to be infused with a special energy that inundated their souls, hearts, and minds, creating an atmosphere conducive to visionary experiences.

Rabbi Nachman empathized with his students as individuals and as a group; he felt their pain and poverty, their spiritual and often their physical hunger. He was also fired by a messianic zeal, he wanted to remedy what he considered to be the decadent ways that had infiltrated the Hasidic movement, originally so vital a force. Superstition and ignorance were gaining ground; greed and the struggle for power seemed to have become the motivating force. He longed to restore the purity of the ancient Hebrew religious tradition. The zaddik's, or Master's, goal should be to inspire the follower through the Word of God, and thus expand consciousness, reawaken the spirit, reinvigorate the whole being—to turn "the wilderness of the hearts into a dwelling-place for God."[4]

Rabbi Nachman's fervent desire was to go to the land of Israel. There he would be in touch with the spirit of Moses; he would tread on the ground where Simeon bar Yohai who lived in the second century and allegedly wrote the *Zohar* (the *Book of Splendor*), one of the most important works of Kabbala, had made his home. Rabbi Nachman's desire to reach the Promised Land became an all-consuming flame. No earthly force could stand in his way.

Family and friends did their best to dissuade the young rabbi. His decision was unalterable. Since so many Jews after the diaspora were imbued with an all-pervasive desire to return to the Holy Land, Rabbi Nachman's longing to see the ancestral home of his people fulfilled a dream. In Israel, too, in keeping with Ezekiel's vision, the Messiah would resurrect the dead:

Therefore prophesy, and say unto them, Thus saith the the Lord God; Behold, O my people, I will open your graves, and cause you to come up out of your graves and bring you into the Land of Israel.

And shall put my spirit in you, and ye shall live, and I shall place you in your own land: then shall ye know that I the Lord have spoken it, and performed it, saith the Lord. (Ezek. 37:12, 14)

Rabbi Nachman did not fear the many obstacles that he knew would confront him on the journey to the Holy Land. He had no illusions about them but considered such difficulties a "test" that every zaddik must endure to prove himself worthy of his calling. He looked upon the struggle to overcome them as a spiritual exercise, a form of self-discipline that not only would lead to the achievement of a desired goal but also strengthened the soul, allowing it to pass into the next phase of its rising course to God.

In 1798, he departed with his disciple Nathan on the long and arduous trip to the Holy Land, leaving his wife and three daughters to the care of others. Perils of every kind were experienced en route. When Rabbi Nachman finally arrived, he is reputed to have said: "I have attained the fulfillment of the whole Torah."[5]

The following year when Rabbi Nachman returned to Medvedevka and rejoined his family, it was evident that his pilgrimage to the land of Israel had been a turning point in his life. A renewed zeal and a fresh vision inspired his being. "One must not despair!" he would repeat again and again. To be righteous and pure in each thought, word, and deed should be one's goal. In this way everyone may experience God's thought, His infinite light, his music, that indwelling of an ineffable force. In other religions, Nachman contended, the devout believe that God acts "through messengers," the "princes of the upper sphere," but the Hebrews experienced God directly: "Thou art one."[6] The inner passion that had been kindled within him inspired him to bring forth a fresh message of religious renewal through which he hoped a more profound understanding of the beatific religious experience could be imparted to others in his community.

Wherever he settled thereafter (Zlatopol, 1800; Slatopol, 1802–10), his teachings became the subject of controversy, and he, the target of vilification by certain members of the Jewish communities in which he lived. Although he accepted the slights aimed at him, his sense of isolation and exile increased. He likened himself to Moses and to other great prophets who had suffered at the hands of implacable enemies. The greater his anguish, the more certain he was of being the appointed wise man of his generation—the *zaddik hador*.[7]

Sorrow on a personal level was also the lot of Rabbi Nachman. Although his daughters lived to grow up, married rabbis, and had children, his two sons, for both of whom he had had the greatest hopes, died in infancy of tuberculosis. His first wife also passed away from the same disease (1806) and shortly after his own remarriage the following year, he too contracted it.

Rabbi Nachman died in Uman where forty years previously so many Jews had been martyred. The window of his room faced the cemetery. On the day of his death, he asked that his bed be turned in a certain direction, that his shirt and robe be buttoned in a specific way, as though he was preparing himself as best he could to meet God. Members of the Jewish community filed into the house to pay their last respects. His disciple Nathan recorded the occasion in his diary:

We thought that he had already passed away and began crying, "Rebbe! Rebbe! To whom have you left us?"

He heard our voice and lifted his head, turning his awesome face to us as if to say, "I am not leaving you, heaven forbid!"

It was not long before he passed away and was gathered to his fathers in great holiness and purity. Bright and clear, he passed away without any confusion whatsoever, without a single outward gesture, in a state of awesome calmness.[8]

Rabbi Nachman's spiritual message, implicit and explicit in "The Master of Prayer," remains an inspiration to many even today. It arouses, imparting to the reader its spiritual fervor. Words and sequences may be experienced on various levels not only for their discursive meanings but also for their spiritual nourishment, and as multiple unfoldings of an ascending soul.[9] Rabbi Nachman declares: "At times my words enter like a silence into the hearers and rest in them and work later, like slow medicines; at times my words do not at first work at all in the man to whom I say them, but when he then says them to another, they come back to him and enter into his heart in great depth and do their work in perfection."[10]

For Rabbi Nachman and for Kabbalists in general, the word is an exoteric vehicle for the reception of esoteric knowledge. The word like the number is archetypal, a particle of cosmic energy. Hummed, chanted, or meditated upon, a word or sound may, therefore, pave the way to a unitive mystical experience. The word is a vehicle which may lead to a believer's inner transformation: from an earthly condition to a sphere where God makes his love and will known. The word is the *vessel* into which God channels his fire, breath, and spirit. According to the Kabbalists, each word in the Torah—the first five Books of Moses—possesses six hundred thousand "faces" or "layers of meaning, of entrances."[11] Each person must find his or her own way of entering the Word, so that he or she may experience the divine mystery, the effulgence—that is the primal source of life.

The alphabetical letters that form words are also of significance to the Kabbalist: *aleph* (A) is considered to be "the source of all articulate sound," the "spiritual root" of every letter, in essence and in fact.[12] In the *Zohar*, which modern scholars believe was written not by Simeon bar Yohai in the second century but by the thirteenth-century Castilian Kabbalist Moses de Leon, God makes the presence of his mystery known through the Word, the thought, and his own creative process, The Sefiroth, in a "highly differentiated *coniunctio*.[13] The Sefiroth, God's ten divine emanations, are also his attributes. Each is an archetype, an aspect of his eternal being. As such, the metaphysical concept of the Sefiroth may be looked upon as a complex personality structure that permeates the entire universe. Imagistically, it is identifiable with a human body, a tree; conceptually, as a divine language; psychologically, as the Self.[14]

Isaac Luria, whose works were known to Rabbi Nachman, added his own speculations concerning the Godhead in keeping with the symbolic image of the Sefiroth. Rather than adhering to the conventional doctrine of God creating the world out of himself, Luria conceived of the *Tzimtzum*: God contracted or withdrew into himself in order to create the world, thus causing a vacuum that paved the way for the creation of a "kind of mystical primordial space"—the universe. Such a process is not an exteriorization but rather an interiorization, a "falling back upon oneself" or withdrawal into oneself. It is therefore the reverse of what had long been considered the method of creation. Gershom Scholem considers the *Tzimtzum* to be a metaphysical reaction to a psychological condition—representing that archetypal exile experienced so profoundly, both on an unconscious and a conscious level within many Jewish psyches. Luria could neither forget the exiles that took place in ancient times nor ignore the oppressive results of the Spanish Inquisition, where those Jews who chose to remain in Spain had outwardly to convert to Catholicism and become marranos, forswearing their true religious identity. A secret, introverted attitude may have been unconsciously adopted by them as well as by those who fled Spain, fearing that another round of persecution awaited them in their next port of call.

When the Sefiroth came into being, that is, when God began the creative process out of himself "in a free act of love,"
divine light remained in the "primordial space." As creation became the revelation of the divine Self, a second ray of light came
forth, activating the entire cosmogonic process. Duality thus was
created, causing separation, differentiation in form and meaning, tension. The dynamics of the Sefirotic process have been
compared to "divine inhalation and exhalation," implosion and
explosion. As long as this supreme being remained undifferentiated, light existed undisturbed. Once divinity took his course
downward and became manifest, light, too, became differentiated and required some form or vessel to contain it. An an-
thropomorphic figure, Adam Kadmon—the primordial man—
was therefore created. This first cosmogonic being, a personification of the entire Sefiroth, was androgynous and was known
as pneumatic man: a living spirit.[15] The light that flowed from
his eyes, mouth, ears, nose, was so powerful that it shattered
the vessel containing them. The Breaking of the Vessels, one of
the most important concepts in Kabbalistic thought, is the first
cosmic catastrophe—leading to exile from the Godhead. Nothing thereafter in the created world would be flawless. Adam,
God's second creation—psychic man—a living soul—was a
"reflection of Adam Kadmon" but imperfect.

With the Breaking of the Vessels, God's "divine sparks" of
light became mixed with matter (*Kelipot*, or "shells") and thus
with impurity or evil. Henceforth every person's obligation
throughout his or her earthly existence is to gather up these
"divine sparks of light" to be found in good or bad deeds. This
process of gathering or repairing (*Tikkun*) will eventually restore all the broken fragments and pave the way for their reintegration or elevation into the Sefiroth. *Tikkun* places a sense of
responsibility on every person; it also endows him or her with
a sense of accomplishment—the feeling of well-being that results from doing a good deed oneself or encouraging someone
else to do one. Every action on a human level is identified and
associated with the Sefiroth; it affects and is affected by it.
Everything within and without the Sefiroth is therefore interconnected. To create a condition of unity and harmony within
the Godhead is therefore to accomplish a balance in the psycho-

logical condition of an individual or group: to reintegrate the ego into the Self.

ARCHETYPAL ANALYSIS

The mystery that lies within "The Master of Prayer" is to be unraveled by each reader in accordance with his or her own level of understanding and depth of experience. Because feelings cannot be conveyed in words, emotions expressed in abstractions, Rabbi Nachman chose not to reveal his religious credo through a sermon or exegesis in the traditional way but to disclose in the form of a legend or tale the mystical emanations of a soul yearning for redemption and touched by grace.

A quest is undertaken by a Master of Prayer. The Master, or zaddik, is an enlightened holy man, a kind of prophet who has a hidden message to reveal to his students and disciples, clarifying certain inexplicable events for those who are able and ready to receive them. The Master imparts his knowledge in symbols and in accordance with Kabbalistic procedure. In the Sefirotic image, the zaddik is an embodiment of *Yesod*. Psychoanalytically he represents ego-consciousness: the ego projecting its personality on the world, relating to people and things in the exterior domain in a basic and active manner. In that the Sefiroth is considered a progressive manifestation of God, it is part of an organic whole, participating in the activities of both upper (heavenly) and lower (earthly) spheres. A kind of vessel the zaddik, who is devoid of personal existence, acts as a channel, a funnel, through which the divine spirit flows. When King David, considered one of the great zaddiks, said "My heart is hollow within me" (Ps. 109:22), he was describing the earthly condition of the religious seer or visionary.[16] The Master in Rabbi Nachman's tale has emptied himself of all extraneous thoughts and attachments, both personal and worldly, devoting his entire existence to God's work. Following in the footsteps of Simeon bar Yohai, Isaac Luria, and the Baal-Shem-Tov, all of whom experienced heightened awareness, he develops a connection within his own being between the upper and lower spheres of his spiritual world and in a parallel process between his unconscious and conscious in the psychological domain.

The Master in Rabbi Nachman's tale experiences an *imitatio Mosi*. Such an identification might well be indicative of spiritual pride, but this is not so in the Master's case. On the contrary, like Moses, he feels honored by the responsibility God has accorded him; he is grateful, too, for being one of the chosen or elect of God. In accordance with biblical tradition, to be one of the chosen people is an expression of divine love:

The Lord did not set his love upon you, nor chose you, because ye were more in number than any people; for ye were the fewest of all people:

But because the Lord loved you, and because he would keep the oath which he had sworn unto your fathers, hath the Lord brought you out with a mighty hand, and redeemed you out of of the house of bondmen, from the hand of Pharaoh king of Egypt.

Know therefore that the Lord thy God, he is God, the faithful God, which keepeth covenant and mercy with them that love him and keep his commandments to a thousand generations. (Deut. 7: 7–9)

The Master is imbued with divinity's love: he feels its warmth, its effulgence, and seeks to convey to others what it means to him.

A father image, a patriarchal figure, who represents the moral precepts of his religious tradition, the Master is also endowed with inner strength, prepared to confront whatever obstacles might prevent the fulfillment of his mission, whatever humiliations might lie in wait for one who tries to arouse consciousness and inner vision in others. Psychologically, the Master possesses a strong ego: one that lives in harmony with the Self, that will not falter under the weight of pain or disappointment nor become overbearing with success. He is certain of the positive nature of his goal, gaining in strength as he continues to pursue the frequently lonely path leading to understanding and insight.

Prayer is the most efficacious way to channel spiritual energy, to open oneself to God. It is a *rite d'entrée* and *rite de sortie*, going from the terrestrial to the celestial spheres. It unties the "knots" that constrict and bind one to the material world that blocks off so much of the psyche, thus preventing a free-flowing interchange. A transformatory ritual, prayer stirs that "archaic heritage within man"; its findings are then blended with one's present situations. Once the psyche is aroused through this spiritual experience, this energizing process, the doors to the perception of the unknown are forced open and images from the collective unconscious arise autonomously. It is in these depths that believers come to terms with the God within them (or the Self), thus constellating fresh spiritual points of view. The archetypal images that flow into consciousness through prayer release in turn new psychic energies, infusing the individuals with the strength and power to forge ahead. Prayer is an effective device for it fills the psyche with a kind of animal vigor, allowing hitherto repressed instincts to flow unrestrictedly. It is a link between telluric and celestial existence—past, present, and future—an anabasis and katabasis.[17]

1. Archetypal Eden

The Master has chosen a distant land "on a silent sea, shaded round by trees"[18] for his dwelling place. A secluded crystalline area, far from the tumult of city life is "the abode of his concentration" (p. 115). The image of the "silent sea" indicates a fecundating force, a world *in potentia*, according to Thales, who considered water the source of existence. In this inspirational atmosphere, the Master knows the power of divinity and is renewed by it. The liquidity of water is a mediating agent.

Even though he lives alone, the Master is in no way alienated from himself or from human society. He feels at home in every area of life, whether he is alone under the vastness of rural horizons or with others in the crowded noisy city. Unlike Adam who was expelled from paradise because he disobeyed God, the Master leaves his Eden-like domain to further God's work. When entering the collective domain during his journeys to foreign lands, the extroverted attitude needed to communicate with strangers balances out the introverted ways the Master experiences in his secluded environment by the sea. Like inhalation and exhalation, the rhythmic flow within the Master increases his sense of interrelatedness within his own being as well as within those whom he encounters. His conversations with strangers are described as "ascending" as though he were "uplifting" souls. He feels connected to the world, both horizontally and vertically, within and without, secure in his individuality as well as in his messianic calling.

The Master's energy seems limitless, as if it came directly from God. Each word he speaks is life-giving, life-creating. As in the Thirty-third Psalm, "By the word of the Lord were the heavens made; and all the host of them by the breath of his mouth" (Ps. 33:5), so the Master speaks with such power that he seems to kindle fire, arouse emotion in the listener as "the ear and heart of the other opened to him and allowed his word to enter" (p. 116). The individuals to whom the Master directs his discourse are so overwhelmed by the vitality of the archetypal words, that they follow him back to his realm as if in "holy flight," there to experience a higher awareness in the calm of meditation. A primitive enthusiasm, a nearly pantheistic fervor, flood the converts.

Since the Word is considered concentrated divine energy, it becomes a catalyst, a creative force, allowing cosmic rhythms to flow into and out of it. When Moses was given the Torah on Mount Sinai, God's message was revealed in divine language: an expression of his "pure thought," a mirror image of the absolute that contained "the hidden meaning and totality of existence." [19] Words, then, are bridges that permit intercommunication between the finite and infinite worlds, the material and immaterial spheres of being. Because each letter and each word, whether audible or not, visualized in the mind or simply sensed, can become an object of meditation to the devout, allowing the projection of his or her being onto various levels or depths of consciousness, it is not surprising that excitement and jubilation were experienced by those who listened to the Master's words. He possesses a charismatic force that attracts, hypnotizes, and envelops those who are prepared to receive his message and to be taken into his fold.

There exists another land, however, far from the serene area where the Master dwelt, where the acquisition of gold is the sole reason for existence. It is not the spiritual gold equated with God's light but the material gold, identified with the golden calf of the Israelites. Everything in this society is valued solely in terms of money and wealth. The more gold one possesses, the greater is one's power and reputation. This obsession with wealth has created a psychological climate of terror within these people. Fearing that their gold might be stolen from them and that they might be robbed of all their treasure, they have gone to live in a secure mountain retreat, isolated from the envirous.

All roads leading to their mountain redoubt are sealed save one "secret approach" (p. 117).

That these gold-worshipers are identified with the mountain, an ascensional image, indicates the depth of Rabbi Nachman's satire. So-called spiritually oriented areas, such as mountains, contain profane elements. Whether Mount Meru for Hindus, Mount Sinai for Hebrews, the Mount of Olives for Christians, Mount Kaf for Muslims, the mountain is a materialized symbol of inner loftiness. The gold-lovers, however, have secreted their treasure to serve selfish, self-serving purposes and not the superior or glorified fourth state of the mystic.

The Master who lives in a world of opposites—in his remote realm of spiritual concentration and in the material sphere as teacher and guide—wants to awaken these enslaved people; he wants to lead them away from their removed peripheral existence and direct them toward their true task on earth, which is to bring about harmony within their human (ego) and divine (Self) aspects. He therefore goes to them and struggles to bring them the divine Word, to enkindle a love for the spiritual and not the material forces in life. So powerfully do they cling to their "divinity of gold," however, that his words fall on deaf ears. Although he is discouraged, the fire of his messianic zeal prevails. The Word archetype—the divine Word—empowers him to voice his credo in rapturous tonalities as centuries earlier, Isaiah intoned his: "Sing unto the Lord a new song, and his praise from the end of the earth, ye that go down to the sea, and all that is therein; the isles, and the inhabitants thereof" (Isa. 42:10). Still he fails.

A synchronistic event occurs. The archetypal Hero appears on the scene. In keeping with the Sefirotic image, he may be identified with *Netash*—male vigor, "lasting endurance," a force able to subjugate enemies and rescue the righteous, a host of God that actively performs the divine will. The archetypal Hero is a conqueror. Kind to those who submit to him and cruel to those who oppose him, the Hero archetype frequently appears in periods (or in the unconscious of a person) when circumstances are particularly difficult and new force is needed to open the way, to find a new course that will lead to a balancing of tensions. As *Netash*, the Hero struggles to maintain what his

King dictates—to further the governing principle of the society of which he is a part. He also seeks to fulfill his own needs and characteristics, displaying force, strength, and authority in his dealings. Psychologically, the Hero stands for the ego's desire to evolve, to improve its rapport with the exterior world both actively and emotionally. Identified with the risen sun, the archetypal Hero is also linked with surging psychic energy, with the libido, as it arouses the disparate elements within the psyche, calling them into activity and awakening them from their lethargy. The Hero is also an aspect of the Master, since the entire Sefiroth is a complex of interrelationships. As representative of the Word, the Master needs the Hero, an active force to carry out his message in the earthly domain. What the Master generates spiritually, the Hero enacts concretely in the workaday world.

Meanwhile, the gold-lovers grow increasingly terrified. What they do not know is that the Hero is not interested in the material property of gold, in worldly power. He wishes only to alter the course of these obsessed individuals, to free them from their false subservience. When the Master, working with the Hero, ascends the mountain to the gold-lover's retreat, he tells them that "God, the source and goal of all inner life" should be their focus (p. 210), they listen. Now that fear has entered their world, they seem to be more receptive to his teachings. The Master has made some headway, he now realizes, because each individual person must be allowed to approach the Godhead in his or her own way, apprehend and experience it as best he or she can.

The greater the light, the more extensive is the shadow. The Mammon worshippers entwined in their lust for gold unconsciously fear losing what it represents: earthly security and power. They project their anguish on to the Hero, who seems to them to be their enemy, and long to rid themselves of him. They are unaware of the fact that unless they alter their course, they will be the source of their own destruction: their shadow or negative characteristics will envelop and finally obliterate them, blinding them as blazing metal has already done to their superficial values. The material world, subject to the law of change, is governed by birth, growth, deterioration, and death. Security, therefore, can never be gained by means of material objects. It stems from an inner condition, from spiritual gold (*aurum* is the Latin word for gold, in Hebrew, however, *aor*, which means the metal, is given additional value, since it also stands for light, spirit, intuition.) The gold-lovers have not evolved either spiritually or psychologically. They see only the metallic luster and not the ineffable aspect—the inner mystery. Their faces are focused on the ground, the telluric domain. As such, their spiritual and psychological growth is stunted, paralyzed; their progress barred.

Rather than assuaging their terror, the Master encourages it by stressing the negative course they have taken in life. To worship the tangible object is to overemphasize the transient physical side of life: the outer garment rather than that mysterious element which lies within. Angered by what they consider to be the Master's blasphemies, the gold-lovers take him to court and question him.

2. *Archetypal King* (Hokhmah) *and Queen* (Binah)

The Master tells his inquisitors about how once he served a King and Queen. In their palace hung a picture of a *hand* with five fingers upon which were inscribed every kind of symbol or sign: "a map of all the worlds at all times" (p. 121). Only the King, however, could understand its meaning.

The King may be identified with *Hokhmah* in the Sefirotic image; with "wisdom or the primordial idea of God," the "inner intellect," the flash of genius, the power of revelation, the Father, the beginning. Since each of the ten emanations is an archetype of divine or psychic energy, acting and reacting upon the other elements within the whole, everything that the King does, or all that happens to the King, reflects upon the other nine attributes. So the psyche functions in a similar way, according to its own mysterious or unconscious laws. Few experience the full power of the King in the religious sphere; the same may be said of the psychological realm, since only a fraction of human beings are involved in developing their potential to that degree. The goal of the religious individual, as in the therapeutic domain, is not only to reach the highest or most profound of levels, but also to *participate* in them consciously, as a working element, the way Moses did on Mount Sinai. The King is a transpersonal figure, since he is an archetype; an energetic principle representing a cluster of abstract qualities, including that of supreme consciousness, which encompasses genius and the power of revelation and prophecy.

The Crown, *Kether Elyon* (the Supreme Crown), which occupies the primary place in the Sefiroth and symbolizes the unknowable, invisible aspect of God, is alluded to in Rabbi Nachman's tale but never made visible. No human being can gaze upon it. To do so would be to experience the very heart of mystery: the created/uncreated. Translated into psychological terms, this means that when the ego (the center of consciousness, or man) attempts to look at the Self (the entire psyche, God), the finite world is exposing itself to the infinite. Dangers await the uninitiated. One may be swept into death by the shifting currents within the cosmos or the collective unconscious, drowned by its tumultuous waters, blinded by its radiance, deafened by its tonalities. Insanity is then the outcome. In the Book of Exodus we read: "Thou canst not see my face: for there shall no man see me, and live" (33:20). So the Crown made of gold in its most purified and rarefied state does not take on reality: it exists as pre- and post-thought, pre- and post-reality, an abstract condition prior to manifestation, even in the mind; inaccessible, therefore, to human understanding. The Crown, a paradigm of the Infinite or Hidden God, is reminiscent in many ways of the Gnostics' *deus absconditus*. The golden Crown of Nachman's tale which ideally rests on the King's head when all is in order, is identified with the divine spirit in man. Its circular shape underscores its eternal and celestial nature; it binds the Crown to the crowned, God with man, the temporal with the atemporal spheres. Beams of light radiate from the Crown, suggestive of creative thought, energetic power. Psychologically, the Crown may be considered a representation of the Self: transpersonal, immanent. It permeates the psyche, which Jung defined as "the totality of all psychic processes, both conscious as well as unconscious" and extends from its most hidden, deeply unconscious form to its most accessible state.[20]

The hand upon which the cosmic map and its signs and symbols were represented, indicates the various interrelationships in the Sefirotic world and its multiple reflections in the temporal sphere. Allusions to the hand of God are to be found throughout the Bible. The hand of God has been compared to the eye of God in the Scriptures because it both sees and feels. When the Master in Rabbi Nachman's tale refers to the hand he saw, he may have been describing an apocalyptic vision—a deeply moving moment in his own spiritual evolution, similar in power to the times when God's hand touches a human being, empowering him to translate divinity's message.[21] When the Lord touched Jeremiah's mouth, for example, he was endowed with the power to preach.

Binah, the Queen Mother of whom the Master speaks, represents wisdom and understanding, the traditional capacity for the intellect, alluded to as the supernal *Shekhinah*. The Queen is identified with the palace, the royal home, that protects and nurtures, fostering growth and change within a changeless domain. When the King—*Hokhmah*—works in harmony with the Queen—*Binah*—echoing the balance between the active and passive, the masculine and feminine, constraint and expansion, harmony prevails within the Sefiroth.

Because the King *knew* the Queen and *understood* the signs and symbols of the hand, "he knew the place where each art and skill had its primal source which flowed out of the depths of eternity; and he knew the ways of these places" (p. 122). He was connected with himself and therefore, with all his other archetypal attributes—to his source of being. Due to this interconnectedness within and without, he was empowered to revive what was withered, water what was parched, restore the dead to life. When people came to him drained or disturbed, he knew exactly how to inspire them with his "grace," to renew them physically and spiritually.

When a Singer "who had the gift of finding enchanting words and tones" and "moving all hearts" (p. 123) came to the palace, the King showed him where the "inexhaustible melody that sounds forth from itself back into itself" was located. Just as the spoken Word is an attribute of the Sefiroth, so is sound, whether audible to the human ear or not. Used by some as a mantra for meditation, sound puts one in touch with the time/ space continuum; as such, it can become the source for prophecy. It revolves around waves, timbers, rhythms, serial patterns, form, as ordering devices, in the same way as meter and number. Pythagoras first suggested the existence of the "music of the spheres," but the thirteenth-century Spanish Kabbalist Abraham Abulafia wrote of "the music of pure thought" that one experiences when divested of sensory involvement.[22]

For the Kabbalist, the sound of music is of utmost importance. It breaks down man-made barriers, melts feelings, "cuts through" the "husks of Evil" in the world.[23] The dynamism created by a voice, by the intoned word, the musical pitch, are ways of ascending and descending from the mortal to the immortal sphere—coherent techniques for progressing to infinite heights, reaching sublime interplanetary spheres as some mystics have allegedly accomplished. King David channeled his love for God in his song, as both an active and a passive participant in the creation of divine harmonies.

O Sing unto the Lord a new song; sing unto the Lord, all the earth. (Ps. 96:1)

Make a joyful noise unto the Lord, all the earth: make a loud noise, and rejoice, and sing him praise. (Ps. 98:4)

Let the roar, and the fulness thereof; the world, and they that dwell therein. (Ps. 98:7)

The Wise Man comes to the King. He, too, is led "to the place of light where the last foundations open and no level can withold itself from the eye" (p. 123). Eye and light are once again equated, indicating that vision is the source of light and spiritual understanding. Although the eye indicates clairvoyance and wisdom in some (as in Siva's third eye), others have the physical organ but fail to use it. "Son of man, thou dwellest in the midst of a rebellious house, which have eyes to see, and see not; they have ears to hear, and hear not; for they are a rebellious house" (Ezek. 12:2).

The King leads the Master to "the place of the soul where the fountain of fire beat against me, and the power of my prayer has rejuvenated its stream" (p. 123). The fountain, symbolizing a perpetual source of renewal, emerges from the very central point of being—the soul—where the eternal manifests itself, feeds and nourishes the life-force. It is within this font, this hallowed area, this *temenos*, that the transpersonal experience becomes accessible. When ascending toward divinity in an ecstatic visual experience, fire is seen liquidly glowing, heating its cold surroundings, blazing in its transparency. The symbol of libido (psychic energy), fire is a generative demiurgic force that can both purify and destroy. It sears those who try to draw too close to its mystery, annihilating those who cannot accept its double nature, its tension of opposites, but paving the way for those ready to experience a theophany. It was through flame and lightning—the flash produced by the discharge of atmospheric electricity—that Moses saw "black fire on white fire" on Mount Sinai—the preexistent Torah given him by divinity—that instrument upon which letters and words were not yet completely formed, where spirit and matter still lived inchoate.

The Kabbalist believes in the existence of two Torahs: the one that came into being prior to the Creation, and the one written in "black fire on white fire," its meaning indicating a world in *potentia*, which is not "perceptible to a spiritual or sensory eye."[24] Only Moses was empowered to read this Torah because he was prepared to do so, his protracted contemplation of its letters had endowed him with primordial wisdom. The Torah known today is the one made accessible to the human mind, each letter and word bearing its own level of meaning or consciousness, its own exterior and interior definition.

The Master was permitted to view the flame of divine mystery and was illuminated by the experience. The living heart of the Torah—the center and root of all things—concentrated its energy on his heart and soul. It became the object of his meditation. When he saw the flashing sparks and gleams that appeared, displaying particles of blazing letters, he felt he had participated in primordial thought—in the very fabric of existence.

The King also took the Hero to the source of being; he showed him the course that destiny had ordered him to take. The victorious sword was to be his instrument. The King gave him the weapon with the admonition that "from time to time he must return to its place and plant the sword in the earth, which nourishes and consecrates it for new wars" (p. 123). A sword is double-edged. Its shining blade serves to both protect and destroy. The cherubims guarding paradise, for example, were each given "a flaming sword which turned every way, to keep the way of the tree of life" (Gen. 3:24).

It was decided that the Hero would marry the Princess, referred to on the Sefiroth as *Malkuth* or the lower *Shekhinah*, thereby uniting polarities in the lower triad as well as reaffirming their relationship in the upper one—the more remote sphere of being. The Princess represents the kingdom of God in the existential sphere. She is the mystical archetype of the community of Israel, of the earthly mother—body consciousness. She is the presence and immanence of God in the whole earthly creation and is represented in mystical literature as the Bride, the Matrona, the earthly Jerusalem. She is the aspect of divinity that dwelt in the Temple of Jerusalem, and after the Temple was destroyed, she went into exile with her people. Her return from exile is celebrated weekly on the Sabbath in two ritual feasts, one at noon and one before sundown, welcoming both *Shekhinas* back into God. During the rest of the week, however, she is separated from the Sefiroth. Only when permanently reunited, it is believed, will harmony exist throughout the universe.

A son was born to the Princess and the Hero, a "sheer miracle of beauty," who radiates light and joy. In time he becomes perfection incarnate, save for one fact: he cannot talk. Although he knows everything, both temporal and atemporal in his own way, he is not sufficiently developed to experience the Word/thought. Still enjoying a *participation mystique* with the Godhead, the child—psychoanalytically identified with the ego—is not yet sufficiently strong to have an identity of his own; consciousness has yet to develop, it is not ready to be articulated.

The child archetype also represents the future, the emerging or awakening life-force. The product of a *coniunctio*, his structure is not yet solidified, his essence is still malleable. Morally he may be equated with Adam prior to the Fall. Psychologically he is identified with the formative potential and still unrealized forces in the unconscious. The mystic child, a child of the soul (Moses, Christ, Buddha, and others), is usually associated with knowledge in its pristine state. As such, he remains in touch with the "secrets" of the universe, understands both formed and formless worlds. Like the birth of new insight that has just emerged into consciousness, the child archetype seems an expression of beauty and light because it still bears the promise of perfection, the hope of realizing the ideal: "For unto us a child is born, unto us a son is given; and the government shall be upon his shoulder; and his name shall be called Wonderful,

Counsellor, the mighty God, the everlasting Father, the Prince of Peace" (Isa. 9:6).

The child, devoid of conflict, lives in the palace in a paradisiac atmosphere. He laughs, runs, smiles, plays. Paradoxically, such an Edenesque atmosphere cannot last forever. The storm that is about to rise with whirlwind force represents dissociation in the psychological sphere; fragmentation, a shattering of the psyche, ensues.

3. The Exile Archetype

Archetypal exile has both negative and positive aspects. The former, which is experienced as severance from one's source or roots, may result in alienation, extreme fear and agitation. Such an outcome with all the emotions clustered around the original experienxce may to some extent explain the yearning of the Jews for the land of Israel.

In its positive workings, archetypal exile may be considered a *rite de passage*. When Moses led the Israelites out of Egypt to wander in the wilderness, where they spent the next forty years, they suffered much physical and spiritual agony. The experience, however, helped to rid them of all vestiges of their earlier state of subservience (their slave mentality), while developing in them a sense of their own worth and ability to survive. The same may be said of Moses himself. Before he was considered fit by God to lead his people out of bondage, he too, had to go through a period of discipline and training. It was in the desert that he met Jethro, his future father-in-law, who was also his spiritual mentor. Jethro's wisdom and guidance and the deprivation Moses knew during this period of isolation helped him evolve from the temporal to atemporal visionary sphere.

In Rabbi Nachman's tale, the reader now learns of the ravages of the terrible storm that descended on the King's palace. It "mixed up the elements with one another, made the ocean into mainland and the mainland into ocean" (p. 124). Everything was disrupted, altered, turned into its opposite; psychologically, a condition of *enantiodromia* prevailed. In the Bible, storm and chaos usually precedes a theophany: "Thou shalt ascend and come like a storm, thou shalt be like a cloud to cover

the land thou, and all thy bands, and many people with thee"
(Ezek. 38:9).

The mystic believes that devastation and disruption of *what
is* are manifestations of God's radiance, that stirring the elements, paves the way for a new consciousness to take form, for
new ways to come into being. A storm, which may be identified
with the aspect of *Gevurah* in the Sefiroth, signifies God's "stern
judgment," His capacity for "punishment," gushes forth, and in
so doing disrupts the stable established order, destroying and
uprooting everything in its wake. Yet, in so doing, when calm is
established, so is greater awareness. After the Flood subsided,
Noah saw a fresh world emerge from where had formerly been
only troubled waters, giving humanity another chance.

A violent storm permeating the atmosphere is the external
manifestation of an unsatisfactory inner condition within the
Godhead, the Self. By destroying the accustomed order of things,
a storm roots up what binds one to earthly conventions. Psychologically, it displaces the ego's patterned existence, thus
awakening it from an enslaved or routine condition.[25] Ezekiel
describes it in the following way: "And I looked, and, behold,
a whirlwind came out of the north, a great cloud, and a fire
infolding itself, and a brightness was about it, and out of the
midst thereof as the colour of amber, out of the midst of the
fire" (Ezek. 1:4).

During the visionary experience, the individual's nervous
system becomes such a finely tuned instrument that whatever
occurs either without or within is magnified in intensity. Inter-
ruption in meditating, perhaps imperceptible to another, may
lead to an unbalanced state. An individual, in his ecstasy, "brings
down the light" to the root of his being.[26] It is at this juncture
that the *Ruach Hakodesh*, the Holy Spirit, is experienced; higher
levels of enlightenment are known and the soul itself in its three
levels may be apprehended. The soul, as defined in the Bible, is
identified with wind and breath: *Neshamah* (or breath) is the
highest and most remote area of the soul (Gen. 2:7); *Ruach* (or
spirit [Joel 3:1]) is the second level; *Nefesh* (rest) is the state of
the soul most closely related to the earthly condition; it is the
most accessible to humankind.[27]

The imagery used to describe the storm in Rabbi Nachman's tale—the wind disrupting the calm in the King's domain,

blowing through the palace with gale force—encourages an identification to be made between this divine force and the *Ruach* and *Neshamah* levels of the soul. A confirmation of this premise can be found in the following description: the "roaring" storm entered the palace as a bird and "took the marvelously beautiful child of the king's daughter on his wings and bore him away in whirling haste" (p. 124). The bird is a spiritualization of the entire sequence. A male principle standing for enlightenment, the sublimation of thought and feeling, the bird is that force that whisks the child away on wings of spirit.

The conflagration which erupted throughout the King's palace, compelling everyone to leave the domain, shattering traditional harmonies, is reminiscent of the Breaking of the Vessels, when divinity's light was scattered and shattered throughout the universe. Now, the *scintillae*, or sparks of light, would also travel. To discover them would be the focus of the next sequence.

Meanwhile, when calm returned to the kingdom, "the men stood there helpless and scattered, estranged from their accustomed homesteads" (p. 126). Everything had changed. The royal family had vanished. Rulerless, the people seek to replace the King but on what basis should they choose one? What should their criteria be? They tremble in their loneliness and their feelings of alienation. Thirty-two different paths of wisdom exist for the Kabbalist, each leading to the supernal point, to a new beginning—the creative center of the "Unmoved Mover." To find the path best suited to each requires an arduous initiation period.

The people discuss various attitudes toward life. The path of wisdom was considered the best by some. Others, argued that it leads to dryness, to overintellectuality, syllogistic thinking, cerebral concepts with no basis in reality, nonsensical chatter, an "idle game." Another group suggests speech as the best choice, since the word entails thought which may be made to act in "the realm of working and happening," as *praxis*. Beauty was advanced as another possibility. Beauty, an expression of God's feeling, it alone "rests eternally in itself." Unless it has an object upon which to focus, "one who rejoices in her," it is unmanifest, experienced merely as an after image, a reflection. Only in the world of manifestation does Beauty lose its absoluteness; then "she is nothing other than a thing and image of joy, born mysteriously out of joy, begetting wonderful joy everywhere, embraced by joy; joy is the sun in whose warm light life perfects itself" (p. 127). Death was also offered as the ultimate value. All else is fleeting, it was contended, only death is eternal. But then, so is Honor.

The disputation pursued its course for seven days: the seven days of Creation, the seven days of the week, the seven notes of the musical scale, the seven alchemical processes leading to gold. Yet, no decision was reached. It was agreed that each person should embark on his own quest and seek the value that most conformed with his view of life. The Hero—the only member of the royal family to remain—and his warriors did not enter the discussion. He knew that without force and power, nothing can be achieved in the physical world, passivity is no solution: "we felt in our blood and in the beat of our hearts how without force life would lack meaning" (p. 128). Thoughts, feelings, concepts, if not followed up and expressed by deeds cannot in this world bring about change. There are occasions in life when aggressive action must be taken to will a new way into existence. Although the Hero's followers did not understand his views, they were touched by his vigor, his love of action and the fire of his spirit—his sense of commitment. Whether it is by the sword or the Word, the Hero sought to reconnect the severed— the upper the lower Sefiroth. To serve his cause with dignity, compassion, and understanding was his goal.

A period of time elapses. The dramatis personae separate. The Master again meets the Hero. Their encounter is vital to enlightenment. Their meeting is providential, synchronistic, as was Moses' when he met Jethro who, at the time, was being attacked by a group of shepherds. When the Master joins forces with the Hero, the spiritual and visceral sides of the Sefiroth are being reconnected—Word and deed, inner and outer domains.

The Hero tells the Master how upon his return to the palace after the storm, "I found my house deserted and all my dear ones vanished from me. Then my steps no longer obeyed the way, but strayed about at random" (p. 129). The Hero was disoriented; his equilibrium and zest for life had been shattered; bereavement encapsulated his entire being. He wandered about in his condition. His mind and body were psychologically disconnected, indicating his ego's inability to cope with the rigors of the situation. Dissociation between ego and Self, represented by his loss of orientation and fragmented condition, paralyzed his every activity. He was withering, parched, dying. His meeting with the Master, therefore, more detached from earthly conditions and more oriented toward supernal climes than the Hero, is of vital importance.

When a Hero conquers too quickly and attempts to dominate outside events too swiftly, as the Hero did prior to the storm, when he went around the earth conquering all the peoples and lands, thereby frightening the gold-lovers—it reveals an overly extraverted condition in the psyche; an overemphasis on the masculine aspect at the expense of the inner being and the feminine component. The Hero failed to pay sufficient attention to the Princess, the *Shekhinah*. His overly aggressive side took precedence: focusing on expansion, victory, impulse, while neglecting his bride-wife-mother and child. A storm, therefore, was needed to rectify the imbalance. The winds, thunder, and lightning destroyed the status quo. The kratophany that ensued forced the Hero to seek new paths, to find a way of rectifying the devastation his attitude had fostered. Only by reviewing his past acts, can he understand the meaning of what has happened: the loss of the *Shekhinah* as relatedness, as love, as futurity. The Hero has already wandered all over the earth in a fruitless search for the royal family: "the abodes of all my dear ones without finding one" (p. 129).

4. *The Archetypal Quest*

In the next sequences the Hero and the Master set out to search for the King, Queen, Princess, and child. At times they are together, at others, separated. Strange and providential encounters occur; many difficulties and obstacles are also met, in accordance with the initiation ritual through which they must pass.

Sometimes they hear lamentations sounding from the trees, the mournful song bewailing their sorrow, pain emerging from the very heart of nature. Like fleeting memories, the sounds and images increase the yearning for what was once integration with deity. Trees may be considered hierophanies in Rabbi Nachman's tale. They seem to greet the travelers wherever they go.

Terrestrial replicas of the tree of life, the tree of knowledge that existed in its most absolute state in paradise, with their proliferating branches, seem to welcome the beleaguered wanderers. The birds they hear remind them of angels—God's messengers—flying from the supernal to the earthly spheres, with God's word, or soaring back, bearing earthly souls to the celestial region.

The Master tells of a hill he has seen, upon which "spread a golden glaze that did not vanish even in the twilight, and the glaze painted on the stony summit of the hill [was in] the shape of a crown" (p. 129). The "golden glaze" he describes is like an afterimage, a memory, indicating the presence of a transcendent force. Nevertheless, the shape of the Crown, invisible and inaccessible, has left its impress as an irradiating or iridescent sun, blazing and lighting the way like the scattered sparks after the Breaking of the Vessels. It is in the hard "stony summit" of the hill that these sparks of light are embedded in strong, cohesive, and durable geological layers. Stones, considered hierophanies as we have seen (the Kaaba in Mecca, the Greek Omphaloi, Beth-el House of God), are believed to have been heaven sent and are, therefore, imbued with spiritual value. That the Master has seen a mirror image of the Crown indicates that he, like Ezekiel before him, has experienced a theophany: "This was the appearance of the likeness of the glory of the Lord. And when I saw it, I fell upon my face, and I heard a voice of one that spake" (Ezek. 1:28). The image of the Crown that the Master saw is archetypal in dimension. It fills him with spiritual light like that of the *Ruach Hakodesh* (the Holy Spirit). It activates his soul, elevating and purifying it as a soul in flight, finally freeing it from all worldly thoughts and feelings. There it stood, poised, in all of its glazed splendor.

Throughout their wanderings, however, neither the Master nor the Hero succeeds in finding the royal family or their abode. Their quest (or spiritual initiation) has not been completed. They are evidently not ready to meet the divine face to face, to gaze upon the sacred countenance (to experience the Self). On one occasion, when the Master is wandering alone in a desert place, he sees "great drops of blood" on the sand, which neither dry up nor trickle. From them emerge "the glance of two eyes" (p. 130). They are the Queen's tears, he realizes, those of *Binah*, exiled from the Sefiroth. He listens as "the sand whispered the lament, soft and broken" (p. 130). Unlike the "golden glaze" and the "stony summit" where the Crown blazes as a reflection of God in all his glory, the Master has encountered a divided, scattered condition. The sand in the desert area symbolizes aridity, a withering of life. Overexposure to the sun, to the light of consciousness in the psychological sphere, causes whatever seeks to grow to fail. Sand, composed of tiny crystals, cut up, divided, each sparkling in the brilliant sunlight, is like so many fragmented souls, disconnected, deenergized, passive. These "divine sparks," however, are ready to be gathered and reintegrated into the Sefiroth, as is the supernal *Shekhinah* in the form of Binah, whose bloodied eyes whispered their soft lament. Blood, which represents life energy, passion, a vital and active principle, is represented in this image as paralyzed, immovable, and nontransformable. It no longer flows and cannot foster new relationships. Its mysterious side (in the divine service) is not activated; and it does not spell the excitement of danger, power, or sacrifice.[28]

The two eyes bathed in bloodied tears, like primeval oceans, had once been able to liquify what had been stiff and unbending. The spirit of God had enucleated them. Without this vital force, they had hardened: feeling had been severed from the rest of being. The atrophied eyes, looking at the Master, never slept; these eyes always observed, stared, were transfixed, waiting for the moment when the gates leading back to the palace would again open, paving the way for her reentry. The supernal eye of the Queen, like providence, follows, aids, and indicates ways to salvation and redemption. The Master understands this; he knows that his search for the sensitive, beautiful, maternal aspects of the feminine principle are near at hand. The numinous properties she represents, although immersed in pain, will one day experience the rapturous embrace of her divine consort.

The Master pursues his course. He comes upon a brook in "which flowed a thin milky streak that did not mix with the water" (p. 130). He observes the alternating currents, the instability of the waters, replicating both the fluidity of nature's course throughout the universe and the circulatory system in the human. He stands before the waters. "He shall drink of the brook in the way," the Psalm says (110:17), imbibe the food of life. Milk, a nourishing principle in nature "has sprung from the

breast of the king's daughter as she stood there and pined for
her child" (p. 130). What the Master has seen is another vision,
a reflection of the Princess (*Malkuth*, the lower *Shekhinah*). Like
so many memories that sustain the devout in their search for
the Godhead, but never quench their thirst or appease their
anxiety, so he pursued his course. Yet, the Princess was there in
essence, though her presence was missing. The *Shekhinah* stood
alone—far from the Hero—cut off from divinity.

Discouraged and distraught, the Master sits down on a stone.
Suddenly he sees that it is covered with all kinds of signs and
markings "engraved in the mysterious hand that belonged to
the king" (p. 130). The Master feels himself to be in the very
heart of mystery, as if he were witnessing that "white fire on
black fire" known to Moses on Mount Sinai. The very essence
of nature seems to burst into lamentations as he penetrates more
deeply into the atmosphere, enclosing himself still more powerfully in its sacrality. The spatial and ascensional vision described, which seems to carry the Master back and forth from
filled to empty space, from heights to abysmal depths, lulling
him into a state of receptivity, also fosters an atmosphere of
terror and awe. Seemingly lost in space, in gravitationless spheres,
he encounters in multiple transparencies and opacities the very
inner, secret, beating heart of an unfolding universe.

The Hero meantime has seen "a forest valley" and "on
gray moss a lock of sun-blond hair that shone of its own light"
(p. 131). Such an encounter shocks and startles him, paving the
way for increased spiritual awareness. The juxtaposition of forest and light, of primeval and rarefied areas, of unchanneled
and sublimated instincts in the image describing the glow of the
child's hair, increases the tension. Like God's glory this image
takes on the power of a religious visitation. No separation exists between the light glowing from the lock of hair and the gray
of the moss: each flows into the other in multiple gradations, in
rhythmic patterns accelerating in movement. Antitheses and
paradoxes pursue their course: light buried in darkness, spirit
encased in matter, purity inhabiting the most sordid dross. Like
a halo or nimbus, this supernal radiance emanating from the
child's hair glows with its own energetic power flying off in sparks
of light. The entire area resounds with the child's footsteps, voice,
laughter, song. A timeless universe has been encountered, di-

mensionless, spaceless, replete with feeling. Though the child is unseen, his presence is sensed; though invisible, the images bound and rebound. Hope is instilled in the Hero's heart, since the connection between external and internal world is intimated.

The Hero takes seven strands of the child's hair, which are mysteriously transformed into "the seven colors of the rainbow." Like the ladder of angels in Jacob's vision, the rainbow is also a symbol of divinity. After the Flood, the rainbow was God's sign to Noah and his descendants of a new covenant; it was symbolic of God's protective force for humankind (Gen. 9:7). In gentle and rounded form, heaven reveals its feminine element as it casts its warm spectrum of colors on earth, awakening mortals to ineffable beauty—serene joy, which comes from the calm after the storm.

The Master and the Hero know that whatever the difficulties, struggles, and evils life has in store, only the individual "through himself" can "establish his life" (p. 132) and find fulfillment. The Master once again tries to teach this lesson to the gold-lovers, but they are still unprepared to understand that the value of gold as a material object is only an illusion. Blind to the fact that salvation is an individual matter, that understanding of one's inner being comes with the experience of wholeness, they refuse to believe that all else is peripheral, transient, a fantasy. Still fearing for their wealth, they send out messengers to a land they have heard is even richer than their own. They want to ally themselves with these people, strengthen their defenses. As they set forth, however, they take the wrong turning and lose their way.

They come upon a man who is carrying a golden staff in which are embedded stones which radiate like so many constellations. His hat is "encircled with strings of pearls that seemed in themselves the treasures of all the seas" (p. 134). It is as if they have come upon some memory from a distant past—anterior existences. They learn that this man was once the King's treasurer. The staff he carries for support points to the way he is to follow, directs his journey toward lighter areas. The sparkling stones and energetic factors stand for power, sovereignty, commandment, but also mean light blazing in darkness. Reminiscent of the rod used by Moses when he struck the rock and water gushed forth, enabling the Israelites to quench their thirst

(Exod. 17:1–6), so the King's treasurer gives the beleaguered lost wanderers food for thought. To lose oneself in the woods or along the path of life is to experience time to come to terms with one's problems, a period in which seclusion and meditation are of extreme importance. The Talmud recounts the story of Moses who was told to pull up a sapphire rod from deep within the ground because upon it were engraved the names of God. Only then would his initiation be deemed complete and he, ready for future instruction.[29] So, too, the wanderers would have to tap other dimensions, and follow the bearer of the staff.

The hat worn by the King's treasurer corresponds—on a lower level—to the King's Crown. Head and thought, consciousness and unconsciousness, are blended in this image, and so are intellect and wisdom. That the hat is encircled with pearls, unites masculine attitudes of mercy, kindness, emotionality, and love with feminine characteristics of wisdom, judgment, punishment, discrimination, and power. It is interesting to realize here that the attributes usually alloted to men are in the Sefirotic configuration identified with women and vice versa. Pearls, come from the sea, from water—the woman's realm—are like so many fetuses enclosed in the womb. Once the pearl evolves from the mystical center, building on the grain of sand, it emerges transfigured in its transluscence and iridescence. So is instinct sublimated and transfigured: in the cavern, cavity, or shell, it lives unregenerate as it reveals itself in the light of day. After the evolutionary process, it becomes one of the most important factors in the salvation of humankind. One understands why the Hebrews and Gnostics looked upon the pearl as essential to redemption.

Upon first seeing the King's treasurer, this archetypal protector of wealth, the gold-lovers believe he will further their cause. They prostrate themselves before him, and ask to see all his treasures. He leads them into a mountain cavern where they can glimpse the splendor it contains. When they ask if they can remove it to their domain, he agrees but warns them "not to desire these things in the manner of money" (p. 135). To misuse such wealth is to seek destruction. Just as gold must undergo a slow process of refinement to become pure metal, so must perfection be earned in the spiritual and psychological domain.

The gold-lovers start to transport the treasure to their own land, but they do not dare look at it outright, but glance at it obliquely, "furtively," fearfully, as if the presence of some blinding force, too great to experience directly. In their homeland, they again believe that the gold acquired will free them from fear, from the Hero's sword. Illusion upon illusion—fear only increases as the worldly treasure grows. They ask the King's treasurer to see the Hero and persuade him not to attack. He complies. When the King's treasurer returns, he reassures the gold-lovers of the Hero's good intentions, and explains to them that the only way for them to find safety is to search for "forgotten paths," in some distant land for "there lies in twilight magic the place from which the sword of the hero takes its mysterious strength." Only then will they be truly free and secure.

The Master and the Hero's search pursues its course. Only by forging ahead, can they experience liberation and detachment, and by the same token, reunification with the Godhead (the Self). After days of wandering, they reach a walled land. They see a man outside the gates who tells them about the storm, the destruction, his search for wisdom which he believes is the highest criterion for kingship. They next come upon a stargazer who also tells them about the storm, the destruction, and his search for *gnosis*. He tells them "I know the life of the stars and so I know the world" (p. 137). The wanderers are incredulous. They doubt the reality of such simplistic answers. "And when the tremor comes over the stars on the day of transformation and dashes them to pieces, what do you know then?" (p. 137). Silence greets the question. Knowledge is limited. To feel that one knows is to reveal a condition of inflation.

Stars, representing the source of light, intuition emanating from the remote black vault of heaven, are also identified with the mind, with intellectual and cerebral knowledge. For the Jews, stars are very significant. The six-pointed Star of David represents a fusion of opposites—water/fire/earth/air—involution and evolution, active and passive—the central point from which all else radiates. In the apocalyptic Book of Enoch, each star is said to be cared for by the other, each is personalized, the man's fate is written in them (Dan. 12:3). Because they twinkle, they frequently indicate an unrealized state, incomplete psychological and spiritual development.

So the wanderers beset with a need for wholeness and

competion, meet with unsatisfactory answers, unfulfilled yearnings. Other philosophers and thinkers present their views on the way. One states he knows the life of the sea and, therefore, of the world. To be sure, water, a preformal substance, contains unconscious contents as yet unmanifest. But does it alone contain the answer? "And when the sun has drunk up the sea on the day of the turning, what do you know then?" (p. 138). Silence. Heat forces evaporation, distillation. So the mind when fired with activity also causes elements to disappear, thereby drying up the source of life. If the mind dominates the body, instincts and emotion dry and wither.

The Master and Hero, and other wanderers displaced by the storm that destroyed the peace and calm of serenity, see an old man sitting on a stone. His eyes are wide open; he gazes out in space as if what he saw were "enclosed it itself" (p. 138). When they ask him if he knows the world, he replies, "I know my soul," which defines as "the firmament that no one can break into pieces. It is the sea that no one can swallow up" (p. 138). It is through the soul, the eternal and collective aspect in man, that the individual becomes receptive to divinity, and experiences a connection with the Self. "Not my will but Thy Will be done," as the prayer states.[30]

So the soul anima/animus complex extends through several levels of experience unconscious and inaccessible, functioning autonomously; its presence is made known in the feelings it generates, both beautiful and ugly, serene and chaotic; as sensations pour fourth and the supernal *Shekhinah* is connected to the Sefiroth. As the soul levels itself down to a less sublime state, so it increases in consciousness, and increasingly takes part in wordly matters. Identified with *Malkuth* (the lower *Shekhinah*), it acts both positively and negatively in the material world; it participates as a projection in humanity's conflicts and difficulties as well as in their joyous events.

The Master and the Hero, along with the rest of the group, realize that the old man must once have been the King's counselor. He encourages them in their search and tells them that they will be healed only after they journey to a dark mountain, they are to encircle it and search for a small crevice in it, within which is a door with two gigantic birds nesting above it.

The metaphoric dark mountain in this image is quite different from the earlier one where the gold-lovers hid their treasure. This mountain is elevated beyond measure so that transcendence may be felt, the height stretching from earth to heaven. That they must encircle the mountain indicates a rechanneling of energy and of spirit, bringing a new frame of reference into being. The crevice—a narrow crack in the mountain's surface—is an indentation leading to a door; the outer core, the "Husks" or the "Shells"—that each person must penetrate if the next stage in the process is to be achieved. The door, suggestive of the Japanese *torii* at the entrance to a Shinto shrine, leads to another level of consciousness, the area containing the Holy of Holics. It is here that the Ark of the Covenant rests—the Torah—the threshold leading to the *sefiroth*, to divinity's innermost inwardness. Only those prepared for the creative center, where the Self encircles the ego, may enter. "And he was afraid, and said, How dreadful is this place: this is none other but the house of heaven" (Gen. 28:17).

The gigantic birds, referring to a superior state of being, carry God's message, as they once had to Moses. When they swooped down from on high in the form of two cherubs, resting above the door, as *Nefesh*, the most accessible of the soul states.[31]

The group penetrates deep into the mountain, into a cavern. There they find a kitchen where "the true food of the human race" is being "prepared in brazen kettles" (p. 139). The fire cooking the ingredients emanated from the deepest levels of the earth, from "invisible paths" leading from "the fire-mountains of the earth." The birds participated in the cooking process by fanning the air with their wings. Those who partake of the food, who enter this cavernous region will be healed.

The cavern, an archetypal image of the womb, is identified in many religions with a place of mystery: Eleusis, the Christian grottos, and so forth. Elijah spent a night in a cave prior to his vision (1 Kings 19:9–14). Simeon bar Yohai spent thirteen years in a cave hiding from the Romans. Since energy is imprisoned in the cavern, as force exists in a dehumanized state as latent existence, so chthonian powers are at work in this darkened and secluded area, aiding in the germinating process.[32] The cavern, a place where gestation occurs, is also conducive to the ego's replenishment. Feeding on the nutritive elements offered by the Self, acquiring renewed vigor through contemplation, meditation, and analytical probing, so the ego experiences the evolutionary process.

Food is fire; it is energy which heats and fluidifies during moments of heightened vision. In Kundalini yoga, energy mounts from the lowest parts of the body to the head, through willed inner discipline. The communion, or partaking of food in the cavern, will cause growth, life, and generate transformation: the agape, the realization and unification of spirit and flesh. Reminiscent of the manna from heaven that the Israelites received during their desert wanderings, so in this instance, food brings insight into the gold-lover's condition. It is through the tasting and eating of the food/life, that the initiate is able to expand his consciousness and to experience God in his blood-stream, coursing throughout his vital organs in the most powerful of ways. Only then is the ego freed from entanglement, allowing it to cross the threshold into eternity.

Even after the cavern experience, however, the gold-lovers still have not learned their lesson. They must wander still further. The group comes upon a marketplace. There they are moved and touched by the words they hear, as if a hand had brushed against them. Their emotions heighten, but once again, the fire grows cold, their fervor diminishes. Only surface warmth had been experienced; emotions are cheap. They reach a garden where youths seated in a circle are listening to a man talk. Interest is aroused, once more, but diminishes soon after: "the word had died in their spirit and lay there like heavy slag" (p. 141). They continue their march through clearings and forests, burning and hungering for an answer. Finally, they come to a clearing and see a man leaning against a tree. He is singing to himself; then he remains silent and trees take up his song. "Great voices came forth from the rocks" as well, as though nature had emerged in giant symphonic overtones, awakening the very forces of life. The birds enter the orchestral flow; the brook counters with its tonalities, beats, and rhythms. Everything is new, clean, fresh; yet it is the same tune, the same air, the same tonalities—all had been heard before. Now, however, it was as if "the air itself became a singing mouth and bore the melody into the world" (p. 142). Nature in its entirety glowed with fire, erupted into activity, swayed as it breathed out its cosmic inhalations and exhalations, encapsulating all of creation in its embrace.

The Master of Prayer realizes that what he is experiencing now is the Singer of the King: the words emanating from his mouth are divine, functioning energetic principles incarnating themselves in structured incantations: those stemming from ancient traditions, sacred musical chants, lamentations dating back far into time—reminiscent of the psalms King David sang when experiencing the depths of despair and the heights of jubilation. Music is that element that connects and creates worlds, unites feeling and thought, implores humankind to participate in the audible feast of life. The mystery of creation is taking root in harmonies of numbered sounds, expressing itself in the plenitude of a sensible yet unintelligible world, communicating in the manifest sphere as an emotion, a feeling, implicit in the nervous system.

The Singer of the King joins the people in their quest, wanders throughout the earth, confronting distress, distortion, and greed. In virtual despair, they finally enter a "deserted wilderness," an arid land where extraneous and superfluous thoughts are nonexistent. Although outside the visible domain, it is paradoxically, an accessible area devoid of growth and movement. Yet, it is here that they meet a "strange woman" whose face is "white and motionless." They stare in amazement. "Never had we beheld such beauty and never such anguish, for it possessed her without destroying her beauty" (p. 143). They kneel before her and request that she become their sovereign. She acquiesces. They recognize her as the King's daughter, the Princess—*Malkuth*, the lower *Shekhinah*. It is she who understood the woes of humankind and experiences their emotions, which has left its indelible imprint on her face.

She joins them, and they continue on their way, arriving in the land of death. At the end of a grotto they see another woman. Her white hair shines in the blackness. She is immovable, like a statue under "the spell of death." From her eyes "bloody tears fell upon the barren ground, for they had destroyed all life, blade and bud" (p. 144). Only after the Master and his friends have spoken to her and her daughter has embraced her does life flow into the Queen, the upper *Shekhinah*, God's intelligence, his understanding, his wisdom.

The Queen takes part in the journey now; the stars light the way, shining throughout the cosmos and leading the way-

farers through the world of darkness. The invisible God becomes a glowing reality now through His stars that sparkle like
dazzling heterotopic eyes, guiding them in their heavenly quest.
Suddenly the King himself becomes visible: "He sat on a hill,
his crown lay beside him, but his head was surrounded by a
mysterious luster" (p. 145). Then they know they have penetrated another sphere of existence and have crossed another
threshold into greater timelessness and spacelessness. The King
speaks in all of his munificence: "The time is fulfilled, the ways
are opened, error is transformed into knowledge, want into
abundance. Let us march forth to the country of the child" (p.
145).

They do so and find the child "laughing," his "shining locks
fluttering about," his hands outstretched to feel the wind as it
flows by. Joy radiates from his face; his golden hair is like a
nimbus, incandescent, effulgent, inspiring humankind with hope.
It is in the child that the earthly and the spiritual fuse, that
differences are nonexistent. The child is playing with some golden
coins which he throws about; these "glittering disks" are like
so many toys—fun objects—amusing, pleasurable, no more and
no less.

The gold-lovers observe the child and their eyes are filled
with anxiety. The Master again leads them back into the cavern,
gives them the food of life to eat. Only now does shame fill their
beings, and with it consciousness awakened. They feel inner
healing taking place; the path they are to follow increased in
substance and consistency. Their faith is renewed; dignity and
purity follow them now, and so does serenity. They understand
the meaning of balance and inner harmony in their personal
and spiritual lives. The *Shekhinah* in its two aspects of Queen
and Princess is now reintegrated into the Sefiroth, as wholeness
in their soul. Just as during the Sabbath the religious Jews celebrate the *Shekhinah's* return to the Godhead, so those who have
been wanderers until now experience the plenitude of their own
individuality (ego), as well as the fullness of their being within
the collective (Self).

The King, however, does not let them rest long. He sends
"them out into all countries, to heal all madness, to enlighten
all illusion, and to disentangle all bewilderment and perplexity"
(p. 148). Their task is to search out the "sparks of light" scat-

tered throughout the world, even in the unlikeliest of places, the smallest of deeds, and the most evil of people. Such is the spirit of godliness, the sanctity of life, and the meaning of the individuation process.

Tradition and Revelation as delineated in Rabbi Nachman's "The Master of Prayer" take the reader through various levels in the religious and psychological experience, from enslavement to the material to a transcendental world that breathes and vibrates with archetypal images. The dramatis personae, revealed by the spiritual and characterological traits identified within the Sefirotic image, disclose a condition of interrelatedness when there is a balance between the various attributes; they show, too, how imbalance, dispersion, and fragmentation ensue when one element within the psychical complex takes on obsessive importance. "The Master of Prayer" leads the reader forward from a state of unconsciousness, psychologically speaking, to one of commitment, from blindness to sight, from aridity to fertility, dissociation to integration. The various spheres of experience the beleaguered wanderers know reveal the dynamics in the ego/Self axis, the increased awareness that comes to one during the unifying psychotherapeutic process—whether by means of meditation, prayer, or dream.

One of the many truly remarkable aspects of the Sefirotic concept is the interconnectedness one finds between the mysteries of the Godhead—its inner workings on a spiritual level—and the therapeutic process. Each of the ten emanations, as viewed as an archetype springing from the collective unconscious, has the power of an energy charge. Each emanation arouses not only itself but also everything else within the whole complex, either by disrupting the inner balance or paving the way for harmony. In the world of absolutes, where the Sefiroth exists in the form of a network of interrelationships, concretized frequently as a tree or human body, it may be experienced as an organic force—one and multiple—the prototype of all existence. So the reader may also experience it as the prototype of his existence, project upon it in such a way that his course is both spiritually and psychologically enlightened.

In that "The Master of Prayer" inflames the soul and compels the search for new spiritual values, new states of being and levels of consciousness, it opens the door to revelation, to the mystical experience, to insight, and causes a flow of archetypal images to stream forth that may be experienced both on a personal and on a collective level. Each is intertwined with the other; each is indelibly marked in the Book of Destiny as "white fire on black fire."

4. Yeats (1865–1939): *At the Hawk's Well*—An Unintegrated Anima Shapes a Hero's Destiny

At the Hawk's Well (1916), the last of Yeats's five plays based on incidents in the life of Cuchulain, the legendary Celtic hero, not only resurrects elements from a bygone mythical age but incorporates into it the religious and intensely stylized and controlled emotions of the Japanese Noh theater. A fusion of Western extroverted drama with its bravura and tragic discontent and the ancient aristocratic art of Japan in all its subdued, introverted, and cosmic beauty, *At the Hawk's Well* synthesizes temporality and atemporality into one deeply moving vision. A composite of mobile images, a mosaic of haunting energy patterns, the play achieves a vivid life of its own, all the more virulent and succulent, because of its containment, searing because of its impersonal and archetypal dimensions.

An initiation ritual, *At the Hawk's Well* dramatizes the predicament of the Yeatsian hero/poet who comes to the well containing the treasure hard to attain—and seeks the waters of immortality—the source of eternal inspiration. Undaunted, driven by the radiance of his own sun/fire personality, by the pulsions which lie at the heart of his instinctual being, he fights to subdue the guardian of the well: the rapacious Hawk Woman (his anima figure). Rather than dominating her, however, he becomes her votary, pursuing her in various ways and allowing this primal image to shape his destiny. *At the Hawk's Well* is poetry of the soul; rare in its own day, unique in ours.

ECTYPAL ANALYSIS

Yeats had been interested in occult sciences since his early days. He began his serious experimentations in psychical research with

George Russell (or Æ as he was called) and two other friends
with whom he founded the Dublin Hermetic Society (1885).[1]
The members probed such matters as Buddhism, Theosophy,
the fourth dimension, theurgy. The theosophical beliefs of Madame H. P. Blavatsky, the granddaughter of a Russian princess,
fascinated him for a period. She believed in the universal over-
soul into which all other souls would eventually be merged;
reincarnation was also implicit in her doctrine. Doubt, however, began infiltrating in Yeats's mind about Madame Blavatsky's integrity and her conduct during her séances. He resigned
from the Theosophical Society in 1890 and that same year joined
the Hermetic Students of the Golden Dawn, a theosophical organization which emphasized Kabbala and Western mysticism,
rather than the Eastern wisdom. Yeats studied the Christian exegesis of Hebrew occult works by Pico della Mirandola and
Eliphas Lévi. He and his newly acquired friends MacGregor
Mathers and his wife (Henri Bergson's sister), held séances at
which supernatural phenomena emerged in all of their esoteric
Christian-pagan accounterments.[2]

Psychologically speaking, Yeats was a divided human being.
It is not surprising, therefore, to learn that the creatures of his
fantasy suffer *antinomic conflict* in every domain: life/death, ego/
Self, man/God, masculine/feminine, individual/ collective, pas-
sive/ aggressive. As mystic and monist, Yeats believed that each
of these polarized forces contained the seed of its opposite: death
existed within birth and vice versa, the ego in the Self, and so
forth. The *All* coalesced in *Unity of Being* or the *Absolute*, a
state in which antithetical conflict no longer existed. During
earthly life, however, when the differentiated world predominates, Unity of Being may be glimpsed through flashes of intuitions, visions, and the like. Only when no longer in the terrestrial sphere, either before birth or after death, may *oneness* with
the universal flow of the Absolute be experienced. Yeats has
recourse to the image of the great wheel, a mandala, which moves
about eternally in circular and elliptical spheres; it contains not
only the pairs of opposites of all existence but the perpetually
recurring death-rebirth cyclical patterns.

When an individual perceives elements beyond his own
limited framework, such as exist in the mythical sphere, one can

transcend the physical dimension and glimpses Unity of Being, thus opening a world of analogies and of correspondences. He immerses himself into networks of intricate feelings, complexes of sensations, and ideations that link him (microcosm) with the collective sphere (macrocosm). For Yeats, the domain of the myth enabled him to expand his consciousness, to return to an *illo tempore*, thus bathe in the pleromatic sphere. Celtic heliolatry was perhaps most meaningful to him because of his origins, and for this reason, he returned to it time and time again in his writings.

Theatrical conventions were also in keeping with Yeats's antinomic beliefs. His concept of the mask, for example, which he so frequently used as a metaphor, could be considered a "stage face." It represented the dominant personality trait the character sought to reveal to the external world. When a negative or distraught mask is donned by a character, it indicated ominous powers coming to the fore, shadow characteristics emerging into consciousness. The mask may take on the numinous power of a spirit, as in Noh drama, endowed with both realistic and supernatural values. The mask, Yeats suggested, is a "disembodied look," a manifestation of another plane of existence; a ghost, a dead being come to life, or some mystical force enacting feelings, desires, needs; an arcane essence that has floated into the phenomenological domain. The mask is both abstract and concrete; it defines and thus limits, humanizes, thereby reduces the godlike qualities in this metaphoric creature to understandable dimension.[3]

Yeats's dramatic goal is to concretize this mysterious world, to reveal a hidden dimension on stage via the mask as well as through the poetry of the play. The dramatist took on the function of those ancient Orphic priests, more specifically the Druid poets who had inhabited Ireland during that heroic and mythic age when Celts dominated the scene. The poet's powers, like those of the Druids, expanded beyond the visible world, right into the *anima mundi*. Poets and playwrights, Yeats felt, are part of a priesthood, a secret society, as are shamans and other esoteric beings. The theater, therefore, should be looked upon as a ritual, a religious ceremony steeped in magic and mystical climes. He rejected the naturalistic bourgeois theater, the well-made play, the thesis dramas with their representational decor, flesh-and-blood characters, three-dimensional plot lines. Such theater Yeats considered peripheral, transitory, accessible to the common man and peasant, therefore, not to the restricted few. What Yeats sought was a symbolic drama, hidden, forbidding, eternally mysterious. Influenced by Maeterlinck, Villiers de L'Isle-Adam, and Mallarmé, Yeats also wanted to deal with universals, with myths, and with the poetic principle, not as an instrument for furthering rationality and a logically ordered universe, but rather by fostering dreams, fantasies, and the Otherworld. Words should take on the force of incantations and, as such, would infiltrate the heart and the mind of the listener. Nuances, suggestions, subtle sonorities, would inhabit the stage space. Speech for Yeats was not a matter of cerebral or intellectual techniques, to be mastered and used. It was a way of introducing a mystical abstract dimension to the stage play to evoke balance and inner tension, sustain duality and conflict.[4] "The theatre began in ritual, and it cannot come to its greatness again without recalling words to their ancient sovereignty."[5] Falsity, artifice, overtheatrical effects, were banished by Yeats in favor of "an asceticism of the imagination," and "an interior variety."[6]

The Yeatsian protagonist combines human and superhuman characteristics. He is, therefore, a prey to conflict, his ambitious and rapacious earthly nature being at odds with his mythical and eternal goals. His life is characterized by a series of struggles; indeed, he lives in conflict and rarely achieves a sense of fulfillment. Only during those fleeting moments, when he can transcend his personal ambition, and the increasingly intense conflict, does Unity of Being come to be known. Struggle for Yeats is on a higher plane than passivity, and though the protagonist must bear the brunt of his clashing interests, it is more admirable to spend one's life the butt of these chaotic powers within the human personality than to yield to stasis and oblivion.

The hero's tragic fate is experienced when he realizes that the universal or supernatural forces (Unity of Being) are impersonal: they remain uninvolved in his individual fate. Rather than assuage his suffering, they look upon him with "sublime indifference." The hero's earthly existence, therefore, becomes admirable only when he struggles against the odds that he faces daily on both a personal and impersonal level: an eternal conflict because it is aimed not only at the workaday world—the status quo—but at his own limitations, his own lack of dimension, his own finitude. He is defeated by the very knowledge revealed to him. He is attempting therefore the impossible; failure is the only outcome. His dignity and stature depend upon his ability to overcome his human condition through a passionately lived and superhuman deed—through the creation of a great work of art which will last, if not eternally, at least beyond its creator's present stay on earth.[7] The hero's imagination, the instrument that prods him to yearn for the impossible, is generally responsible for his tension; yet this very life-force enables him to "reconnect" with the anima mundi, thus to experience Unity of Being. "Because there is submission in a pure sorrow, we should sorrow alone over what is greater than ourselves, nor too soon admit that greatness, but all that is less than we are should stir us to some joy, for pure joy masters and impregnates; and so to world end, strength shall laugh and wisdom mourn."[8]

A dramatist must convey the above-described paroxystic emotional condition onstage: that intensely lived sequence of moments when the hero reaches a state of incandescence, of emotional and passionate intensity, and can go no further on a mortal level but must be reabsorbed and transformed. At this "supreme moment of tragic art there comes upon one that strange sensation as though the hair of one's head stood up," Yeats wrote.[9] Then the heliotropic hero rises above his individuality and gains immortality as he incorporates within himself the complex of conflicting coordinates, surrendering to the sublime vortices of joy: "for the nobleness of the arts is in the mingling of contraries, the extremity of sorrow, the extremity of joy, perfection of a personality, the perfection of its surrender; overflowing turbulent energy, and marmorean stillness; and its red rose opens at the meeting of the two beams of the cross, and at the trysting-place of moral and immortal time, and eternity."[10]

Poetic drama in Yeats's hands was to become the meeting ground of spiritual and physical antagonism: "I seek not a theatre but the theatre's anti-self," he wrote, that is, the very heart of dichotomy.[11] The world of analogies, correspondences, and symbols aided him in achieving his ends. Diametrical forces generated peace or dissention, tragedy or comedy, pain or joy. Symbols were signatures or emblems, visible or understandable expressions of the arcane and invisible spheres. They were the instruments by means of which mysteries became accessible to humankind, spiritual forces merged and converged. Symbols for Yeats were catalysts able to trigger emotions, liberate feelings, bringing contents of the unconscious into consciousness. Symbols renew, alter the "great mind and great memory" of all existence.[12] A word/symbol, may be likened to a magician's wand, a priest's censer, a shaman's effigy, a musician's sound, a poet's simile, a painter's color/form—it sweeps the uncreated into the world. "All sounds, all colours, all forms, either because of their preordained energies or because of long association, evoke indefinable and yet precise emotions, or, as I prefer to think, call down among us certain disembodied powers, whose footsteps over our hearts we call emotions; and when sound, and colour, and form are in a musical relation, a beautiful relation to one another, they become, as it were, one sound, one colour, one form, and evoke an emotion that is made out of their distinct evocations and yet is one emotion." [13]

At the Hawk's Well is endowed with mythic quality. As such it transcends linear space and time and may be simultaneously experienced in both its microcosmic and macrocosmic dimensionalities. Plot is reduced to a minimum and events move ineluctably to their dramatic conclusion, as if prodded by Otherworldly forces. Intimacy is rejected in favor of mystery; remoteness and elusiveness take the place of accessibility and tangibility.

Yeats's adoption of certain Noh techniques seemed to create the ideal vehicle to express his strange and refined ideas about drama. He, along with Arthur Waley, Edmond Dulac, and Ezra Pound, had become fascinated with Noh theatre, and although they had never seen plays performed, they studied its conventions and rituals. Thanks to Pound, who discovered the poverty-stricken Noh dancer, Ito, living in a London flat, Yeats and the other devotees of this Japanese art form were able to experience its complexities firsthand.

Yeats was fascinated with Noh theater, a controlled, disciplined and serious art form that came into being during the fourteenth century. Noh usually included a chorus of eight to ten musicians playing flutes and small drums, wearing elaborate and opulent costumes that contrast sharply with the stark and austere stage. Unlike Greek drama, where the chorus becomes involved in the action and actively addresses the characters, the Noh chorus "describes" what is occurring, "interprets" the thoughts of the main actor, even speaks for him or her at times. Decor consists usually of a single painted pine tree. Remote, elusive, and supernatural in its power, it adds its own lyricism and mystical beauty to the proceedings. The characters emerge— there are rarely more than five in a play—like mobile hieroglyphics, endowing the stage space with feelings of both reality and unreality. The stage thereby becomes a meeting place for the living and the dead, the human and the divine. Noh plays are usually divided into two parts. In the first part, the protagonist enters the stage as a human being or a reincarnation of a humble person. In the second act, he reappears not as he was in reality (either God or hero) but as his ghost, a supernatural being who must experience punishment for a violent action committed during his mortal existence. It is in the second part of the play that the incredible dance is performed, which expresses the protagonist's climactic suffering and excoriating pain. As he mimes his emotions, he poetizes his experience. The intensity of the inner struggle is spun in rhythmic stances, nuanced vocalizations, and hieratic movements—an indelible visual experience. The mask, acting in consort with bodily movements, transfixes the view, hypnotizing and luring the spectator into a more profound level of experience—incarnating, along with his subdued gyrations—the very heart of mystery. It is in the spectacle as a whole, and the dance in particular, wrote Yeats, that "we summon rhythm, balance, pattern, images that remind us of vast passions, the vagueness of past times, all the chimeras that haunt the edge of trance." [14]

At the Hawk's Well was not designed to appeal to the public. "I have invented a form of drama, distinguished, indirect, and symbolic, and have no need of mob or Press to pay its way— an aristocratic form," Yeats wrote. [15] In keeping with the secrecy

required during initiation ceremonies into occult societies, Yeats
wanted no more than fifty "enlightened" people to be present
at a performance.

ARCHETYPAL ANALYSIS

Yeats's Cuchulain cycle, which includes *At the Hawk's Well*, was
drawn from events delineated in the ancient Celtic epic *Táin Bó
Cuailnge*. Written between the fourth and the eighth centuries,
the events described took place at the outset of the Christian
era. Yeats also based his dramatic incident on Lady Gregory's
Cuchulain of Muirthemne, which was her rendition of the legendary Gaelic hero's life.

Cuchulain, like many heroic figures, was endowed with both
mortal and superhuman faculties and was also born under mysterious circumstances. His father, the sun-god Lugh, incarnated
himself into a mayfly and flew into the mouth of the beautiful
Princess Deichtine, the sister of Conchobor, the ruler of Ulster,
as she was gulping down a drink to quench her terrible thirst.
Identified with the primal element water from the very outset,
it is not surprising that shortly after his birth, Cuchulain was
described as being able to "swim like a trout." He was named
Sétanta and was endowed with incredible energy and an equally
fiery spirit. Physically strong, his ways were archaic; his attitude, crude. From the age of seven he performed great feats
with javelin throwing, and manipulated the sword with dexterity. He was taught the art of warfare by his foster father, Fergus,
and magic by the Druid Cathbad. It was Cathbad who told him
that he would have a choice in life. If he took up arms on a
certain day—and he was told the day—he would achieve fame
but his life would be a short one. To this statement, Cuchulain
retorted: "If I achieve fame I am content though I had only one
day on earth."[16]

Women adored Cuchulain for his bravery, his remarkable
beauty, and even perhaps for his violence.[17] He married Emer,
but not before proving his worth: which meant killing hundreds
of men. Cuchulain's relationship with women was complicated.
He had a roving eye and was known to have indulged in many
amorati. Some of the women who responded were not shrink-
ing violets. On the contrary, they were amazons, strong, pow-

erful, militant women, known for their prowess in battle. Aoife was one of these—a fierce warrior queen. Conlaech, the son born of their union, was brought up by his mother who keeps his father's identity secret.[18] In adhering to the oath his mother had demanded of him, the young lad went to the kingdom of Conchobor, and without revealing his name, challenged Cuchulain to battle. Unknowingly Cuchulain killed his own son. When he discovered the truth, his grief was so great that he went mad and began fighting the sea.

Yeats's protagonist is not the pagan warrior of the *Táin* but rather a deeply troubled and divided figure. His coming to drink of the well water is to be understood symbolically as a poet's effort to recapture the creative energy known to him in his youth—when inspiration seemed inexhaustible and forever replenishable. As the play opens, a climate of aridity impresses itself upon the stage proceedings. The hero/poet's struggle consists in his attempt to reconnect himself with the source of immortal life as well as with the feminine principle, both represented in the play by the water image. It is this aspect of his personality that the hero has not only neglected but has also mutilated in his pursuit of his male-oriented role as fighter.

There are three characters besides the chorus of Three Musicians in *At the Hawk's Well*: the Old Man and the Young Man (Cuchulain) wear masks; the Guardian of the Well and the Three Musicians (chorus) are made up to look as if they were wearing masks. In each case, the aura of timelessness is impressed upon the stage happenings, as if these things were forces emanating from supernal or infernal spheres. Anything can happen in this magical and mysterious environment. The only reminder of earthly reality onstage is a wall upon which a "patterned screen" has been placed. A drum, a gong, and a zither have been placed next to the screen. Two lanterns are attached to posts on either side of the stage; a chandelier is also lit, thus retaining the atmosphere of Noh as it was originally performed in the fourteenth century during daylight under the brilliant Japanese sun.

The First Musician, carrying a folded black cloth walks to the center of the stage where he stands immobile. The other Two Musicians enter and stand on either side of the acting area, then walk toward the First Musician; chanting their song, they begin unfolding the cloth slowly and ceremoniusly. They are initiating the spectators into their arcane ways. During the slowly paced ritual, a gold pattern "suggesting a hawk" becomes visible. The hawk is the play's essential symbol. A totem figure, gradually it takes on the occult power of an emanation from another plane of being. It hovers over every facet of the drama, evoking sensations of fear and awe. The Musicians have set the tempo for the activities with their chant, repeating certain words and phrases, designed to lull the audience into a state of receptivity, a trancelike mood, during which time the conscious world lowers its defenses, empowering the unconscious to gain dominion.

The Musicians, Yeats suggested, with their "sunburned faces" are to give the impression of having "wandered from village to village in some country of our dreams."[19] The Musicians unfold the black cloth, and in so doing, create an aura of mystery; as though the book of life were being opened, the web of fabulation unraveled.

> *I call to the eye of the mind*
> *A well long choked up and dry*
> *And boughs long stripped by the wind,*
> *And I call to the mind's eye*
> *Pallor of an ivory face,*
> *Its lofty dissolute air,*
> *A man climbing up to a place*
> *The salt sea wind has swept bare.*
>
> *(P. 136)*

"I call to the eye of the mind," the Musicians intone, blending cadence and rhythm into one meaningful formal expression. In referring "to the eye of the mind," Yeats is alluding to those inner truths existing within the depths of the intellect, to an arcane world that must be invoked in viable form. A soul is to be cut open; passions externalized and feelings concretized in subdued, suggestive, and mysterious emanations. The eye of the mind, referring to Siva's third eye, represents wisdom, that receptive and internal force abounding in light and spirituality that will apprehend perceptions, will prognosticate—its clairvoyance reducing past and future into the mystic's eternal present. Not only did Siva's third eye understand the antinomies of life, but it also contained them within its orbit, propelling fluid analogies to radiate throughout the cosmos in infinite opacities. Yeats's creatures also bore through matter in incisive and energetically reactive fire images, reducing everything within the visible world to ash. For Plato, Plotinus, and Augustine—and for Yeats the spiritualist—the eye allows for inner sight, and though it is "capricious" and "variable" and "cannot shape or change" its focus, it can be summoned by the mind as well as banished. During such activity, visions evolve, feelings and moods crystallize, allowing for the partial disclosures of the arcana to follow.[20]

In keeping with Noh convention, the well on the stage, symbolized "by a square blue cloth" (p. 137), is not representational. A universal mythological motif, the well may be looked upon psychologically as a containing structure, framing the vision, focusing on the play's theme. Like a telescope that points to celestial spheres, so the well extends into the terrestrial one: the earth, the feminine principle. Reminiscent of Jethro's well in front of which Moses stopped to experience feelings of spiritual completion, so Yeats's play is associated with the Druid Connla's well near Tipperary, which was known as a source of knowledge and inspiration.

Yeats's well waters may be identified with the unconscious, the very essence of being and renewal. Considered a numinous force in Goidelic times, springs and rivers were thought to assure fertility and were venerated and for this reason associated with the feminine principle.[21] Water, considered the *fons et origo* of life itself, is a paradigm of concrete mass reduced to its liquid state, or a condition of stasis transformed into a fluid one. It spells life *in potentia*. That the well is "choked up and dry" indicates that growth, germination, and abundance are no longer possible. Nourishment has ceased. An arid, sterile climate reigns. Since we may also consider the waters of immortality as an aspect of the creative principle, we may infer that inspiration has also stopped functioning, that purity of thought, insight, and motility of feeling, elements essential to the apprehension of new and vital poetic perceptions, are at a standstill. A dry and barren climate emerges. Even the stones near the well are no longer moist.

As the Musicians intone their lines in stressed metrical patterns, endowing each word with delicate yet precise shadings, we learn that a hazel tree stands above the well, its "boughs long stripped by the wind." Only the bare branches of this one fruitful tree remain. Its green, lush foliage has vanished. The wind has torn the leaves from the boughs, reinforcing the barren nature of the scene. In this mountainous region, remote, devoid of warmth, the fire of passion has long since died. Feelings have congealed. Antithetical to this vision of stasis, however, is the wind. Not merely a negative force which wrenched and stripped the tree of its foliage, it may also be considered a divine spirit (*ruach*), that rips asunder that which is no longer productive, paving the way for its transformation and eventual rebirth in the following season or lifetime. Ambiguity about the source of the wind and its focus leaves the spectator with concomitant feelings of devastation/doom and also with a sense of awe/numinosity.

The hazel tree, known for its blossoms and nuts, can also be identified with the Druid Connla's well: it represents beauty and wisdom respectively. According to the Celtic legend, it was said that nine hazelnuts grew above the well "out of which were obtained the feasts of sages." These nuts used by Druids for prognostication and incantatory rites were in time identified with the tree of science and of knowledge. Wisdom, like the nut, requires a period of time to ripen; during this span, it must be protected by a shell strong enough to prevent destruction by outer forces. Once ripe, the nut falls or is plucked from the branch, its shell is cracked and the fruit is eaten. So, too, thoughts are born and evolve in a protective climate which aids in the maturation process. Undisturbed, they take in their nourishment until such time as the burgeoning ideas are encapsulated into the creative work. The same may be said for the ego as it takes root and develops within the individual. In Yeats's play, the hazelnuts had once fallen into the well causing its water to then bubble up with inspiration. Such activity has ceased.

The chalk whiteness of the mask, as in the "Pallor of an ivory face" (p. 136), ushers audiences into a colorless and bloodless domain. Life has been withdrawn, feelings congealed, a "marmorean stillness" pervades.[22] The "ivory face" may also refer to the masks worn by the protagonists. Frequently carved from ivory, they maintain their deathlike glazed glances for all eternity and appear onstage as disembodied faces, eerie reminders of earlier existences. All is bleak and gray in this sun-less realm, the whiteness and purity of the unlived and unre-deemed have overtaken. Nature invites the surreal to verge and converge with the real.

"Its lofty dissolute air" (p. 136) emphasizes the dichoto-mies that are to be dramatized. The juxtaposition of "lofty" with "dissolute" underscores the spiritual clime in this moun-tain scene: spirit as symbolized in the wind, which purifies the dross and decayed matter by scattering and blowing it away. The "dissolute" underscores the anthropoid nature of these characters who will appear on the stage: their obsession with earthly and elemental forces. Yeats pointed out in the cosmolog-ical chart he made for *A Vision*, that *At the Hawk's Well* re-volved around the first phase of the great wheel which he iden-tified with earth, the dark of the moon. The height and depth of the visual image (lofty/dissolute) evoke a mental association of arrogance and spiritual and moral decay. The symbols of the tree, the hazelnuts, the well, and the mountain upon which the action takes place are differentiated, in that they are to be ex-perienced on the metaphysical level, as universals, aspects of the great memory of *anima mundi*—they are forces that work their wonders throughout the cosmos.[23]

The spell has been cast; emotions stirred; the divine essence has made its presence known, Yeats suggests. As elements begin to emerge from their somnolence, forces stir and crystallize, beings animate. The Musicians pursue their invocations in language reminiscent of religious ritual: poised and potent, they link spa-tiality to a timeless dimension, holding each in delicate bal-ance—a prelude to the parapsychological experience yet to come.

> *A man climbing up to a place*
> *The salt sea wind has swept bare.*
>
> (P. 136)

Heights and depths are called into play in this cosmic vi-sion; while the parallelism between air and sea, images in states of perpetual transformation (air condensing into liquid, then evaporating, and so forth) and thus of extreme motility, gener-ate tension. Salt has particular significance in Hebrew and Ara-bic tradition; it seals a bond of friendship, indicates incorrupti-bility of intent. For the Japanese, salt is used in ritual purification ceremonies; it is also placed in front of homes to rid the area of impurities. In *At the Hawk's Well*, the mountaintop is cleared of all putrid elements and, therefore, growth and gestation have been banished. Sterility prevails. During such periods, when a tabula rasa is experienced, it invites mystery. As such, the alchemists, and Yeats was familiar with their ideations, considered salt a mediating power between the four elements of earth (visible, solid), air (gaseous, occult), fire (subtle matter), water (liquid, visible).[24] That salty spray swept onto the mountaintop from the ocean floor, represents both a cleansing and a restoring process: old ways were removed, but the quintessence of unknown thoughts and crystal clarities was coming into being.

The Musicians chant anew, their formalized verse accompanying a further unfolding of the cloth of life reveals the "gold pattern suggesting a hawk." This image underscores parallel associations between the sacrificial agony experienced by Prometheus, as an eagle tore at his liver nightly, and the celestial spirit Yeats introduces into his drama. A totem personality, the hawk is a transpersonal force which takes on the might of a theriomorphic deity, dominating the stage when it sees fit, withdrawing when the personality traits with which it is associated no longer serve a purpose. A frightening omen, however, this rapacious, aggressive bird is a feminine symbol in Yeats's play. Although associated with Uranian climes, since it ascends to celestial spheres and is masculine-oriented in its warlike, fearless, and avid encounters; the hawk is also an avatar of the mother goddess, a *vagina dentata* ready to destroy and mutilate those who defy her rule. Here, too, however, the symbol of the hawk is ambiguous. When the feminine principle is repressed and rejected, it emerges in its most dangerous and wrathful aspects—its talons ready to ravish. When understood and accepted, and allowed to participate in the culture or the psyche as a whole, it offers its most caring and nurturing side.

Since suffering and death are the realities of life, the Musicians question the reason for mortal existence. They describe the Old Man as he takes his place at the well. For fifty years he has remained in this desolate spot, waiting for the waters of life to bubble up from the well. In vain he has sought to transcend his mortal condition, but to do so is to negate the very essence of life which is based on change and the cycle of death and rebirth, whereby the living become the dead who in turn nourish the new life yet to come. Nevertheless, and implicit in the heroic struggle, is the individual's desire to counter nature's perpetual flux, to arrest what must alter, and fuse what must shatter. Every mother, the Musicians proclaim, seeks longevity for her child, the "speckled shin," as Yeats writes, implying a lengthy earthly stay leads to a conventional existence, with marriage, childbearing and spirituality as a guiding force. The Old Man, we learn, has lived his life according to the rules, never varying from traditional standards and routines, satisfying society's dictates as he passively pursues his obligations. Excitement, passion, the lure of the intangible and flecting, are unknown to him. Still he seeks to drink the waters of immortality. Each time the waters have risen in the well and there has been the possibility of his drinking them, he has been asleep. When awake, the waters have vanished, choked, blocked by some undefinable force. In sleep all semblance of thought, all will, have vanished. No connection exists, therefore, between the subliminal/feminine world (in sleep) and the rational/masculine sphere (awake). Personality characteristics are similarly jumbled and chaotic as values disintegrate in a blocked, pulverized environment.

The young woman who is the Guardian of the Well has also taken her place. Draped in black, she crouches on a stone near the well, injecting a somber note into the already macabre atmosphere. She remains immobile as if in a trance or the deepest of sleeps. The task of guarding a treasure such as the Golden Fleece, for example, in ancient myths, was usually given to a dragon, monster, snake, or genie of some sort. These hideous beings had but one function, to keep the treasure inviolate and to maintain the sanctity of the surroundings. Only the initiated were allowed to view the treasure. Hiddenness and inaccessibility increased their power and impact upon the imagination. In legends, heroes must destroy the hideous forces in charge of guarding these hierophanies. Psychologically, unless the male/hero annihilates these dragons and snakes (in Yeats's play the hawk) identified with the Earth Mother, he cannot hope to experience ego-consciousness. Such battles have been fought by Saint Patrick, Saint George, Saint Michael, Saint Sylvester, to mention but a few, for the same psychological reason. The struggle to destroy these *vagina dentata* types is the individual's way of

disentangling himself from the tentacles of the devouring mother.
Until such a time as the Guardian of the Well is possessed by
the hawk aspect of her personality, she must remain motionless.
Only when imbued with this transpersonal feminine force is she
energized, thereby bringing to life her hostile, aggressive nature.

The Musicians have now retreated to the wall at the back
of the stage. There they take up their instruments, the gong,
drum, and zither, and continue their incantatory chant:

> *The boughs of the hazel shake*
> *The sun goes down in the west.*
>   *(P. 137)*

Rather than crying out the heightening feelings of terror, Yeats
has recourse to the Noh technique once again: a shaking of the
branch indicates a quivering of the heart; trembling gives rise to
profound anguish and unrevealed sorrow. The subtle use of the
image is more potent here in its ushering of the sorrowful mood
to come. That the sun has withdrawn to the west indicates the
emergence of the moon world, the unconscious, where imagination and fantasy emerge full-blown. It is a world of somber
tonalities; a sterile, ominous wasteland.

Juxtaposed against the still and austere atmosphere of this
isolated area, is the beating heart—the human being who has
penetrated the scene—revealing emotions of pain and sorrow;
also bearing out the idea introduced with the quivering branch
of the hazel tree.

> *The heart would be always awake,*
> *The heart would turn to its rest.*
>   *(P. 137)*

Now that the sun has dimmed and the moon gains strength, the
intuitive domain acquires dimensionality. For the Easterner, the
heart is the organ of divine intelligence and perception. Brah-
man inhabits the heart. This vital organ, the center of the circulatory system, where the double movement of systole and
diastole takes root, is a paradigm for a cosmic force—the in-
haling and exhaling of the universe as a whole. The word *cridhe*
in Celtic means heart and is also identified with center, indicating the focus and locus of being. As the organ of love, affection,
and relatedness, it works as a counterpoise to the previous sen-

sations of iciness, austerity, immobility in this alienated environment.

Like sequences of atonal threnodies, the First Musician adds his comments, fostering the sinister side of this mountaintop. As night descends, as the unconscious takes over, so the dream world allows the floodwaters of instinct to express their needs: the *prima materia* rises up, inchoate.

> *The mountain-side grows dark*
> *The withered leaves of the hazel*
> *Half choke the dry bed of the well;*
> *The guardian of the well is sitting*
> *Upon the old grey stone at its side.*
> *(P. 137)*

Stone, mounds, tumuli, cairns, used as burial places in megalithic times, rise out of the Sligo countryside, lonely vestiges recalling ancient ceremonies in honor of the dead. Above the tombs, three gray stones arranged in a specific order and decorated with cryptic symbols and signs, were usually set in specific arrangements. So the smooth gray stone may also be viewed: its matt surfaces giving the impression of thirsting for water. The ascensional symbolism identified with the mountains or mounds, triggers a sense of wistfulness for the spiritual domain, an urgent need to reach up to some higher sacred force. Mountains, as we have seen in previous chapters, are areas where theophanies have occurred. Isolated, conducive to meditation, it is here that Yeats has placed his characters to magnify their inner turmoil—on lonely slopes, remote, distant, detached from the workaday world.

That the Guardian of the Well is crouched on the "old grey stone" adds an eerie, half-magical quality to the surroundings. Stone, representing durability, strength, as well as enduring and staying power, is considered by the Hebrews, Muslims, and Christians to have been heaven-sent. As such, it has been looked upon with regard to religious edifices, as a kind of cornerstone (Beth-El, Saint Peter's, the black stone in the Kaaba). For the Celts, menhirs and dolmens (similar to tripods with capstones) were used to form burial chambers which are still visible in County Sligo where Yeats spent so many years. These stones, believed to have been used in Druidical ceremonies, contained a secret doctrine which was carried on by word of mouth. At times, stones were known to become sonorous, as was the case with the Lia Fail (the stone of destiny) in Ireland, a talisman for the Tuatha De Danann, the race of superhuman conquerors who moved into and took over Ireland. When a prince in those early times was to assume his governmental post, it was said that the stone sounded. In the *Táin*, however, it is noted that when Cuchulain put his foot on a sacred stone, it remained mute, indicating that he would never be king. Angered by the outcome, he smashed the stone. It is understandable that Yeats would use the stone as a hierophany, ushering in a religious flavor to the work.

Although immovable and silent in *At the Hawk's Well*, stones are active forces, paradoxically, spokesmen for another realm, a subliminal, dark, and fearsome world where dry, parched, "withered leaves," provoke "choking" sensations. The Guardian of the Well, we learn, is "worn out from raking its dry bed,/ Worn out from gathering up the leaves" (p. 137). Hopelessness prevails, fatigue, decomposition, the alchemist's *putrefactio* condition, when the seeds of decay work their wonders.

> *Her heavy eyes*
> *Know nothing, or but look upon stone.*
> *The wind that blows out of the sea*
> *Turns over the heaped-up leaves at her side;*
> *They rustle and diminish.*
>
> *(P. 137)*

Wind, identified with spirit, is a generative force in this image, aiming the spray of the stormy seas in the direction of the sterile mountaintop. Within this gas (wind) and liquid (sea spray), invisible to the naked eye, are nutrients of all kinds. These aid in the blending process which must come to pass for the initiation ritual—the play—to come into being. It is from the sea, then, that living creatures and particles of life will renew the dormant and catalyze the stationary. A mysterious universe is coming to life beneath the wave; informal and preformal elements are going to erupt onto the stage space, spreading growth as well as disquietude, stability as well as uncertainty and indecision. It was by the sea, let us recall, that the race of the gods of Dana, those primordial people, came to Ireland, those superhuman conquerors who brought forth Celtic culture. Dana (or Danu), the Earth Mother and chief goddess of the Tuatha De Danann, incarnating fertility, spread her riches onto this wind-swept, masculinely oriented land. So Cuchulain crossed these seas and made his way to this mountain.

The wind pursues its course regenerating and renewing what is stilled and lifeless. The Druids looked upon the wind as a sign of spiritual power: it was used in magical ceremonies to direct and control extraterrestrial forces; to drive away enemy ships from the Irish coastline or to attract them and their booty to their shores. This Druidic wind, as it was called, was recognizable because it blew into the sails, not away from them; it could be captured and directed through incantations and spells. The wind in *At the Hawk's Well* serves a similar purpose. It paves the way for the arrival of Cuchulain, and it also becomes the prelude to a magic ritual.

The wind turning the dead leaves over and over, scatters them, forcing them to "rustle." The Musicians describe the setting in muted arcane tones. As one pile "diminishes" in size, indicating a transformation is about to take place, another grows larger. Suddenly all is quiet; occult forces encapsulate the stage. The Second Musician speaks of his fear of unknown beings that may take over, changing conditions, causing chaos and cataclysm. Mist and fog in increasing density cover the mountaintop as it is rocked by a tormenting and ominous wind, which terrifies instead of comforts the protagonists. The Guardian of the Well sinks ever more deeply into her slumber, oblivious to the howling wind that has now taken over the area.

> "For the wind, the salt wind, the sea wind,
> Is beating a cloud through the skies
> I would wander always like the wind."
> (P. 138)

Turmoil, not torpor, prevails in convoluted and convulsive force. Reminiscent of the alchemist's *aqua permanens* which infiltrates the cosmos, so here, too, liquids, gases, and solids interact. The psychological picture has also changed; ego now flows into the Self, the individual into the collective. Movement rather than stasis is now encountered.

The First Musician speaks of the Old Man who has been watching the well for fifty years, observing it endlessly, relentlessly. "Doubled up with age," similar to the "old thorn-trees" (p. 138), he pursues his painful quest. Like the individual who spends his time planning, hoping, and yearning to find some secure answer to life's abounding mysteries, so the Old Man waits for the waters of immortality to appear. Yet, as we have learned, each time they bubble, he sleeps. That he is compared to a thorn tree in the above quote, symbolizes the excoriating obstacles which beset his path, preventing the completion of his quest. A dragon or serpent—a hawk—hinders the fulfillment of his dream. His patience has been useless; his needs have not been met. Yet, he walks among the jagged rocks, reminiscent of painful moments during a life experience, which dig deep into his flesh like a crown of thorns. The Old Man walks with difficulty as he attempts to reach his destination. Everything about him is ancient, gray, and impersonal, as though a witness to the very death/growth process. Unlike the pater familias of the Romans, whose strength and power aroused feelings of respect and awe, we are introduced to a *senex* figure in all its negativity; depressed, senescent, sterile, unimaginative, living only in the rational sphere, severed from his unconscious and from the waters of life. Unwilling to accept human limitations, he cannot bear the stress or strain required to transcend his condition.

The Old Man stands immobile with his head bowed. He raises it, however, when he hears a drum roll, crouches, then moves about, perhaps in sharp, jagged, staccatolike gestures, as if he were assuming the personality and stance of a marionette. Puppets, known since earliest times, may be considered vessels for heavenly spirits, ghosts, gods, or demons of all types. Spreading their ambiguities onto the stage happenings, these impersonal forces were endowed with human characteristics, accentuating one or two traits rather than a complex of opposites. Puppets assumed even greater stature in the Japanese *bunraku* which, after the nineteenth century, used half life-size dolls manipulated by three people usually dressed in black and wearing masks. Regarded as representatives of some outer worldly force, these archetypal figures lent a new and startling dimension to drama. Two worlds faced each other on the prosecenium, human and inhuman, each playing out its real and unreal struggle, their mortal and immortal battle.

The Old Man, similar to the passive *bunraku* puppet, is also an intermediary figure, for the poet and the atemporal forces. Controlled, automatonlike, he gestures his way about as he begins gathering sticks and leaves to light a fire. He is not merely a passive pawn. He will become an active force; use the elements about him to his advantage, he believes—heating up the flames of desire. Not really, however, since he is manipulated and manipulates; each force onstage becomes the pawn of the other, acts and reacts to the next. The Old Man is the prototype of those who seek to change conditions and who are duped into believing that the will alone can achieve its goal.

The Old Man kindles the ceremonial fire, in accordance with alchemical ritual. Fire, symbolizing a stirring of the sensate world, engenders conflict, emotion, and change. Without combustion, which occurs with fire, sparks cannot alter darkness and turn it into light, inertia into movement. The ceremonial or alchemical fire is a necessity if the transformatory process is to pursue its course: if passion, rage, sexual love, are to ignite and fight the cold, wind, salt, and spray. The lethargy implicit in the disconnected forces onstage, until now catalyzed by the wind, will be heated via flame. In Shinto ritual, fire represents renewal and is a part of the New Year's celebrations. In Celtic lore the fire of Bel, designed to protect animals from epidemics, was lit by the Druids. Saint Patrick later altered the meaning of this ritual to indicate Christianity's victory over paganism. As the Old Man gathers the leaves, "shivering with cold" as well as with fear and anticipation, he is preparing the stage for blackness to be devoured by light, immobility with activity. The rational sphere will fight the unconscious, diurnal and nocturnal will be at odds.[25]

The Old Man's fire may be linked to the prototypal flame at Uisnech, Ireland's midpoint: representing the hearth or fire altar, the germ of all flamboyant images. We are now at the heart of the transformative ritual: the Old Man's memories are activated; the past is renewed and becomes a segment of the present reality. As such vanished times are reborn, usable once again, able to pave the way for still another life. According to Druidic ritual, the first fire of the year must be kindled with a "fire-drill" which is the instrument used by the Old Man; salt must also be included in the ceremony. The Musicians describe the process:

> *"O wind, O salt wind, O sea wind!"*
> *Cries the heart, "it is time to sleep*
> *Why wander and nothing to find?*
> *Better grow old and sleep."*
>
> *(P. 138)*

The Musicians speak to the elements, personifying and activating them. In concert they encourage the Old Man to cease
his wanderings, his search for the impossible ideal. To pursue
his thankless task is to allow chaos and turbulence to prevail in
a nomadic psyche. He should yield to the sleep of eternity, to
stasis, rather than actuating conflict implicit in earthly existence. Instead of accepting the advice, the Old Man speaks to
the Guardian of the Well, who, like the Cumaean sibyl or the
Delphic oracle, remains silent, lips sealed, immovable like the
gray boulders among which she crouches. Immersed in her unconscious realm, she knows only an undifferentiated world—
timelessness of cosmic life. There is no common denominator
between her and the Old Man, which makes his request to her
even more pitiful. He addresses a vacant spirit:

> *Why don't you speak to me? Why don't you say:*
> *"Are you not weary gathering those sticks?*
> *Are not your fingers cold?" You have not one word,*
> *While yesterday you spoke three times. You said:*
> *"The well is full of hazel leaves." You said:*
> *"The wind is from the west." And after that:*
> *"If there is rain it's likely there'll be mud."*
> *To-day you are as stupid as a fish,*
> *No, worse, worse, being less lively and as dumb.*
>
> *(P. 138)*

The juxtaposition of "yesterday" and "today" in this mon-
ologue serves to underscore the antithesis existing between es-
chatological and cyclical time, a personal and collective past,
mortal and mythical dimensions, sacred and profane moments.
The Old Man recalls his youth, when life seemed full, filled with
inspiration and hope. Enlightenment, he believed, was merely
for the asking: after the hazel tree was in flower the nuts would
ripen and they could be plucked with ease; the waters of eternal

life would always be there to drink. The inevitability of death is rarely understood by the young. Only as age takes hold does the fact of one's own mortality become real; it is no longer a vague abstract intimation, but a certainty, a concrete actuality. The wind from the west indicates the coming of sunset, the onset of the dark vision. "Mud," representing the *prima materia* is a blend of earth (*adama* in Hebrew) and water, the substance out of which man was formed. Infused with *ruach* (spirit), God endowed man with soul. So as the Old Man lights the fire, the elements are present for the creation ceremony, the birth of the new man—a *renovatio*.

The Old Man is discontented. He calls the Guardian of the Well "stupid as a fish," again using a provocative antithetical expression. Fish, so important in legends in general and in Celtic mythology in particular, are identified with knowledge: the salmon ate the hazelnuts that fell into the Druid Connla's well and thus were associated with wisdom.[26] Fish are numinous in that they represent potential life and were, therefore, symbols for the divine: Christ, for example, is identified with the fish— the anagram for the Greek word for fish, *ichthys*, as we have seen in a previous chapter, means *Jesus Kristus Theou Uios Soter* (Jesus Christ Son of God, Savior). Since fish swim in watery depths, so thoughts remain buried within subliminal areas until they surface, then identified, understood, and externalized by the conscious personality.

That the Old Man calls her "stupid as a fish" indicates his inability to penetrate her sphere of being; he is cut off from the subliminal, elemental world and cannot communicate with the Guardian of the Well. She lives in the unconscious world and he in the conscious one. Since he is unable to connect with her, he hastily concludes, that she is inferior: two dimensions at odds with each other, each centered upon its own struggle and needs.

Although motionless and uncommunicative as is all matter for the nonmystic, the moment the seer/poet glimpses it, he peers into its depths, and what appears "stupid" to the insensitive eye, yields its multiple meanings to the perceptive one. In the Kabbala, which Yeats had studied, divine sparks reside in dross and must be picked out, gathered, sought for by individuals, then returned to the higher spheres from which they originated.

The visible world, therefore, may be considered a veil, a wall, a mask for a hidden domain—a deceptive screen behind which a treasure is hidden away. When the Old Man says:

> *Your eyes are dazed and heavy. If the Sidhe*
> *Must have a guardian to clean out the well*
> *And drive the cattle off, they might choose somebody*
> *That can be pleasant and companionable.*
>
> (P. 138)

He misunderstands the function of the Guardian of the Well and rather than experiencing the cosmic dimension of the mystic, he lives incarcerated in his paltry domain. The Sidhe whom he mentions, were a "highly cultured" nation of warriors and poets who made their home in the raths (fairy mounds), the most famous being the New Grange on the Boyne. They were known for their blue eyes, pale faces, and long curly yellow hair.[27] Identified in time with fairies and supernatural beings, they were said to inhabit a region beyond the known world— that Otherworld existing outside of the space/time continuum, located in the west and in the north—far out in the seas. An enchanted area which did not know death, sin, or illness, it was looked upon as a utopia, a paradise. Its dwellers remained forever young and beautiful. The goal of the Sidhe folk was to enchant mortals, to numb and benumb them, lulling them into a state of inactivity. Their music—some were poets and singers—evoke the deepest sensations, allowing contact to be made between the phenomenological world and the secret source of life. When strange sounds and tonalities were heard by mortals, emanating from unexpected spheres, it was thought that the Sidhe were at work in the Otherworld and were heralding their coming.

When the Old Man remonstrates that the Sidhe sent such a "stupid" person to guard the well, he misunderstands the role of these archetypal beings, these feminine principles. Aside from not being in touch with his anima, as projected in these archetypal forces around him, he is also working at odds with this autonomous force within him. He again questions the Guardian of the Well and wonders why she wears that "glassy" look?

> *Why do you stare like that?*
> *You had that glassy look about the eyes*

> *Last time it happened. Do you know anything?*
> *It is enough to drive an old man crazy.*
>
> (P. *139*)

Eyes are the vehicles of perception, knowledge, illumination, although in apposition to the infinite here, are antithetical to the Old Man's view. He understands nothing of their power. Her eyes, like the sun and moon for the ancient Egyptian, fire and water for the alchemist, look out into an infinite expanse. These eyes, transfixed as they now seem, we will later learn, have the power to destroy any mortal who gazes within their "unmoistened" depths. So strong is the light they contain, so powerful is their divine force, that they can dissolve and crush any object. The human eye cannot perform such deeds alone. Only when a divine or extraterrestrial spirit is in them—the Sidhe in this case—can they burn and sear. The Guardian of the Well is possessed: her eyes glow, shine, intensify; they vibrate with light, blinding all that peer into their "moistless" depths. An aspect of the anima mundi lies within the eyes of the Guardian of the Well. Like the Self, as it surrounds and incorporates the ego, so this Sidhe force will destroy everything that is subjective, personal, in the Guardian of the Well. She is a medium and thus an agent of the collective being for a transpersonal will. She dwells in a remote, intangible fourth dimension. Unable to act upon her own, she experiences her solitude without remorse or pain in a detached, soulless state. The Old Man's complaints, therefore, remain unheard. Alienated from the world of the living, she responds only to those supernal forces that emanate from extratemporal climes.

A Young Man from the audience moves onto the stage, as in Kabuki theater, thereby encouraging communication between actor and spectator. We learn that it is Cuchulain, the Celtic hero whose passionate existence, warlike games, and amorous nature have already made him famous. He has lived fully and powerfully and now seeks the immortal waters. He admits to being in a hurry, "youth is not more patient than old age"; he has had a long journey, climbing to the mountaintop for "half a day," thereby reintroducing the idea of time on both a temporal and a mythical plane. Identified with the sun, his costume glitters with golden accouterments of all types. His

presence announces a kind of theophany; it is as disruptive as a
vision. He blazes with activity, warms the cold climes, triggers
the seemingly inactive moon-dominated sphere. Antithetical
factors glare; sun and moon vying for dominion, gold and silver, light and darkness, youth and old age.

Cuchulain looks at the Old Man, the shadow aspect of his
own being: his pedestrian, conventional characteristics which
never vibrate or shudder with passion or poetry. Cuchulain filled
with the fiery blood of his father, the sun-god Lugh, is not one
to meditate or indwell. He informs the Old Man of his intention
to drink the waters of immortality, to capture eternal inspiration. He brags about his earthly adventures, his prowess and
fame. The Old Man has never heard of him. "What mischief
brings you hither?" (p. 139), he questions. He considers this
impetuous fiery young man "crazy," wasting his time in fruitless
activity, such as "shedding of men's blood," or loving women:
both transient occupations. Cuchulain, whose very being seems
to pulsate with life, tells the Old Man how, after drinking until
dawn,

> I rose from table, found a boat, spread sail,
> And with a lucky wind under the sail
> Crossed waves that have seemed charmed, and found this
>   shore.
>
> (P. 139)

Cuchulain's allusion to wine indicates that he is following
the proddings of his instinctual, and not his rational, sphere.
His unconscious has taken precedence. The ship that carried
him across the waves symbolizes the protective force that guided
him safely over the watery depths of his subliminal realm. Another factor is also involved in his journey: it is the Druidic
wind, that breath of the spirit which forces its way into the
poet's fantasy world, compelling him to seek out new experiences.

A "lucky" wind as Cuchulain calls it, steered him into unknown ways, unconquered lands, offering the excitement a hero
needs. Although Cuchulain was still creating his essence, still
forming his personality, he is at a crossroads in his own life. The
activity and aggressivity of adolescence had diminished. A more
reflective period is in the offing, when a personality must seek

deeper territories as it molds its way. Until now, he said, his existence was "charmed." He never reflected or evaluated: he was all instinct, acting and reacting. His life, should he pursue the same course, would be lived in a symmetrical pattern; it would become as routine and as corrosive as the Old Man's. To transcend his limitations, to discover his ground-bed, was unconsciously the reason why Cuchulain has come to this barren land, to seek the waters of immortality—hoping to renew inspiration and revitalize perceptions.

Cuchulain, like many other heroes, was not known for his intelligence. He challenges and taunts, brags of his exploits, flaunts his accomplishments not only verbally and in gesture but also in the gold of his armor and jewels. The ancient Celts loved to bedeck themselves particularly after victory. Cuchulain was no exception. The Old Man remarked:

> *If I may judge by the gold*
> *On head and feet and glittering in your coat,*
> *You are not of those who hate the living world.*
> *(P. 139)*

Cuchulain grows impatient. Libido is forever flowing out of him in contrast to the inactive Old Man who fits in well with the bleak landscape. His tongue is "rough" Cuchulain says of the Old Man, and parallels this "barbarous" spot. Where, he asks, are the well, the tree bearing hazelnuts the solitary girl that lives among "grey boulders."? Cuchulain has envisioned a beautiful maiden, antipodal to the unfolding reality. As an anima figure, he sees a sylphlike woman, tender, gentle, understanding, easily conquerable by the brash hero. As for the waters of immortality, surely they were located in a paradisial sphere. Cuchulain's utopian vision may be likened to the domain of the Sidhe, certainly not to this windswept mountain peak.

When the Old Man points out the "grey boulders," the "solitary girl," the "stripped hazels," in the dismal, misty, windswept, and darkened clime, Cuchulain is taken aback. He does not understand. What does the Old Man mean? "Can you see nothing yonder?" the Old Man questions. The paradise Cuchulain has imagined with crystal-clear waters, green fields, trees, flowers, and the melodious harmonies of talking rocks and animals is nowhere to be seen in this barren place. Youth is prone to folly the Old Man declares. Does he believe that simply by reaching the well he will immediately be able to drink the waters?

Water in this case represents esoteric knowledge for the mystic. Unlike cerebral thought or factual intelligence, the deepest spheres cannot be acquired by asking. Wisdom in the mystical sense of the word is tantamount to revelation. It is not required; it is a gift and one that is given only to those who have proved they are worthy to receive it by going through protracted periods of initiation. Cuchulain is incomplete, only the active or physical side of his life has concerned him: the conquest of the inner world still has to be undergone. His titanic nature has to be transformed into a more spiritual force.

The Old Man urges Cuchulain to retreat, to leave the mountain, to return to his former existence. It is only after he agrees to share the waters of immortality when they rise in the well that the Old Man accepts his presence and warns Cuchulain not to be benumbed by the Sidhe who will attempt to lure him away from achieving his goal. The Women of the Sidhe are "Fishers of men," who, like the Greek sirens, lure their prey away, distracting, captivating, and dominating them. Unlike the sirens, those monstrous beings with heads and breasts of women but bodies of fish, never able to satisfy a man, so the Hawk Woman, an avatar of the Sidhe, will also fascinate, hypnotize, and deaden her victims. Hetaira types, the Women of the Sidhe, understand better than anyone else how to captivate, entice, and turn the conquering male into a passive and listless being. Iconographically, this type has been featured as a devouring vampire woman; born of human desire, she is a projection of man's unsatisfying relationship with women. Forever desirous, he yearns for the impossible.

Cuchulain is confident. He is different, he muses, strong, powerful, invulnerable. He will remain vigilant and not be lulled into a state of oblivion. He tells the Old Man that he will "pierce" his foot and that the pain will keep him awake. The foot, representing one's relationship to the earth, to the workaday world, is then considered a steadying force. It also symbolizes the phallus. To hurt it would indicate Cuchulain's willingness to sacrifice his instinctual nature for the time being—foreshadowing a change in personality—while strengthening his spiritual outlook.

Suddenly the Guardian of the Well shrieks like a hawk.

When Cuchulain refers to the sound made by "that bird," the Old Man counters, "There is no bird." Although it "sounded like the sudden cry of a hawk," Cuchulain realizes that "there's no wind in sight" (p. 141). The atmosphere reverberates with the piercing cry, which ushers in a mood of terror, even startling the elements into activity. Cuchulain remembers that as he was climbing the mountain he had seen a strange "great grey hawk" which "swept down out of the sky" (p. 141). Although he thought he knew every kind of hawk, he had never seen one like this before:

> *It flew*
> *As though it would have torn me with its beak,*
> *Or blinded me, smiting with that great wing.*
> *I had to draw my sword to drive it off,*
> *And after that it flew from rock to rock.*
> *I pelted it with stones, a good half-hour,*
> *And just before I had turned the big rock there*
> *And seen this place, it seemed to vanish away.*
>
> (P. 141)

Cuchulain senses his own vulnerability as he observes the hawk flying in and out of the heavens, circling, ready to destroy him at a moments notice, to pluck out his eyes—masterful in its strength and in the pursuit of its ineluctable goal.

Provoking, taunting, aggressive, powerful in its warlike grandeur, the hawk is the herald of Cuchulain's defeat. A theriomorphic symbol, the hawk represents those contents within Cuchulain's unconscious that have not yet been humanized. Existing at a level beyond human understanding, they are divided between the daemonically superhuman and the bestially subhuman. Since the hawk is identified with soaring high in the sky, intellect and gnosis are usually associated with this bird. Its power to mutilate, crush, pulverize, and dismember is implicit in its downward plunge to earth after its prey. It is this very spirit of rapacity (also inhabiting Cuchulain) that has now entered the Guardian of the Well, causing her to shriek.

Psychologically, the hawk is Cuchulain's anima: it is his soul, in its sinister, fearful, and destructive aspects. The Old Man even says that the hawk is not really a bird but a transpersonal force, a feminine deity, an aspect of the Sidhe.

The Woman of the Sidhe herself,
The mountain witch, the unappeasable shadow.
She is always flitting upon this mountain-side,
To allure or to destroy. When she has shown
Herself to the fierce women of the hills
Under that shape they offer sacrifice
And arm for battle.

(P. 141)

Rather than the beautiful girl of Cuchulain's dreams, the hawk personality which entered the Guardian of the Well is defined as a "mountain witch," a female dragon whose lust for flesh is unappeasable. The witch is an archetypal figure, a negative avatar of the mother goddess. In Christian civilization, the dark and light aspects of the psyche are always at odds; the Virgin Mary representing the celestial, benevolent, and redeeming aspects of the anima; the witch, its counterpart.[28] Owing to the extreme polarities involved, a split occurs within the psyche of the person projecting on the Christian myth: Satan is the black element within the universe; Christ, the all light. The greater the role Mary plays in the individual's personal life, the more powerful and frightening will the opposite aspect become. Since the prevailing conscious attitude rejects the negative principle rather than assimilating it within the psyche, evaluating its function relevant to the wholeness of the personality, this so-called negative evil force—the Jungian shadow—will increase its dominion making the psyche more and more vulnerable.[29] Only when consciousness comes into being could Cuchulain or the Old Man fight off the witch personality by absorbing it into themselves, accepting it and transforming it into a life-giving force.

Having taken the form of the Hawk Woman, an avatar of the Women of the Sidhe (of the Earth Mother), those ancient fertility goddesses who lull their victims into a state of sublime rapture, the Guardian of the Well attempts to gain a stranglehold over Cuchulain's conscious mind. By arrogating to herself his every thought, feeling, and sensation through her sensual powers, she will attempt to transform him into a will-less being, a follower rather than a leader. Reminiscent of Goya's fearful witches, she is a redoubtable and heinous force, injecting her victim with benumbing and bedazzling fantasies. Still despite her negative attributes, this anima figure represents positive features: the instinctual and undisciplined activity she fosters within the unconscious, if aided by the rational sphere, could be transformed into new and ordered patterns of behavior, paving the way for a *renovatio* condition. Thus the individual's understanding of subliminal forces can increase his powers over the creative principle. Pacts with sorceresses and witches, with devils as well, have often been man's way of attempting to solve the anima problem.

The Old Man again warns Cuchulain to leave while he is still unharmed. Once he peers into the eyes of the Hawk Woman he will be cursed. Never will he know the love of woman again and be able to keep it, nor will he be free to live as before. A premonitory image emerges:

> *Never to win a woman's love and keep it;*
> *Or always to mix hatred in the love;*
> *Or it may be that she will kill your children,*
> *That you will find them, their throats torn and bloody,*
> *Or you will be so maddened that you will kill them*
> *With your own hand.*
>
> (P. 141)

Cuchulain, unwise, unknowing, unyielding, dominated by his own overinflated ego, filled with a sense of masculine power and achievement, does not listen. Deploring the Old Man's lack of confidence and limited vision, he tells him: "You seem as dried up as the leaves and sticks" in this barren, windswept spot. Tired of life, the Old Man suffers from decrepitude and can no longer understand the vigor and vastness of life.

Suddenly the Guardian of the Well emits another cry, ominously piercing the stilled atmosphere. Cuchulain is unaware that each time the Guardian of the Well yields to her hawk instinct, she is possessed by an outer-worldly force: a demon, a spirit that lives and breathes through her. The hawk, Cuchulain's totem figure during his heroic years, had always been his protector and guide. As such, he owed an obligation to this animal. The totem is a guardian spirit or tutelary power which belongs to an individual: it is through the totem that one enters into a relationship with one's animal state—the instinctual world. In Cuchulain's case, it represents life energy. When identifying with a specific personality trait within the hawk, allowing it to guide him as it had in his youth, such a relationship had worked in Cuchulain's favor. As the years passed, he never learned to relate, to come to terms, with this aggressive and brutal side of his personality, nor did he ever learn to understand it sufficiently to integrate it into his psyche. He had, therefore, never acquired maturity. Growth demands struggle and sacrifice. What had been positive during his youthful days—the totem in him—will now lead him astray and pave the way for his destruction—a dissociation of the personality.

The Old Man speaks:

> *Look at her shivering now, the terrible life*
> *Is slipping through her veins. She is possessed.*
> *Who knows whom she will murder or betray*
> *Before she awakes in ignorance of it all,*
> *And gathers up the leaves?*
>
> (P. 142)

The Hawk Woman's shivering is, indeed, an indication of her possession by an aspect of the Woman of the Sidhe. She represents the devouring woman, who, rather than giving up her prey, dismembers it. Such power does this Hawk Woman wield that anyone who gazes into her "unmoistened eyes" is cursed. Just as Medusa in Greek mythlogy—who had serpents for hair, brazen claws, and enormous teeth—turned the beholder into stone, the Hawk Woman's personality is wholly destructive. Perseus was saved from annihilation because he carried a mirror with him and did not look directly at her. Psychologically no one may peer into a God's domain: the Self. To experience the absolute, either in its horrific or beauteous aspects, is to invite the destruction of the ego, to welcome its fragmentation. To peer into the Hawk Woman's "unmoisterned eyes" is to encounter a universe without time or space, to allow the collective unconscious to take over, to open the floodgates. Drowning ensues—insanity.

Controlled and propelled by transpersonal energetic factors, the Hawk Woman now ventures forth, subtly, deceitfully, unrelenting in the pursuit of her goal. The Old Man senses the change in the atmosphere. The waters will soon rise, he predicts. He yearns for that moment; he virtually licks his lips at the thought of the liquid sound of those bubbling waters that will bring to him immortal life and bliss—the final realization of his decades of anticipation. Cuchulain is possessed by a different fervor. He looks straight at the Hawk Woman. Again the old Man warns: "She has felt your gaze and turned her eyes on us" (p. 142). He cannot bear her eyes because "they are not of this world" (p. 142). They reveal an infinite domain and do not belong to the Guardian of the Well but to the spirit that activates her.

Suddenly the Guardian of the Well throws off her cloak and rises from the ground. Her dress suggests the form of a hawk. An unconscious content, then, is surfacing. It is an undifferentiated aspect of the psyche, still unconscious or repressed, and therefore untamed. As the Hawk Woman rises from the ground, it is as though life itself were being created: the unknown takes on dimensionality and concretion—it is sustained in one viable metaphor. The theriomorphic deity in all of her power and grandeur fixes her eyes on her prey. Unabashed, Cuchulain speaks:

> *Why do you fix those eyes of a hawk on me?*
> *I am not afraid of you, bird, woman, or witch.*
>
> (P. 142)

He stares, glares into those "unmoistened eyes," like two incandescent terrifying forces, exulting as they cast their spell, their curse, into the legendary warrior hero, still thirsting for a world of eternal creativity.

Fearless, Cuchulain walks toward the side of the well. He will not leave, he states peremptorily, regardless of her activities. He will conquer this demonic force, experience her captivating ways but never become dominated by them. He looks into her eyes, those brilliant, gleaming vessels, those circular orbs—mandala images—that sun and moon which the Egyptians believed spoke their own language, articulated their own thoughts and words.

The Old Man has already fallen asleep. He is dead to the happenings, to the world of life with its agonizing as well as its ecstatic moments. The Hawk Woman circles about as she begins her dance. Her gyrations and arabesques are geared to haunt, mesmerize, and intoxicate her victim, dizzying him in her spatial intertwinings, dulling his senses as vertigo swells his being and the irrational reigns. Similar to the dance in the Noh theater that represents the climax of the emotional situation, so in Yeats's drama, the dance expresses the deepest of feelings. The intensity of the beat parallels the energetic charge implicit in the inner friction. The Hawk Woman and Cuchulain are like forces of nature which vie with each other in determining the outcome of their destiny: the individual mortal ego/consciousness pitted against the Hawk Woman, a collective transpersonal force whose vital powers know no limits.

Dance, which orders and structures the space/time continuum, linking it to the creative factor, brings an entirely new frame of reference into being. Like Siva who danced the world into existence by establishing relationships between earthly and cosmic forces, so the Hawk Woman enacts her needs and calls into being an active and reactive realm which demands the *participation mystique* of her prey.[30] It is through the mimetic art that she brings the nonmanifest into being: signs, symbols, and gestures usher in a world of analogies, associations; cosmic depths are called upon and reached. Similar to the trance caused by the dervish's dance, Unity of Being is experienced as feelings of elation and deliverance pervade the psyche, while the world of differentiation and fragmentation vanishes. Only mythical time exists: past, present, and future are experienced simultaneously; happenings occur in an eternal present. For Plato, dance originated in the divine: prior to its becoming movement, he wrote, it was sign and symbol—the key to the invisible domain. Instead of a chaotic, hysterical outburst on stage, as frequently occurs in Western theater, when "the disordered passion of nature" is experienced, dance, Yeats wrote, "is a series of positions and movements which may represent a battle, or a marriage, or the pain of a ghost in a Buddhist purgatory" in an ordered, sustained, and vital way, since it is an expression of the energetic factor within man, working in harmony with the thinking function.[31]

As the Hawk Woman pursues her gyrations onstage, Cuchulain at first remains detached. Gradually he observes more and more closely the spiraling, coiling interwoven forms created in space by this archetypal figure: her sensuality taunts and tantalizes him. She ushers in visions of what could be a phantasmagoria of beauty wedded to cruelty. She has become transpersonal—that "vessel for the creative power of God"[32] which the mortal mind cannot grasp yet seeks to understand and which appears at certain moments in insights and intuitions. Were it to innundate the soul, it would destroy it. The Hawk Woman as an oracular force motivates, animates, the world about her, not in the human sense or in the visible form she personifies, but in the rhythmic power with which she moves, the intensity of the emotions she arouses. Yeats's description of the Oriental dancer may be applied to the Hawk Woman's motions: "There are few swaying movements of arms or body such as make the beauty of our dancing. They move from the hip, keeping constantly the upper part of their body still, and seem to associate with every gesture or pose some definite thought. They cross the stage with a sliding movement, and one gets the impression not of undulation but of continuous straight lines."[33]

Slowly Cuchulain is aware of the waves of energy infiltrating his psyche, the desire invading his bloodstream. Like deadly venom, it seeps into his system, invades his being. He yields to the circular and spherical patterns she weaves about him.

The First Musician informs the audience that "madness" has taken hold; Cuchulain has grown "pale" and he "staggers" to his feet. We observe him as he speaks to the hawk, as he starts to chase her about: "Run where you will. . . . you shall be perched upon my wrist" (p. 143). The dance pursues its course; and as the Guardian of the Well was possessed by the hawk spirit, so Cuchulain is also mesmerized by this archetypal force, obsessed by it. Will-less, as if in a trance, he follows the Guardian of the Well in her circumambulations, dropping his spear before leaving the stage in pursuit. The waters rise, splash, and bubble, wetting the gray stones, like so many creative thoughts emerging from the depths of being—converging like inspiration which foams unexpectedly and without warning. "Our thoughts and emotions are often but spray flung up from hidden tides that follow a moon no eye can see," Yeats wrote. So the Hawk Woman, in consort with the Woman of the Sidhe, works in her secret ways, her moon aspect, arousing the tides and the waters of the subliminal world during her nightly trajectory, stirring, inciting, agitating those depths within which incandescent forces live inchoate.

"He has lost what may not be found," the Musicians sing. The immortal wisdom that Cuchulain envisions—beauty, truth, reality—is not within his mortal grasp. The world of the Absolute is closed to mortals: Unity of Being can only be experienced in fragments by those still wedded to the phenomenological realm. To yield to the Hawk Woman—to the Woman of the Sidhe—is to ask for oblivion, to end the ever-changing struggle for existence which is the stuff of life.

The Old Man awakens; he "creeps" to the well, blames the "shadow" again for the evil perpetrated; he fails to accept his own inadequacies which he projects outside himself. Deluded and distracted by the Hawk Woman's power, he looks about at the dark moist stones, the emptiness of the well, the desolate sky. He understands that once more the waters have bubbled forth while he was asleep—the treasures were again reabsorbed by mother earth. To be victimized by these demonic forces is to indicate that his unconscious is no longer his: it has been dominated or inhabited by the Guardian of the Well; she has stolen his shadow and made it her own for a period. To steal an identity, even temporarily, reveals the presence of a nonfunctioning ego.

Unaware that his individual personality no longer belongs to him, Cuchulain returns to the stage, and he and the Old Man in nearly parallel refrains castigate the Guardian of the Well for having eluded his grasp. She is hiding in the rocks, in the cairns that dot the Sligo countryside, those burial mounds where the Celtic heroes of old lay in wait for their own immortal journey through death and rebirth. Suddenly the Musicians cry: "Aoife! Aoife!" and strike a gong. "What are those cries?" Cuchulain questions. The queen of the amazon warriors, Aoife, "the greatest woman warrior in the world," who understands enchantment and witchcraft better than anyone else, has aroused her female companion to action.[34] Cuchulain has violated their sacred rights by attempting to capture the Guardian of the Well for himself, thus leaving unguarded the waters of perpetual wisdom—the source of life itself. His punishment will be written into his karmic pattern: unknowingly, he will kill his son, his instinctual being prevailing over his rational sphere. (The theme of Yeats's play *On Baile's Strand*.) In the hills, Aoife and her warriors have lit their fires; singing out their incantations, reciting prayers and threnodies, they pay homage to the great earth goddess—the Woman of the Sidhe—in her hawk avatar. Similar to the fertility divinities of the ancient world (Gaia, Rhea, Hera, Isis, Demeter) whose presences spell birth and death, who nourish and destroy, so these amazon types who appear so powerfully in societies when the masculine principle is either in a weakened condition or in disarray are ready to pounce and mutilate the male. Aoife and her cohorts, priestesses in their own right, represent the woman castrater, the maimer and destroyer of young boys, the virile matriarchal principle who has opted to alter the status quo, dismembering the patriarchal stronghold, imitating the male in his way rather than establishing their own ground of being. Extremists, they seek to satisfy their own inner needs and cravings, to impose their image upon a world that has rejected them or relegated them to an inferior position. Unlike the Hindu goddess, Kali, who represents in her single person three aspects of life (creator, maintainer, and destroyer) and is depicted in images and sculptures in so many of her avatars, ranging from the ugliest to the most beautiful of women, the Hawk Woman symbolizes only one aspect.

Cuchulain henceforth will never again know rest; his soul, his psyche, will be forever tormented, cut in two, divided. His life will pursue the same course as before, a life of extroverted action, rather than evolving into the next phase of experience. His masculine needs would encourage more bloody battles, fiery rages, heated love affairs. Their outcome will bring death to him and to those he loves. He shoulders his spear once again and leaves in search of his destiny.

As the Musicians unfold the cloth anew, they sing of Cuchulain's reentrance into the human realm, his return to earth. The Old Man, who had stooped behind it, leaves the stage unnoticed. The play of antinomies has not led to higher consciousness, nor have the conflicts plaguing the protagonists been resolved. Cuchulain's journey which might have paved the way for deeper insights and greater understanding has only increased his "folly." Like Yeats himself, he will be driven by a force beyond his understanding, a "lamentable shadow" forever drawing him back into a strife-filled life. These are the dangers that the hero and poet must brave in order to carve out the new, the poignant, the eternal aspects of the life experience. Such a being may never know happiness. Cuchulain's father was divine, his mother mortal. So the poet, who also experiences temporal and atemporal spheres, is forever seeking to penetrate the All, to know Unity of Being; realizing always the impossibility of the task. "Wisdom must live a bitter life" (p. 144), the Musicians sing.

The cloth is folded; the play is over; mortal man's effort to gain transcendence has been defeated once again. Yet it is this very struggle to attain the unattainable that Yeats continued to celebrate in his later works. The poet, he wrote,

must not seek for what is still and fixed, for that has no life for him; and if he did, his style would become cold and monotonous, and his sense of beauty faint and sickly. . . . but be content to find his pleasure in all that is forever passing away that it may come again, in the beauty of woman, in the fragile flowers of spring, in momentary heroic passion, in whatever is most fleeting, most impassioned, as it were, for its own perfection, most eager to return in its glory. . . . Is it that all things are made by the struggle of the individual and the world, of the unchanging and the returning, and that the saint and the poet are over all, and that the poet has made his home in the serpent's mouth?[35]

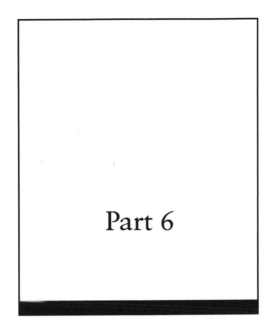

Part 6

The Kalevala (500–1300?):
Finnish Shamanism—The Senex Hero
and the Faulty Anima

The Kalevala, the Finnish national epic, is based on groups of
ancient poems and ballads gathered together by Elias Lönnrot
(1802–84), physician, philologist, and scholar. Comparable to
Homer's *Odyssey* and *Iliad,* and to Firdausi's *Shah-Nama* in
that it takes its readers back to an *illud tempus* where purity of
thought and feeling cohabited with whirlpools of evil energies,
The Kalevala sings of primordial times when gods and heroes
roamed the earth.

    Lönnrot gathered songs from every corner of Finland, trav-
eling from the humblest to the most prosperous areas, talking
with old and young, looking through cellars and attics, any-
where and everywhere for all possible information concerning
his literary and musical heritage. Runes (*runot*) songs were usually handed down from one generation to another by simple
farmers, vagabonds, or *kantele* players. (A *kantele* is a five- or
seven-string zitherlike instrument plucked by hand.) The *Kalevala,* or *Old Karelian Songs,* was published in 1835 (pt. 1) and
1836 (pt. 2); a new edition appeared in 1849. It has been suggested that Lönnrot was overly subjective in his approach to
The Kalevala. Yet Homer and Firdausi, who gathered the material availble to them in the same manner, so it is claimed, may
be accused of the same tendency when composing their epic
poems. Such is the poet's and the scholar's prerogative. Since
mythologies of all nations and of all times are subject to innu-
merable variations, Lönnrot, who heard and read many var-
iants to one song or multiple and different plot delineations of
one hero's life, chose the one he felt best suited to his endeavor,

the one he felt best represented the Finnish soul. His choice, based on a lifetime of study and meticulour scholarship, was one of deep feeling for his nation and its people.

Whether ancient or modern, fact or fiction, the events delineated in *The Kalevala*, as well as those recounted in other great myths, reveal archetypal patterns in peoples; they are like psychic structures which expose conscious and unconscious impulses, needs, desires in a living culture. In that archetypes form the bases of religions and legends, they dramatize dimensions of understanding and feeling which are eternal, dating back to archaic times and still powerful in the Finnish psyche today. Specific archetypes (creation, shaman/hero, shadow, anima, night-sea journey, giant, the treasure) will be analyzed within both the framework of the epic poem, *The Kalevala* and in a more universal vein, in an effort to determine their meanings and impact upon modern readers.

ECTYPAL ANALYSIS

The Finns were first mentioned by the Roman historian Tacitus in his *Germania*. He was in reality referring to the Lapps, Finland's first inhabitants. The Finns began migrating to the land named after them from the Baltic areas in small tribes and clans. By the eighth century they took the land from the Lapps who were driven northward. By 1000 A.D. settlements had solidified and a national culture was growing which would be reflected in *The Kalevala*.

The adventures dramatized in *The Kalevala*, according to Lönnrot, dated from 500–1300 A.D. Other scholars, such as Julius Krohn, suggested 400–1000 A.D. as the period upon which *The Kalevala* was based. The romantics, fired with feelings of national pride, were convinced that the events poetized in *The Kalevala* were drawn from some remote, nebulous time, probably from the Creation period.[1]

Whatever the date, the situations, dramatis personae, feelings, and atmosphere created are of mythical quality, reflecting a culture and period in history which was difficult and rigorous. Farmers, living in remote areas, eked out livings for themselves and their families; fishermen, loggers, and hunters combed the areas for food. Epidemics of cholera, typhoid, tuberculosis, and dysentery were more the rule than the exception. During the winter months, particularly in the northern regions of Finland near the Arctic Circle, months of darkness clothed their world. Travel in such isolated regions, where waterways were ice-covered, was possible only by sleigh or carriage, pulled by horses or reindeer. Fear of evil spirits haunted the people always during these lugubrious and depressing months. When spring came and the sun was reborn, jubilation was felt in the hearts of the people, and hope was renewed. The southern regions of Finland were not so harsh or extreme, and terror would be mitigated by reason. Nevertheless, here, too, blinding snow storms, congealed lakes, canals, and seas, made winter travel difficult.

Life in Finland, as well as in northern and central Asia, focused around the shaman: he was magician, healer, educator, adjudicator, demiurge. The virtual patriarch of the tribe or clan, the wisdom residing in him was believed to have been transmitted from extratemporal sources. His powers stemmed in part from his ability to communicate mystically with spirits and perform miracles. The most important protagonist in *The Kalevala*, Vänämöinen—a hero/musician, shaper of events—was a prototypal shaman.

Shamanism, an animistic religion, existed in ancient times, according to some mythologists, dating back to 3000 B.C., and it continues in certain areas in Asia today, in a mitigated form along with Christianity, Hinduism, Taoism, Buddhism, depending upon its location. The Finns were converted to Christianity in the eleventh century; at first they practiced Catholicism, but now the majority are mostly Lutherans. It is understandable, therefore, that many Christian elements are interwoven in the happenings in *The Kalevala*.

Shamans are not only looked upon as "Masters of Fire" but also as "Masters of Spirits." Unlike other religious groups who pray to God or gods, saints or holy people, asking for their beneficence, shamans dominate extraterrestrial forces. Their effectiveness resides in their skill and knowledge over a world that lies beyond the visible domain: it is an animistic sphere, where an invisible domain tingles with life, and mysterious spirits make their feelings and intentions known in happy or sorrowful events. The shamans intercede when evil spirits seek to harm an individual or clan; their art/science aids them in rendering certain enemy forces ineffectual or in manipulating them as they wish. Shamans call upon spirits or demons (or former shamans) to help them heal the sick, fight wars, or discover specific secrets which lie hidden in nature and would, if known, help them perform their magical feats with greater brio. Shamans indulge in a variety of fascinating techniques which they master only after long periods of ascetic practice.

A shaman, for example, may sit in his yurt (dwelling) staring for hours or days at a wall, until he enters into a deep trance state; he may litanize or meditate, hallucinate, trying to evoke helpful spirits, which would feed the needy and cure the sick. During the shaman's trance states, or other parapsychological conditions, his soul may ascend to heavenly regions or descend into infernos peopled by monstrous creatures. Communication between the living and the dead is accomplished by the shaman, since he dominates these forces and is not possessed by them. He is capable of accomplishing other miraculous deeds: transforming himself into an animal, mineral, or vegetable. If he decides to become a horse, rock, or flower, he takes on the personality of the entity upon which he projects, thus acting, speaking, or resembling the persona he has invoked. The intimacy he knows with natural forces as a result of his metamorphoses takes him back to a primordial condition, an archaic state of being which replenishes his psyche, reinvigorates, and restores what has been delimited by the difficulties involved in his life experience.[2]

The shamans, so it has been reported, have been known to accomplish astounding feats: walking or lying on hot coals, even swallowing them; enduring extreme cold; cutting themselves deeply with knives; flying; transforming themselves into animals, birds, or minerals; and more. Such incredible activities require long and arduous initiation periods which vary according to the regions where shamanism is practiced. In all cases, shamans demonstrate a high degree of intelligence and insight, as well as remarkable memories and great sensitivity.

Shamans may inherit or be elected into their vocation. Bloodline, however, is not sufficient to prove one's calling. The signs indicating a youth's propensity for such a religious life are frequently manifested in behavioral patterns. A neophyte may become moody, introverted, sleepy, and seek out lonely and isolated areas in the woods, lake regions, or wilderness where he can experience nature in its fullness and primitive conditions. At this period in his life he may be prone to visions, hallucinations, convulsions, hysteria, or other nervous disorders. These very special neurological disturbances on the part of adolescents are considered signs of God's favors: a call for an encounter with divinity or with special spirits with which the hierophant will communicate and from whom he will receive instructions as to the type of initiation he will undergo.[3]

During initiation periods, a neophyte must learn to harden and strengthen himself against life's difficulties. He may climb a mountain and live in complete isolation for seven days or more, subsisting on the animals which he catches with his teeth alone, not by using any instrument. In seclusion, he experiences intense cold and may enter into trance states during which time he sees his soul becoming detached from his body and traveling toward the heavenly or infernal regions. Expanded consciousness, to which he has now opened himself, teaches him a new vocabulary; it also makes known new musical tonalities, poetry, a variety of dance steps (mandalas) which will aid him in acquiring new and very special magical powers. Initiation periods are also spent learning the secrets of the clan's elder shaman: how to survive and dominate physical agony; how to acquire knowledge concerning the most important of all rituals—death and rebirth. If, after the completion of his trials, the neophyte is deemed acceptable, capable of exiting from the profane world and being born into a transpersonal kingdom, of curing the ill, communing with invisible spirits, he is ready to become a shaman. He will not only perform astounding physical feats but will also enter into an intimate spiritual relationship with nature and the cosmos; he will astound by his incredible memory and his abilities as singer, poet, musician, priest, doctor, and seer.

Once he has become a shaman and has, after years of practice, proven his abilities, he becomes a patriarch of his tribe or clan, leader of religious ceremonies carried on in a yurt or public area. Called on to heal the sick or guide alienated souls, help enfeebled tribes to fight for their rights over aggressive neighbors, see to the land's fertility or the return of the sun after months of darkness, the shaman practices his magico-religious art for all to experience. His rituals usually begin with meditation or mental contemplation during which time he sees himself with greater clarity: such objectivity leads him to virtually sever psyche and body—ego and Self. He sees, at this time, his soul separated from his body, wandering through the spheres of being. He may observe his own skeleton, see his flesh and blood separating from his bones; he may lacerate his flesh, yet stem the flow of blood. His language made up of sacred phonemes, labials, gutteral, sonorities of all types, has the power to invoke spirits and guide the confused. If he seeks to journey to heavenly spheres, he may choose to sacrifice a horse in the yurt, its spirit aiding him in his ascensional ride. The horse in such cases is killed in a very special manner: its spinal column is crushed so that no blood will fall upon the worshippers in the yurt. The flesh and skin are then hung. Offerings are made to ancestors and protective spirits. A communal meal is then prepared, to be eaten by the shaman and those who seek the protection and aid of gods and spirits. At times, a heavenly bird is invoked, or other ascensional animals. The shaman now begins his skyward journey. He will climb a sacred tree, looked upon as the world axis or cosmic tree. Sometimes the shaman uses the post in the center of the yurt (meant for the smoke to exit) which he climbs and from which he leaves the yurt. The roof of the yurt is itself considered to have holy aspects: it is constructed to resemble a heavenly vault, the center of the world—linking earth to heaven.[4] At other instances, he rides on horseback to a nearby tree.

During the ceremonies, the shaman, or Master Musician and Poet, rolls his drum, plays the kantele, or simply intones or litanizes, thus invoking the supreme deity, Bai Ulgan, through special sonorities and rhythmic patterns. It is Bai Ulgan who assures fertility, whose attention is focused on humankind, who lends a helping hand whenever needed. He is neither remote nor cut off from those who seek his help. He dialogues with his people. A *psychophoric* interchange takes place during which time not only is the deity concretized, but the shaman is visited by him, takes on his characteristics, and in this state reaches a condition of ecstasy. With Bai Ulgan's aid, the shaman may not only ascend to heavenly spheres but can also visit the domain of the dead. During such journeys, the shaman's voice, vibrating in strange and haunting fashion, may take on piercing overtones and rhythmic counterplays. If he incarnates a bird's persona during the ritual, or that of an animal, he may cry, screech, bark,

beat, howl, and chant in what we would call states of protracted delirium. Such moments may include willed seizures
(unlike the neurological condition, which, unless medicated, is
uncontrollable). Here, the shaman is considered to be experiencing a transpersonal existence, reliving a nonlinear space/time
continuum, where it is said, he has now reconnected what had
once been divided within him—heaven, earth, and the lower
sphere—or in psychological terms: the conscious and the personal and collective unconscious.

Just as his psychological sphere has now been fused, so his
heights, depths, and various sensations are also united. He lives
in a state which was known prior to the great cosmic schism:
when nature and gods spoke the same language—in a *participation mystique*. Such "ontological mutation" is reenacted by
the shaman in spiritually ordered religious rituals which make
of him—as is the case of all great religious leaders and prophets—a supreme poetic artist.[5]

ARCHETYPAL ANALYSIS

1. The Creation Archetype
Creation, whether referring to the cosmogonic process, the birth
of a child or an idea, or a new psychological attitude, is both a
solemn and a sacred moment in the life experience: when the
primordial condition of *wholeness* or *oneness* is transformed
into differentiated zones. In psychological terms, it may be described as the ego breaking away from the collective unconscious.[6]

In *The Kalevala*, the creative process ushers in an archaic
mode of thinking and feeling. Earth, mountains, trees, springs,
seas, and land masses are humanized; they vibrate with elemental life and personality, as if participating in a giant awakening.
Each entity, paradoxically, experiences itself in a *participation
mystique* with the cosmos, yet contains its own energetic (*mana*)
personality. The dual nature of this relationship aroused wonderment and excitement—the *numinosum*.

The opening scenes in *The Kalevala* make us privy to an
amorphous condition. Ilmatar, the Virgin of the Air, a transhu-
man presence, an invisible force, has grown tired of living alone.
The coldness and remoteness of the barren regions in which she

exists pain her, as does her purity and voicelessness. She emerges
as a psychic image, a kind of world soul, reminiscent of Plotinus's "unending All of life."[7] In her loneliness, she experiences
sensations of disorientation, anguish, as though she were losing
herself, perpetually, irrevocably. She yearns for another form, a
responsive force that will put an end to the stillness of her spiritually immobile condition. Metaphysically, solitude permeates
her identityless being; it stirs feelings of dissatisfaction as well
as fear.

There was a virgin, maiden of the air, lovely woman, a spirit of
*   nature.*
Long she kept her purity, ever her virginity
in the spacious farmyards, on the smooth fields of the air.
In time she got bored, her life seemed strange
in always being alone, living as a virgin
in the spacious farmyards, in the vast wastes of the air.
Now indeed she comes lower down, settled down on the
*   billows.*
On the broad expanse of the sea, on the wide open sea.[8]

The Virgin of the Air's sense of alienation increases, causing her
a kind of overwhelming panic. An inability to alter her condition, to transform her sterile state into a fecund one, arouses
chaos within her, a condition which manifests itself as a catalytic force. Such tumult is important in that it fosters in the
Virgin of the Air, a climate conducive to the creative process.

Virginity, such as Ilmatar experiences, has taken on a negative connotation. Not yet a *spiritus creator*, the Virgin of the
Air is but a wandering and lonely soul who longs to incarnate,
to leave the infinite and solitary expanse which is her air home.
To be inseminated would bring vibrancy to her being, she feels;
it would transform her abstract, transparent presence as formless matter into a viable, concrete entity. As an idea seeks incarnation in the work of art, and an individual yearns for companionship and communication, so the Virgin of the Air decides to
mingle with the moisture of life, the sea beneath her. She slips
into the waters which poets compare to an infinite space/time
continuum, which Thales considered the principle of all things,
psychologists identify with the amniotic fluid of the uterus, as
well as with the colletive unconscious. She absorbs and reab-

sorbs this liquid realm, this preformal state of existence into her being. Then she waits.

"There came a great blast of wind. . . . The wind blew her pregnant. . . . she carried a hard womb, a stiff bellyful for seven hundred years" (p. 5). Wind, frequently regarded as divine spirit (*nous, pneuma*) is looked upon in Genesis as a fructifying force: when God "breathed into his [Adam's] nostrils the breath of life; and man became a living soul" (1:2). Anaxoras wrote of a "whirlwind" which created the world from itself.[9] It is the wind/spirit that injects inert matter with energy, that foments movement. Similarly, we may say that an idea, when activated, propels the mind, injecting thought clusters with increased momentum, allowing an idea to snowball, to acquire density and avalanche force, as it makes its way into existence.

A tempest rages. Its fury blows the Virgin of the Air round and round in the waters, causing foam to whiten the horizon. Such an image is reminiscent of the Old Testament Creation story when the Spirit of God covered the waters; of Hesiod's *Theogony*, when Aphrodite was born from the foam of the sea; and of the Vedic hymns, when Vayu moved over the waters like an invisible magic power, inspiring cosmic creativity in each of his breaths.[10] Such an event, symbolized in *The Kalevala* by the storm of divine, psychic, and poetic origin, disrupts the heretofore balanced cosmic rhythms and paves the way for a new center of gravity, impelling fresh attitudes and orientations.

The fetus remains within the Virgin of the Air for seven hundred years. It must be noted here that in myths time is not measured according to linear concepts but in terms of the fourth dimension. There is, therefore, no beginning, no end; time bathes in a limitless and spaceless sphere. Such an expanse is impossible to measure or experience in an intellectual frame of reference. That the Virgin of the Air could not expel her creation may indicate that the gestation period had not yet been terminated; the fetus had not taken on the proper consistency, form, depth, or breadth to withstand the rigors of the outside world. It still needed to be protected, to remain invisible. Nevertheless, dangers beset all phases of life. Should her pregnancy continue too long, the fetus could experience a condition of stasis; worse, it could rot, disintegrate, and then fall back into the *prima materia*. As long as the womb/unconscious does not communicate the fruit of its inner process to the outside/conscious world, the living being does not emerge; the idea remains waterlogged, the psyche egoless.

The Virgin of the Air is assailed with torment. She regrets having allowed herself to be inseminated, preferring her lonely airborne state to the freedom and sameness of her present un-differentiated liquid condition. As she roams about in the end-less waters, senses of worthlessness and inadequacy overwhelm her. She fears a stillbirth, in the same way a poet would the emergence of an unfinished or imperfect work. Depression is not unknown in the individual who brings forth the new and untried. Frequently, when on the verge of completing a magnum opus, a lull descends upon the artist or writer just prior to that moment when inert energy is transformed into kinetic or active fields—when the idea is about ready to erupt into conscious-ness. The inner domain senses the future loss of what had once belonged to it, experiences feelings of bereavement. The Virgin of the Air knows this listlessness, this sensation of helplessness.

In desperation, she calls upon Ukko, the heavenly god, the luminous father image. This living organism, considered a uni-versal fructifier because he is the source of unlimited energy, "radiates through and in every particle of nature."[11] Omniscient and omnipotent, he may be looked upon as the creative point, that sustaining force which gives impetus to life. As the repre-sentative of infinite wisdom, he is empowered to regulate, order, and guide unlimited and inaccessible expanses. He listens to the supplications of the Virgin of the Air as they resound in sound-less waves throughout the universe.

Time elapses. "A goldeneye," a type of wild duck, begins flying about the waters seeking a place to nest. The Virgin of the Air raises her knee from beneath the sea. When the bird sees this smooth surface, he decides it is the perfect place to incubate his young. He alights on the knee, the eggs are then formed and warmed.

Like the Paraclete, the comforter, the intercessor for the Virgin Mary, so the bird—a soul-force, a bridge between Ukko and water, a messenger aiding in the transformatory process—is instrumental in giving body to spirit, materiality to an amor-phous condition. The bird, representing a superior state in the hierarchy of being, a totem, is a paradigm for spiritual realization, as attested to in the drawings of birds as soul-bearers in the Lascaux caves; and as mystical soul-forces in Farid ud-din Attar's *The Conference of the Birds*.

That the bird should have chosen the knee (a part of the body which plays a role in several episodes in *The Kalevala*) as its nesting place is significant. A connecting link between the thigh and the lower part of the leg, the knee enables walking, ambulating—the carrying out of a willed idea. Insofar as the Virgin of the Air is concerned, the knee makes it possible for her to realize her potential, to nurture a new element both passively and actively.

Meanwhile, the eggs take on warmth. Concomitantly, the Virgin of the Air suddenly feels herself burning, her "sinews" melting, "her skin scorched" (p. 6). The fire of creation has heightened the intensity of her emotions. Love begins flaming within her; movement takes on energy. Oneness has vanished and is giving way to multiplicity, diversity—the future earth-born state. The birth process in general may be regarded as an ordeal by fire: Siva created the world with fire; Brahma was identified with fire; the phoenix is reborn from its ashes; the Holy Ghost appeared to the apostles as flames (Acts 2:3–4). Since shamans experience the flame of mystical heat during their moments of magical ecstasy, it is not surprising that the Virgin of the Air should also feel burning sensations. As life grows within her, she is involved in the transformatory process: eggs turning into earth/matter. While she continues to swim in the vast expanses of water, she fashions coasts, bays, reefs, islands, and mountains, giving birth, so to speak, to myriad facets in the form of earthly configurations.

Humankind has not yet come into existence; it remains an illusion, a spiritual force buried deeply within the belly of the Virgin of the Air. For another thirty summers and thirty winters, the gestation period will pursue its course. The Virgin of the Air swims here and there, always hoping that the treasure contained within her will emerge. Not until the *fascino sum* ends, however, not until the fruit of the womb grows sufficiently weary of an inner existence, will it emerge from the dark waters of cosmic existence.

The archetype of emergence in *The Kalevala* may be considered a paradigm of exogamy: the ego refuses to be repressed any longer and seeks as best it can to eject itself from uterine waters, to sever itself from a symbolic condition of incest. Within the mother's womb, reminiscent of Jonah's incarceration in the whale, the fetus, prototypal man (we later learn, by the name of Väinämöinen), begins to reflect upon his condition. He wonders how he can endure this "dark hiding place," this "cramped dwelling where he never saw the moon nor spied the sun" (p. 7). He grows impatient and longs for the outer world, the earth, air, and the freedom to live and grow independently. He begs the moon and the sun to free him, to "Escort the traveler to land" (p. 7). No outer force will come to his aid. He must strive, fight for freedom himself. To struggle for self-government is a lonely affair, as is death. It is a voyage, a *rite de passage* which must be traversed single-handedly. It is in the very anguish provoked by the ordeal itself, that inner strength is earned, that fortitude comes into being.

Väinämöinen, future shaman and poet, is already endowed, we are told, with certain personality traits: he "ponders," he "reflects," he "thinks." Unemotional, he thinks first and then acts. To extricate himself from his incarceration, he takes his ring finger, looked upon by ancients as an important factor in divination, and his left toe, to move "the gate of the fort," to turn "the bony lock." The analogy made between the Virgin of the Air's uterus and "fort" and "lock" would indicate the iron or metallic forces with which Väinämöinen would have to struggle. He will stop at nothing. If his finger and toe do not help him, his nails will serve him. He will use them to cut his way out of the "threshold" and his knees will give him leverage. He cuts, rips, tears at the flesh, using every instrument at his disposal to create a large enough birth passage. An accumulation of energy channeled in this area enables him to propel himself outward in one final thrust.

Väinämöinen "plunged straight into the sea," then surfaced, and made his way into a treeless land. In joy and ecstasy he gazes at the moon, sun, Great Bear, and the stars. The "stouthearted singer" (p. 7), as he was to be known, understood that his connection with the Virgin of the Air had ended. His mother had given him life. It was he who would now have to shape his destiny. As a future culture hero, he would have to form his own essence, create his personality, and become the psychopomp future generations would look upon as leader and wise man. He felt the strength to fulfill what he already knew to be his mission.

Väinämöinen, primordial man and future shaman/poet, was unique among culture heroes. He was born old. A *senex* figure who had lived so many years within his mother's womb, he emerged as a patriarch in all senses of the word: magician and worker of miracles. Throughout *The Kalevala* he is alluded to as "steadfast," as "an eternal sage," as "reflective." He is *logos*, "reason," the Word, verbalized thought, characteristics which presuppose inner awareness. A reflective and meditative being, Väinämöinen would not act rashly as long as *logos* dictated his ways. A creative force, a poet and singer who accompanies himself on the kantele, he is reminiscent of Orpheus. His gifts are also born from supernatural spheres. Stones stir to his music and grass, flowers, trees, bend to his harmonies, filling the universe with song. Väinämöinen holds nature in thrall.

Väinämöinen possesses vast powers, as do many culture heroes. From his mother he was given autonomy over the forces of the air (spirits, demons); the birds, instrumental in his birth, endowed him with spiritual attributes, sublimating capabilities; the waters, which had been his home for so long, allowed him to feel at ease in a fluid, constantly transforming and shifting world. Now Väinämöinen would have to learn to cope with earth: matter—encounters with people. If he succeeds in understanding the factors involved in the phenomenological sphere, he will have proven his mettle as shaman and poet: he will have learned to rectify imbalance, heal what is impaired, salvage what is damaged, remedy what is flawed. Väinämöinen's trajectory has consisted thus far of three stages:

air: an amorphous, invisible condition; similar to an idea which remains immersed in the *prima materia;* hypostatized abstract concept; a formless ego existing in the collective unconscious.

water: a fluid, tactile, still invisible entity; an idea in the process of taking on sustenance and consistency; the ego emerging into consciousness though still enjoying a *participation mystique.*

earth: the incarnated being; the solid, invisible, phenomenological sphere; the idea realized, manifested. Ego-consciousness comes into being.

2. *The Archetypal Shaman Hero*
After having crossed the "threshold" from an unconscious existence in his mother's womb to the differentiated world, Väinämöinen is in a position to fulfill his destiny. As future archetypal shaman/hero, he now stands for an awakening consciousness, which brings new values and experiences to the society which projects upon it. The world of light, which has now replaced the years of darkness Väinämöinen had known, may be looked upon as the ego's giant impulse toward life and activity; libido (psychic energy) cascading forth, erupting into existence. Energy is no longer closeted, it is being expended externally, helping him form, shape, and determine a worldly existence.

Väinämöinen faces a "treeless" land on earth. Such a condition spells sterility, loneliness, and isolation and in no way answers his needs nor fulfills his longings. In tune with nature, because of his affinity with the air and water elements previously described, he knows how to use its powers to his advantage. He already understands the myriad sounds he hears, incomprehensible to those who have been severed from the wonders of the so-called inanimate world, but for him, representing an endless treasure trove of riches. Väinämöinen feels connected to the external sphere as he does to his inner domain. Confident in his abilities and capacities to fend off destructive encounters, such as despair, he acts overtly in coming to terms with difficulties.

Väinämöinen's first task is to transform barren into fertile land; psychologically, to subsume the talents which lie fallow within his inner world, to discover and develop his potential. He calls upon Sampsa (Spirit of Arable), a helpful agent, a creative factor, to fulfill his needs. A tiny lad, similar to the dwarfs of the Icelandic *Eddas*, Sampsa may be looked upon, psychologically, as an impulse or intuition, an unconscious force which leaps or falls (*Einfall*) into consciousness when needed, appearing to the writer or mythmaker as a glimmer or a minute crystallization, an aspect or expression of a larger idea/form.[12] Such spirits or dwarfs as described in *The Niebelungenlied* live within

the earth or in the hills and are said to possess childish characteristics. Sampsa fits this definition: he is small and young; he is
human, but incompletely formed. On the other hand, dwarfs
are known to be industrious and active in whatever their spe-
cialties. Sampsa sows a crop of trees for Väinämöinen, and colorful, regal, graceful pines, towans, willows, and junipers emerge
quickly and densely.

Forests become thick and lush. One oak in particular grows
to such heights that its branches hide the sun. Väinämöinen "reflects" and "ponders" (p. 9). To allow the creative urge to run
wild, unchecked, which is what such overfertility implies, is to
incite chaos and not cosmos. Such a way would allow impulses
(the dwarf factor), glimmers, insights, sparks—never a completed or well thought-out work—to inundate the world. To
permit this condition to pursue its course is to invite darkness,
the irrational and undifferentiated vision—to encapsulate the
universe. It would pave the way for regression, a return to uterine condition. Väinämöinen had spent too many long years in
the *nigredo* phase of existence to allow such a situation to prevail. Sight, not blindness, is what he wished; light, not dark,
nebulous opacities. He wanted consciousness as opposed to unconscious quantities. Clarity of vision brings order, orientation,
and point. Without these factors Väinämöinen's existence would
not attain universal/eternal stature. Never would he earn the
powers of shaman/poet if he allowed darkness to prevail; such
penumbra would find him groping about, stumbling in dank,
bleak, mephitic realms. Greatness is achieved when experiencing a *hieros gamos*: a felicitous relationship between inner and
outer domain—the sun/moon principle within the psyche. Only
when such balance reigns, would Väinämöinen succeed in
arousing wonderment and dazzling the world with his powers.

A future culture hero, Väinämöinen understood the need
for ego-consciousness. As such, he realized that the oak tree in
question had to be cut down: a paradigm for shearing and shap-
ing of primal forces within himself. To evaluate his earthly situation, therefore, was of utmost urgency. He looked at a world
resonating with infinite sonorities, redolent with incredible
growth. Although he felt attuned to universal forces, he was
"wise" and understood that whatever obliterates consciousness
must be eradicated. The oak had to be felled so that sight, *gnosis*,

and clarity of vision could develop. Only when he could see outside of himself and observe the vast expanses before him, would he be able to objectify his situation, thus developing an identity of his own and discovering his potentials. Similar to the hierophant who must experience the initiation ritual in order to evolve to the next level of being, so Väinämöinen will have to test the extent of his powers, his stamina, his thinking and feeling capacities. The spectacularly large and beautiful oak tree had to be sacrificed. To divest the world of this fertile force, which, psychologically, represented such a creative element within him, was the price to be paid for future development.

Psychologically speaking, to cut an oak is an intensely meaningful experience to the Finnlander and Lapplander. To allow a tree to blot out the sun is a dangerous omen: it may be a prelude to the disappearance of this flaming force, an idea which strikes terror in the heart of people living in upper latitudes. Should darkness take over, evil would grow unchecked throughout the earth. Wizards with their superior powers would be able to annihilate humankind, pitilessly and unmercifully. Coldness would envelop the earth; water would congeal, killing the fish, robbing man of his sustenance! Solitude would fill the cold lunar light on earth; impersonally still stars would cast their eerie shadows upon a dead planet.

To cut a tree in areas where shamanism/animism is alive and active is no easy matter. Trees are believed to be inhabited by living souls and, if not properly cut, may offend or hurt the being in question. The punishment meted out for such an offense may be grave: the wood spirit might refuse to burn in the hearth, or other, more serious evils might await the perpetrator of such a crime. To fell a tree also has positive implications. As a future shaman, Väinämöinen would be able to fashion a drum from its body. Drums are extremely important to shamans. When they pound, strike, beat, roll out certain rhythmic sequences, the sound waves energize them, help them take off on their mystical journeys to "the Center of the World" or fly through the air in rapidly paced gyrations. As the sonorities amplify, diminish, and filter throughout the atmosphere in whole or partial tones, the shaman feels himself empowered to seek out and contact helpful spirits while, at the same time, immobilzing evil demons. Both the tree and the drum, iconographically, are paradigms of the shaman's ecstatic sojourn: when he opens himself up to the cosmic experience.[13] Important, too is the fact that the shaman's drum is comparable to the sword of the Westerner during medieval times: given a name, it is thereby endowed with a personality and legend. Trees are also used to make bows and arrows which are not only used for hunting but also in the fashioning of musical instruments. A bow is whittled from a tree, then tied from end to end with the gut of an animal, thus is the "singing-bow" made. With a single string, Siberian shamans play for long periods of time, the monochord sounds encouraging them to slip into a trance or arousing their spirit sufficiently to begin a spirit/dance. Although sounds emanating from the singing-bow seem to focus on but a single note, its multiple tonal colors lend such variety, that a whole set of emotional values emerges from the wood.[14]

Still Väinämöinen "ponders" and "reflects" (p. 9). He attempts to assess the situation logically to put his thoughts in order. For him, killing a tree, still so bound to the natural world, is like severing a limb. The future shaman/poet, however, knows that for a life to gain dimension, for a cretive work—the poem/song—to take on an existence of its own, deletions of segments, interludes, and images are salutary to strengthen the personality as well as the work of art as a whole. Light and discernment, therefore, must prevail if the magnum opus is to emerge unencumbered and sweep into being, catalyzed by its own exquisite and eternal radiance.

Yet, Väinämöinen hesitates. He speaks out his turmoil: "Maiden mother, you who bore me, Nature spirit, my upbringer!" (p. 9). In his agony he calls forth a helping spirit. "A man comes up from the sea" at this moment; a person rose from the unconscious. Similar to Sampsa, this new Einfall, is "as tall as a man's thumb" and emerged into concretion when Väinämöinen was overwhelmed with feelings of desperation. Scintillae, glimmers, ideas, impulses, adolescent or unformed in the main, work effectively as catalyzing agents to trigger activity within the individual's being. What was novel about this dwarf was the fact that "on his shoulders was a copper helmet, copper boots on his feet" (p. 9).

That this new helping force which leaped into consciousness was compared to a finger again calls a digit into play. The

finger, which Väinämöinen had used so aggressively and effectively to break out of the birth canal, was now being identified
with the dwarf that would fell the oak. The finger would thus
be used to sever, cut, rip, and tear a life-force whose roots were
buried deeply within the earth: a parallel image to Väinämöinen's first liberation from constriction. That the dwarf wore
copper was in keeping with the period dramatized in *The Kalevala*. Metals were believed by primitive peoples to have been
heaven-sent. They were, therefore, to be considered a linking
force between celestial and terrestrial spheres. Copper, which
was used in toolmaking as far back as 3100 B.C.[15] was also
believed to have medicinal value. It cleansed "foul ulcers" and
protected against cholera. In addition to these virtues, this
malleable, ductile, and relatively soft metallic element was endowed with miraculous qualities: when the crude ore is heated,
it gives off certain fumes which can turn the workmen's hair
green. To the scientist, this reveals the presence of some invisible
force or substance, but to primitive peoples it means the presence of a deity or spirit.[16] That the dwarf which Väinämöinen
called upon to help him fell the tree wore copper on his head
and feet, created an energetic climate favorable for the *numinosum*. When a blazing sun shone upon the dwarf's copper ac-
coutrements a dazzling image came into being, reminiscent of
Jakob Boehme's experience: when the sun's rays blazed on a tin
plate—and at that very moment opened him up to enlightenment, to a cosmic revelation.[17]

Suddenly, Väinämöinen's attention was drawn elsewhere.
When he later looked back upon the dwarf, this "oddest" person had grown into a giant. A superman of sorts, this titanic
force in nature had reached enormous size: his head almost
touched the clouds. Psychologically, this once little man was no
longer to be experienced merely as an impulse or a *scintillae*
emerging from the unconscious, but had now assumed the intensity of an affect, a creative élan which had been energized by
an inner light, thus expanding its size and powers. Representative of brawn rather than brain, this vestige of an archaic heritage symbolized the giant effort made by Väinämöinen to build
his new world, his individuality. For the creative artist that he
was, it indicated the presence of enormous instinctual power

which lay buried within him and which, when tapped, might aid in the fashioning of his life as shaman/poet.

The copper giant cuts the oak with his axe, piercing through the thick bark and trunk like an intuitive idea which slices and lacerates clusters of thought patterns as it battles fiercely to reach consciousness. A paradigm of enlightenment and discernment, the copper giant aims his blows at uneven growth, unreasoned thinking, unformed and deformed propagation. To hide the sun— the rational principle—is to allow untutored, unmanicured forces to proliferate. A structureless condition must be sacrificed so that the future shaman/poet may create with discernment, strengthen his visionary powers, thus enabling the very spirit and heart of *renovatio* to come into being.

Fire ejaculates from the oak tree as it is being struck down. The friction created from the contact of copper and wood pours out its energy in flame; a blaze comparable to the "devouring fire" experienced by Isaiah when God brought into existence the creative Word (30:27). A rainbow becomes visible after the severing process, again linking terrestrial and celestial worlds, greeting Väinämöinen's new thrust for freedom with signs of welcome. The rainbow's colorful and rounded beauty spreads feelings of relatedness and comfort throughout the cold and fog-enclosed surroundings. The sense of isolation which had permeated these heavily forested regions vanished momentarily; replaced by melodious color tones chanting their vibrations and sonorities in emanations ranging from highly pitched to velvety low tones—in keeping with the vital energy centers so crucial in the cutting ceremony and so important in fostering a climate conducive to the creative act.

Now that the sun shines anew and the earth is warmed and befriended by the great celestial force, Väinämöinen decides it is time to grow barley and oats. The mood of the land must be just right if the earth is to yield its riches. So, prior to the planting of this vital food, the terrain must be cleared of extraneous growth and rubble. To tame, cleanse, prepare, filter the earth so that ordered and willed insemination may come to pass requires another difficult ordeal. Another cutting is in order. All the trees must be felled, Väinämöinen reasons. Only one birch will be left standing, to be used by the eagle to build its nest. Out of gratitude, the eagle enables Väinämöinen to clear the land. It "struck fire, caused flame to flash" (p. 12). With the help of the wind, the forest was reduced to ash—the purest of states.

The eagle, able to fly directly above the clouds and into the sun without being blinded, is identified with the masculine solar spirit: *gnosis*, the conscious act. It is this factor which Väinämöinen put to use—his thinking principle—when he decided to destroy the forest land and create arable fields. In so doing, Väinämöinen dealt a blow at the dark state of identification with the collective world; in so doing he was assuming his own identity, deepening his understanding of himself, his worth, and his future as an individual in a collective society.

Väinämöinen sowed the seeds, scattering them everywhere, as far as the eye could see. Never neglecting the religious ritual which accompanied such a creative act, the moment of insemination was solemn and awe-inspiring. Väinämöinen sang the "Sower's Charm" invoking the "Woman living under the earth," the great mother, the "old ruler of the soil, mistress of the earth" (p. 12). He begged her to make the land fertile and to allow the plantings to burgeon. Ukko, "the heavenly father" was also called upon to furnish the proper ingredients, to balance *spirit* and *soul* in nature so that each would work in harmony with the other, bringing prosperity throughout the land and to its people, who had now come into being.

3. The Shadow Archetype: The Ordeal of Wisdom

The terrain had been cleared, the seeds planted. Väinämöinen had laid the groundwork for his future activities as shaman/ poet. Similar to the creative process in general, when the mind is no longer bombarded by extraneous events, unfocused tensions, or wandering thoughts, it concentrates on the seed/idea, enabling it to take root, grow, burgeon, giving cohesion to the disparate elements it encapsulates in the completed work. Thus far, Väinämöinen functioned well when *logos*—sharpness of thought and orderliness—dominated. Fate, however, frequently intervenes, breaking up the smooth-running course of existence, disrupting rational sequences, even the creative process. Fate, which the Gnostics called *heimarmene*, may dismantle, disrupt, alter what would otherwise have been continuous and solid. Were it not for fate, however, life could become one long period of conformity: unbroken, undivided, never allowing for an influx of fresh ideas to catapult into existence. Using a parallel line of reasoning we may say that when unconscious contents force their way into the existential world, consciousness is momentarily shattered and stasis is fragmented.

Väinämöinen's courage, perseverance, and psychological health are again ready to be tested. Fate calls upon a trickster, a youthful force, an impish young man to arrive on the scene. He may be looked upon as Väinämöinen's shadow archetype: representing those characteristics in an individual which the conscious personality considers negative and deems unacceptable. Rather than considering them in terms of the whole personlity, they are rejected and, in Väinämöinen's case, projected onto the impish "scrawny Lappish lad" called Joukahainen (p. 14).

An unthinking and rash young man, Joukahainen is described as forever acting on impulse. Despite his parents' warnings and admonitions, he decides to challenge Väinämöinen's wisdom and his power, to confront the culture hero and future shaman. He seeks to prove that he is more learned, more intuitive, more innovative than Väinämöinen, and that he and not his rival should be the psychopomp—the community's leader. Envious of Väinämöinen's talents as poet and singer, he is certain that he too can "bewitch' anyone and everyone who surrounds him. Nor does he intend to be outdone by Väinämöinen in the domain of magic. He had studied sorcery and enchantment and considers himself a master in these art/sciences. Joukahainen's brashness and lack of caution succeed in clouding his vision, and blocking his sense of reality. Too eager to reign supreme, he is unable to see the dangers at stake.

Joukahainen's plan did not have perspicacity. First, he decided to battle Väinämöinen on a physical level. He drove his sleigh into his rival's, hoping to smash it and its rider. Miraculously, Väinämöinen emerged unharmed. The Lappish lad then suggested a singing contest between the two. A wizard with words, imaginative, sensitive, endowed with great clarity in his thought processes, Väinämöinen's colorful vocalizations and lilting harmonies emerged in haunting metered verse, clever and astute epithets, striking images, and innovative metaphors. Joukahainen's by contrast, were labored, dull, and flat; the platitudes with which his song was replete, palled. Angered and

ashamed by his performance, the reckless young man challenged Väinämöinen to a duel. Here, too, he lost to superior
thinking. Väinämöinen parries each of his unguarded thrusts
and finally grounds his enemy. Master of Magic, Master of Word
and Deed, Väinämöinen grows annoyed at the affont caused
him by the Lappish lad and changes him into a swine. With a
sense of jubilation, the Master Musician sings out his feelings
for all nature to hear. His bracing words of rapture, his tonal
modulations entrance streams, flowers, trees, shrubs, which bend
and sway to the magic strains. Lakes begin to splash, the earth
rocks and shakes as Väinämöinen's superhuman powers manifest themselves in song and poetry. Only then did Joukahainen
accept the fact—at least outwardly—that he had lost.

> *O wise Väinämöinen, eternal sage!*
> *Reverse your magic charm, revoke your enchantment.*
> *Free me from this predicament, get me out of this situation.*
>
> (P. 18)

Weak-willed, unformed, egoless Joukaihainen promises
Väinämöinen anything and everything if he releases him from
his enchantment. He offers material gifts: a boat, bows, a stal-
lion. None is acceptable. Finally, he proposes his beautiful young
sister, Aino, to the old sage. The gift he offers, however, is not
his to give. No matter, for Joukahainen has again yielded to
impulse. Never does he once consider his sister's reactions; never
does he respect the feelings of others. He is driven by his desire
for immediate gratification.

Väinämöinen is delighted with Joukahainen's suggestion.
He revokes the magic spell and allows the lad to return to his
district. Väinämöinen follows. Though immensely displeased with
her son's comportment, Joukahainen's mother is happy with the
prospect of Aino's marriage to Väinämöinen. Aino, however, is
unwilling to accept the old man as her husband. To do so is to
go against nature. Youth seeks youth. She cannot, however, fight
her mother, brother, and the wise sage. Her sense of frustration
is such that she begins to weep. The tears, however, do not assuage her pain. She longs for life, youth, love. The mother remonstrates. There is "no reason to get gloomy," she tells her
daughter. She accuses her of having gone mad, of harboring a
ridiculous outlook. Not to accept Väinämöinen in marriage is

unthinkable. Representing the status symbol, the bourgeois and settled aspects of life, the mother is the paradigm of conformity. She wants things to be easy for her daughter and for herself. To invite Väinämöinen to become part of the family is to bring honor to it. The daughter's need for romance and love is in no way compatible with the old woman's ideas. Aino bewails her destiny while walking into the woods. Dark, eerie, unconscious forces now take hold in this archaic domain. She senses the fact that to marry "the terrible old man" would bring her sorrow. As she goes through the forest and down to the sea, her grief grows ever more strongly. Unknowingly, she begins splashing in the water as if to purify her being, to salvage herself from the senex figure's presence in her mind. To wash away her sorrow ever more completely, Aino strays too far into the fluid realm— too deeply into its wavelike flow—and drowns.

Aino representing the emerging feminine principle, is Väinämöinen's anima figure. She is that autonomous image of woman the male carries within his unconscious. As representative of the feeling world, Aino is so underdeveloped a component within his psyche that she dies when confronted with the possibility of unifying with the thinking senex figure. She yearns to live out her maidenhood. She had harbored the illusions and dreams of so many adolescents, hoping for future love experiences which would make them tingle with joy. Her unthinking brother had put an end to her world of fantasy, forcing the dormant and unformed anima to emerge into the phenomenological realm. Unprepared, unable to find a way out of her predicament, Aino/anima lost her footing and drowned in the waters of the unconscious: her ego had been dismantled, shocked, traumatized, and fragmented by her encounter with the senex figure, never again to be revitalized in this form.

Once in the waters, Aino took on the contours of a fish. When Väinämöinen saw her swimming about in the clear limpid waters, he tried to pull her out, to grab her and make her his own. She evaded his grasp each time. Even in this episode, she remained true to her anima nature, as an autonomous image in his unconscious she slips through his net and floats back into the deep waters where he experiences her as a reality.

Väinämöinen, poet and senex figure, had not yet learned to relate to his anima anymore than to his shadow. The feeling/

anima principle was foreign to his being. For Väinämöinen, feeling resided only in poetry and music, aspects or split-offs of the feminine principle. He had not yet learned to relate to a real woman. The magic he spun with his voice and his kantele, the power evoked in his words and harmonies held no charm for the young girl. He needed to learn another magic formula—nonintellectual—which would allow him to viscerally experience woman as a flesh and blood human being and not merely from the cerebral, thinking, and abstract spheres. Music and poetry created by and with the mind exist in structured tonalities and colored resonances. These are products of art/artifice/artificial and do not relate directly to life. What Väinämöinen had offered Aino corresponded to *mind and not to heart*.

Nor had Väinämöinen's shadow been integrated into his psyche. Joukahainen was a paradigm of all those lively, impulsive, and youthful elements which erupt into the existential sphere without rhyme or reason. Joukahainen lacked foresight and did not understand the repurcussions of his acts. He was a Finnish Epimetheus and not a Promethean type: afterthought was his way. As a shadow figure, Joukahainen's characteristics were rejected outright by Väinämöinen who functioned so well in his *logos* centered universe. He had encouraged the instinctual domain to participate as a functioning force in the whole psyche, rather than as a split-off, assuming autonomy and power of its own, he might have transformed what was so destructive into an energy-creating positive force. Joukahainen would remain stunted and unformed. As a result, what he represented in Väinämöinen, emerged spasmodically, hurting and bruising those with whom he came into contact.

Although Väinämöinen had defeated Joukahainen and had put him to shame, his victory caused him hubris. So much so, that his vision became clouded and he wrongly believed he had rid himself of Joukahainen. He neglected to take the *revenge principle* into consideration. Once he allowed his defenses to drop, he invited trouble. Väinämöinen had not yet reached the stage in life when he could afford the luxury of serenity. Unguarded, Joukahainen was left to his own devices. Angered by his defeat, he watched Väinämöinen's every move for the right moment to strike back. It happened one afternoon when Väinämöinen was riding his horse through fields and shallow lakes.

Joukahainen took his bow and arrow, aimed, and struck his enemy. Väinämöinen fell into the water and was carried off by its strong currents into the sea. Joukahainen rejoiced, certain this time of having killed the culture hero.

Väinämöinen had returned to the element of water, the fluid and formless realm, to the Virgin of the Air in whose womb he had lived for so many winters and summers. He needed a period of introversion, a *regressus ad uterum* in order to reimmerse himself in the feminine principle, to undergo a watering down of uneven and blocked unconscious contents. His views needed reworking, expansion in preparation for the world of conflict in store for him. As he experienced the fullness and foam of the nutritive waters, he saw an eagle fly by. It was the same one which had nested in the birch tree that he had not cut down. It was the eagle's turn to help Väinämöinen. He took him on his back to the shore. The masculine force, represented by the eagle/savior figure, brought the culture hero back to consciousness. The combination of the feminine principle (water) and the masculine force (eagle) working together, healed the bruised body, strengthened the ailing psyche, and brought equilibrium to the formerly unbalanced condition.

The eagle takes Väinämöinen to Louhi, the mistress of North Farm—a cold and icy region in Finland. She treats him well. Yet, despite her kindness, Väinämöinen longs for home. He feels uprooted, alienated, depressed. Nor can he fathom his reactions: "I can hardly know even myself," he says (p. 40). Why should he feel strange and out of place at North Farm? Joukahainen's arrow had pierced so deeply, his drowning had caused him such trauma, that the shock waves were still potent factors, still disrupting the course of his existence. He needed to reconnect with his roots, to experience the sustenance of familiar landscapes, trees, mountains, and lakes he knew so well.

Louhi promised she would see to Väinämöinen's homeward journey and would also give him her daughter in marriage, if he would forge a Sampo. The Sampo, similar to the philosophers' stone, the Grail, the Glorified Body of the mystic, is an immortal substance, a cosmic process, a unitary psychic concept which solidifies an inner experience: it reveals the link existing between ego and Self; it transforms the disparate facets of a personality into a cohesive whole. The Sampo is an ideal, a panacea, the outcome of a projection which fills an inner need, either on an individual or collective basis. Owing to its magic powers, the Sampo is supposed to bring prosperity and happiness to those who possess it.

Väinämöinen agrees to Louhi's plan. He will send Ilmarinen, the smith, to North Farm to forge the Sampo. Only a metalworker of renown can blend, mix, and heat the elements in such a way as to create a Sampo, a mysterious and miraculous alloy.

4. *The Anima Archetype*

Väinämöinen left North Farm with joy in his heart. On his way, he spied Louhi's daughter. She was dressed in traditional costume and sparkled with beauty and vibrancy on this crystal-clear day. So taken is Väinämöinen by the young girl that he asks her—unthinkingly—to become his wife. She accepts, but he must first fulfill certain conditions, such as fashioning a boat without *touching* it.

Tests and difficulties have frequently been part of the love game. In medieval times knights had to fight for their amorata, accomplish daring and dangerous feats to be worthy of affection. On the surface, Väinämöinen's compliance with the young lady's demands do not seem overly strange; however, he should have considered the circumstances and the impact of the tests themselves. Instead, he allowed instinct rather than *logos* to prevail and was unaware of the fact that he had little or no understanding of the feminine principle—his feelings had only reached the bud stage and were like clusters of under developed impulses. The schism existing between his inferior feeling function and his dominant thinking characteristics had not been breached. He yielded, therefore, to the Joukahainen in him — his shadow—and so, acted rashly. To impress the young lady, Väinämöinen bragged about his great building ability. In reality, he had never constructed a ship, which represents the thinking principle. It is a solid force that would see Väinämöinen through the dangerous waters of the unconscious, bringing him safely to the other side. Blind to his limitations, allowing his inflated ego to guide his speech, he neglected to consult the rational sphere of his personality. Without wisdom on his side, Väinämöinen courted disaster.

Väinämöinen begins building the ship. While splitting some logs with an axe, it slips and cuts his knee severely. Blood gushes forth, uncontrollably. As we have already learned, the knee plays an important role in *The Kalevala*: it was on his mother's knee that the bird rested and then built its nest, thus allowing the eggs to be born, and creativity to emerge. The knee, therefore, represented the origin and source of Väinämöinen's own identity—his strength and energy center. Now that his knee had been so severely severed, he could no longer walk with ease, indicating that his relationship with earth—with reality—had been impaired. Since the knee spells motility and power, it may be subsumed that Väinämöinen's own thoughtlessness had immobilized him. That blood, which is life, warmth, and spirit, flows out of him so powerfully symbolizes a decline in his energy, a diminution of that magical force which distinguishes the life/death condition.

Väinämöinen tries every manner and means to stanch the flow of blood. He puts moss on his wound, herbs of all types, even applies pressure. To no avail. He must find some other way to heal the split, to fuse what has been severed. The dichotomy within his personality, psychologically speaking, has grown too broad: the shadow factor and anima figure are experienced only unconsciously, therefore, projecting themselves as autonomous split-offs, thus as dangerous powers.

Väinämöinen sets out as best he can in search of some power conversant with the magic healing formula. He happens upon an old man who tells him that before he can make his knee whole again, he must find the source of the element that had caused his injury. No remedy can be effective, in the psychological domain, until one understands what brought on the disruptive condition, what caused the break. Since Väinämöinen's axe was made of iron, he would have to discover the origin of this element and in that way learn how to control or work in harmony with this force.

The old man represents age-old wisdom. He may be identified with a shaman long since dead, reputed for his extraordinary insights and powers, whom Väinämöinen has called on for help. Just as Sampsa and the copper man had emerged into consciousness when the need arose, so the old man was a vestige of some primordial past. Similar to the elders of a community, a priest, doctor, or rabbi, the old man stands for that mana personality, that force existing in the collective unconscious which surfaces in moments of deep stress. The old man is a warning principle. He puts Väinämöinen on guard to the dangers involved when dealing with impulses, rash ways, anima, and shadow types when these forces are not integrated into the psyche.

Väinämöinen, however, fails to look within, to assess his deeds, feelings, and thoughts, He projects them on outer forces, namely a host of evil spirits whom he blames for his accident: the wizard Hiisi, Väinämöinen declared, made the axe's handle shake; Lempo, turned its cutting edge toward his knee; Paha, misdirected the blow and caused the wound. These negative entities succeeded in assuming great power over him simply because Väinämöinen neglected to understand the role they played in his life, allowing the rational principle to diminish in force and scope. He did not weigh the problems involved. Overcome by the maiden's beauty, he allowed himself to be carried away once again by his inferior feeling function. He failed to consider the fact that he had no ship-building experience and that to create one without *touching* it, was an impossibility. Hands, which enable humankind to reach out, grab, fashion objects, are means of relating to the outside world. Without being able to grasp, manipulate, and feel life, ingredients so important in primitive societies, Väinämöinen would surely fail. Important, too, is the thought that harm awaits those who believe themselves capable of accomplishing feats which call them outside of their field of expertise.

Väinämöinen had still not accepted his past defeats: Aino's departure and death, his second encounter with the anima figure in the person of Louhi's daughter, and the inordinately difficult demands she made upon him. Bravoura, the persona which hides inferiority, was used to face the world. The split knee, one might say in Väinämöinen's case, was a manifestation of his broken heart.

The culture hero realized that the wise is the right course to take and followed the old man's advice. He went to seek the origin of the metal which had caused him his accident. Iron, similar to copper and other metals, was believed to emanate from heaven. Strong, powerful, hard, and inflexible, its use has both positive and destructive consequences. As a plow, it helps in planting and, thus, feeding humankind. As a knife, sword, or other warlike instrument, it destroys as well as defends. Shamans use iron utensils during their ceremonies to evoke spirits and to prove their mettle. Smiths' ovens, dug deep within the earth, are made of iron. In these recesses metals are heated, bent, and fashioned to serve humanity's needs. Considered as a type of demiurge, because of the "miraculous" works it brings forth, iron is also known to have therapeutic powers. Prior to Pliny's time it was used to stay the flow of blood. Dr. Sydenham (1665) was one of the first physicians to have patients ingest the metal in a refined form, because he believed it was effective in increasing red blood corpuscles.[18]

Väinämöinen's quest to learn the source of this crude and energetic element would, therefore, aid him physically as well as psychologically. The forging and melting process which iron must undergo in order to become ingestible by humans, requires time and knowledge. Its consistency alters from hard to fluid; its color, from black to red, similar to Väinämöinen's nervous system which was heated and burned with ardor for love of Louhi's daughter. The redness he had felt in her presence had aroused sparks within him, influencing his countenance as well as his actions. Its incandescence had liquefied what had once been solid within him, spreading chaos, blindness throughout his system. So sightless had he become that when felling the tree to make his ship, he failed to pay complete attention to his task. His thoughts, like ductile metallic elements, flowed toward the object of his passion, the girl. The anima figure, unpredictable as an autonomous force in his unconscious, had caused him great harm. The joint that had allowed him to walk, run, jump through life on a steady keel had been injured. Now he would have to apply particles of iron in their flaming state to his wound, to cauterize it and stanch the flow of blood. Only then would he contain the life-force within him and purify the noxious and debilitating powers which had brought such damage.

In time, Väinämöinen learns the secrets of iron. He returns to the old man and tells him: "I know the origin of iron" (p. 47). Satisfied with Väinämöinen's progress, the senex figure uses the charm which checks the flow of blood. He also prepares an ointment that will "exorcise" the pain experienced during the healing process. Pain and discomfort are experienced not only in the physical sphere, when bones and flesh mend, but also psychologically, as the components of the personality fuse. To test the efficacy of the unguent, the old man mends some huge boulders, seals crevices in the mountains. He then bandages Väinämöinen's knee with strips of silk.

> *Then old Väinämöinen already felt a real relief.*
> *He soon got well, his flesh grew fair . . .*
> *healthier than before, finer than in the past.*
>
> (P. 54)

Väinämöinen raises his head in thanks. The pain of the ordeal he had experienced had taught him that bravado and arrogance had nearly severed his knee—his personality. What he had not yet understood, however, was that despite the iron's hardness and strength, it rusted and flaked when exposed to the elements too long. So the anima, when projected indiscriminately and unconsciously onto outer figures, can likewise lead to a fragmented psyche.

When Väinämöinen finally reaches home he suggests to Ilmarinen, Master Forger and beater of iron, that he make a Sampo. Second in hierarchy to the shaman, the smith in northern climes is constantly at work in the community to ward off evil spirits. Since he handles fire, forging instruments for war as well as for sorcery, he is also believed to be a visionary able to see into inner realms where metals are born and evolve.[19] *The Kalevala* gives the entire history of iron, from its creation and gestation to the finished product. Identified with human intelligence the forge and forger (Ilmarinen in this case) are frequently associated with the warmth of thought and meditation, and with libido as well. That a forger succeeded in creating *something* out of a *formless object*, made of him a miracle worker and his forge, a hierophany in primitive societies.

Ilmarinen arrives at North Farm and brings the Sampo into existence. In a breathlessly exciting as well as terrifying interlude, the reader views Ilmarinen at work. The fire blazes, burns, and glows. From within its flowing embers, which Ilmarinen observes with extreme attention, there emerges the bow of a boat. He removes it from the flames, is dissatisfied, smashes it, and throws it back. The same things happens with other forms which have been fashioned: a heifer with golden horns, a plow with silver handles. A perfectionist, only a flawless object would fulfill his creative urge.

> *Then on the third day*
> *he came upon a marbled stone, a big block of rock.*
> *There the craftsman stopped, the smith built a fire;*
> *one day he made a bellows, the next he set up the forge,*
> *the craftsman Ilmarinen, eternal smith,*
> *thrust the things into the fire, his work down to the bottom of*
> *   the forge.*
>
> (P. 59)

Ilmarinen's furnace is reminiscent of the great ovens worked by the Taoist masters, those organizers of the created world, fashioners of so many wonder-working instruments. It also recalls the Nibelung dwarfs, miners who shaped the magic helmet, Tarnhelm, and the mysterious sword, Nothung, in Wagner's *Ring* cycle.[20] As the fire blazes, the bellows sound, the anvil rings, so the patron of smithies indulges in the alchemical dictum: *solve et coagula*—nothing substantial and valuable can be made until the hardest of elements is made to flow like water; only then are new unions, fresh essences, and alloys brought into existence; psychologically, a reconstituting of views and attitudes toward life.

Ilmarinen's forging of the Sampo ushers in a whole new dimension into *The Kalevala*: the personification of metals, the humanization of inanimate forces. Nature, both within and outside of the earth seems to awaken, to tingle with life and activity, energized as if by some supernatural spectacular force. As the fire burns and glares, the metals become audible. The pain and howling of the metals as they are being burned and shaped—during the transformation process—is again an indication of the difficulties involved in changing a life course, in focusing on a different way, in altering the thrust of certain relationships, diminishing their brutalizing effects while encouraging the positive factors involved. The Sampo, like the philosophers' stone is a *complexio oppositorum*. Within its essence lies a treasure, a mysterious *aliage*, a meditative device similar to a mandala, healing those who see into it and learn from the experience.

Ilmarinen, Master Forger, brought the Sampo to its perfected state on the third day:

> *he bent down to look at the bottom of his forge;*
> *he saw that a Sampo was being born, a lid of many colors*
>   *forming.*
> *Then craftsman Ilmarinen, eternal smith,*
> *taps away fast, pounds away spiritedly.*
> *He forged the Sampo skillfully: on one side a grain mill,*
> *on the second side a salt mill, on the third a money mill.*
> *Then the new Sampo ground away, the lid of many colors*
>   *went round and round;*
> *it ground a binful in the dawn, one binful of things to eat;*
> *it ground a second of things to sell, a third of household*
>   *supplies.*

> (P. 60)

The Sampo incarnated the needs of a culture, of a people whose
lives were arduous and whose future always precarious. As such,
it brought happiness and prosperity to North Farm. It was composed of commodities of all types, foods and staples which were
lacking in the workaday world. The Sampo, therefore, fed, both
spiritually and physically, the hungry and starving communities.
As a hierophany, it answered a deep-seated desire: humankind's
wish to be connected with celestial and earthly spheres, thereby
empowered them to block out and immobilize evil forces. Winter snows and iced-over waterways which made hunting and
fishing so difficult were some of the nearly overwhelming odds
against which these northern peoples struggled. The Sampo's
presence developed in the people a new sense of belonging which
helped them stave off melancholy, feelings of loneliness and
alienation which corroded their beings during the long black
winter months. The Sampo represented activity, fertility, and
hope for those who believed in its power.

5. Väinämöinen's Night-Sea Journey

As Osiris and Christ, as well as countless other historical and
mythical figures, experienced their night-sea journeys, so Väinämöinen would have to go through his supreme initiation—
the ego's encounter with the Self. Such an ordeal is important
heuristically. It requires the hierophant to overcome the terrible

vicissitudes which take place with a regression into the collective unconscious: the drowning of the ego within its tumultuous waters; its fragmentation and assimilation by components; its reemergence into light. Only after passing such a test is the ego strengthened, able to function in harmony with the Self; only then is the shaman/poet born into a higher sphere of consciousness. To come through the night-sea journey successfully requires enormous inner strength and great psychological health; it is comparable to a life/death struggle.

Shamans must go through such a night-sea ordeal in order to become thoroughly conversant with their art/science. In Väinämöinen's case, he must *build* the ship he will use to take him to his insalubrious lower depths: he must, symbolically speaking, *build* his psyche into a cohesive whole. An outer core—the ship—is a carapace which must be capable of resisting attack from all types of infernal entities, as represented at times by jagged rocks and ocean swells. Similar to a vase or womb, the ship encloses and protects; it allows everything within to circulate and ambulate, as blood through the arteries. All parts of the psyche, therefore, are attended, and fed, cooperating in the struggle facing the shaman/hero. When called upon consciousness will prevail, even when cataclysmic events seek its obfuscation. Thus will the ego be saved from possible mutilation by the Self.

All of Väinämöinen's knowledge and art will be put to work in the construction of his ship: in the pursuit of *his* goal. This time he sets about his task, not by the proddings of an autonomous anima figure, but because of an inner necessity. Väinämöinen again has recourse to Sampsa, "the Spirit of Arable," that dwarf figure whom he called upon to help him seed the land with trees, that small being who lies buried within his unconscious—as an impulse, an *Einfall*—and summoned into consciousness during moments of need. This little spirit works meticulously. First he consults the trees around him—aspens, evergreens, oaks—inquiring of them which wood is best suited to ship building. He is told that the oak is the finest and richest of them all.

Then old Väinämöinen, eternal sage,
made a boat skillfully, by magic singing fashioned a vessel

from the shattered remains of a single oak, from the fragments
    of the fragile tree.
He sang a charm, made fast the bottom; he sang a second,
    joined the planks,
soon he sang a third charm, too . . .

                                                        (P. 97)

Väinämöinen chants as he builds, intoning but a single note
for long periods of time, relating this basic tone to others in
sequences of nuanced vibrations which drone on and on with
hypnotic effect. The singleness of purpose activates the physical
and psychical powers, inciting them to work in his favor. Wood
is entranced and bewitched by the poetry which fills the earth;
it awakens, catalyzing the instruments needed by Väinämöinen,
helping to place each piece of wood into the other. The wood
allows itself to be shaped, molded, fastened into one powerful
architectural form. Each plank, as if responding to Väinämöinen's breathing, sways in kinetic velocities, ensnared by the
momentum of the sequential rhythms.

Despite the harmonies intoned, Väinämöinen lacked three
charms to make his ship seaworthy. To acquire this knowledge
meant descending to the Abode of the Dead, to an unknown
and frightening realm, where apparitions in monstrous regalia
stalk about. It is within the deepest strata of elemental and subliminal spheres where entities live inchoate, diffused, dissem-
bled, that Väinämöinen must descend. Only there will he find
the nutritive elements capable of replenishing and revitalizing
the creative élan. Overexposure to the light of reason leads frequently to spiritual and creative impoverishment.

Väinämöinen will now begin his night-sea journey. Unlike
Charon's ship, which took the shades from one shore of Hades
to the other, or Amida Buddha, who considered himself a pas-
serby in the waters of life, Väinämöinen of his own free will
decides to immerse himself in the insalubrious domain of the
dead—there, to find the answer to his puzzling existential problem. The chthonic powers he encounters are archetypal in dimension; they are forces with which he has not yet had to contend. Death's daughters, for example, are "stumpy," ugly, mean,
vicious. Negative female figures, as is the case of most guardians
of secrets and treasures in myths and fairy tales, they are de-

scribed as voracious dragon types; their spiritual and psychological claws and jaws are ever ready to pounce and crush any victim approaching them. That Väinämöinen encounters these spirits and is unafraid of them indicates his growing inner strength, his ability to face the most insidious and invidious of beings.

These horrific maidens, who call themselves Death's Daughters, are destructive anima figures—poisonous in all senses of the word. They are carriers of spiritual and physical disease. To expose oneself to these goddesses is to experience the very origin of a thousand scourges. Described as black-faced and having pustulating skin, each reigned over a particular sickness: pleurisy, colic, gout, phtisis, ulcers, scabies, canker, plague, and a "fatal spirit, a creature eaten up with envy" who was not given a name. Since disease was believed to be caused by the soul's departure from the body, a cure consisted in the recapturing of this force through exorcism. Plagues, interestingly enough, have been embodied throughout history in womankind. She is the disease-spreading force which must be routed. Like the Erinnyes, the Greek goddesses of revenge, who also worked for the terrible mother, so Death's Daughters perform their terrors in vulnerable areas, where darkness, fear, and repression reign supreme.

Despite the horrors viewed by Väinämöinen, he remains fearless. Rather than shrink from their sight, he makes demands upon Death's Daughters. He wants to be taken to the "other" bank of the river—to the land of the really dead. They comply. He is received by Tuonetar, the queen of Tuonela, the Abode of the Dead. She offers him beer to drink.

Steadfast old Väinämöinen looked long at his stoup;
frogs were spawning inside, reptiles crawling on the sides.

                                                        (P. 100)

Väinämöinen refuses to imbibe. To get drunk, to lose his lucidity, would be his undoing. Another reason was also instrumental in his refusal: to drink beer (or water) in the Abode of the Dead in myths of many lands meant to remain bound, imprisoned in this darkened domain, to forgo ego-consciousness. To withdraw into such a state of oblivion, into the whirlpool of eternally circular energetic powers, is to be shut up in the collective unconscious—to allow insanity to prevail. Shamans, masters of magic, are on the contrary, always lucid, even, paradoxically, when experiencing their cataleptic trances. They observe their activities at all times and are not enslaved by their subliminal worlds: they see their souls leaving their bodies; they watch every limb function in their voyage heavenward or within the earth.

After Väinämöinen refuses to drink the brew offered him, the queen of the dead, angered by his abstention, informs him that he will never leave her realm, never return to the upper world—to consciousness. He had entered a sphere from which there was no return. Suddenly, Väinämöinen fell into a deep sleep. While in this condition a net of iron mesh a thousand fathoms long, with sharp iron teeth, is thrown over him and the entire area surrounding the nearly lifeless body. Never would he succeed in extricating himself from such a barrier, the queen of the dead maintained. Väinämöinen, however, shaman/poet, was also a Master of Magic. He called upon his knowledge of wizardry, which had been developed during his previous ordeals. Väinämöinen transformed himself into a snake and "crept in the form of an iron reptile" (p. 101) through Death's Domain, slithering through the sharp metal teeth, unhurt. Väinämöinen knew that difficulties may be broached from several vantage points and if one way is not efficacious in solving a problem, another may be. That he chose the form of a snake—a paradigm of wisdom in the East as well as of immortality (the annual molting of its skin)—indicates that he needed to be in touch with the elements this primeval force represented: the earth's eternal rhythms, that is, instinct. Snakes are also considered in Kundalini yoga, as energy centers. Every individual has his own snake which is coiled up in his lower extremities; its energetic powers are exercised and strengthened through special rituals during which time these lower forces are made to travel upward within the body until they reach the head—then focus upon a centrally located spot on the forehead which is believed to be endowed with "divine intelligence." The fusing of energy and mind augments spiritual and physical insight. Snakes in their ambivalence and mysterious ways also cure as well as kill. If properly approached and handled with care, a serpent may yield its knowledge as it did to Aesculapius who immortalized it on

his cadeusis. By transforming himself into a snake, Väinämöinen, similar to Ulysses, used ruse as well as intellect to extricate
himself from the tentacles of impending doom.

Väinämöinen slithered through the vast iron net: its mur-
derous teeth, arranged in soldierlike formation, proved to be
harmless. His night-sea journey had further increased his understanding of the ways and wiles of the world; his patience had
also been tested and strengthened as had his insight. When he
finally reached the outer world and saw the sun shedding its
brilliant rays throughout the universe, he experienced the quintessence of joy which comes from having undergone a terroriz-
ing experience and having survived by means of one's own ingenuity and perspicacity. "Many have got there, few have come
from there, from the home in Death's Domain, from the eternal
cottages of the Abode of the Dead" (p. 102). Väinämöinen, sha-
man/poet, had completed his night-sea journey—his period of
indwelling—during the course of which he had unearthed certain secrets which would be put to use in his next adventure.

6. The Giant Archetype
Väinämöinen's ordeals were not yet over. He still had to discover those charms which would enable him to construct his
ship. Only by seeing a task through to its finish does one experience a sense of accomplishment and fulfillment. To this end,
Väinämöinen consults the giant Antero Vipunen. He finds this
primitive archaic force, stretched out on the ground, a poplar
tree growing from his shoulders, a birch from his temples, an
alder from his cheeks, a willow from his beard, a fir from his
forehead, and a wild pine between his teeth.

According to the Edda, giants were born into the world
prior to the gods. They relied on strength for power and were
usually looked upon as spiritually indigent. Neither good nor
evil, the giant, a primal or vegetative entity, represents quantitative amplifications of ordinary beings: he surpasses human
nature from a physical point of view. As such giants have frequently retained certain qualities of a terrible father of childhood reminiscences, of a harmful force such as Goliath or Og
(the Amorite king of Bashan [Num. 21:33]), the Cyclops Poly-
phemus, the Christian's Satan, the Sumerian's Humbaba. Väinämöinen was fully aware of the dangers involved in confronting

a giant—a titanic force which could destroy him in one fell swoop. All depended upon Väinämöinen's approach to this primitive being, the source of many secrets which the shaman/poet sought to discover.

Väinämöinen was pragmatic; his method, well reasoned. First he cleared a path to the giant's mouth by cutting down the trees which blocked his way. Such proximity to the mouth would enable him to hear the giant's words of wisdom.

He drove the iron cowlstaff into Antero Vipunen's mouth,
into the grinning gums, the rattling jaws.
He uttered a word, spoke thus: "Slave of mankind, get up
from lying under the ground, from sleeping a long time."

(P. 104)

Vipunen felt the pain of Väinämöinen's axe, saw, and other cutting instruments which had bitten into him. He awakened. His body throbbed. Meanwhile, Väinämöinen's "right foot slipped, the left foot slid," and suddenly, he found himself in the giant's mouth. The immense creature then opened his jaws wide and Väinämöinen was swallowed up along with his sword. Once again darkness prevailed. Ingenuity, Väinämöinen's strong point, had been heightened to even greater peaks resulting from his previous ordeals. He accepted his fate as Jonah had. Instead of withdrawing into a state of passivity, he built himself a small boat within the giant's belly: "he rows, he glides lightly from end of gut to end of gut" (p. 105).

That Väinämöinen's foot slid during the course of his work indicated, once again, the importance of the fate factor. No matter how reasoned is humankind's way, forces beyond his control and understanding are ever-present, ready to disrupt the ordered. What is of import is the individual's ability to take nature's unpredictable ways into account and not to allow them to destroy one's course, but to adapt to them, building upon them. Such attitudes increased Väinämöinen's energies: they forced him to draw upon himself to seek out his answers. That the giant swallowed the shaman/poet is also of great significance. The mouth, from which breath, nourishment, and the word are ingested and emerge, represents an ontological condition. *Logos, spiritus, consciousness,* make their secrets known through the mouth. The mouth is a vessel through which man reveals his creative principle. An aggressive force, the mouth is armed with teeth and tongue, connecting the uncreated realm of darkness with the created world of light. It is a vehicle through which fantasy is transformed into fact, energy into activity. That the giant opened his mouth indicated his willingness to allow Väinämöinen access to the treasures of the inner man, those archaic forces within him. Unlike the volatile female principles Väinämöinen had encountered in the Abode of the Dead, the giant's components were inactive. Slumbering most of the time, immersed in brawn rather than in brain, the giant offered Väinämöinen direct contact with vital organs: knowledge buried far within the *flesh* of existence. Unimpeded, Väinämöinen traveled far into the giant's stomach. Identified with the transformatory process, since this organ takes in food in one state and alters its consistency and quality via its gastric juices, so knowledge, too, is to be unearthed by Väinämöinen within the *gut* area, calling upon the heart, liver, intestines, and bladder in the process. The giant's entire inner system works on behalf of Väinämöinen. Each organ imparts its special knowledge to the shaman/poet. Still Väinämöinen seeks to discover more. He has recourse to art/artifice. He will practice metallurgy: from his shirt he makes a forge; his sleeves and fur-lined coat serve as bellows; his knee becomes the anvil; his funnybone, the hammer. He strikes away, blow after blow at the giant's belly. The pain Vipunen knows is excruciating: "hot coals are coming into my mouth, fire brands onto my tongue, iron slag into my throat" (p. 105). Despite the jabs, thrusts, and searing sensations, the giant refuses to reveal the deepest of secrets. Väinämöinen threatens him.

> *I will set my anvil deeper in the flesh of your heart*
> *press my sledge hammer more firmly on the more painful*
>   *spots, too,*
> *so that you will never get free, never, never at all*
> *unless I get to hear charms, take along propitious spells,*
> *hear enough charms, thousands of magic formulas.*
>
>   *(P. 111)*

Finally, Vipunen begins reciting charms of all types: against injuries, disease, misadventures, exorcisms, intimidation. Still Väinämöinen has not heard what he wants to know. Only in the *heart*—the center of being, the focal point of life—would the answer be forthcoming.

The heart and lungs are the seat of the soul according to mystics, ranging from the ancient Egyptian sages to the Hindu practitioners of occult arts. For this reason, warriors in certain cultures, eat the heart and lungs of vanquished peoples to better absorb their vital force. The heart is the focal point of feeling and affectivity. The knowledge emanating from this organ is not cerebral, but emotional; its responses, therefore, are frequently more important and more profound than those resulting from the cerebral cortex. That blood emanates from the heart and is pumped throughout the entire body, indicates that this organ is responsive to the needs of the whole person rather than to specific areas. The Taoist masters understood that the heart was the focal point of cardiac rhythms and, for this reason, learned to master it according to their will. They thereby combined intellect and feeling; in so doing, life's polarities worked together rather than at odds. What had been an inferior or superior function within the psyche was better balanced. Such was the lesson Väinämöinen had to learn.

When Väinämöinen, therefore, strikes at the heart (the heart of the matter), the giant yields, and "opened his chest of words" (p. 111). His "chest" contained the secrets hard to attain—the Treasures of Tradition, the Tables of the Law—verbal sperm. Unlike Pandora's box which had been opened out of curiosity, Väinämöinen's quest was a mature one; it reached the "heart" of nature, allowing consciousness to grow. He perfected himself as shaman/poet and in so doing, aided humanity in overcoming its ordeals.

Once Väinämöinen experienced the sacred chants emerging from the vital organ itself, the words and sounds communicated to him took on greater meaning and impact. Vipunen intoned his knowledge in the stillness of mind/body—in the timeless universal world soul. The shaman/poet learned how to cure souls of depression and sorrow, of worldly cares. Not from the head exclusively, as Plato had dictated in his world of Ideas, but also from the bodily sphere. Both areas had to enter into complicity, thereby including feeling and emotion into what would otherwise have become a dry and lifeless cerebral realm. Vipunen's harmonies spoke to Väinämöinen of planets, stars, heavenly bodies, which responded to his emanations by vibrating in multiple frequencies, variegated cosmic dimensions. Vipunen knew how to stretch sound, slim it, so it would be received in sympathetic ways by natural forces: the rock, tree, waters, and so forth.

Vipunen's pain grew intense. Still Väinämöinen hammered, cut, and fired his metals within the giant's abdomen. Then, Vipunen opened his mouth wide and allowed his captive to step into freedom—to reveal his message to humankind.

Old Väinämöinen set out from the mouth of the man of great learning,
from the belly of the man of great resources, from the bosom of the man of great magic knowledge.

(P. 112)

Väinämöinen builds his boat and sails onto other adventures as shaman and poet. Solitary, as is the trajectory of the chosen one—the being who has been designated to lead his people—Väinämöinen understands and accepts his lot. He now knows that he will never be able to live on a human level. He cannot, therefore, seek out love in mortal terms nor know personal relationships in earthly contexts. He is a collective figure, eternal in his imaginings and fantasies, universal in his concepts, answering society's needs in the spiritual as well as the creative domain.

7. Archetypal Music: The Kantele

One of Väinämöinen's most moving adventures takes him on another journey through the seas. While sailing through some rapids, a large pike emerges from the deep. Since it obstructs the boat's course, it had to be killed. From its jawbone, Väinämöinen fashions an "instrument of eternal joy," the kantele.

From what was the harp's frame? From the great pike's jawbone.
From what was the harp's pegs? They are from the pike's teeth.
From what are the harp's strings? From the hairs of the Demon's gelding.

*Now the instrument was produced, the harp got ready,
the great pikebone instrument, the fishbone harp.*

(P. 274)

   Bones of fish or animals are considered living entities, positive forces, frameworks for the soul and body. They are, therefore, rarely destroyed. The Finns and Lapps believe that the gods use the bones of the dead in the reconstruction of new beings and animals. Since the kantele was fashioned from the pike's jawbone, it may be looked upon as a hierophany in *The Kalevala*. It was considered such in the *Eddas*, as heroes were burned with their harps at their sides on the funeral pyres, making sure the instruments would follow them to the next world. Väinämöinen's kantele was that vehicle which allowed him to tame his adversaries, to lull natural forces to sleep, and to experience relatedness with the universe at large.

   Generous as always, Väinämöinen allowed those who wished to play his kantele. Only he, however, was capable of modulating its tonal essences, which emerged like litanies, threnodies, as well as songs of jubilation and exultation. For the shaman that Väinämöinen was, the notes, chords, and overtones sounded in subdued registers and imperceptible to many, were apprehended by inanimate forces. Tree, water, earth, rock, experienced its superb resonances in sympathetic ways, pulsating when touched, hesitating when concerned, paused when reflecting and joyful in the ebullience of staccato rhythms. Nature in all of its multiple manifestations, sensed the minutest gradations in volume and intensity, as Väinämöinen's strange and haunting soundings seemed to strike each entity in its own center of being.

   That a solar hero such as Väinämöinen had reached such heights as musician and shaman, meant that a plateau and then a descent were in order. In keeping with this pattern, we are told of a storm which arose at sea. Giant waves covered the ship in which Väinämöinen and his friends found themselves. People and objects, including the kantele, were washed overboard. The very instrument which had made Väinämöinen Master of People, Master of Song and Word had vanished forever. "There has gone my creation," Väinämöinen cried out, "gone my lovely instrument, vanished my eternal source of joy!" (p. 286). Although the creative factor had been washed away, and with it the pleasures of life, no regret existed on Väinämöinen's part. "In a boat there must be no lamenting, in a in a vessel no whimpering." Life must pursue its course. Distress, pain, loss are all part of the life process. The new, fresh, and the future must forever be considered. "Weeping does not rid one of distress nor howling of evil days!" (p. 287). To face the realities of existence was Väinämöinen's way now that he had passed his *rite de passage*.

So too did the Sampo vanish during the storm. When shattered, its disparate parts floated into the sea, others were washed onto the shore. In keeping with the great mystical traditions of Orphism and Kabbala, Väinämöinen started to gather up the bits and pieces of this sacred force. He expended his energies seeking to fix what had been broken, renew what had been destroyed. Hope, therefore, superseded the despair which could have overwhelmed him.

Time passes. A boy is born to a virgin called Jarjatta. So "strange" is he, that Väinämöinen suggests he be put to death. His advice is not taken. Instead, he is christened king of Karelia. Väinämöinen, angry and distraught, realizes that his powers and authority are over. He prophesies that one day he would be called upon again to guide his people, to instill them with strength, fiber, and energy. Before leaving in a copper boat, Väinämöinen bequeaths his newly fashioned kantele, along with his songs, to those remaining behind.

> He sang magically for his last time,
> sang up a copper boat, a copper-decked vessel.
> He sits down in the stern, set out for the clear expanse of the
>   sea.
> He was still speaking as he was going, remarking as he went
>   along:
> "Let time pass, one day go, another come;
> they will need me again, be looking, waiting for me
> to fetch a new Sampo, to prepare a new instrument,
> fetch a new moon, free a new sun
> when there is no moon, no sun nor any worldly joy."
>
> (P. 336)

Earth-oriented, *The Kalevala* exudes its spiritual and creative yearnings via words, music, and the spectacular images and colorations. Its message, which reflects the culture of the Finnish people, as do myths in general, is one of hope, but not blind or utopian, rather realistic, residing in the very heart of the conflict and the struggle of daily existence. In keeping with the importance accorded to nature, *The Kalevala* focuses on forests, plantings, seas, waterways, and animals, to teach its lessons and reveal its mysteries. That Väinämöinen was forever building boats, journeying in them from one end of the land to another, even within the giant's belly, underscores the importance of travel by ship in a land dotted with shoals and rocks, where navigation is one of the most efficacious ways of bringing produce from one area to another; it is also a deeply pleasurable experience for the Finn—a great adventure even today.

Väinämöinen, senex figure, shaman/poet, is archetypal in dimension. He represents an ideal for a people so deeply rooted in the earth. He is a thinking principle, a solar force, a light-bringer to a land immersed for so many months in darkness and cold. In their wisdom, however, the Finns understood that an overly rational attitude also has its dangers: it brings aridity to a culture and to the psyche. Only with a balanced *hieros gamos*, can a working relationship between the polarities implicit in the life experience, be effected. Such was the lesson Väinämöinen learned. With fulfillment, he offered the best to humankind.

The Kalevala has been an inspiration for many artists. Lafcadio Hearn (1850–1904) believed that it contained "all the elements of a magnificent operatic episode . . . an universe for startling and totally new musical themes."[21] Sculptors such as Erik Cainberg (1771–1816), who was the first to treat *The Kalevala* motif in this medium, inscribed his vision of Väinämöinen for eternity. Aksel Gallen-Kallela (1865–1931) created a pictorial version of *Aino* (1891), and a fresco entitled *The Forging of the Sampo* (1893). A film, *The Day the Earth Froze* (1959), shot in Finland but produced in America, was an adaptation of the Sampo episode.[22] Perhaps the greatest spokesman of them all was Jan Sibelius (1865–1957) who composed his orchestral works in the profoundly musical spirit of *The*

Kalevala. With magic and artistry, he brought Väinämöinen to life, as the shaman/poet and kantele player had predicted at the conclusion of his saga: "Let time pass, one day, go, another come; they will need me again, be looking, waiting for me."

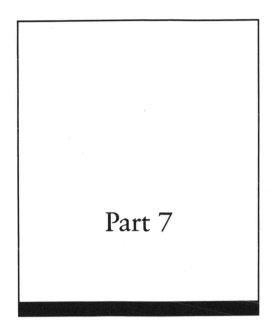

Part 7

Attar (1120–1230): *The Conference of the Birds*—A Sufi's Mystical Experience and the Dehumanization Process

The Conference of the Birds (Mantiq ut Tair) by the Persian mystic poet Farid ud-din Attar is a long allegory describing the philosophical beliefs and religious practices of the Sufi. It depicts the quest of myriad birds, endowed with human characteristics, from their terrestrial condition to their final absorption into the Simurgh—a metaphor for Allah, the supreme being or God. During the stages of their difficult trajectory each of the birds in this veritable comédie-humaine develops its own potential, but only thirty of them are destined to achieve their goal. Hidden within Attar's lyrical work is the entire Sufi mystery revealed in the seven levels of religious experience attained by the birds. Also implicit in *The Conference of the Birds* is the psychological process that takes the protagonists and the reader from an ego-centered condition in the external world to annihilation and reintegration into the Self: a dehumanizing process.

Similar in its theme of trials and pilgrimages to the thirteenth-century French *Romance of the Rose*, Chaucer's fifteenth-century *Canterbury Tales*, and Novalis's nineteenth-century *Heinrich von Ofterdingen*, Attar's work relates a religious and psychological experience that permits the protagonists/initiates to reach out beyond the world of contingencies and ego limitations into a celestial sphere where feelings of wholeness and completion are fully realized. Sufi mystical poetry, as found in the works of Rūmī Attar, Sa'dī (1184–1291), Hāfiz (c. 1325–89), and Rūmī (1207–73), the founder of the whirling dervishes, may be interpreted according to the reader's level of illumination or psychological awareness.

The seven stages of spiritual consciousness traversed in *The Conference of the Birds* are part of the Sufi system of initiation. Expressed in metaphor, symbol, hyperbole, metonymy, and other figures of speech, Attar's work combines a deep poetic experience with an equally deep religious and psychological one. Love, for example, which is described as a flower, tree, pearl, water, desert, and mountain, has far more than its literal, physical meaning, just as love has in the Song of Solomon or the *Rubaiyat* of Omar Khayyam; love is a metaphor expressing a shifting emotional factor, the essence that links man and God. It is the Sufi way of conveying the ascensional climb from the sensate world of multiplicity to the sublimated experience of oneness— from concrete form to the annihilation of shape; from sense to extrasensory perception.

Attar's imagistic language, which is often stylized and elaborate, allows the reader to focus on certain recurring paradigms, such as a garden, a body of water, a rose, all mandalas: graphic symbols of the universe that mirror the various stages of spiritual consciousness for both the initiate and the reader.[1] Archetypal in dimension, such images reveal a parapsychological condition: the initiate attempts to go beyond the spatial-temporal sphere of sense perception, then merges in the All. There also exists yet another level of *gnosis* beneath the plethora of visualizations, a secret language that only the Persian Sufi understands. It consists of cryptographic elements—similar to the Kabbalists's *gematria, notarikon*, being assigned to each letter and to the way the words are placed in the sentences, devices that supposedly encourage communication between the individual initiate and the collective force which is God.

The style and content of Attar's poem thus represents in itself a mystical and psychoanalytic progression. The initial confessions made by the birds, for example—revealing their intentions, feelings, and attitudes toward life—may be viewed as corresponding to the anamnesis, the amplification of certain problems, situations, and emotional conditions that disclose the personality and prepare the groundwork for further analysis. The anecdotes and allegories, metaphors, symbols, images, and incidents described by the birds throughout the tale are also paradigms of Attar's remarkable psychological technique. Such intrusions or interruptions in the free-flowing narrative delay the action and interrupt the reader or listener's train of thought, forcing comparisons and parallels to be made, thus altering mood and tension, and thereby changing the attitude and level of understanding.

The seven stages of spiritual growth to be traversed, or of obstacles to be overcome, in *The Conference of the Birds* are designed to awaken the novitiate's inner eye, to arouse the sub-liminal contents in the sphere, permitting apperception of spir-itual and psychological conditions to which he might otherwise have been oblivious.[3] Reminiscent in certain respects to Aris-totle's entelechy—humankind's conscious and unconscious de-sire for wholeness—the Sufi's indoctrination process is designed to expand consciousness. The Sufi's task in life is to complete what is incomplete, cleanse what is stained, and train the inner being to yearn for the experience of perfection. Transcendence lies at the root of Sufi mystical experience, as it does for so many mystical cults. Constant striving, therefore, is the Sufi's way: from the seed to the flower, from the sperm to the quin-tessential being.

ECTYPAL ANALYSIS

Farid ud-din Abu Hamid Muhammad ben Ibrahim, to give his whole name, later known as Attar ("perfumer" or "druggist"),[4] was born near Nishapur, the birthplace of Omar Khayyam. Little is known about his actual life. The following anecdote is told, however, that Attar had inherited a successful pharmacy from his father. One day a stranger, a Sufi, entered the shop and looked around. Suddenly his eyes filled with tears. Attar told him to leave. "It is not difficult for me," the stranger answered, "I have nothing to carry, nothing but this cloak. But you, with your costly drugs? You would do well to consider your own arrange-ments for going on your way." Moved by this statement, Attar replied that he too hoped to end his life as a Sufi. "We shall see," the man of God answered, and thereupon, lying down on the floor of the shop, he died. This incident made such an im-pression on Farid that he immediately sold his pharmacy and sought entrance into a Sufi order. After completing his initia-tion, he went on a pilgrimage to Mecca, then left the Sufi circle, and spent the next thirty-nine years of his life wandering from place to place, from country to country. He finally returned to his native town, where he died.[5]

Attar wrote over two hundred thousand verses and many works of prose; among the latter is *Tadkhirat al-auliya*, which contains biographies of many Islamic saints. His knowledge was vast; his poetic sensibility, equally profound. Rumi, who as a child had met the one-hundred-and-ten-year-old Attar, is reputed to have said: "Attar is the soul itself."[6]

The semimonastic Sufi order started during the eighth century as a protest against the worldly riches and moral laxity of the Umayyad caliphates in Damascus. Hasan Baṣrī, who died in 728, is said to have been the founder of Sufism. To prove the depth of their feelings and intentions, the truth of their religious convictions, he and his followers, ascetic in nature, began wearing a simple cloak made of wool (ṣūf), as a result of their renunciation of worldly values. As time went by, the Sufi's cloak, or *khirqa*, took a more and more esoteric meaning; it signified the cloaked or hidden spiritual doctrines of the Sufi. Only the chosen could be initiated into the mysteries involved—not the untutored mass who might bring catastrophe upon themselves and the world were such knowledge to fall into the hands of the unprepared.[7]

Muhammad himself was said to have first placed the *khirqa*, the cloak of "concealment" over the shoulders of his daughter Fatima, her husband, Ali, and their two sons, Husein and Hasan, thus transmitting spiritual power to their descendants, the future Imams. The *khirqa*, then, represents "the transmission of universal spiritual power"—the eternal knowledge that comes from above. Each Sufi who has earned the right to wear the garment is said to have this transpersonal force within him.[8] The novitiate receives the *khirqa* only after a long training period that may last for three years or more, depending upon the order and the century. During this time he must repent, trust in God, and undergo extreme physical and emotional hardships. He must never complain, fast frequently, sleep for only a few hours nightly or not at all, meditate for a period of forty days, paralleling, according to the Koran, the time Moses spent awaiting the theophany: "And when We did appoint for Moses thirty nights (of solitude), and added to them ten, and he completed the whole time appointed by his Lord of forty nights;

and Moses said unto his brother: Take my place among the people. Do right, and follow not the way of mischief-makers" (Surah 7:142).[9]

Sufism, although varying according to the time and place practiced, was greatly influenced by Shiite (Arabic "sectarian") belief. The Shiites, who represent one of the two great divisions in Islam, broke with the orthodox Sunnites during the struggle over Muhammad's successor. The Shiites considered that the ruling caliphates had been taken over by usurpers and recognized only Ali and his two sons as the rightful caliphs, but the three were murdered. Shortly thereafter, they were elevated to the rank of sacred martyrs. The divine line must be kept, the Shiites maintained, which began with Ali, continued with his nine successors, the last of whom was alluded to as the Twelfth Man, alive today but hidden in the world, and who will appear on the Last Day.[10]

In keeping with Shiite doctrine, the Sufi rejected what he considered to be the more dry, didactic, and scholastic approach to religion advocated by the Sunnis. Emphasizing the inward and subjective spiritual world rather than the outward, objective, and terrestrial condition, Sufi thought represented a compensatory factor within the unconscious, counteracting the more orthodox literal and cerebral interpretation of the Koran.[11] Neoplatonism, Buddhism, Christianity, Kabbala, and Gnosticism were important elements in forming the philosophical basis for Sufi thought. Opting for a highly sensitized approach to God, the Sufis claimed to have experienced ecstatic union with divinity—moments when they felt completely detached from the telluric domain—and integrated into the Godhead. Because the "He" became "We" for the Sufi mystic Al-Ḥallāj (858–922), he was considered a heretic (suffering from inflation that he dare compare himself with God or feel he had experienced Him) and executed. Hasan Baṣri declared his love for God, also measuring himself with divinity, when he said, "I desire Him and He desires me." One of the most important Sufi philosophical treatises was Al-Ghazālī's (1058–1111) *The Revival of the Sciences of Religion*, a compendium of deeply spiritual religious statements concerning God: a paradigm of the Sufi initiation ritual with all the mystical and psychological overtones implicit in such doctrine.[12]

Prayer, recitation, incantatory invocations, anaphoras, as opposed to theological exegesis, were advocated by the Sufi order. Devoted to a *via contemplativa* and a *via illuminativa*, a path leading from the world of multiplicity—that is, from darkness—to one of unity and light, the Sufi's goal was to remove the veils that separated him from Allah—the ultimate reality. To this end, he sought to annihilate (*fanā*) his ego that remained attached and so enslaved to terrestrial wants, needs, and thoughts, and incarnated or created with his human condition. Free from this world's dross, the Sufi was able to pursue his course into the pleromatic sphere: *baqā*, his reintegration into the Godhead, the Absolute—the original condition of primordial untiy, the state of being prior to earthly creation.

Psychologically speaking, the ordeals required to become a Sufi are extreme: designed to redirect one's life course—from mortal to divine goals, from ego to Self. A dehumanizing process that rejects mankind's "weaknesses" by suppressing them—which is also the technique used by many ascetic and mystical groups—the Sufi cuts himself off from the workaday world of the senses and from all relationships. The energy previously expended in extroverted (outside) activities can then be refocused into introverted (subjective or spiritual) channels. Ritual prayers and ceremonies, therefore, take on great importance, aiding the neophyte to achieve his goal.

The initiate must forgo any life or desires of his own. He must surrender his will to the *sheikh* (Islamic teacher) who is in charge of helping him through the transformatory process. Looked upon as a holy man, the sheikh plays the role of guide and master; absolute obedience is owed him. Accepting this condition, the neophyte must also perform the most menial tasks for the sheikh and other members of the brotherhood. Opposed to institutionalized precepts, intellectual and abstract reasoning, the sheikh teaches through experience—the act. The novice, therefore, must work both physically and metaphysically. Important, too, is the fact that the postulant must share all his feelings, thoughts, dreams, ideas, and sensations with the sheikh. Should the sheikh not be cognizant of his most intimate feelings, the novice might be prematurely overwhelmed by an ecstatic experience, thus endangering his sanity.[13] The confidence he places in his sheikh relieves the disciple of all responsibilities.

According to Sufi doctrine, the reason for such dependence is not to allow the neophyte escape from life but to provide the desire for transcendence, to go beyond the limited linear space/time view of ordinary existence and gain cosmic consciousness through the ecstatic experience.

Emotions play a strong role in Sufi training. Fear, for example, is considered vital in arousing certain affective conditions. Fear of God, fear of judgment, and fear as a warning during the neophyte's initiation are instrumental in arousing an unfixed inner spiritual climate that leads to an alteration in the state of consciousness. Hope is likewise of utmost importance. The polarization of fear and hope increases the tension of opposites and creates a dichotomy conducive to emotional upheavals that gives rise to a kind of purgative process within the neophyte, taking him out of his world of disparate forms into a supraformal existence. Under these circumstances, past, present, and future are wiped away, giving rise to the emergence of anterior worlds into consciousness. The initiate then feels himself to be the repository of eternal mysteries—those that existed prior to Creation. As the initiate accomplishes each step of the process of purification, encountering and surpassing his previous condition, enlightenment becomes more intense and a plethora of new sensations and color tones imposes itself on the adept—blue to colorlessness.[14]

To experience God's being through ecstatic trance states requires great devotion and faithful recourse to various practices: prayer, breathing techniques, rhythmical physical movements, and the *dhikr* (recollection) are all means of attaining unity with divinity. Identified with the Hindu *mantra*, or *yantra*, the *dhikr* consists of repeating certain words or phrases, such as "Glory to Allah" and "There is no God but Allah," for hours, days, weeks on end. The harmonious relationships created by the various tonalities, rhythms, vibrations, repercussions, and bodily movements open the way to the atemporal godly domain. The formula repeated, with closed eyes and in a seated position with the legs usually crossed, having had little or no sleep and still less food, diminishes one's conscious outlook. As the *dhirk* is spoken, either silently or aloud, alone or in group formation, the name of Allah absorbs the initiate, fills his entire being, is inhaled and exhaled by him, thus increasing his energetic power and the force of the meditative device. It is during the *dhikr* that the Sufi worships Allah as if he were actually visible and to the Sufi, he is—since he is certain that Allah sees him.

During the initiation period, the process of separation between his personal and impersonal existence (earthly and celestial condition) must also be enacted: the initiate must cut away his physical or carnal (*nafs*) breath from his spiritual one (*rūh*). *Nafs* consists of breath emanating from the bowels and passing up to the glottis; it stands for "animal activity" and belongs to the sensient existential sphere. *Ruh*, on the other hand, is breath emanating from the brain and makes its way through the nostrils, that is, from the immaterial and spiritual realm. It is *ruh* that allows the initiate to increase his spiritual capacity, thus paving the way for the ecstatic state, the rational or conscious being obliterated. When reciting the Koran, the disciple unites *nafs* and *ruh* by vocalizing or nasalizing consonants with special sonorous tonalities and rhythmic principles, thereby preserving and reviving the initial divine breath which had originally been revealed in the sacred text.[15]

It is during the state of ecstasy that the Sufi experiences God's glory and light: a transparent opaline luminescence that takes him into a suprasensible world. Sufi masters warn strongly against a lighthearted attitude toward such practices. Only after rigorous training should such an endeavor be undertaken, too much light can only blind one both physically and psychologically. Only a few are capable of rigorous self-discipline; still fewer should attempt an encounter with God—the Self for the Jungian psychologist. A shattering of the personality, a burning of being may ensue.[16]

The Sufi's God is very close to being pantheistic. He is not the "One Transcendent God of Islam" but rather "One Real Being who dwells and works everywhere." His throne is located in the human heart as well as in the supernatural sphere. Love, therefore, is the generating force, the fusing archetype that unites lover and beloved, each acting through and with the other to form the "pure soul" that merges with the Godhead. Since God is present everywhere in the tangible world—from the smallest of atoms to the spacelessness of unlimited galaxies—the whole cosmos is a theophany. Behind every visible form (image, word, letter, number) or intangible entity (idea, feeling; sensation, thought) lies divinity. A flower, a bird, or a serpent is a manifestation of a higher sphere of being, a purified soul, absolute beauty or ugliness.

The Sufi's training takes him through what are alluded to as *permanent stations*, which are acquired, and *passing states*, which are given by God.

> *Permanent stations* (maqām) *(consist of repentance,*
> *conversion,*
> *renunciation,*
> *trust in God.*
> *Passing states* (hāl) *consisting of favor,*
> *grace,*
> *gift,*
> *end to ego life (he exists*
> *in the "state" God gave*
> *him originally).*[17]

The permanent stations are looked upon as being self-taught and self-imposed, earned through the practice of constant disciplines, such as fasting, prayer, self-mortitication, and other ascetic practices. The knowledge acquired by the initiate is considered permanent because he must have passed through the previous stations in self-development in order to reach each higher level of understanding. His achievements, therefore, are cumulative, each level of consciousness paving the way for the next. Passing states, however, are God-given. They permit the initiate to know exaltation, experience divine light, and pierce through the veils separating him from God. Such insights may illumine his entire being and flood him with feelings of transcendence. Because divine grace flows throughout the universe, it may also overwhelm the uninitiated individual, inundating his being with forces that may be beyond his capacity to integrate within his psyche, thus leading to insanity or other psychological problems; or it may allow him to leave the imprisonment of his earthly form and leap into pleromatic spheres, thereby increasing his consciousness. In *Gullistan*, Sa'dī defines *hāl* in the following manner:

> *My state is that of leaping lightning.*
> *One moment it appears and at another it vanishes.*[18]

The very concept of permanent and transient represents, of course, a dichotomy: each seems to be one kind of object, a separate entity, yet each in its own way progressively transforms the initiate spiritually and psychologically. This is the case in *The Conference of the Birds*. The novitiate gradually frees his being from the impurities of his earthly form, thus fostering his reintegration into the supreme being, the Self.

ARCHETYPAL ANALYSIS

The Seven Valleys that must be crossed by the birds in Attar's poem represent the seven stages in the Sufi process designed to bring enlightenment. The seven steps are comparable to the seven alchemical stages, the seven days of Creation, Allah's seven attributes, the seven heavens that exist according to the Koran (Surah 36:11), and serve to purify and clarify what is insalubrious and cloudy. Each stage reveals a new center of consciousness to the initiate, an opening into a supresensible world. A beginning and a return, each state is a stepping-stone requiring a progressive disorientation and disassociation in the conscious/rational attitudes, if the transpersonal sphere is to be reached.[19]

As the birds reveal their needs, wants, and thoughts, in what might be termed a veritable psychodrama, the entire atmosphere is imbued with the verbal conceits of myriad volatile elements. That Attar chose birds to be the protagonists of his allegory is not surprising. Other Persian Islamic poets, such as Firdausi (941–1020), author of the great epic *Shah-namah*, also did. They were attracted to birds not only because birds symbolized superior states of being—associated with the element air—but also because of Muhammad's miraculous Night Journey and Ascenscion (*Mi'rāj*). When the Prophet went to heaven and saw the tree of life, he observed countless birds of variegated colors on its leafy branches, singing so melodiously that he knew each was inhabited by the soul of a faithful follower.[20]

In that birds are spiritualizing forces or soul images, they inject the allegory with supernal and outer-worldly sensations. These bird/humans, which the ancient Egyptians identified with *Ba* (soul) because they fly away after the death of the body, endow the tangible world with energy and power—forces that reach deep into the heart of the being in need of light, health, and awakening. As the birds begin their chatter in Attar's poem, barriers seem to lift, painful inhibitions vanish, secrets are slowly revealed. Songs and melodies stir the atmosphere from the outset, imbuing it with excitement, terror, love, and trepidation.

Sound (musical and otherwise) is a highly important element in Sufi initiation rituals. By means of repeated sonorities (litanies, chanting, humming, breathing, the *dhikr*, and so forth), the initiate is able to practice a kind of autohypnosis that causes him to enter a state of ecstatic trance. Persian music does not consist of halftones, but of thirds, capable, according to the Sufi, of evoking the most tender of feelings and arousing altered states of consciousness. There are several incidents in *The Arabian Nights*, for example, when the characters swoon as they listen to beautiful poems or verses from the Koran or sounds from a lute—as if these tonalities had descended via some heavenly "voice."[21] Every living form, the Sufi believes, expresses his feelings for Allah in his own language, thereby injecting an infinity of tonal forms, timbres, and energy patterns into the universe. In *The Conference of the Birds*, sounds and rhythms excite the flow of emotion, trigger an upsurge of ideas, and thus pierce and penetrate into the further world beyond. Such innervation activates retinal vision, allowing haptic sensations to firm. Corroborating the belief held by Pythagoras and Plato that music awakens the soul, Attar's poem triggers anterior modes of existence; it stimulates recollection and penetration into unheard-of blendings—absorption into symphonic celestial harmonies. Rūmī wrote:

> *The song of the spheres in their revolutions*
> *Is what men sing with lute and voice.*[22]

Birds, which represent unconscious contents in Attar's poem, also symbolize a life attitude, the need to volatilize and sublimate earthly feelings and sensations. As they pass through the seven stages, the birds' outward physical natures become less defined and diminish in importance—they rid themselves of the earthly dross that holds them down. A concomitant transformation of noetic values occurs: an overly involved condition in the workaday world is replaced by a purer quintessential state residing in truth/Allah/totality. Attar writes: "The soul has a share of that which is high, and the body a share of that which is low; it was formed of a mixture of heavenly clay and pure spirit. By this mixing, man becomes the most astonishing of mysteries" (p. 5).

The Conference of Birds opens with an invocation to the Creator, followed by an enumeration of heavenly bodies and human types, and then concentrates on the animal, vegetable, and mineral kingdoms. Allah permeates every image, breath, and sensation described in the poem, and "there is none but Him, no one can see Him." Mortal eyes are blind to him because he is formless; yet the world radiates his brilliance. "Should you catch even a glimpse of Him you would lose your wits, and if you should see Him completely you would lose your self" (p. 4). The Sufis understand the psychological damage that can come to one if unprepared to experience the Self. To open oneself up to the Self could mean an eclipse of the ego, a permanent cutting of all ties with the real world. The neophyte might be too overwhelmed by the visionary experience and never again reestablish contact with the mundane sphere. Attar suggests that each bird "walk carefully" and allow the heart to lead, that is, feeling, rather than the intellect. For the Sufi, cerebrality, which proceeds from a logical and rational way of functioning, is cold, insensitive, and incapable of taking the adept into the pleromatic sphere, where he will apprehend the mysterious world beyond—the invisible and impalpable domain that exists for the person who *sees*.

"To each atom there is a different door," Attar writes, "and for each atom there is a different way which leads to the mysterious Being of whom I speak" (p. 4). Each bird, therefore, must find his own way on the journey, in keeping with his own psychological makeup, yet adhere to the rituals and traditions set down by Sufi masters. Each bird, then, is to fulfill its own individual destiny as well as that of the collective. As a bird, he is identified with destiny.

The birds are told that during the course of their initiation they are to be purified and thus become *fire*. All peripheral attachments in the concrete and spiritual domains must be annihilated, destroyed—become ash. A state of nothingness may then be experienced, "But God will remain" (p. 10). In the process, all thoughts and feelings that might distract the initiate from meditation upon the Godhead will be eliminated, so that a climate conducive to the experience of supraconsciousness can prevail. Factors as yet unrevealed will be disclosed and formless matter will come into being. As such, a kind of "epiphany of knowledge" takes place during which the initiation is open to inner revelation, inner sight: *gnosis.*[23]

The cult of fire, implicit in Sufism and demanded of the initiate, may well be considered a vestige of Zoroastrian ritual. Zoroastrianism (also called Mazdaism), an ancient Persian religion allegedly founded by Zoroaster in the sixth or seventh century before Christ, was based on dualism: on the struggle between the forces of light/good (Ormuzd, or Ahura Mazdah) and those of darkness/evil (Ahriman). Purification of the soul by fire and the discovery of a new earth and heaven allowed the initiate to experience what has been termed the vital fire: that incandescent flame that inhabits the innermost area of each individual and emanates from the primal fire which was and is Allah. Since he is the light, radiation and irradiation exude from him eternally and immanently. To experience him is to know and enter into light. In Attar's poem, the birds have to be bathed in fire and seared by flame so as to gain entrance into their pure essence, their opalescent tonalities, and be able to shine with supernal clarity and prismatic luster.[24]

The Hoopoe bird is to become the "Master of the Path," that is, for the Sufi, the sheikh, or the analysand, the psychotherapist. Mentioned in the Koran as well as in other Islamic works, the Hoopoe is the mythological bird that guided King Solomon along his path (Surah 27:20) and brought about Solomon's meeting with the queen of Sheba. Endowed with sacredness, the Hoopoe bird takes on a numinous nature for the Muslim, and to this day is not to be killed.[25]

In *The Conference of the Birds*, the Hoopoe is feminine in gender and therefore may be considered an anima figure. It is she who directs the flight of the birds and determines their destinies. It is she who sets in motion the individuation process, who interprets the others' dreams, reveals their secret situations to them, narrates their confessions, and underscores the philosophical and mystical points that must be understood.

Psychologically speaking, as we have already pointed out, the anima represents man's unconscious attitude toward woman (just as with the sexes reversed, the animus for the woman). As anima and animus appear in dreams, myths, and literary works, they usually are considered repositories for feelings that are not discernible in a person's outer attitude. Thus they are highly revelatory of the unconscious state of those who project onto such beings. That the Hoopoe should be in charge of transform- ing the birds' orientation from a centroverted, ego-centered, earthbound condition to a collective and celestial sphere, im- bued with all the spiritual values implicit in the *sublimatio* con- dition, is not surprising. Islam is the most patriarchal of reli- gions. Woman is considered to be an object destined only to please man and ensure procreation. She is according to the Ko- ran definitely inferior to the male: "Men are in charge of women, because Allah hath made the one of them to excel the other, and because they spend of their property (for the support of women). So good women are obedient, guarding in secret that which Allah hath guarded. As for those from whom ye fear rebellion, admonish them and banish them to beds apart, and scourge them" (Surah 4:34). Since woman is considered merely as a collective entity, functional in purpose, existing only as a way of gratifying masculine desire, man does not see her as an individual being in terms of her own wants, needs, or feelings. Real relationships between the two are rare because little dis- crimination or individuation takes place. Unable to deal with the feminine principle in daily life, man experiences woman only on the unconscious level as an anima figure. Thus she remains an autonomous power, and the result is that she is either spiri- tualized or vilified: described either as saint or sinner. She is deprecated still further, since the Muslim believes that woman is the cause of evil: it is she who seduces man and lures him away from his obligations—as a jinn or peri (invisible spirits)— thereby taking the blame for man's lusts and instinctuality. The man in this manner is able to project his shadow characteristics on woman and thereby to justify his negative attitude toward her. Or the anima may be a sublimating force, an idealized cre- ation, as is the Hoopoe in *The Conference of the Birds*. As an anima figure in Attar's poem, the Hoopoe contains all those qualities that the prevalent conscious masculine attitude lacks. Only as a spiritualized force can man come to terms with the feminine principle.

The birds listen intently as the Hoopoe describes the conditions and characteristics needed to begin and pursue the search for the Simurgh. "No country is without a king," the Hoopoe states (p. 11). Some form of ruler or rule seems to be vital for any culture if it is to survive and yield its fruit. Representative of order and of the ruling attitude in life, and a projection of divine power, the Simurgh in *The Conference of the Birds* stands for the judging principle. He is thus the intercessor between humans and God, life as we know it and the great mystery that lies beyond. The Simurgh injects ethical and spiritual values onto individuals and the collective. Psychologically, the Simurgh helps the birds to develop feelings of detachment and independence, and a desire to know and experience the Godhead. He is the archetype of perfection in Attar's work.

As the Hoopoe begins relating the details concerning their projected pilgrimage in search of the king/Simurgh, she grows "excited and full of hope" and places "herself in the middle of the assembled birds" (p. 10). In so doing, a mandala is formed. The mandala, a circular image used for meditative purposes by Tibetan Buddhists, centers and concentrates energy within a given area. To concentrate on a mandala is a psychologically unitive experience; it forces concentration rather than dispersion of libido. The energy center thus formed activates the psyche; it prepares the groundwork for the irrational or metaphysical experience to occur. The mandala is a self-renewing, self-restoring technique used to arouse sensory perception. It revitalizes rhythms, sounds, and feelings into a synchronous whole. When Sufis pray in unison, they generally sit in a circle and chant and sway according to various rhythms. Thus phenomena within the unconscious are activated and divest the brain of extraneous matter, idle thoughts, or random feelings. The inflow of energy encourages psychological transformation. The mandala may also be looked upon as a microcosm of divine power: it actualizes cosmic energy. A psychologic image is thus created, a sacred space that enters the initiate's focus and interiorizes spatiotemporal energies. Comparable to the cave, empirically speaking, one used by ascetics, it is conducive to the visionary experience as reported in patristic literature as well as in biblical and Buddhist works.

The mandala images, suggested C. G. Jung, appear in the dreams of individuals when order must be maintained or reestablished. It is an archetypal image that activates not only the imagination but also the subliminal sphere, thus altering states of consciousness, transforming meaning and sense data, even a person's basic orientation. Such archetypal images, as viewed in *The Conference of the Birds*, permit a suprasensory universe— a world beyond the visible one, known as the sphere of mystery—to take on dimensionality. Forms and figures of all types now make their impress known, becoming virtually tangible entities. Hence, the mandala may be instrumental in the discovery of another way of knowing—a *hierognosis*—bring a super-consciousness into existence.[26]

The Hoopoe/anima, as leader of the group of birds, has "entered the way of spiritual knowledge," writes Attar. As she stands in the center of the multitude of birds, "the crest on her head was as the crown of truth"; representing "the crown of glory" (p. 143).[27] The Hoopoe has experienced the world of duality; she is able to distinguish between good and evil. Her crest, therefore, stands for intellect, wisdom, the highest human faculty according to Neoplatonists and the Sufis. The circular crest on the Hoopoe's head, which also forms a crown and a mandala image, represents supraterrestrial forces; superior knowledge, power, elevation, and a dome of sovereignty. Sparks of light emanate from the Hoopoe's crest/crown. Slowly and dignifiedly, she informs the birds that she has "knowledge of God and of the secrets of creation" (p. 11). Similar to an angel or the Holy Spirit—or to an intuitive thought, all of which have frequently been represented by a bird, the Hoopoe seeks to fulfill her ministerial functions as guardian, leader, and executor of the Word and the Book, such important factors in Islam. Like the angels Gabriel, messenger and initiator; or Raphael, guide to travelers; or Michael, vanquisher of dragons, the Hoopoe is a member of Allah's army.

The Hoopoe must help the birds to rise above their limited earthborn existence, to reach out and free their lower souls from imprisonment in matter. Extreme introversion is needed to effect the change required. To look within necessitates a descent into the unconscious, to discover the divine residing within man's central organ, the heart. "He who hears with his heart is genuine, he who hears with his soul [*nafs*, or "lower soul"] is a fraud." [28] The heart thus referred to by the Sufi is not to be confused with the physical organ; it is spiritual and must be cared for and fed, as a seedling must be nurtured if it is to grow into a beautiful tree. Each of the birds, the Hoopoe informs them, must develop his own potential in order to experience grace. Each must cross the desert of despair, so that the carnal elements within the psyche may be annihilated; stations of the heart must be experienced to foster a condition of sacredness, thus creating a climate conducive to the apocalyptic visionary experience—an encounter with God.

The way will be arduous, the Hoopoe warns. Great suffering will be the lot of all. If, however, heart and spirit are determined on this course, ardor and will can be used to burn the outer core of being, the flabby garb of flesh that prevents deeper understanding. Only through the experience of difficulties and pain, even despair, can the initiate gain entrance to those supernal spheres where the Simurgh exists. "Wash your hands of this life," the Hoopoe counsels, meditation persists.

Since the Simurgh symbolizes the Self/God, it is natural that this symbol of totality or circularity would make its home beyond Mount Kaf, which also exists outside of our objective world. As a representative of wholeness, the Simurgh's function is to unite what is disparate, to reconnect what has been severed during the course of life. In that the Simurgh stands for the higher collective soul of all the birds brought together by the Hoopoe, it is a manifestation of an unconscious attitude: the desire of each to become part of this fabulous creature, which promises completion.

As a metaphor for the Self—that is, as the psychological equivalent of God—the Simurgh exists at a certain level of experience, or *gnosis*, within each being. It represents each person's inner immortal sphere, his transpersonal point. It is this psychic center that each individual bird must tap. To discover this deepest of levels, this point of creation for the mystic in general, the Almighty Spirit, the Sublime Intelligence hidden within each being, the Sufi disciple must burn away all peripheral entities; he must annihilate those veils of matter that prevent him from ascending to God's dwelling place—that "inaccessible" area in which luminosity coexists with darkness.

1. *The Valley of the Quest*

The quest itself may be seen as a *rite de transformation*, giving rise to a displacement of values, an alteration in the conscious dominant. "He who is not engaged in the quest of the inner life is no more than an animal . . . he is a nonentity, a form without a soul," the Hoopoe declares (p. 101). In keeping with the process of the metaphysical experience, as the journey pursues its course, what seems important at the outset will diminish in value. The inner world will become more and more meaningful as exterior things, events, and relationships lessen in vitality.

The Hoopoe tells them, "Wash your hands of this life if you would be called a man of action" (p. 13). Forge ahead. As the Koran sttes: "He who Allah leadeth, he indeed is led aright, while he whom Allah sendeth astray—they indeed are losers" (Surah 7:178).

The Simurgh makes his home beyond Mount Kaf. A mountain range that according to Islamic dogma surrounds the earth, Kaf is a cosmic region located outside the known and visible world. One cannot reach this domain unless shown the way by a supernatural being. Psychologically, Mount Kaf represents self-development, higher being—the Thou. That it is very high or stands as a mountain indicates that one must ascend to reach it, sublimate what is uncontained in the *topos*. One must, paradoxically, go beyond or outside of it in order to reach it.

Mount Kaf represents an inner condition or inner reality. It is an internalization of space: *ubi/ubique*. Because it exists beyond the physical universe, it is intelligible only to the supranatural world or psychic sphere. Although it is ontologically real, it eludes the temporal senses; therefore, to experience it, one must develop special heightened perceptive faculties—noetic or cognitive understanding of a metaphysical nature. An archetypal image, Mount Kaf also takes on the contours of a mandala because it surrounds the world. It is a circular area that lies preordained within the psyche, imbued with a sacred topology formed by thoughts, desires, feelings, and premonitions. This image form or energy pattern, this substratum or layer, is the goal each of the birds seeks. It is the central and equilibrating force. A level beneath consciousness that appears through projection, the archetypal image of Mount Kaf exists within the psyche as a *phainomen*: it comes into being only as a mirror image upon which the inner climate becomes visible or is engraved, etched, reflected. It takes on actuality in both inner and outer domains: becoming substance and, as such, remaining *suspended* in the mind's eye or spiritual world, as a physical body in a three-, four-, or five-dimensional world as long as concentration lasts.

The Hoopoe whets the bird's appetites by telling them that the Simurgh first manifested itself in China. One of its feathers fell on the land. A mental picture is thus engraved on the minds of all those who come into contact with it: "All souls carry an impression of the image of his feathers" (p. 13). Each bird is invited to understand truth and reality according to the levels of his initiatory experience. A flutter of excitement permeates the throng as the birds listen in rapt wonder to the glories of the Simurgh. They try to visualize this fantastic being; but only a fragment of his total essence, the most concrete aspect of his image can be comprehended because they are still contained in the material.

As we have already mentioned, the Hoopoe frequently interrupts her homiletic sequences by intertwining little stories, anecdotes, and moral tales, pointing to the special conditions that must be observed or rituals that must be undertaken during the course of the initiation. In effect, she disorients the birds, interrupts their self-centered thoughts, breaks up their preconceived ideas, and thus is able to guide them still further into the realm of the unknown.

The Hoopoe recounts the story of a well-known Muslim ruler, Mahmud. One day as Mahmud was riding alone in the desert, he saw a man sifting the earth looking for gold. He threw him a bracelet, then left. The next day he returned and saw the same man occupied in the same way. Why? he asked. "I found the bracelet you threw me, and it is because I found such a treasure that I must continue to search as long as I live" (p. 101). Each initiate, the Hoopoe states, must pursue his search throughout his worldly existence, even if he is convinced he has attained the ineffable state of sublimity. "Seek the door, but even this is not sufficient; the door must be opened—the unknown penetrated" (p. 101).

Patience and confidence are virtues that aid in reaching that transcendent state beyond the individual condition. Only by objectifying acts and feelings, by examining them slowly and precisely, will object and subject be separated; each must be considered as a separate entity to enable the depotentiation of what was heretofore considered a unified whole. The procedure must be continuous, the Hoopoe affirms. There must be no stopping because of despair or remorse, no turning back in the noetic experience if the Godhead or universal Self—the Simurgh—is to become known.

The Hoopoe calls for an anamnesis, a recalling or reminiscence of facts concerning the birds. Each bird then gives its own case history. Its earthly experiences are bared, and its numinous or extratemporal dimensions disclosed—giving the reader the impression that he or she is at the threshold of a mystery.

The Nightingale[29] is the first to speak. Known for the sweetness of its song, the melancholy, fragile, and distant yearnings of its lyric tone, the Nightingale symbolizes the soul—in metaphysical sense—longing for eternal beauty and quietude— a soul in love. The Nightingale confesses that it is pining away for its beloved rose. Its entire life is centered on this flower despite the fact that its breast has been bloodied and cut by the rose's thorns. Unfulfilled desire inundates the Nightingale's being, while the rose, in all its beauty, stays aloof, inspiring the bird to pour forth its most exquisite melodies.

For the Sufi, yearning is essential if the soul is to develop from its lower condition to its highest essence. The Sufi's goal is to develop his potential as the egg hatches and then becomes a bird. To be caught in the web of satisfaction, to allow an earthly incarnation, a mere form or fragment of a personal force, to seduce a being by its perfume or beauty, is to yield to immediate gratification. If the Nightingale seeks the universal being, the Simurgh, it must divest itself of all earthly desires, step out of its obsession with the rose into a silent invisible world, a universal sphere. Earthly desire corrodes the longing for wholeness, incorruptibility, and eternity; it prevents the loss or surpassing of ego-consciousness, of a concern with earthly conditions, and does not pave the way for detachment necessary to advance to the next level in the Sufi initiation procedure.

The Nightingale sings movingly of its pain; emotionally, fitfully, and passionately, it unveils the mysteries in its heart. It hovers around the rose, seduced by the flower's aromatic essence, its beautiful form, and color. As if overcome by some magic philter, some strange force that inundates its being, the Nightingale's will has grown weak; the energy needed to seek the Simurgh has slackened.

The Hoopoe is disappointed in the Nightingale. Because of the rose's exterior beauty, the Nightingale is devoting its life to what is transient and fleeting. Distant, proud, protected by its thorns, the rose stands for that force in life that seduces the innocent and destroys the desire to penetrate further. To illustrate her point, the Hoopoe tells the story of a dervish who fell in love with a beautiful princess after she had smiled at him. For seven years he pined away, thinking only of her. "Passion was awakened by her sleepy eyes and by the sweet intoxication of her presence" (p. 15). One day, when he chanced to meet her again, he asked her why she had smiled at him that first time. "O you fool," she answered, "when I saw that you were about to humiliate yourself, I smiled from pity" (p. 16). The pious man had spent years in fruitless devotion caused by a fleeting glimpse, an insignificant chance experience. Only the eternal being is worthy of love.

In this same story, Attar satirizes what he considers to be the innocuous existence of obsessive devotion. Whether it be the Nightingale's love for the rose or the mystic's feeling for the princess, in either case the condition of rapture or ecstatic trance is misdirected because it is not for Allah's sake that ecstasy is sought. A Sufi must divest himself of all desire or emotional needs that center on his own self-gratification and focus exclusively on divinity; appearances must vanish; the phenomenological sphere must disappear. Religious ecstasy must lead to regeneration, that is, to a refocusing of energy, an alteration of course. If this does not come about, these spiritual practices are useless.

The Nightingale's obsession, psychologically speaking, can only lead to an impasse. It is an escape mechanism that creates a condition of stasis rather than encouraging further struggle. The Nightingale's potential can never be developed by clinging to a fruitless relationship that leads to nothing, that merely encourages a false sense of security. When love leads to nothing, neither heart nor soul can renew the ego/Self axis, and thus it remains stationary. The veils of matter separating the Sufi from the Simurgh thicken and expand still more powerfully.[30]

The Parrot now makes his desires known. Sparkling in the sun's rays, which highlight its exquisite green and gold feathered array, it looks down with disdain and anger at the other birds. Its entire life is focused on one desire: find the waters of immortality guarded by Khizr, a man who is said to have been alive during Abraham's time and who possesses the answer to life's mysteries. The Hoopoe remonstrates that the Parrot's goal is as fruitless as the Nightingale's. Why long for the impossible, for eternal life in the temporal sphere? "He who is not willing to renounce his life is no man," (p. 17), the Hoopoe states. One should not seek immortality in the created world, which has a beginning and an end to it; to do so is to go against nature, against God. Eternal life is a condition prevailing in divinity alone. Life and death are both part of the cosmic process—two halves of a whole. The circular experience, which makes for transfiguration and rebirth is implicit in the life experience—as it is in the mystical and psychological domain. To entertain thoughts of a personal immortality is a sign of spiritual pride—of hubris.

Those who fear death are obsessed with the tangible world, preoccupied with external and fragmentary notions; the Hoopoe claims: "You are not an almond; you are only the shell" (p. 17). The Parrot is living in a state of arrested development; it is no longer able to grow and change. Psychologically, it has become paralyzed, which is manifested by its constant repetition of gestures and words. Its arrogance, coupled with feelings of resentment at the servile condition in which it is forced to exist, dominates the Parrot's outlook. Paradoxically, it enjoys the security of its condition because it seeks to retain it, yearning to live forever as a handsome youthful bird. The imprisonment it so resents in the physical domain, however, is symbolic of a psychological attitude: it is incarcerated in its own limitations, dominated by an idea that runs counter to its spiritual growth. The Parrot is locked in its own egocentrism. A bird that merely mimics what others say and never originates an idea of its own is incapable of delving into profound spiritual realms. The Parrot's superficial view of life is a mockery, a travesty of existence.

The Peacock struts vainly about.[31] With its shimmering irridescent tail of a thousand eyes, it is one of the most colorful creatures in existence. The Sufis have likened its unfolding tail to the spirit as it expands, to fire in its incandescence of activity and purity. In Islamic iconography, the Peacock symbolizes the cosmos, as viewed as a wheel that turns perpetualy upon itself. In this regard, it takes on the contour of a mandala, a center of energy, arousing emotions of all types. The Hoopoe in Attar's poem now calls the Peacock "the Painter of the world" (p. 17) for both its exquisite colorations and the energy patterns depicted on its feathers.

The story is told that the Peacock has once been in paradise where it became friendly with the Serpent and was then cast out. Now it lives only with the hope of finding a "benevolent guide" who will lead it back to the world of everlasting light (heaven). The Hoopoe tells the Peacock that the Simurgh's palace is far more perfect than any Edenic experience. "You cannot do better than to strive to reach it" (p. 18). The Peacock does not understand the importance of such a mission, the value of struggle, the need for truth-seeking within "the vast ocean of existence." *Gnosis* as well as love are implicit in a spiritual quest, the Hoopoe suggests. Emotions help in the conflict one must wage in order to overcome transient needs and in the search for deeper values. Only through meditation could the Peacock succeed in untangling its confused feelings and sensations, gathering together those energetic principles that could then be focused on spatial and adimensional spheres.

The Duck is also preoccupied with its own beauty and its own pleasures. It roams about the earthly waters in a glorious state. "No one has ever spoken to a creature prettier or purer than I," the Duck says. Such a complacent outlook bars any chance of clear-sightedness, the Hoopoe intimates. Blind to any other way of life, the Duck is content to live as it does. "So, since my concern is only the water, why should I leave it?" (p. 19). To seek the Simurgh would necessitate leaving the element it loves best to fly across valleys and mountains. Survival under such circumstances would be uncertain. The Hoopoe chastises the Duck for its indolent self-satisfied ways.

The Partridge, too, does not want to sacrifice its pleasures. In Persia, the Partridge was frequently compared to woman for its elegance and haughty gait, its grace and beauty. When eating partridge, it was said that one was absorbing the "philter of love." Christian ascetics considered this bird the incarnation of a demon for the above-mentioned reason. In *The Conference of the Birds* the Partridge states: "I like to wander among the ruins, for I love precious stones" (p. 20). Colored gems of the most dazzling kind fascinate the Partridge. "He who possesses the perfume does not seek the colour; he who has the essence will not forsake it for the glitter of outward form. Seek the true jewel of sound quality and no longer be content with a stone," the Hoopoe declares (p. 21).

The Humay is also "a slave of pride," and so is the Hawk, that royal bird which seeks the company of kings. The Heron is vigilant but indiscreet and melancholy; it lacks the strength to search for the Simurgh. The Owl makes its home amid ruins and mysterious areas where treasures abound. Noted for its mournful solemnity and nocturnal solitude, it often symbolizes wisdom, but in Attar's poem, it represents weakness; comfortable in its own limitations, it seeks nothing more. The Sparrow, fearful and frail, trembles like a flame. A journey is surely too difficult to undertake. "O you, who in your despondency are sometimes sad, sometimes gay," the Hoopoe exclaims, "I am not deceived by these artful pleas. You are a little hypocrite. Even in your humility you show a hundred signs of vanity and pride" (p. 28).

When all the birds congregate together, they seem to divest themselves of their individual emotions and characteristics and experience a *participation mystique*—which is true of most collective gatherings. Their common emotions are activated, and a lowering of individual consciousness takes place. The birds find themselves yielding to the suggestive power of the group; they act without reasoning and defer to the wishes of the majority. The collective in such cases is not a responsible agent. The individuals caught up in group energies regress and identify with the whole. There may, however, be another result as well. The group may give the individual bird the courage it lacks alone; it may also arouse the bird's enthusiasm and nobility of purpose. The Hoopoe's function now is to encourage and energize solidarity, to put an end to individual and collective wailing with regard to this group of birds.

The Hoopoe speaks out forcefully inspired by her goal, and group energy is rechanneled, directed to flow into another dimension. Centroverted feelings within the participants are reshuffled; ideas rearranged. The birds are ready to strike down barriers, to abandon the rationalizations that prevented them from pursuing their goal. A transference of feeling from the outer to the inner realm occurs. A "subjective process," feeling is the function within the human being that judges not according to intellectual notions, that is, cognitively, but according to an affective climate—"bodily innervations."[32]

The Hoopoe channels feeling, which is the most powerful of the functions among the birds, as discerned in their anamnesis. Because feeling is incapable of intellectualization, it cannot be transformed into an impersonal concept or abstraction; it is an active apperception of value and thus may be redirected by an act of will, as, for instance, from a passive to an active condition: rather than being loved, one loves. An active effort must be put forth. Undirected feelings will not succeed in altering the birds' way or redressing an imbalance in their psyche. Only by participating in a feeling way in a joint collective venture will their ontological experience be heightened, their lethargic egos awakened, and the veils of worldly attachment that bar their vision into the pleromatic sphere disappear.

2. *The Valley of Love*

The second stage in the Sufi initiation process enlists love and sacrifice in the metaphysical experience, the initiate's relationship with his sheikh, and the emotions of pain and suffering engendered.

In *The Conference of the Birds*, as well as in poems of Saadi, Ḥāfiẓ, and Omar Khayyam, hedonistic physical love is banished. Only divine love can so intoxicate the Sufi novitiate that he is cured of his worldly obsession. Then Allah becomes his ear, eye, and mouth and invades every part of the Sufi's being. Love is the catalyst. It is the power that works toward the unification of disparate components within the psyche. As *eros* (earthly love), however, it may be experienced only on a metaphysical level—as a disinterested and nonpersonal feeling that focuses not on an individual wish or joy but on the gigantic experience of knowing divinity. Paradoxicaly, since love is that

force which enables the novitiate to experience higher sentiments and transmundane essences, it does, interestingly enough,
focus on individual being. As an intermediary stage in the Sufi
discipline, love paves the way for expanded consciousness. In
the Koran we read: "Say (O Muhammad, to mankind): If ye
love Allah follow me; Allah will love you and forgive you your
sins. Allah is Forgiving, Merciful" (Surah 3:31). Love, however,
is to be decanted discretely in purified form, focused always
upon the Creator and never on his physical counterpart. Hence
sympathy develops in *The Conference of the Birds* that flows
from the earthly to the divine spheres. It grows and deepens in
power within the birds' hearts and paves the way for an eventual theophany, paralleling the divine yearnings of Allah who
sought to be known to his creatures and so brought them into
existence.

The Hoopoe illustrates her concept of metaphysical love by
the tale of "The King and the Beggar." The king knew that the
beggar who professed deep love for him was being disingen-
uous. He gave the beggar the choice of either going into exile or
having his head cut off. The beggar chose exile and the king
thereupon had him beheaded. When the chamberlain inquired
why an innocent man had been put to death, the king explained
that if the beggar had truly loved the king, he would have chosen death rather than leave his beloved. "Had he consented to
the execution," the king answered, "I would have girded my
loins and become his dervish. He who loves me, but loves his
head better, is no true lover" (p. 56). There is no half measure
in Sufi training. No choice, no gradations. It is absolute, as extreme as it can be and still remain within the human sphere.

For love to be truly effective, the Sufi's heart must be pure
and untarnished—like a brilliant mirror which reflects the entire world. Thereby the eyes of the soul may become receptive
and perceptive, and read the as yet unwritten word of the mystery that lies on the other side of the mirror. The *vita purgativa*
broadens the heart, casts off corrosive elements, and paves the
way for free-flowing emotions focused on God.

Love, which the Sufi experiences as a sublimating force, is
extreme in nature and, as such, is described as *flaming fire*. No
afterthoughts, no feelings of abandonment, no regrets, must intrude upon the Sufi's complete concentration on the Godhead.

Good and evil no longer exist in this incandescent state of passionate love. Each bird, therefore, is now completely engaged in the quest and cauterizes any *eros* principle which might link him with earthly intents. The Sufi does not reason about his love. To do so would invite evaluation and differentiation, the very elements he seeks to unite in one brilliant and glowing flame. "Love is represented by fire, and reason by smoke. When love comes reason disappears," the Hoopoe states (p. 102). Love burns every vestige of reason away; it engulfs and consumes everything else. Thought no longer intrudes; discernment and reflection are incompatible with flaming emotions. The Hoopoe sums up the condition needed to further the intuitive function: "If you possessed inner sight, the atoms of the visible world would be manifested to you. But if you look at things with the inner eye of ordinary reason you will never understand how necessary it is to love (p. 102).

The Hoopoe then narrates the story of one of Islam's great saints, Rābi'a al 'Adawiyya (/17–801). The prototype of the pious woman, she is said to have brought the concept of "pure love to an austere ascetic outlook" into early Sufi tradition.[33] In view of Islam's ambivalent attitude toward woman, Rābi'a's sainthood was not extraordinary. Indeed, it was quite in keeping with the *sublimatio* condition to which womankind was relegated, as is the Virgin Mary for the Christians.

Born in Bastria, she was sold as a slave early in life, then freed by her master who understood the fervent nature of her prayers and her inner spiritual radiance. She did not want to marry and spent the rest of her life in self-denial and performing works of charity. She worshiped Allah out of love for him, not because of any fear of hell or hope of paradise. She is reputed to have said that love of God was her only goal. She meditated and contemplated for days "enflamed by love and longing . . . lost in union with God." In the spring she used to close her windows because she knew that "the gardens and the fruits are inside, in the heart."[34] Rābi'a spent eight years making her pilgrimage to the Kaaba, the "cube-shaped stone building in the center of the Great Mosque at Mecca," by measuring her length on the ground. "Now, at last, have I performed my task." On the appointed day, however, when she was about to enter the Kaaba, which contains the sacred black stone that came from heaven (originally it is said to have been white, but it turned black because of humanity's sins), her women deserted her (p. 144). Rābi'a retraced her steps, anguished and distraught, because her eight years of travail had been unsuccessful.

The Hoopoe then explains the importance of such a lesson: "So long as you float on the deep ocean of the world its waves will receive and repel you, turn by turn" (p. 51). One must become detached from all worldly desires, which includes penetrating the Kaaba—the most sacred place for the Muslim. Love leads to heights, but it must know its place, must withdraw and temper its flame when the occasion arises. Only when love knows how to act can greater force and power emerge from it. It must know the sacrificial act to be of true value.

The spirit of sacrifice is implicit in Sufi training. Sacrifice implies the removal of everything that is considered incompatible with a God-oriented life. Whatever centers around the ego, which stands between the inner and the outer world, must be banished. The psychic energy which is normally expended in carrying out everyday activities must be withdrawn from the outer world and directed inward. Such extreme introversion paves the way for a return to a state of unconsciousness and a veritable sacrifice of the whole human experience, of human consciousness. This condition disrupts the instinctual foundation of the personality. The sacrifice of the ego allows the novitiate to fall under the dominion of the sheikh to whom he owes complete obedience, the way a child does to its parents. As a result, the novitiate abandons all sense of his own identity and of individual direction in life.

The sheikh's function is to channel the novice's psychic energy into new sources and fill the vacuum caused by the initiate's withdrawal from active participation in the conscious outer world. Once the neophyte surrenders himself completely to his sheikh, he begins his journey into new dimensions, fresh subliminal realms. This total surrender to another is the more difficult because the novice is in a sense transformed into a living corpse, divested of all will and initiative. The sheikh then plays the role of the Prophet Muhammad for the believer; it is through him that Allah speaks. "The Master to his disciples is as the Prophet to his congregation," states Suhrawardī, a Persian Sufi.[35] The sheikh's role is to clarify and define Allah's wishes, and to see that they are spread and carried out throughout the Sufi brotherhood.

The sheikh is also a healer. His goal is to cure whatever ailments afflict the novitiate. Henceforth, no act, no matter how small and seemingly insignificant, may be performed by the novice without the sheikh's knowledge and consent. Just as man can do nothing without God, the Sufi novice can do nothing without the sheikh. Such a condition is paradoxical, however, because man cannot strive without God, and yet God is ever omnipresent within and without. "His act is the cause behind all things,"[36] wrote Kalābādī. Consequently, the sheikh is not only God's intermediary, as the angel Gabriel was for Muhammad, he is also a projection of his beloved of sorts. The love, or *eros*, factor, which the initiate experienced in the everyday world, has been rerouted to the sheikh.

In order to redistribute the novitiate's psychological and spiritual system, the sheikh must sever him from everything outside of the God/love experience so that he will not be distracted by worldly matters. Called the "whore" metaphorically, the initiate becomes the target or butt of every passing thought, feeling, or sensation that seeks to take him away from his spiritual obligations. He becomes more and more closed to the outside world, however, and accepts the life of poverty, asceticism, and sacrifice that he took on when he assumed the woolen cloak of the Sufi. His inner being develops, empowering him to hear, touch, smell, and feel on an interior plane—without having recourse to the exterior one.

The novitiate's blind obedience to his sheikh is a metaphor for his complete submission to Allah's will: it reinforces his faith in the all-powerful and in his bodily representative on earth. It also frees the novice from all mental constructs and conflicts, allowing his personal problems to vanish. Obedience to the sheikh, nevertheless, must not be considered as a purely passive state nor as a form of passive suffering. Such a situation would reduce the initiate to a condition of physical sterility, like that of a dog. His subservience must be looked upon as a state of *active suffering*, the purpose of which is to insure the destruction of all worldly attachments. Only the religious pilgrim who has renounced all personal possessions, whether spiritual or material, can comprehend how the veils shrouding God's realm from mortal sight may be lifted, how the shades of darkness may yield to enlightenment. Obedience is not merely renunciation; it is, in effect, a confession of faith—to believe fervently that "There is no God but God" is the great paradox (based on negation and proof) which lies at the heart of the Muslim religion.[37]

Active suffering is an integral part of the transformation process; the ability to withstand the ordeal by fire or torture, bodily pain, is considered proof of the genuineness and incorruptibility of the initiate. Physical mortification tests the purity of the novice's emotional condition and the strength of his faith. Only under such trying conditions—when physical and emotional anguish pierce and crush, can the psyche experience the violence of chaos, of the *massa confusa*, leading to a blacking out of all outside life. At this point, libido may be redirected into higher channels.

As a patriarchal figure, the sheikh reigns supreme. It is he who teaches higher wisdom and the secrets of ancient mysteries to the novitiate. The sheikh unties the knots and opens the door to the pleromatic sphere where the inner eye experiences the ecstatic flames of fulfillment—unitive experience with Deity.

3. The Valley of Understanding

Understanding helps the Sufi novitiate to alter his attitude and prepares him for greater awareness between subject and object: the loved and the beloved. During moments of contemplative thought, each is seen as interacting with the other in mutual sequences and relationships. The understanding of the disciple, as viewed by the Sufi, is comparable in psychological terms, to a projection between analysand and analyst: each of the participants sees the other with increasing clarity, discovering new depths and levels of consciousness within the psyche. The image perceived takes on increased consistency and ushers in an entire new hierarchy of colorations, rhythms, and chain reactions. "When the mystery of the essence of beings reveals itself clearly to him the furnace of this world becomes a garden of flowers. He who is striving will be able to see the almond in its hard shell. He will no longer be preoccupied with himself, but will look up at the face of his friend. In each atom he will see the whole; he will ponder over thousands of bright secrets" (p. 108).

It is in the Valley of Understanding that the novitate's psyche develops and deepens its ontological realization. According to the Koran, the soul was created prior to the body. During its human incarnation, the soul strives to rid itself of its faults and foibles in order once again to reach its original pristine state— that of pure light. It may succeed in this endeavor through renunciation of all desire and dreams of power, fame, honor, and love on a worldly level. To do so, however, the *nafs*, which is the lower or instinctual soul, must be destroyed. A soul may be hierarchized as follows:

1. *The* nafs, *or lower soul.* It indicates evil, passion, a sensual nature. The Koran describes it in the following manner: "I do not exculpate myself. Lo! the [human] soul enjoineth unto evil, save that whereon my Lord hath mercy. Lo! my Lord is Forgiving, Merciful" (Surah 12:53). (See also Surah 75:2.)
2. *The blaming soul.* It criticizes the activities of the ego and is identified with the intellect. In the Koran we read: "Nay, I swear by the accusing soul (that this Scripture is true)" (Surah 75:2).
3. *The pacified soul.* It is equivalent to the pure state of the heart and exists in a condition of actuality. The Koran states: "But ah! thou soul at peace!" (Surah 89:27).[38]

Fear is associated with the lower soul, negative in essence. Terrified that the initiate may become dominated by what the ruling collective attitude considers evil, the earthly, or feminine, principle must be done away with corporeally as well as spiritually. The anima, now identified with evil, becomes a seductive and alluring force: sometimes represented in life or in religious works as a demon, a jinn, a peri, spirits in Islamic belief that may mesmerize the otherwise straight, clean, and pure Sufi. What these forces represent must be shorn. Such a psychological attitude, Dr. Marie-Louise von Franz writes, accounts for Islam's violent attitude toward paganism and for the extremely repressive measures used to destroy the polytheistic mystery religions in early days of Christianity.[39]

The Hoopoe describes the *nafs* as "one-eyed and squinting . . . vile, slothful and unfaithful . . . dazed by the tinsel" of life (p. 57). Because man allows himself to be enticed by worldly existence, he often ends his days "with nothing in him except desire for the superficial things of exterior existence" (p. 57). But the lower soul may be redeemed. If the novice is conscious of the *nafs* and realizes its power, he will constantly be on guard against it. In this "awakened" condition he will be able to seize this insidious force, control it, repress it, and purge himself of it.

The *nafs*, or what psychologically speaking we would label the shadow, exists in the novitiate's world as a reality. It is a concrete entity that the Sufi believes he may experience in the form of a fox or mouse emerging from his throat, or in the form of a dishonest woman or a whore who attempts to win his affection, or in the form of a cheat, and so on. *Nafs* are concretized in Sufi works as horses, mules, or snakes, always hungry, intent upon sucking out the life-force of their prey. Resisting the power of the *nafs* may be accomplished through solitary fasting, prayer, silence, and meditation. Under these conditions the *nafs* will perish from want of nourishment; and the ego dominated by the *nafs* will also expire. The worldly being or outer realms must be done away with so that man's individual nature may be reborn in God.[40]

The Hoopoe reinforces her teachings by relating the story of a king (God/Self) for whom thousands died because they loved him. Although they longed for his presence, his subjects could not endure the blaze of his presence for any length of time. It would cause their annihilation. The king therefore has a mirror made "so that his face could be seen indirectly" (p. 31), through reflection. Similarly, only in the diluted form of a reflection can the birds observe the pacified soul—the Simurgh—in his glory. Were he to view the totality of his being, he would be blinded and darkness would prevail. The initiate can, therefore, experience divinity only as an afterimage. The Hoopoe adds: "With good fortune, you will see the Sun in the shadow; but if you lose yourself in the shadow, how will you achieve union with the Simurgh?" (p. 32).

The Hoopoe is preparing the birds for the next level of experience. As finite beings with reasoning minds and physical bodies, they cannot yet comprehend the infinite realm where multiplicity blends into unity. Only through sudden sparks of intuition that erupt into consciousness and flood the being with light can they cope with so powerful an irradiating force. The "Light of Allah" can also blind and leave the being in perpetual darkness—in a shadow world to be consumed by the embers of an implacable sun. The *blaming soul* recognizes these inadequacies and will prepare the initiate with special protective devices to aid him to withstand the intense experience. The intellect apperceives and senses all the missing factors and rectifies the condition. As the object of consciousness is projected before the novitiate in a mirror image, noetic values are kindled; situations, sensations, and conditions empirically experienced, faced in this afterimage, may now be dealt with and finally dominated. Heightened understanding now allows the novitiate to gain greater and greater insight and to approach the Self/Simurgh indirectly through the mirror for longer period of times and in deeper spiritual and psychological levels of experience. Although tension within the outer and inner realms still exists and the disciple's sacrifice is not yet complete, his one all-encompassing need for the world of the absolute conditions his ascent to the world of the *pacified soul*.

The *pacified soul* knows rapture of the most sublime kind. Obsessive personal needs and longings have been sublimated. Everything within the initiate's psyche now works toward the final goal. The cosmos suddenly fills with silence and emptiness, yet bursts with activity, noise, brilliance—all stilled in the sphere of pure being. The noises, complaints, and longings that once occupied the birds with fruitless activity (an attitude antithetical to the search for the infinite) have ceased. They now know a sort of celestial music of the spheres, perceived in tones, rhythms, and colorations that give birth to a new sense of quietude and serenity—as well as to the expectant tremulous feeling that comes with the anticipation of bliss.

The dual dynamism of mortification and the nourishing principle implicit in the Valley of Understanding, which created a *horror vacui* within the initiate, has now been filled. The conscious mind has now been fed on new substances, still invisible and impalpable, but that serve to alter and rectify the imbalance that previously impeded the Sufi's growth and evolution in the mystical sphere.

4. The Valley of Independence and Detachment

At this stage of his development the Sufi novitiate is in what has been termed a state of suspended animation: neither is he troubled by the desire to possess anything nor does he seek to discover new elements. He feels himself to be between two extremes and drawn to neither. The Hoopoe describes the condition as follows: "In this state of the soul a cold wind blows, so violent that in a moment it devastates an immense space: the seven oceans are no more than a pool, the seven planets a mere spark, the seven heavens a corpse, the seven hells broken ice. Then, an astonishing thing, beyond reason! An ant has the strength of a hundred elephants, and a hundred caravans perish while a rook is filling his crop" (p. 110).

Allowing this state of indifference to continue would lead to a condition of stasis, a paralysis that would surely impede the novitiate's progress. The Hoopoe therefore counsels the birds to "Go still further" because remaining suspended at midpoint would mean to languish and experience a sort of living death.

It is in this halfway condition that the birds begin to discover their own resources—their inner reserves, their self-sufficient natures—not on a personal level but on a transpersonal one. The knowledge the bird experiences, thanks to the Hoopoe's guidance, inflames them anew. They again become the passionate seekers they had once been but at a higher level of understanding and experience, with greater power to consume "a hundred worlds" (p. 112). The Hoopoe tells the story of "The Fly and the Honey": to illustrate this aspect of her lesson: A fly saw a beehive in a garden and wanted to enter it so desperately that it paid an obol to do so. Delighted with the honey, it soon realized that its wings were caught in the substance, and it was unable to move. The more the fly fluttered, the more deeply imprisoned it became. The lesson is plain: to become too deeply ingrained in one phase of existence or dependent upon one level of consciousness is to divest oneself of the spirit of independence and detachment one has so desperately sought to obtain. Detachment is defined as severing ties with as many ontological and phenomenological states and conditions of being as possible.

Fear and apprehension again intrude as the birds begin to understand that their journey will lead to even greater difficulties and sacrifices. There is no stopping, no resting, no relaxing or abating of tension. According to the Hoopoe, eternal mystery is a "road without end." The Hoopoe fosters fear in the birds, just as the sheikh does in training the Sufi novitiate. Considered salutary if properly understood and handled, the emotion will usher in a new life of fresh dreams and perceptions. Consciousness is sometimes a prey to lethargy and inactivity; a desire for unlimited horizons must be reawakened within the initiate. A *jihād* (holy war) must be waged against sloth, particularly now when comfort and serenity might become the dominant attitude.

The fear that saturates the atmosphere paves the way for spiritual renewal. The initiates must suffer and feel distress at this juncture in their evolution. The turmoil that prevails destroys the previous feeling of quiet which came with suspended animation. Renewed activity traumatizes the novitiate. His extreme desire for *wholeness*, the mandala experience, forces him on at the expense of his life. "It is better to lose your life in the quest than to languish miserably" (p. 49), the Hoopoe affirms. Life is a relative experience, and though there is no guarantee that one will reach one's goal, the effort expended in search of fulfillment is what counts. Each of the birds experiences his journey in a different way; each absorbs the Hoopoe's message within his own understanding. Only when the *knower begins to know himself* is true progress made.

Even spending an entire life ostensibly worshiping the Simurgh is no guarantee that the birds will finally reach their goal. The Hoopoe tells them the story of a Sufi who spent forty years adoring God in the desert. There he was with but a single tree and a bird in it to keep him company, but the bird sang so sweetly that it was as if a veritable symphony were pouring forth from nature's deepest secrets. The Sufi was enchanted by the heavenly tones, which kept him in a state of glowing rapture. Allah, however, saw through the Sufi's long devotions. "Tell the Sufi," He said, "I am astonished that after so many years of devotion he has ended by selling me for a bird. It is true that this bird is admirable, but its song has caught him in a snare. I have bought him and he has sold me" (p. 61). The Sufi's detachment was incomplete. He had not really advanced in his training; his spiritual learning had remained on the primary level.

The Hoopoe proceeds to castigate those who feel that they are living religiously in a state of sanctity when in fact they are merely mouthing for their own reasons empty phrases. It is not the world alone that must be renounced but everything that binds and chains a person to a routine, be it one of enjoyment or pain, beatitude or conflict. The Hoopoe illustrates this by the story of "The Spider." It weaves a marvelous web, and a fly gets caught in it. The fly is killed by the spider, who feeds on it. But then the owner of the house takes a broom and sweeps the web away. Nothing is left: spider, fly, and web have all been destroyed, or rather transformed. Similarly the birds must be capable of complete detachment—of sacrificing their very being. Only then will the abandonment of their mortal transient condition be complete, and they will become worthy of encountering the Simurgh.

5. The Valley of Unity
Antinomy is the rule of the day. Everything that was considered smooth, connected, and related is now reexamined and fragmented—dismembered so that it may be reintegrated into another sphere of being. "In this valley, the Hoopoe states, "everything is broken in pieces and then unified" (p. 115). Problems are again subsumed, conflicts explicated, emotions parceled out, but in closer proximity to the goal—the Simurgh. No longer burdened with the weight of a persona and centroverted ego, or the dross of worldly existence, the birds experience a sense of lightness and weightlessness that precedes their *sublimatio* condition. Important now is the understanding of the breaking-up process and the need of reviewing what had seemed to be unified: the elements that link number and time; past, present, and future; the visible and the invisible.

Similar to the ancient religious mysteries of dismemberment (Osiris, Dionysus, Orpheus, Christ, for example), the I and the Thou of the novitiate separate. In so doing the Sufi novice experiences a second mortification leading to a rectification, making certain that henceforth the ego can never again identify with the Self, thus avoiding any possible state of inflation. In this process of breaking up the conscious and unconscious components within the psyche, feelings as well as intellectual concepts are reexamined. Letters, words, sentences, are analyzed as single units and as atomized particles, linguistically, phonetically, numerologically. What seemed secure and understandable in a previous phase of development is no longer true. Disconcerted and lacking identity, the Sufi novitiate again feels disoriented—but this time, however, in a different way—as if he had "fallen into the ocean of exterior life." In this collective sphere he flounders, experiencing the waves of conflict, antagonism, contrariety, now and then achieving some semblance of security. Despite the inner chaos, his feelings, thoughts, and intuitions are slowly transforming themselves; analogies reblend into new entities; the invisible and unimaginable become concrete. The heightened libido and the surging tumultuous activity experienced by the Sufi disciple slowly recede, slacken, and pave the way for a new and more profound illumination, when "the Sun will draw aside the veil which covers it" (p. 116).

Disassociation, which prevails at this stage of development, allows the Sufi novitiate to review his past states in a fresh frame of reference, shedding new light on his motivations and sensations. Life seems to be burgeoning in an altogether new manner.

The birds listen to the Hoopoe as she describes the vigilance required of those who refuse to be ensnared by the charms of the devil. "Whenever I wish to enter the Way, the devil rouses my vanity and prevents me from seeking a guide. My heart is troubled, for I have not the strength to resist him. How can I save myself from Iblis [evil] and be revivified by the wine of the Spirit?" asks one of the birds (p. 58).

Just as the analyst tries to ferret out each segment of a problem from the whole, in order to explicate its nature and impact, so the birds pursue their probing during this phase. Experiencing both their weakness and strength allows them to deal with their particular psychological makeup in a different manner. Every desire must now be understood and dealt with individually; each "demonic force" or shadow characteristic will be depotentiated as the light of consciousness intrudes. The knight pursues his incessant struggle, never yielding to the dog that follows, for should he once allow that instinctual world to attract him, he would encourage a pack of hounds to follow every step. "This world is a sweating room or prison, the domain of the devil; have no truck with it or with its master," The Hoopoe declares (p. 59).

The dismemberment or dissociative stage invites the reunification of disparate parts through the *dhikr*, the ritual that helps integrate the unsubdued contents within the psyche.[41] The *dhikr* may also be envisaged as representing in symbolic form the *khirqa*, The Sufi's woolen cloak. The adoption of it forces the novice to concentrate on the inner world, following the movements of *ab extra ad intra* (from without, within), thereby tapping profounder realms in him. A progressive descent into the collective unconscious allows the seeker to penetrate the universal Self and to consolidate those forces that pave the way for *transconsciousness*.

It is the ritual of the *dhikr* that links the Sufi disciple with the world around him. Objects are no longer seen in three dimensions but as psychospiritual forces, suprasensory entities. Space seems extended, time stretched, a dimensionless universe comes into existence. Consciousness is not lowered as it was earlier during the *participation mystique* phase; it has been altered and heightened instead by noetic values, understanding, depth perception which have become actualized. The novitiate's entire being is now open to his soul—no longer in the state of instinctual *nafs* or of blaming ones; it has reached the pacified level, that is, it has become serene; freed from the burdens of darkness. It is fire and light.

The Hoopoe quickly informs the birds that their travail is not yet over. "The light you think you have in the Spiritual Way is only a flickering flame. . . . Do not let yourself be seduced by the glimmer which you see" (p. 86). Such glimpses of revelation are plateaux only, heights of sorts; they also may well be obstacles, lulling the neophyte into a state of contentment and dispersal of attention which must still be extreme. A fluid condition has resulted: intuitions of immortality are glimpsed, a transsensory condition has taken on reality; nonspatial and nontemporal spheres have been subsumed; telepathic phenomena are sensed; timelessness within the deepest recesses of the mysterious universe is about to be encountered. As multiplicity slowly withdraws, the birds concentrate on the Whole—the Infinite.

The part will become the whole, or rather, there will be neither part nor whole. In the School of the Secret you will see thousands of men with intellectul knowledge, their lips parted in silence. What is intellectual knowledge here? It stoops on the threshold of the door like a blind child. He who discovers something of this secret turns his face from the kingdom of the two worlds. The Being I speak of does not exist separately; everyone is this Being, existence and non-existence is this Being. (P. 116)

6. *The Valley of Astonishment and Bewilderment*

As if engulfed by a giant wave, the birds are heaved back and forth. They experience sadness and joy, the bitter and the sweet. "It is at once day and night. There is fire, yet a man is depressed and despondent," the Hoopoe states. Surprise and bewilderment are the Sufi novitiate's lot. Nothing is certain: Is he or isn't he? Nothing is fixed or recognizable; everything is now seen in variegated color tones, including feelings and sensations. "Have you or have you not the feeling of existence?" And of the world outside, the initiate realizes that he belongs to neither world completely: "My heart is at the same time both full and empty of love" (p. 119).

Disorientation implies detachment for the Sufi; orientation is in effect attachment. Such a state of being cannot exist for an overly long period. The most profound experiences, nevertheless, may be kindled during the course of each of the seven phases of the Sufi initiation process. In the Valley of Astonishment and Bewilderment, the initiate probes into even more profound levels of consciousness; he becomes a *nabi* (a prophet). Undirected feelings allow intuition to take hold, leading the initiate into myriad channels permeating the universe. Although such a psychological condition may be termed irrational, for the highly disciplined Sufi, as well as for certain creative individuals, its value lies in activating dimensions within the unconscious that may lead to further investigation in the bodily and spiritual domain. The initiate becomes the sounding board for physical sensations that focus on him from external areas and rebound from him into the cosmic infinity. He feels as though life outside of him is sinking into his pores. He is being absorbed and enriched by these energy patterns. Such a phase of experience may not be conceptualized nor categorized. As Jung has suggested, thinking and feeling are "incommensurable" with one another.

Astonishment and bewilderment are composites of that very

special moment that precedes reintegration of the created and the Creator, the beloved and the lover—the initiate's flowering into the one supreme being. No longer earth-oriented, the soul looks toward the "Unseen World," which is self-subsisting yet belongs to a higher sphere. The *I* is virtually nonexistent at this point; it is on its way to becoming Thou: two halves merged into one.[42]

Suffering is still implicit in this sixth stage of development. In this connection the Hoopoe tells the story of "The Grateful Slave." A king gives his slave a rare fruit to taste. When the slave tells the king how delicious it is, the king asks the slave for a piece of it. He puts it into his mouth and is surprised at how bitter it tastes. "Sire, says the slave, "since I have received so many gifts at your hand, how can I complain of one bitter fruit? Seeing that you shower benefits on me, why should one bitter- ness estrange me from you?" (p. 70). Suffering clarifies views and relationships, according to Sufi tradition. It increases *gnosis* if the evaluating principle is put to work along with the pain experienced. Thus, astonishment and bewilderment together with distress yield insights into an infinite beyond.

"The Way is not open to everyone; only the upright may tread it," the Hoopoe points out (p. 73). This statement creates further bewilderment among the birds. The sacrifices they have suffered during their spiritual journey, the nagging pains they have felt in their attempt to direct their feelings onto God, and then to be told that the Simurgh may not show himself, brings despair. To this the Hoopoe counters, boldness is also a factor in spiritual ventures. To reach the Simurgh/Self requires activa- tion; passivity or lethargy are negative characteristics and do not pave the way for self-development. In illustration of this idea she narrates the story of a Sufi who had been the butt of lapidation. To avoid the stones children throw at him, he goes into a building. Even there, he feels stones falling on his head from an open skylight. He begins to insult the children. Finally, he realizes that hail is falling on him, not stones. Rather than trying to assess his situation, he remains in darkness; his shadow world dominates; his evil thoughts are projected onto external entities in a near-paranoid attitude. The world is his enemy, he believes, when in reality he has allowed his shadow to hold sway. Had he seen beyond his immediate problem, had he allowed astonishment and bewilderment and boldness to intercede, sparks of light might have illuminated his situation; thought would have pointed the way to truth.

With increased light and truth that bewilderment triggers because it opens heretofore closed or unified regions, the intuitive function is further activated, allowing the initiate to be saturated in mystical knowledge (*ma'rifa*; in Greek, *gnosis*) heretofore beyond his reach. His new insights diminish sensation and feeling functions and take the initiate outside of the body experience—into heretofore incomprehensible dimensions—always within the level of his understanding. Apocalyptic visions are now apprehended. Such experiences may be looked upon as *events of the soul*, a prelude to the immersion into the Simurgh/Self/Godhead. The initiate who has now evolved to nearly the same level as the sheikh may be considered a *medium* figure: a vessel through which the Supreme Essence experiences himself. Because God/Self is reality and the visible world (ego) comes into existence as a reflection of his form, the vision itself is a mirror image of deity. As such, his reality is present in everything; in images, forms, ideas, shadows—in spirit and substance; in a world ranging from the infinitely small to the incommensurable galaxies.[43]

7. *The Valley of Deprivation and Death*
The Hoopoe flounders at this juncture. She is at a loss to describe the ineffable sensations or theophanic visions to come. Similes, metaphors, metonymies, symbols, and any other figure of speech seem inadequte. To convey the essence of the divine center of being, the God/Self as actualized in the Simurgh, is impossible. "The essence of this Valley is forgetfulness, dumbness, deafness and distraction; the thousand shadows which surround you disappear in a single ray of the celestial sun" (p. 123).

In the Valley of Deprivation and Death the soul experiences its third state most completely. It becomes pacified in light that radiates from its center to its peripheral regions, inundating the cosmos with its subtle energetic particles. It is at this juncture that the initiate encompasses and integrates all of his previous experiences; accumulated sensations, attributes of all types, feelings of pain and joy—all are gathered into himself and transformed into clusters of heightened awareness.

The vastness of the universe is now experienced as an ocean creating eternally mobile and immeasurable surface patterns, each forming and losing its outline and consistency in the other and as rapidly as the mood requires. As a drop in an infinite ocean, an atom in a concrete mass, the initiate could have felt pangs of extreme solitude or alienation but, instead, feels sensations of *quietism* saturating his entire being. He experiences a sense of belonging to Self/divinity. Born into a new existence, a world of mysteries, the intangible seems within reach, participation in the All endows him with notions of ineffable riches. He is both individual and complete; a microcosm and a macrocosm. "When aloe wood and thorns are reduced to ashes," the Hoopoe states, "they both look alike—but their quality is different" (p. 124). Accordingly, identity is experienced in the *nonexistent* state individually and collectively in keeping with each of the bird's soul states.

The Hoopoe suggests that the birds don that *khirqa* of nothingness to become atoms of temporality, drink from "the cup of *annihilation*," then "cover their breast with the belt of belittlement," and place on their "head the burnous of non-existence" (p. 125). The Hoopoe now tells of the moth that was so intoxicated with love that it flew straight into the flame where it shriveled; but it experienced the most ineffable of joys because the flame embraced it so tenderly and completely. "He has learned what he wished to know; but only he understands, and one can say no more" (p. 125).

The state of annihilation (*fanā*) sees to the destruction of consciousness, that aspect which is incarnated in being. The initiate's eternal and amorphous aspect, that which is flame, will live on and be reunited with the universal being. This condition of annihilation and reintegration cannot be compared to the Hindu's *nirvana*. Unlike the Hindu but similarly to the Hebrew and Christian views, the Muslim believes in individuality of the soul. *Fanā*, therefore, is the process that removes mortal man's outer personality but retains that aspect of it which God endowed with His attributes. The condition of *baqā* now follows: the reintegration into the primordial light of God, of the initiate's divine nature—his eternal aspect. The state of *baqā* cannot really be known during man's lifetime; it may be glimpsed in trance states or implied. It is the state of absolute identity with God.

Fanā has been described as a "gathering in of the gathering," when the ego merges into the Self and the Self into the cosmic Self. It is not to be understood as a union with deity because such a concept presupposes in itself duality; nor should it be termed indwelling, which indicates the incranation of divinity into man. Divinity is implicit in man—always. "*Fanā* is the nullification of the mystic in divine presence" and may be explained as a reintegration of the individual into one's primordial condition—into the Absolute. When unity becomes identity in a condition of heightened consciousness, *baqā* is said to be experienced. Black light then permeates the All; divine light blazes throughout the mystic's Self—now experienced as cosmic consciousness—leaving no room for any other tonality. There is, then, a virtual "blackout."[44] (Black is the color associated with God. It is so intense that colors existing within the composite blackness can no longer be differentiated.)

The conditions of *fanā* and *baqā*, psychologically speaking, indicate the end of tangential life, the obliteration of all differences between object and subject, ego and Self. Such an eclipse of consciousness as required in *fanā* and *baqā* would invite insanity for the Occidental, untrained in such practices. The individual would be unable to return to the mundane sphere and remain forever "stuck" in the atemporal realm. For the Sufi, however, whose being has been focused by the aforementioned disciplines, immersion in the pleromatic sphere (not baqā) seems to lead to cosmic consciousness and endow the initiated with a deeper understanding of transcendent immanence.

In either case, the condition of spaceless/timeless/facelessness seems tantamount to death. For Attar, and for the Sufis in general, death is merely a particle of existence—one aspect of being in a condition of flux. Whether life is short or long, Attar implies it is composed of segments of eternity, breaths within infinite rhythms and atomic particles. "Don't you know that life, be it long or short, is composed of a few breaths? Don't you understand that whoever is born must also die? That he goes into the earth and that the wind disperses the elements of which his body was made" (p. 66). Man is with God at all times, the Sufi believes; whether alive or dead, active or inert, mortal or immortal. Each aspect of his being belongs to an infinite process: "a particle of the great whole," similar "to the rose in the calyx" (p. 88).

The Hoopoe looks around. Only thirty birds of the countless myriad that began the journey remain. Weary and dejected, they are now perched at the door of the Simurgh's habitation.

The Simurgh, an archetypal image that came into being as a result of an affective condition, is indescribable: "this Majesty that cannot be described, whose essence is incomprehensible—that Being who is beyond human reason and knowledge" (p. 129) is not to make its presence known. Representing the collective soul of all birds, the Simurgh is an expression of an inner attitude projected onto a single entity or bird; it is the image of the Self on the psychological level, it is comparable to the Hindu's *atman*, the Buddhist's Buddha, the Christian's Christ, the Jew's Jehovah. A psychic center that includes the ego but is not comparable to it, the Simurgh represents totality beyond human comprehension—infinity, God.

As the birds stand outside the Simurgh's door, apocalyptic visions flash into existence, unknown sensations and anticipations of the absolute.

Then flashed the lightning of fulfilment, and a hundred worlds were consumed in a moment. They saw a thousand of suns each more resplendent than the other, thousands of moons and stars all equally beautiful, and seeing all this they were amazed and agitated like a dancing atom of dust, and they cried out: "O Thou who art more radiant than the sun! Thou, who has reduced the sun to an atom, how can we appear before Thee? Ah, why have we so uselessly endured all this suffering on the Way? Having renounced ourselves and all things, we now cannot obtain that for which we have striven. Here, it little matters whether we exist or not." (P. 130)

Suddenly the door opens. A chamberlain steps forward. The birds want to "acknowledge the Simurgh" their king, they tell him. The chamberlain is irritated by them. "O you whose minds and hearts are troubled, whether you exist or do not exist in the universe, the King has his being always and eternally. You bring nothing but moans and lamentations. Return then to whence you came, O vile handful of earth!" (p. 130). The birds are astounded by such treatment. But then the chamberlain informs them that "the lightning of his glory" will manifest itself. The birds are aflame with passion, reducing everything about them to that quintessential element—alchemical ash. The moment is at hand; the door is thrust open

and as he drew aside a hundred curtains, one after the other, a new world beyond the veil was revealed. Now was the light of lights manifested, and all of them sat down on the masnad, the seat of the Majesty and Glory. . . . The sun of majesty sent forth his rays, and in the reflection of each other's faces these thirty birds (si-murgh) of the outer world, contemplated the face of of the Simurgh of the inner world. This so astonished them that they did not know if they were still themselves or if they had become the Simurgh. At last, in a state of contemplation, they realized that they were the Simurgh and that the Simurgh was the thirty birds (p. 131).

Attar's pun on the word *simurgh*, which means "thirty" in Persian, is the perfect mataphor for God as universal Self. It mirrors, incorporates, synthesizes, yet individualizes the dimension/dimensionless aspect of the birds. As they contemplate the Simurgh, that is, themselves, in the collective soul that he represents, they understand that each is both one and many, as the Simurgh is multiple and one. God/Self is a mirror in which humankind observes itself, experiences reality in itself and in others, realizes its own potential both individually and collectively. Humankind is also a mirror in which God contemplates his names and qualities; without the created, the Creator would not exist or know himself. The individual is an archetype into which creative energy is channeled; when this force reaches a certain stage in its development, it returns to its primordial condition in God/Self.

"The Sun of my majesty is a mirror," the Simurgh states, "without the use of tongues" (p. 132). The manifest world, then, is the reflection of God. The word *speculum*, once used for mirror, is associated with speculation, a noetic function. During the course of their pilgrimage, the birds had speculated and pondered, bringing them ever closer to an understanding of the universe and of themselves—their oneness as reflected images of the All. Their theorizing and actions led to spiritualization. Unlike Narcissus, who fell in love with his own image (his ego), the Sufi expanded his field of vision during his initiation period. It is the Self/God, the total being and beings whose elements and factors lie beyond the immediate field of speculation, that has become visible—not the ego, which in Narcissus's case was swallowed up by the Self, leading to his demise. The love of God that the Sufi experiences is lived out consciously; it is difficult to acquire and is gained only after severe trials and disciplines. It requires a willing annihilation to a power superior to it, not a yielding to an infirm ego.

As the birds contemplate themselves in the mirror which now takes on the clarity and perfection of their own highly polished beings, the Simurgh spreads its wings and hides the sunlight. The picture darkens. The birds have lost themselves in the Simurgh as "the shadow was lost in the sun" (p. 132). A giant and overwhelming implosion/explosion seems to have occurred: a cloud vanishes within a ball of fire, a shadow disperses as day dawns. The Simurgh/Self/God—the collective universal soul that contains all forms and colors, tones and overtones—experiences its primordial unity once again in the absolute world of nothingness. As Attar wrote: "Be absolutely not!"[45]

The seven stages of Sufi initiation described in *The Conference of the Birds* take the novitiate from individual forms and mundane interests to an illuminated and atemporal condition. During his training which, as we have seen, includes such religious disciplines as the *dhikr*, meditation, contemplation, ecstatic and apocalyptic visionary experiences, and such ascetic practices as fasting, self-flagellation, sleeplessness, and complete obedience to one's spiritual director, the novice feels absorbed in and being absorbed by the Simurgh/God/Self. As the sheikh sees to it that his disciple is divested of everything personal and human, the initiate's libido is centered inward, energizing the subliminal sphere.

That an anima figure—the Hoopoe—is cast in the role of the sheikh in Attar's poem is fascinating. Allotted to an inferior role in Islamic culture and virtually banished from Sufi tradition, woman is resurrected as a spiritualized, dehumanized, angelic force. As an anima figure, the Hoopoe is heart, intuition, and beauty, an amorphous and yet floating force that represents goodness. It is she who helps the birds to develop their potential and achieve fulfillment, to experience a *unio mystica*. As the meditations and disciplines progress, a *sacrificium intellectus* is realized because it is through feeling and not cerebrality that progress is made. The birds do not pursue their ascesis rationally; their extreme introversion is motivated through the gentleness of the Hoopoe/anima. It is through her that they learn the meaning of oneness, enabling the birds to reconnect what has been severed: they bind masculine and feminine principles, life and death, evil and good in one ineffable experience.

Experientially, the seven stages of the Sufi's ascensional process develop the sense organs of the initiate into finely tuned instruments of apperception. In the fourth dimension, which is revealed to the Sufi when his disciplines have been completed, he experiences a suprasensory sphere where form, shape, context, consistency, depth, coloration, rhythms, and dynamisms are clothed in eternal oneness. In this condition, he becomes a theophanic witness, a mirror in which divinity reveals himself, in which ego sees its reflection in the Self, the transient in the eternal, the finite in the infinite.

The physical and spiritual demands made upon the initiate during his training period mold him into a living manifestation of a metaphysical notion: flux. He becomes "a man of the moment" in the true sense of the word: mobile, never resting, always advocating increased *ma'rifa*. Perpetual striving is implicit in Sufi doctrine. Attar writes in *The Conference of the Birds*: "All that you have heard or seen or known is not even the beginning of what you must know, and since the ruined habitation of this world is not your place you must renounce it. Seek the truth of the tree, and do not worry about whether the branches do or do not exist" (p. 132).

The emphasis placed on asceticism in Sufi ritual, on the annihilation of the ego and of attachment to the present world with its human relationships, is similar to that found in other deeply religious and mystically oriented sects, whether they be Christian, Buddhist, or Hindu. It is a nonexistential way of viewing the life experience: an escape mechanism for some, a discovery of the transcendental sphere for others, depending upon one's point of view and psychological needs. In either case, it is a *dehumanizing process*. The human sphere is downgraded. A transient domain, it is considered a negative entity and unworthy of too much attention. The dehumanizing process divests man of what is essentially his earthly condition and compels him to look to the celestial and transpersonal spheres. It is as extreme a point of view as the hedonist's, which is anchored in the here-and-now, pleasures-of-the-flesh principle. The complete obedience to the sheikh in the Sufi discipline is a positive attribute for those who seek the godly sphere during their temporal sojourn. It is a negative condition, however, for those who yearn to develop their potential in the everyday world. To divest a human being of his will and individuality is to rob him of his uniqueness and sense of dignity. The initiate's forced identification with the sheikh, or father image, stunts his psychological growth; it forces him to withdraw into an undifferentiated realm where noetic values are experienced in heavenly climes. The extreme introversion required of the Sufi novice also creates a *regressus ad uterum*. Used as an instrument to detach the adept from his worldly condition, it succeeds in rechanneling his instinctual needs into celestial climes, opening the doors to the unconscious and keeping them ajar. Under such circumstances the initiate may lose sight of his everyday existence and opt exclusively for ecstasy in the religious experience.

The two paths—existential and transcendental—which have been humankind's choice since the beginning of time, answer specific needs within a personality, represent a cultural factor throughout the world, and are ways of assuaging humanity's eternal longing to experience a realm beyond the space/time continuum. Whatever the way as Attar notes at the conclusion of *The Conference of the Birds*: "If you wish the ocean of your soul to remain in a state of salutary movement you must die to all your old life, and then keep silence" (p. 136).

Conclusion

"The human psyche is the womb of all the arts and sciences," Jung wrote.[1] The literary creation, a manifestation of the subliminal realm working in harmony with the conscious sphere, is a unique expression of an individual's personality as well as the revelation of a cultural phenomenon. When the writer sounds out his depths authentically, if he probes the mythic level of his world, he reaches into archetypal spheres wherein the seeds of past, present, and future exist as living organic entities—acting and being acted upon. Comparable in this respect to the prophet announcing a religion yet to be born, a philosopher collecting his pronouncements which one day will become *praxis*, so the writer reveals his message. Endowed with special powers, he molds the raw material—the amorphous substance—living inchoate within his depths, fashioning it into symbolic configurations.

An explanation of the work of art from a Jungian point of view adds another dimension to the play, poem, essay, and novel. The *whole being* is probed and dilated, soma and psyche, thus bringing new ways of viewing situations to the readers on both an individual and collective level, paving the way for a reshuffling of emotions and a refocusing of empirical and spiritual attitudes. In this manner, it is hoped that the problems ferreted out may be made more understandable to the readers, thus enabling them to cope with them more readily. Reminiscent of the philosophers' stone upon which the alchemists of old projected, so the great literary work also reveals a psychological and an aesthetic condition within the author, critic, and reader. It is a living and breathing entity—a catalyst—which arouses creativity within those who come into contact with it, sparks intuitive flares, churns emotional and spiritual values, thereby paving the

way for a deeper understanding of Self. In so doing, a broadening of the conscious/unconscious relationship within the human
experience can also come to pass—an expansion of knowledge.

The writers discussed in *A Jungian Approach to Literature*
not only subsume imbalances existing within their own psyches
but also reveal the dangerous levels these have reached in the
society in which they lived and worked. When contemporary
readers confront the characters and situations as they spin out
their existences in *The Bacchants*, one questions the meaning of
their comportment. Why, for example, does such an identification between the Bacchants and Pentheus exist? What are the
elements involved? What affective situations are triggered?

A work of art may never be fully explained in terms of the
author's personal psychology nor that of the critic or reader.[2]
To do so is to limit its vigor, to dismantle its impact, to distort
its meaning. What may be apprehended—and what interests us
here—is the urgency of the author's message and its appeal to
many different ages and societies. The forces dredged up by Euripides, stemming from the profoundest levels of his collective
unconscious, the masses of mephitic sensations that are called
into play, answered a need within him—as it does within the
men and women in today's society who keep reading and producing his drama as well as works dealing with similar themes.

Like the snowball that gathers momentum as it rolls down-
hill—to borrow Bergson's metaphor—so the work of art generates energy in the form of mass and light. It assumes the power,
depth, and intensity of an avalanche; it becomes a conglomerate
of violent emotions, active forces operating within the framework of the essay, poem, drama, and novel. To explicate the
resonances and reverberations and their meanings that emerge
from the work of art in the light of present-day values has been
the aim of *A Jungian Approach to Literature*. That each part is
divided into two sections, ectypal and archetypal, allowed me
to ground the work under discussion in the empirical world and
then to highlight its eternal and universal aspects. The ectypal
analysis, like an anamnesis, approximates the historical context
of the work, familiarizing the reader with specific facts perti-
nent to the author and his creation. The archetypal analysis removes the poem, play, novel, or essay from the personal to the
collective sphere. Since we are dealing with raw psychological

material in the essays—fashioned and transfigured by the artist—we not only peer into his inner world but also study his
mastery over his creative impulse. The visionary experience
brought to life in the work, cut and sized by him to his dimension, is then explicated by the critic, also within the scope of his
or her frame of reference. Hopefully, the elements underscored
will activate, stimulate—even jar—the reader's own psyche.

Each part focuses on a special psychological condition
thereby offering throughout the possibility of affinities, identi-
fications between the work of art and those who project upon
it. *The Bacchants*, an outgrowth of a primordial experience,
reveals a society in chaos. Terrifying as it may seem, we are
made privy to extremes which revolve around the struggle between matriarchal and patriarchal forces. Several types of sexual perversion come into play on an individual and collective
basis. *The Bacchants* is reality; not Euripides' alone, but existing in altered and transfigured forms in the contemporary world.
It is a warning by the author to the unsuspecting and the naïve
in certain societies—to examine the conditions in which they
live. It points to the dangers involved when a shadow is allowed
to unleash its fury and rage unchecked. Let us recall that not so
long ago, the supposedly "civilized" state of Germany, considered the pinnacle of learning and culture, when ruled by the
Nazis gave rise to the bloodiest moments in history. During the
Holy Inquisition in Spain, in the fifteenth and sixteenth centuries, when Christianity had reached its virtual apogee, *autoda-
fés* (acts of faith) were the rule of the day. In *The Bacchants* then,
we see unadulterated instincts enacted in ritual form, proliferating their religious frenzy upon the stage of life; in so doing, they
are drawing attention to an imbalance lurking within society.

Parzival introduces the hero figure. Psychologically, he represents the ego attempting to wrench itself free from a *participation mystique*: from a positive mother figure in this case, a
kind, nourishing, and protective force that can all too easily
turn into the opposite were it allowed to cling too long to its
progeny. Should such a condition prevail, the adolescent would
remain stunted in his development; his ego would be arrested.
What made Parzival's task of breaking away from his mother
so difficult was her "goodness" and "kindness." Such a mother
is sometimes more dangerous than the *vagina dentata* type, be-

cause of the pseudo security she offers. Parzival had the strength to fight his way free of his psychological swaddling clothes and though his initial act of liberation was cruel, and the struggle he faced difficult and painful, he succeeded in carving out his own future and experienced the joy of fulfillment.

Montaigne, born during a particularly difficult period when religious strife between Catholics and Protestants nearly tore his country apart, was endowed with a hypersensitive psyche. Instinctively, he knew that his ego had to be strengthened if it were to survive, that a coming to terms with pain and death would not only deepen his understanding of himself but of humanity in general. His study of the writings of his contemporaries as well as of the ancient classics was his way of gaining wisdom and insight into the life experience. Seneca, Horace, Herodotus, Virgil, Epictetus, and many others became role models for him at various times in his life. Each branded him with their *scintillae*, altering and enlarging his frames of reference. A redistribution of values occurred; feelings experienced as energy particles transformed his views, paving the way for a continuous reassessment of his inner condition and personal development.

A young society gave birth to Corneille's Horace, an aggressive and instinctual hero. Primitive conditions are fertile field for primitive psychology: with little room for refined impulses or gentle nuances of feeling. The welfare of the society as a whole is the single concern; the individual is relatively unimportant. In *Rodogune*, a quite different situation prevails. The state has reached its zenith; it is dominated by a powerful queen who, in order to assure her position, commits the most heinous of crimes. Archetypal in dimension, Corneille saw Cleopatra as a transpersonal figure, grandiose and virtually sublime—with "greatness of soul." The question arises as to why such flamboyant types are active throughout the world today? Why are they forever alluring and fascinating, as well as captivating? How is it that society—and the individual—allows such creatures as Horace and Cleopatra, for example, or the Bacchants and Pentheus to pollute the air that surrounds them?

Goethe, Novalis, Rabbi Nachman, and Yeats sought more spiritual and rarefied climes. Dissatisfied with terrestrial conditions, as they understood them, they yearned for greater understanding and serenity. Their pathological fantasies coexist with healthy imaginings, mirroring the emotional disquietude that so often lies at the heart of the artist's nature.

Novalis's literary trajectory revealed a *regressus ad uterum.* The Earth Mother was his inspiration; he also longed for her embrace, for it alone, he felt, would assuage his pain, bring warmth to the world of coldness, consolation to his solitude, love as opposed to dispassionate objectivity.

Elective Affinities may only appeal to those who have reached the middle of life. Marital problems, resulting from a condition of stasis in a relationship come to the fore. Relying upon the material world for stability and not on an inner spiritual condition and the staleness existing between husband and wife paved the way for the aridity which led to the breakup at the end.

Rabbi Nachman's ordeal and his mystical quest stem from a harrowing empirical existence. The persecution of the Jews reached new heights in the eighteenth and nineteenth centuries in Europe. A life lived in constant dread of annihilation—the threat of daily progroms—gave rise to a unique psychological condition. The ego's exile, indicating a diminution of the relating factor in life, might have led to Rabbi Nachman's withdrawal from life. It did not. His creative spirit, activated by his unconscious, paved the way for his night-sea journey that encouraged him to complete "The Master of Prayer." In so doing, he revealed the transformation which had occurred after having experienced his altered states of consciousness: the integration of the ego into the Self—man and God in harmony and balance.

Yeats also suffered from solitude and alienation. His hero, Cuchulain, was a man at odds with himself; his poetical universe always seeking fresh inspiration, longing for unity with his anima figure. Guided by instincts, frequently, which lead to such disastrous situations as Cuchulain's killing of his son, the unity which he so desperately seeks is nowhere to be experienced—except in the work of art.

In *The Kalevala* we are dealing with a different sort of hero. Unprotected by a natural mother, Väinämöinen was forced out into the world alone and friendless. But, because he had been nurtured in his mother's womb for so many years, he was born old and wise. He knew how to befriend the elemental forces of air, wind, water, and fire so that they would come to his aid in time of need. Yet, when it came time to dealing with the feminine principle, Vänämöinen was found wanting. Never having known his mother (a figure who carries the first anima projection), he had difficulty in his dealings with girls and women. Rather than attracting them, he alienated them. The feminine principle was realized within him only in abstract terms, in the poetry and songs he composed. Vänämöinen was the archetypal hero who answered the needs of a primitive society—vastly different from Horace—whose existence was constantly threatened by winter cold and wild beasts.

Farid ud-din Attar takes us into the Sufi's mystical domain, a discipline that involves the dismantling of the ego, its pulverization, and not its growth or evolution. To annihilate the ego, which is the goal of the Sufi experience (and which we in the West generaly consider the most destructive of acts, antithetical to the individuation process), is to reject the entire notion of identity and individuality. The Eastern religions, on the other hand, believe that egolessness is at the root of the cosmic experience; without having achieved this level of growth, the pleromatic sphere and cosmic consciousness remain unknown.

The ten literary works chosen for explication in *A Jungian Approach to Literature* are a living record of aesthetic and spiritual experiences, the revelation of passions clothed in archetypal imagery, as mysterious and elusive as the work of art itself. Because a great literary work belongs to the transpersonal world, as does the archetype, it may never be fully explained, only glimpsed; the interpretation reflecting the psychological depth and understanding of the person making it. Critics and readers approach a work of art through their own eyes, senses, intuitive faculties, which may (or may not) make the novel, play, or poem meaningful to them and to others. Explications, therefore, are never definitive. At best, they are temporary, part of the fluid and changeable world. There is, therefore, no right or wrong to criticism. Each person brings to the work the psychological outlook that composes his world. What is important is the understanding gleaned—its trajectory into the reader's soma and psyche.

Although flux, change, instability, are the rule in the creative sphere, there is a steadying element and relatively fixed factor within it as well: the quest. This quest that the creative venture elicits empowers individuals to deepen their own levels of consciousness, to expand their views, and thus encourages them to develop more fully the unique experience that is their own life. Arduous, frequently harrowing, the sounding out required to allow the quest to proceed is the very element implicit in the individuation process—the force that yields the fruit: "In the wilderness shall the waters break out, and streams in the desert" (Isa. 35:6).

Notes
Bibliography
Index

NOTES

INTRODUCTION

1. Edinger, "An Outline of Analytical Psychology," p. 1. The entire article gives the most explicit definitions of Jungian terminology. It is highly recommended.
2. Ibid., p. 1.
3. Ibid., p 12.
4. Ibid., p. 10.
5. Ibid., p. 7.

PART I

All quotations from *The Bacchants* come from *Ten Plays of Euripides*, trans. Moses Hadas and John McLean (New York: Bantam Books, 1966).

1. Eliade, *Aspects du mythe*, pp. 9–53.
2. Abood and Harris, "The Splintered Personality in Euripides," pp. 60, 62.
3. Edinger, "An Outline of Analytical Psychology," p. 10.
4. Hutin, *Les sociétés secrètes*, p. 22.
5. Bachofen, *Myth, Religion, and Mother Right*, p. 71.
6. Eliade, *Histoire des croyances*, p. 374.
7. Kerenyi, *The Gods of the Greeks*, p. 256.
8. Eliade, *Histoire des croyances*, pp. 373–74.
9. C. G. Jung, *Collected Works* 6:170–83.
10. Ibid., 12:86, 134 ff., 294. Dionysus, interestingly enough, has been identified with Christ, since both their mothers had been divinely inseminated: Semele by Zeus and Mary by the Holy Ghost. Both mothers ascended to immortal spheres, thereby becoming spiritualizing agents. Wine and blood are associated with their worship. Christ said: "I am the true vine, and my father is the winedresser. Every branch of mine that bears no fruit, he takes away, and every branch that does bear fruit he prunes, that it may bear more fruit, . . . I am the vine, you are the branches"

(John 15:1–5). That Jesus changed water into wine when he performed the miracle at Cana bears out this identification. Jung writes that "the wine miracle at Cana was the same as the miracle in the temple of Dionysus, and it is profoundly significant, that, on the Damascus chalice, Christ is enthroned among vine tendrils like Dionysus himself." Even the name Dionysus-Iacchus, Iacchos, and Jesus have common roots.

11. Gilbert Murray, "Euripides' *Bacchae* and the Ritual Pattern of Tragedy," in *The Scapegoat: Ritual and Literature*, p. 105.
12. Abood and Harris, *The Splintered Personality in Euripides*, p. 73.
13. Entralgo, *The Therapy of the World in Classical Antiquity*.
14. Benoist, *L'Esoterisme*, p. 26.
15. Kott, *The Eating of the Gods*, p. 192.
16. Abood and Harris, *The Splintered Personality in Euripides*, p. 69.

PART 2

1. Jung and Franz, *The Grail Legend*, p. 158.
2. All quotations from *Parzival* are taken from Wolfram von Eschenbach, *Parzival* (New York: Vintage, 1961).
3. Will Durant, *The Story of Civilization*, 4:425–50.
4. Ibid., p. 592.
5. Ibid., p. 307.
6. Ibid., p. 573.
7. *Parzival*, p. 67.
8. C. G. Jung, *Collected Works* 9.2:4.
9. E. Jung and Franz, *The Grail Legend*, p. 41.
10. C. G. Jung, *The Visions Seminars*, 2:407.
11. Franz, *Number and Time*, p. 18.
12. Ibid.
13. C. G. Jung, *Collected Works* 9.2:118–19.
14. C. G. Jung, *Visions Seminars* 2:425.
15. C. G. Jung, *Collected Works* 9.2:31.
16. E. Jung and Franz, *The Grail Legend*, pp. 52–65.
17. Ibid., pp. 155–56.
18. Ibid., p. 179.
19. *Encyclopédie des mystiques* (Paris: Seghers, 1977), 2:29.
20. C. G. Jung, *Collected Works* 9.2:224.
21. E. Jung and Franz, *The Grail Legend*, p. 166.
22. Ibid., p. 165.
23. C. G. Jung, *Collected Works* 9.2:165.
24. C. G. Jung, *Visions Seminars* 2:457.
25. Ibid., p. 334.

PART 3

Quotations from Montaigne's *Essays* are taken from Frame, *The Complete Essays of Montaigne.*

1. Montaigne, *Essais*, p. 1204.
2. Frame, *Montaigne: A Biography*, p. 85.
3. Ibid., p. 240.
4. C. G. Jung, *Collected Works* 6:611.
5. Whyte, "The Growth of Ideas," pp. 257–59.
6. C. G. Jung, *Collected Works* 6:471.
7. Ibid., pp. 568, 481.
8. Edinger, "An Outline of Analytical Psychology," p. 12.
9. C. G. Jung, *Collected Works* 11:495.
10. Frame, *Montaigne: A Biography*, p. 259.
11. C. G. Jung, *Collected Works* 18:452. See Albert Thibaudet, *Montaigne* (Paris: Gallimard, 1963); Pierre Moreau, *Montaigne, L'Homme et l'oeuvre* (Paris: Boivin, 1939); Jean Plattard, *Montaigne et son temps* (Paris: Boivin, 1933); Fortunat Strowski, *Montaigne*, 2d rev. ed. (Alcan, 1931).

PART 4

1. Edinger, "On Being an Individual," p. 70.
2. Neumann, *The Origins and History of Consciousness*, pp. 100–150.
3. Whitmont, "The Role of the Ego in the Life Drama," p. 41.
4. Edinger, "On Being an Individual," p. 79.
5. Ibid., p. 43.
6. Whitmont, "Momentum of Man," p. 8.
7. Franz and Hillman, *Lectures on Jung's Typology.*
8. Whitmont, "On Aggression," p. 59.
9. Corneille, "Discours du poème dramatique," in *Théâtre* 1:19.
10. Neumann, *The Great Mother*, p. 168.
11. Otto, *Le Sacré*, p. 29.
12. Zimmer, "Die indische Weltmutter," quoted in Neumann, *The Great Mother*, p. 15.
13. Edinger, "An Outline of Analytical Psychology," p. 11.
14. Zabriskie, "Goddess in Our Midst," p. 38.
15. C. G. Jung, *Collected Works* 9.1:86.
16. Ibid., 5:258.
17. Hillman, "On Senex Consciousness," p. 146. See Paul Bénichou, *Moralistes du grand siècle*; Robert Brasillach, *Pierre Corneille*; René Bray, *La Tragédie cornélienne devant la critique classique*; Bernard Dort, *Pierre Corneille, Dramaturge*; Serge Dubrovsky, *Corneille et la dialectique du héros*; Lucien Goldman, *Le Dieu caché*; Octave Nadal, *Le Sentiment de l'amour dans l'oeuvre de Pierre Corneille*; Georges Poulet, *Etudes sur le temps humain.*

PART 5.1

The translations of *Elective Affinities* come, for the most part from Goethe's *Elective Affinities* (New York: Ungar Publishers, 1962). They have, however, been altered by me.

1. Raphael, *Goethe and the Philosophers' Stone*, p. 48.
2. Ancelet-Hustache, *Goethe*, p. 78.
3. Ibid., p. 86.
4. Raphael, *Goethe and the Philosophers' Stone*, p. 42.
5. Ancelet-Hustache, *Goethe*, p. 78.
6. Raphael, *Goethe and the Philosophers' Stone*, p. 42.
7. Ibid., p. 51.
8. C. G. Jung, *Collected Works* 6:368.
9. Raphael, *Goethe and the Philosophers' Stone*, p. 52.
10. Goethe, *Italian Journey: 1786–1788*, p. 138.
11. Ibid., p. 51.
12. Will and Ariel Durant, *The Story of Civilization* 11:565.
13. Goethe, *Elective Affinities*, p. v.
14. Marie-Louise von Franz, *Aurora Consurgens*, p. 143.
15. Neumann, "Narcissism, Normal Self-Formation, and the Primary Relation to the Mother," pp. 88–89.

PART 5.2

1. Eliade, *Rites and Symbols of Initiation*, p. 111.
2. Hiebel, *Novalis*, p. 9.
3. Birch, *The Disciples at Saïs and Other Fragments*, p. 21.
4. Hiebel, *Novalis*, p. 26.
5. Birch, *The Disciples at Saïs*, p. 28.
6. Ibid.
7. Ibid.
8. Ibid.
9. Ibid.
10. Ibid., p. 32.
11. Hiebel, *Novalis*, p. 36.
12. Ayrault, *La Genèse du romantisme Allemand*, p. 136.
13. Ibid., pp. 132–36.
14. Eliade, "Mysteries and Spiritual Regeneration in Extra-European Religions," p. 17.
15. Franz, "Archetypes Surrounding Death," p. 10.
16. Ibid., p. 9.
17. C. A. Meier, *Ancient Incubation and Modern Psychotherapy*, pp. 34–45.
18. Quoted from *C. G. Jung Letters* 2:45 ff., February 29, 1952, by Franz, "Archetypes Surrounding Death," p. 20.
19. Ibid.
20. Eliade, *Rites and Symbols of Initiation*, p. 111.

PART 5.3

Spellings of Jewish terms follow Gershom G. Scholem, *Major Trends in Jewish Mysticism.*

1. Buber, *The Tales of Rabbi Nachman.*
2. Ibid., p. 25.
3. *Nahman of Bratslav*, p. 17.
4. Buber, *The Tales of Rabbi Nachman*, p. 26.
5. Ibid., p. 196.
6. Ibid., p. 207.
7. *Nahman of Bratslav*, p. 19.
8. Kaplan, *Meditation and the Bible*, p. 25.
9. Buber, *The Tales of Rabbi Nachman*, p. 29.
10. Ibid., p. 30.
11. Scholem, *On the Kabbalah and Its Symbolism*, p. 36.
12. Ibid., pp. 28–30.
13. C. G. Jung, *Collected Works* 14:455.
14. Scholem, *Major Trends in Jewish Mysticism*, pp. 218–220.
15. C. G. Jung, *Collected Works* 14:413.
16. Kaplan, *Meditation and the Bible*, pp. 28–30.
17. C. G. Jung, *Collected Works* 14:522; 5:177.
18. Buber, *The Tales of Rabbi Nachman*, p. 18.
19. Scholem, *Major Trends in Jewish Mysticism*, p. 133.
20. C. G. Jung, *Collected Works* 6:789–781. Edward Edinger wrote in "An Outline of Analytical Psychology," that the Self is "the center and circumference of the psyche."
21. Scholem, *Kabbalah and Its Symbolism*, p. 317.
22. Scholem, *Major Trends in Jewish Mysticism*, p. 133.
23. Kaplan, *Meditation and the Bible*, p. 64.
24. Scholem, *On the Kabbalah and Its Symbolism*, p. 49.
25. Halevi, *Kabbalah Tradition of Hidden Knowledge*, pp. 5–21.
26. Kaplan, *Meditation and the Bible*, p. 50.
27. Ibid., pp. 18–19.
28. Rosenberg, *The Anatomy of God*, p. 57.
29. Halevi, *Kabbulah Tradition of Hidden Knowledge*, p. 19.
30. Kaplan, *Meditation and the Bible*, p. 18.
31. Ibid., p. 38.

PART 5.4

All quotations from *At the Hawk's Well* are from Yeats, *Plays and Controversies*—the 1923 Macmillan (London) edition.

1. Yeats, *Essays and Introductions*, pp. 43–44.
2. Moody and Martin, eds., *The Course of Irish History.* See this volume for an excellent background picture for Yeats's play.
3. Ellmann, *Yeats: The Man and the Masks*, p. 199.
4. Seiden, *William Butler Yeats: The Poet as a Mythmaker*, pp. 206–17.

5. "The Theatre," in Yeats, *Essays and Introductions*, p. 170.
6. "Speaking to the Psaltery," ibid., p. 16.
7. "William Blake and the Imagination," ibid., pp. 112–45.
8. "Poetry and Tradition," ibid., p. 252.
9. Ibid., p. 255.
10. Yeats, *Plays and Controversies*, p. 255.
11. "Magic," in Yeats, *Essays and Introductions*, p. 28.
12. Ibid.
13. "The Symbolism of Poetry," ibid., p. 156.
14. "Certain Noble Plays of Japan," "The Tragic Theatre," ibid., pp. 156, 243.
15. "Certain Noble Plays of Japan," ibid., p. 221.
16. *The Táin*, p. 85.
17. Ibid., p. 150.
18. Ibid., p. 153.
19. "Certain Noble Plays of Japan," in Yeats, *Essays and Introductions*, p. 221.
20. "Symbolism in Painting," ibid., p. 148–51.
21. Graves, *The White Goddess*, p. 12.
22. "Poetry and Tradition," in Yeats, *Essays and Introductions*, p. 255.
23. Yeats, *A Vision*, p. 135.
24. Hutin, *L'Alchimie*, p. 73.
25. White, *The Bestiary*, p. 139.
26. Rees and Rees, *Celtic Heritage*, p. 159.
27. Graves, *The White Goddess*, p. 207.
28. Franz, *Shadow and Evil in Fairy Tales*, p. 104.
29. C. G. Jung, *Collected Works* 9:8–10.
30. "Certain Noble Plays of Japan," in Yeats, *Essays and Introductions*, p. 200.
31. Ibid., p. 231.
32. "The Autumn of the Body," ibid., p. 189.
33. "Certain Noble Plays of Japan," ibid., p. 231.
34. Gregory, *Cuchulain of Muirthemne*, p. 37.
35. "Discoveries," in Yeats, *Essays and Introductions*, p. 287.

PART 6

1. Kolehmainen, *Epic of the North: "The Kalevala,"* p. 189.
2. Eliade, *Myths, Dreams, and Mysteries*, pp. 42–44.
3. *Encyclopédie des Mystiques* 1:45.
4. Eliade, *Myths, Dreams, and Mysteries*, pp. 64–69.
5. Ibid., p. 60.
6. Franz, *Patterns of Creativity Mirrored in Creation Myths*, p. 116.
7. C. G. Jung, *Collected Works* 5:138.
8. Lönnrot, *The Kalevala*, trans. Francis P. Magoun, Jr., p. 4. Because of the

length of *The Kalevala* certain episodes have been omitted from this analysis.

9. C. G. Jung, *Collected Works* 5:49.

10. Eliade, *Shamanism*, pp. 397, 407.

11. C. G. Jung, *Collected Works* 5:61.

12. Franz, *Creation Myths*, p. 172.

13. Eliade, *Shamanism*, p. 171.

14. Hamel, *Through Music to the Self*, pp. 79–80.

15. Gille, *Histoire de la métallurgie*, p. 7.

16. Fernie, *The Occult and Curative Powers of Precious Stones*, pp. 423–28.

17. Franz, *Creation Myths*, p. 56.

18. Fernie, *The Occult and Curative Powers of Precious Stones*, p. 468.

19. Eliade, *Shamanism*, p. 470.

20. Donnington, *Wagner's "Ring" and Its Symbols*, p. 98.

21. Ahokas, *A History of Finnish Literature*, pp. 151, 156, 195, 209, 239, 244–45.

22. *Facts about Finland*, pp. 64–77.

PART 7

1. Schimmel, *Mystical Dimensions of Islam*, p. 285.

2. See chap. on "The Golem" in Knapp, *The Prometheus Syndrome*, pp. 97–123.

3. Corbin, *The Man of Light in Iranian Sufism*, p. 109.

4. The word *attar* decoded according to mystical numerical equivalents means "the fluttering of a bird," the "flash" of light, to "twinkle," to "shine," or to be shaken by the wind."
Shah, *The Sufis*, p. 109.

5. Attar, *The Conference of the Birds*, p. 137. All subsequent quotations are from this 1978 Weiser edition.

6. Shah, *The Sufis*, p. 118.

7. Gardet, *La Mystique*, p. 101.

8. Nasr, *Sufi Essays*, p. 109.

9. *The Glorious Koran*, trans. Mohammed Mammaduke Pickthall (New York: New American Library, n.d.), p. 131. All subsequent quotations from the Koran are from this edition.

10. The extreme beliefs of some of the Shiite sects, all the more powerful because they were connected with Persian nationalism, have led in some circumstances to the creation of fanaticism, as exemplified in the activities of the Ismailis, Fatimides, Assassins.

11. Franz, *Individuation in Fairy Tales*, p. 58.

12. Craff, *The House of Islam*, pp. 63–65.

13. Schimmel, *Mystical Dimensions of Islam*, pp. 100–104. By the tenth century, decadence among many Sufi brotherhoods was great: drugs, alcohol, political and military positions, were taken by the heads, or sheikhs,

of these brotherhoods who controlled the entire group with an iron hand.
The initiates, therefore, were ready to die for their sheikhs and did in
many cases.

14. Nasr, *Sufi Essays*, p. 33.
15. Trimingham, *The Sufi Orders in Islam*, p. 197.
16. Nicholson, *The Mystics of Islam*, p. 8.
17. Nasr, *Sufi Essays*, pp. 73–82.
18. Ibid., p. 75.
19. Corbin, *The Man of Light*, p. 2.
20. Evildoers are incarnated in birds of prey. Martyrs for Allah, it was be-
    lieved, went to heaven in the form of birds. Solomon knew the language
    of the birds (see Koran, Surah 27:16, p. 273).
21. Nicholson, *The Mystics of Islam*, pp. 63–65.
22. Corbin, *The Man of Light*, p. 289.
23. Ibid.
24. *Larousse Encyclopedia of Mythology*, pp. 309–24.
25. According to the Koran, after Solomon built the Temple in Jerusalem he
    went on a pilgrimage to Mecca. He needed water and called upon the
    Hoopoe, who possessed the gift of finding underground springs, to indi-
    cate a spot where plenty could be found. The Hoopoe was also the bird
    who carried Solomon's letter to the divine Balkiss, known as the Queen
    of Sheba, inviting her to his kingdom. See Attar, *Conference of the Birds*,
    p. 143.
26. Corbin, *The Man of Light*, p. 6.
27. One may compare the Hoopoe's crown, a manifestation of the divine crown
    in Hebrew Kabbalism: Kether in the *sefirotic* chart.
28. Trimingham, *Sufi Orders in Islam*, p. 197. Quoted from Ahmad ar-Rutbi,
    Minhat al-ashab (1939), p. 92.
29. See Keats's "Ode to a Nightingale." Plato considered the Nightingale to
    be a symbol of Thampyras, an ancient Thracian bard. For the Japanese
    the Nightingale's melody is implicit in the Lotus sutra.
30. Corbin, "Mundus Imaginalis," pp. 2–8.
31. The Peacock is mentioned in the Bardo-Thodol. It represents Amitabba
    Buddha's throne.
32. C. C. Jung, *Collected Works* 6:544–48.
33. Schimmel, *Mystical Dimensions of Islam*, p. 426.
34. Ibid., p. 39.
35. Persian adaptation of Shrawardi's Awarif (Meier, "The Transformation of
    Man in Mystical Islam," (p. 49).
36. Ibid., pp. 47–52.
37. Palmer, *Oriental Mysticism*, p. 17.
38. Corbin, *The Man of Light*, p. 66.
39. Franz, *Individuation in Fairy Tales*, p. 82.
40. Nicholson, *The Mystics of Islam*, p. 39.
41. Guénon, "The Language of the Birds," p. 301.
42. Trimingham, *The Sufi Orders in Islam*, p. 157.

43. Fritz Meier, "The Problem of Nature in the Esoteric Monism of Islam," pp. 149–203.
44. Schimmel, *Mystical Dimensions of Islam*, pp. 144, 123.
45. Fritz Meier, "The Spiritual Man in the Persian Poet Attar," p. 303.

CONCLUSION

1. C. G. Jung, *Collected Works* 15:186.
2. Ibid., p. 86.

BIBLIOGRAPHY

Abood, Edward F., and Phyllis Harris. "The Splintered Personality in Euripides." *Psychological Perspectives* 8, no. 1 (1977).

Ahokas, Jaakko. *A History of Finnish Literature.* Bloomington: Indiana University Press, 1973.

Ancelet-Hustache, Jeanne. *Goethe.* London: John Calder, 1960.

Attar, Farid ud-din. *The Conference of the Birds.* New York: Samuel Weiser, 1978.

Aynard, J. *Les Poètes Lyonnais. Précurseurs de la Pleiade.* Paris: Boissard, 1924.

Ayrault, Roger. *La Genèse du romantisme Allemand.* Paris: Aubier, 1976.

Bachofen, J. J. *Myth, Religion, and Mother Right.* Princeton, N.J.: Princeton University Press, 1973.

Baynes, H. G. *Mythology of the Soul.* Baltimore: Williams and Wilkins, 1940.

Benoist, Luc. *L'Esotérisme.* Paris: Presses Universitaires de France, 1970.

Birch, Una. *The Disciples at Sais and Other Fragments.* London: Methuen, 1903.

Buber, Martin. *The Tales of Rabbi Nachman.* Translated by Maurice Friedman. New York: Horizon Press, 1956.

Campbell, Joseph. *The Masks of God: Oriental Mythology.* New York: Viking, 1970.

Corbin, Henri. "Mundus Imaginalis." *Spring* (1972).

———. *The Man of Light in Iranian Sufism.* Boulder, Colo.: Shambhala, 1978.

Corneille, Pierre. *Théâtre complet.* Vols. 1 and 2. Paris: Pléiade, 1950.

Cox, Edwin Marion. *The Debate between Folly and Cupid.* London: Louis Williams and Nordgate, 1925.

Craff, Kenneth. *The House of Islam.* Belmont, Calif.: Dickenson Publications, 1969.

Davy, Marie-Madeleine. *Encyclopédie des Mystiques.* Vol. 1. Paris: Seghers, 1977.

Delcourt, Marie. *Hermaphrodite.* London: Studio Books, 1956.

Donnington, Robert. *Wagner's "Ring" and Its Symbols.* London: Faber and Faber, 1963.

Durant, Will. *The Story of Civilization.* Vol. 4. New York: Simon and Schuster, 1950.

Durant, Will, and Ariel Durant. *The Story of Civilization.* Vol. 11. New York: Simon and Schuster, 1975.

Edinger, Edward. "On Being an Individual." *Spring* (1967).
———. "An Outline of Analytical Psychology." *Quadrant,* Spring 1968.
Eliade, Mircea. *Aspects du Mythe.* Paris: Gallimard, 1963.
———. "Mysteries and Spiritual Regeneration in Extra-European Religions." *Eranos Yearbook.* Vol. 5. New York: Pantheon, 1964.
———. *Rites and Symbols of Initiation.* New York: Harper Torchbooks, 1965.
———. *Myths, Dreams, and Mysteries.* New York: Harper Torchbooks, 1967.
———. *Shamanism.* Princeton, N.J.: Princeton University Press, 1972.
———. *Historie des croyances et des idées religieuses.* Paris: Payot, 1979.
Ellman, Richard. *Yeats: The Man and the Masks.* New York: W. W. Norton, 1978.
Entralgo, Pedro Lain. *The Therapy of the World in Classical Antiquity.* Edited and translated by J. Rather and John M. Sharp. New Haven, Conn.: Yale University Press, 1970.
Epton, Nina. *Love and the French.* New York: Ballantine, 1959.

Facts about Finland. Helsinki, Finland: Otava Pub. Co., 1979.
Fernie, T. *The Occult and Curative Powers of Precious Stones.* Blauvelt, N.Y.: Steiner Books, 1973.
Frame, Donald M. *Montaigne: A Biography.* New York: Harcourt, Brace and World, 1965.
———. *Complete Essays of Montaigne.* Stanford, Calif.: Stanford University Press, 1965.
Franz, Marie-Louise von. *Aurora Consurgens.* New York: Pantheon, 1966.
———. *Patterns of Creativity Mirrored in Creation Myths.* Zurich: Spring Publications, 1972.
———. *Number and Time.* Evanston, Ill.: Northwestern University Press, 1974.
———. *Shadow and Evil in Fairy Tales.* Zurich: Spring Publications, 1974.
———. *Individuation in Fairy Tales.* Zurich: Spring Publications, 1977.
———. "Archetypes Surrounding Death." *Quadrant,* Summer 1979.
Franz, Marie-Louise von, and James Hillman. *Lectures on Jung's Typology.* New York: Spring Publications, 1971.
Fraser, James George. *The Golden Bough.* Edited by Theodor H. Gaster. New York: Criterion, 1959.
Frey-Rohn, Liliane. "Evil from the Psychological Point of View." in *Evil.* Evanston, Ill.: Northwestern University Press, 1967.

Gardet, Louis. *La Mystique.* Paris: Presses Universitaires de France, 1979.
Gille, Bertrand. *Historie de la métallurgie.* Paris: Presses Universitaires de France, 1966.
Goethe, Johann Wolfgang von. *Elective Affinities.* Translated by James Anthony Froude and R. Dillon Boylan. New York: Ungar Publications, 1962.
———. *Italian Journey: 1786–1788.* Translated by W. H. Auden and Elizabeth Mayer. New York: Schocken Books, 1968.

Graves, Robert. *The White Goddess.* New York: Farrar, Straus and Giroux, 1974.

Gregory, Lady Augusta. *Cuchulain of Muirthemne.* London: John Murray, 1903.

Guénon, René. "The Language of the Birds." In *The Sword of Gnosis.* Edited by Jacob Needleman. Baltimore: Penguin, 1974.

Guillot, Gérard. *Louise Labé.* Paris: Seghers, 1962.

Halévi, Z'ev ben Shimon. *Kabbalah Tradition of Hidden Knowledge.* London: Thames and Hudson, 1979.

Hamel, Peter M. *Through Music to the Self.* Boulder, Colo.: Shambhala, 1979.

Henriot, Emile. *Portraits de femmes.* Paris: Albin Michel, 1951.

Hiebel, Friederick. *Novalis.* Chapel Hill: University of North Carolina Press, 1959.

Hillman, James. "On Senex Consciousness." *Spring* (1970).

Hutin, Serge. *L'Alchimie.* Paris: Presses Universitaires de France. 1971.

———. *Les Sociétés secrètes.* Paris: Presses Universitaires de France, 1971.

Jung, C. G., *Collected Works.* Vols. 1–20. Princeton, N.J.: Princeton University Press, 1957–79.

———. *The Visions Seminars.* Vol. 2. Zurich: Spring Publications, 1976.

Jung, Emma, and Marie-Louise von Franz. *The Grail Legend.* New York: G. P. Putman's Sons, 1970.

Kaplan, Aryeh. *Meditation and the Bible.* New York: Samuel Weiser, 1978.

Kerenyi, C. *The Gods of the Greeks.* London: Thames and Hudson, 1976.

Knapp, Bettina L. *The Prometheus Syndrome.* Troy, N.Y.: Whitson Publishing, 1979.

Kolehmainen, John I. *Epic of the North: "The Kalevala."* Mills, Minn.: Northwestern Publishing, 1973.

Koran, the Glorious. Translated by Mohammed Marmuduke Pickthall. New York: New American Library, n.d.

Kott, Jan. *The Eating of the Gods.* Translated by Boleslaw Taborski and Edward J. Czerwinski. New York: Vintage, 1974.

Larnac, Jean. *Louise Labé: La Belle Cordiere de Lyon.* Paris: Firmin-Didot, 1934.

Larousse Encyclopedia of Mythology. Hong Kong: Prometheus Press, 1973.

Lönnrot, Elias. *The Kalevala.* Translated by Francis P. Magoun, Jr. Cambridge, Mass.: Harvard University Press, 1975.

Meier, C. A. *Ancient Incubation and Modern Psychotherapy.* Evanston, Ill.: Northwestern University Press, 1967.

Meier, Fritz. "The Problem of Nature in the Esoteric Monism of Islam." *Eranos Yearbook.* Vol. 1. Princeton, N.J.: Princeton University Press, 1954.

———. "The Spiritual Man in the Persian Poet Attar." *Eranos Yearbook.* Vol. 4. Princeton, N.J.: Princeton University Press.

———. "The Transformation of Man in Mystical Islam." *Eranos Yearbook.* Vol. 5. New York: Pantheon, 1964.

Montaigne, Michel E. *Essais*. Paris: Pleiade, 1950.

Moody, T. W., and F. Martin, eds. *The Course of Irish History*. Cork, Ireland: Mercier Press, 1967.

Murray, Gilbert. "Euripides' *Bacchae* and the Ritual Pattern of Tragedy." In *The Scapegoat: Ritual and Literature*. Edited by John B. Vickery and J'nan M. Sellery. Boston: Houghton Mifflin, 1972.

Nahman of Bratslav, the Tales. Introduction and Commentaries by Arnold J. Band. New York: Paulist Press, 1978.

Nasr, Seyyed Hossein. *Sufi Essays*. London: George Allen and Unwin, 1972.

Neumann, Erich. *The Origins and History of Consciousness*. New York: Pantheon, 1954.

————. "Narcissism, Normal Self-Formation, and the Primary Relation to the Mother." *Spring* (1966).

Nicholson, Reynold A. *The Mystics of Islam*. London: Routledge and Kegan Paul, 1966.

Otto, Rudolf. *Le Sacré*. Paris: Payot, 1969.

Palmer, E. *Oriental Mysticism*. Reprint. London: Frank Cass, 1969.

Raphael, Alice. *Goethe and the Philosophers' Stone*. New York: Garret Publishers, 1955.

Rees, Alwyn, and Brinley Rees. *Celtic Heritage*. London: Thames and Hudson, 1973.

Rosenberg, Roy A. *The Anatomy of God*. New York: Ktav, 1973.

Roy, Charles. *Oeuvres de Louise Labé*. Paris: Alphonse Lemerre, 1887.

Schimmel, Annemarie. *Mystical Dimensions of Islam*. Chapel Hill: University of North Carolina Press, 1975.

Scholem, Gershom G. *Major Trends in Jewish Mysticism*. New York: Schocken, 1965.

————. *On the Kabbalah and Its Symbolism*. Translated by Ralph Manheim. New York: Schocken, 1973.

————. *Kabbalah*. New York: New American Library, 1974.

Seiden, Morton I. *William Butler Yeats: The Poet as a Mythmaker*. Ann Arbor: Michigan State University Press, 1962.

Shah, Idries. *The Sufis*. New York: Doubleday Anchor Books, 1971.

Storr, Anthony. "The Psychopathology of Fetishism and Transvestitism." *Journal of Analytical Psychology* 2 (July 1957).

The Táin. Translated by Thomas Kinsella. London: Oxford University Press, 1975.

Tricou, Georges. *Louise Labé et sa famille*. Genève: Droz, 1944.

Trimingham, Spencer J. *The Sufi Orders in Islam*. Oxford: Clarendon Press, 1971.

Weber, Henri. *La Création poétique au XVI siècle en France*. Paris: Nizet, 1955.

White, T. H. *The Bestiary*. New York: Capricorn, 1960.

Whitmont, Edward F. "The Role of the Ego in the Life Drama." *Spring* (1966).
———. "On Aggression." *Spring* 1970).
———. "Momentum of Man." *Quadrant*, Summer 1976.
Whyte, Lancelot L. "The Growth of Ideas." In *Eranos Yearbooks*. Vol. 5. New
    York: Pantheon, 1964.

Yeats, William Butler. *Plays and Controversies*. London: Macmillan, 1923.
———. *A Vision*. New York: Macmillan, 1969.
———. *Essays and Introductions*. New York: Collier Books, 1977.

Zabriskie, Philip. "Goddess in Our Midst," *Quadrant*. Fall 1974.
Zimmer, Heinrich. "Die indische Weltmutter." Quoted in Erich Neumann's
    The Great Mother. New York: Pantheon Books, 1963.

INDEX

Abraham, 117, 189, 336
Abulafia, Abraham, 206
Adam, 199, 208, 275
Adam Kadmon, 184, 189, 196
Aesulapius, 302–3
Aeneas, 37
Africa, 38, 40
Agape, 184, 222
Agon theme, 13–23, 122
Air concept, 279
Alba Longa, 114, 115, 120, 122, 123
Albrecht, Doris, xvi
Alchemy, 62, 139, 140, 141, 147, 149, 150–51, 152, 155, 156, 175, 178, 185, 186, 240, 244, 297, 364; *aqua permanens*, 157, 245; *dissolutio*, 139, 148, 149, 157, 159; metals, 142; *separatio*, 149, 150, 158; universal element, 140, 187
Alcibiades, 93
Alexander the Great, 93, 106
Alfred the Great, 38–39
Al-Ghazālī, 319
Al-Hallāj, 319
Alienation, x
All, the, 150–51, 164, 165, 169, 179, 185, 228, 274, 352, 356, 357, 359
Allah, 315, 320, 321, 324, 325, 326, 327, 330, 332, 340, 341, 342, 343, 347, 349
Almond symbolism, 177, 344
Alsace, 112
Anabasis, 199
Anamneses, 82, 316, 334, 339
Anaxoras, 275
Androgyny, 129, 196

Angelus Silesius, 181
Anglo-Saxons, xiii, 35, 38
Anima, xv, 143, 144, 256; in Attar, 327–28, 345, 360, 361; in *The Bacchants*, 6, 14, 15, 17, 21, 32; defined, xiii; vs. ego, 5–6; in *Elective Affinities*, 148, 152, 153; in *The Kalevala*, 289–90, 293, 294, 295, 296, 370; in Novalis, 161, 167, 170, 172, 173, 174, 175, 176, 177, 179, 180, 181, 183, 184, 186, 220; in *Parzival*, 42, 55, 56, 64, 67–68; in Yeats, 227, 250, 253, 255, 257, 369
Animus, 128–29, 130, 220, 327–28; defined, xii
Annihilation, 356–57, 361
Anthropophagy, 3. See also *Omophagia*
Antihero, xiv, 122
Antiquities of the Jews, 126
Anxiety, 96
Aphrodite, 16, 18, 21, 275
Apollo, 11, 12, 32, 89, 155
Arabian Nights, The, 325
Archetypal analysis, xi
Archetypes, ix, xii, xv, 6, 8, 28, 68, 111, 114, 117, 119, 120, 125, 126, 203, 261, 268, 365, 370; child, 208, 224; consciousness, 85–86, 188; creation, 268, 273–80, 321, 324; exile, 189, 209; gods, 7, 9; hero, xiv, 25, 201–2, 207, 208, 212, 213, 214, 217, 219, 220; 202, 205, 208, 211, 212, 279, 285, 330
Ares, 16
Aristotle, 5, 145, 151, 164, 317
Arnold of Villanova, 157

BETTINA L. KNAPP, a scholar of international renown, is Professor of Romance Languages and Comparative Literature at Hunter College and a Lecturer at the C. G. Jung Foundation. Among her more than two dozen books are *Theatre and Alchemy* (preface by Mircea Eliade) and studies of Louis Jouvet (preface by Michael Redgrave), Antonin Artaud (preface by Anaïs Nin), and Céline (preface by Jacob Javits). She has also edited a volume of correspondence (1923–1968) between her father, the late novelist and playwright David Liebovitz, and Lewis Mumford.

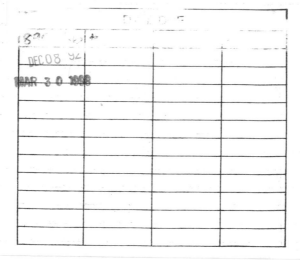